THE NEW MERCENARIES

ANTHONY MOCKLER

SIDGWICK & JACKSON

LONDON

DEDICATION

This book is dedicated to Xenophon the Athenian who
marched so many parasangs; who wrote the best book of
memoirs ever penned by a mercenary; who lived – and
to Clearchus the Spartan, his commander and friend…
who died.

First published in Great Britain in 1985
by Sidgwick & Jackson Limited

Copyright © 1985 by Anthony Mockler

ISBN 0-283-99296-4

Printed in Great Britain by
The Garden City Press
Letchworth, Hertfordshire
for Sidgwick & Jackson Limited
1 Tavistock Chambers, Bloomsbury Way
London WC1A 2SG

Contents

A Guide to Abbreviations

Initials, like jargon, are a curse; and I have tried to keep them to a minimum in this book. Nevertheless they do have to be used; and though it seems fair to assume that everyone who reads this book will know that the RAF is the Royal Air Force, the UN the United Nations, and an NCO a non-commisioned officer, it seems equally likely that there will be understandable confusion between the OAU and the OAS, or the SAS and the SIS, to take only two obvious examples. Hence this list. In many cases, I feel it is less important to know what the initials stand for than what they refer to. I hope baffled readers will find it a useful aid to turn back to when in doubt. It covers all the 'initialese' used in this book.

Military Units

1er REP	The 1st Foreign Legion Paratroop Regiment, now disbanded.
2e REP	The 2nd Foreign Legion Paratroop Regiment, still in existence.
ANC	The Congolese Army.
BAOR	British Army on the Rhine.
SAS	The British Army's semi-secret élite unit.
SADF	The South African armed forces.
RLI	The Rhodesian Light Infantry.

Military Ranks

DMI	Director of Military Intelligence.
CO or OC	Commanding officer/Officer commanding.
2 1/C	Second-in-command.
RSM	Regimental sergeant major.
CSM, CQSM	Company and company quartermaster sergeant majors.

Military Expressions

AWOL	Absent without leave – a lesser offence than desertion.
ASAP	As soon as possible – an immediate order.
'O' Group	Order Group – where orders are issued.
FN	Belgian-made rifle.
AK	Czech-made rifle.
RPG	Rocket-propelled grenade.

Semi-Military, Semi-Terrorist Organisations

OAS   Represented the French who wished to stay in Algeria. Attempted to assassinate De Gaulle.

IRA   Represents the Irish who want to take over Northern Ireland. Has assassinated, and attempted to assassinate, many English leaders.

PLO   Represents the Palestinians ousted by Israel. Basically a political body but indirectly involved in many assassinations.

Intelligence Services

CIA	American	SDECE	French
SIS	British	SID	Italian
		GID	Libyan

BOSS/DONS/   South African (basically same organisation, but with
NIS   different names).

Various Political Abbreviations

OAU   Organisation of African Unity, Africa's mini-United Nations (South Africa excluded).

UDI   Applied to Rhodesia only. Ian Smith's 'Unilateral Declaration of Independence' from the United Kingdom in 1965.

MP   A British Member of Parliament (n.b. not used in this book of the Military Police).

Angolan Political Movements

FNLA   Holden Roberto's, in the north of the country.

UNITA   Jonas Savimbi's, in the south of the country.

MPLA   The Marxist movement that seized power successfully pre-Independence and still forms the official government.

FLEC   The 'liberation movement' in the oil-rich enclave of Cabinda.

Organisations Associated with John Banks

TAE Ltd   Trucking Company

ISO Ltd
SAS Ltd   }   Mercenary-hiring companies
ACRO

Press and Radio

AP   Associated Press, American news agency, with correspondents all over the world.

NBC   American broadcasting network, also worldwide.

CBS   Another of the 'Big Three' American broadcasting networks.

Author's Acknowledgements

My thanks are due to an enormous number of people for active help, information or support in the course of my researches for and writing of this book. Many, I am sure, would prefer not to have their names mentioned in print; and it would be invidious to single out some rather than others. So I will confine myself to thanking them all in general but to thanking by name those who actually helped on the literary side of this book: in the first and foremost place Hope Leresche, my agent, who inspired it and fostered it, a fine and forceful woman, always enthusiastically loyal to her authors and warm to her friends, sadly missed; next Gwendoline Marsh who supported me in my task in a myriad of ways and at great expense to her nerves and indeed pocket but always (well, nearly always) with good humour and – dare I say it? – with devotion; thirdly Patrick Janson-Smith, my editor: unflappable, interested, positive, generously reasonable – and reasonably generous; lastly Kate Fraser who not only typed the manuscript with her usual speed and skill but boosted its author's morale immensely by saying, as his first reader, that she had enjoyed it very much; as I hope all subsequent readers will also do.

Foreword

On Christmas Eve, 1964 I flew in to Leopoldville, the capital of the Congo. It was my first important assignment as a special correspondent for *The Guardian*, and I was apprehensive.

At *The Guardian* the general view was that mercenaries, who had been infesting the Congo on and off for the past four years, were the dregs of Europe – hired killers. The particular reason for my apprehension was that my assignment was to track down the leader of the mercenaries, the hired killer *par excellence*, 'Mad Mike' Hoare. I had no idea where I would find him or how he would react to a journalist from a liberal newspaper. I had visions of trekking into the interior – Kivu? Katanga? Orientale? – in the wake of hordes of rabid, bloodthirsty and murderous mercenaries – if indeed I ever got that far. I had even more worrying visions of being shot out of hand, once my 'mission' was revealed, and being casually floated down a remote stretch of the River Congo, where – so they said in Leopoldville – bodies of all government ministers would sooner or later be seen passing by.

It came therefore as something of an anti-climax when I discovered that 'Mad Mike' Hoare was staying in Room 534 of the Hotel Leopold II where I was myself installed. His physical appearance came as an even greater shock. He bore no resemblance at all to a hired killer or a dreg from a gutter. He was short, dapper and very neatly turned out in light khaki with a major's crown on his epaulettes. He wore a beret but he carried an attaché case, not a weapon. He resembled a British officer from a good regiment, though possibly politer and more courteous than most of that class. He appeared to be in no way insane. That evening he took me out for a drink in a bar on the Boulevard 30 Juin. He drank orange juice himself. He fended off the 'jungle bunnies', loud-mouthed colourfully dressed tarts who swayed up to our table demanding beers. No one seemed to recognise him as the feared and fearsome mercenary leader. He talked of his crusade against communism and told me how in order to instil the regimental spirit he insisted on church parade and football matches every Sunday for the 'volunteers' ('we don't much care for the word "mercenaries" ourselves') of Five Commando.

I went to bed in a haze that was only partly alcoholic. What on earth was I to make of all this? How could I write an article about a 'Mad

Mike' who was so different from the weapon-festooned bloodcurdling mercenary leader I had imagined? Was I meant to take seriously his apparently sincere talk of Western values and the need to defend them? Why hadn't I asked him about the money, for heaven's sake? Just because it seemed indelicate? What were these mercenaries here for? What sort of men were they really? Which were right – my impressions back in *The Guardian*'s newsroom or my impressions out here on the spot? That was the origin of the present book. That is when I made up my mind to investigate, as deeply and as widely as I could, what to me had become the paradox, the mystery, of the twentieth-century mercenaries, and what manner of men they were.

This book is the result of those investigations.

Anthony Mockler
Moulin D'Andé

September 1984

Prologue

THE MAKING OF THE MODERN MERCENARY

1

Genesis: The Historical Background

Friars: (giving their usual greeting to wayfarers) God give you peace!
Hawkwood: God take from you your alms!
Friars: We meant no offence, Sir.
Hawkwood: How, when you pass by me and pray that God would make
me die of hunger? Do you not know that I live by war and
that peace would ruin me?

Froissart's *Chronicles*

Colonel Faucitt scoured Europe for mercenaries. Colonel Faucitt, like so many colonels and captains involved in the mercenary trade both before and after him, was an Englishman. What made the colonel rather different, however, from all the others was that Faucitt was the official mercenary recruiting agent for the British government.

There is something peculiarly hypocritical about the occasional condemnations of mercenary activity issued by various British governments over the past quarter of a century. British governments have always used mercenaries when it has suited their interests, and indeed continue to do so even now. But at no time was their need for mercenaries more desperate, it seemed to the British government of the day, than at the time of the American Revolution. The American rebels, they feared, could put 50,000 militia – citizen volunteers – into the field, whereas the whole British Army was only 30,000 strong and roughly half of that strength was, as so often in British history, permanently tied down by garrison duties in Ireland. In the summer of 1775 the first disastrous news of British defeats reached London; and the British government began, discreetly, to panic.

At first – and this is one of the most extraordinary stories of the American War of Independence – the British had hoped to hire no less than 20,000 Russian mercenaries to redeem the situation. The British Ambassador in Russia was certain that in view of Catherine the Great's 'intimate affection for the British Nation' he could reckon upon 'a strong body of Her Imperial Majesty's infantry'. London was delighted to hear it. It seemed a godsend solution to all the government's military and manpower problems. As soon as the Ambassador's despatch reached the Cabinet, messages went out from London to America, promising the jittery British generals cooped up in Boston and elsewhere that this massive reinforcement of fearsome mercenaries from Tartary would definitely be sailing from the Baltic ports the following spring; and from London to Moscow, with instructions to the Ambassador to offer the Empress £7 per head levy money, half to be paid at once – £70,000 – and half – the remaining £70,000 – when the 20,000 hired troops had actually embarked (they did not trust Catherine's 'affection' too far) on ships of the Royal Navy. 'I will not conceal from you', wrote Britain's Secretary of State for Foreign Affairs to the Ambassador, 'that, this accession of force being very earnestly desired, expense is not so much an object as in ordinary cases.' In other words the British were desperate enough to pay almost any price the Russians might demand. Rumours of the most massive and outlandish mercenary bargain ever suggested in British history spread all over London that autumn. 'When the Russians arrive', Gibbon, the great historian of the *Decline and Fall of the Roman Empire*, wrote conversationally to a friend, 'will you go and see their camp?' Clearly he was looking forward to a spectacle of barbaric splendour and fearsomeness such as many a mercenary-hiring Byzantine emperor must have seen in Constantinople, but never a free-born English scribbler have dared hope to view in London.

In the rebellious colonies meanwhile fear of the Russian hordes and indignation at the threat of using mercenaries at all against free-born citizens were growing. 'He has plundered our seas, ravaged our coasts, burnt our towns and destroyed the lives of our people', as the American Declaration of Independence was later to put it. 'He' – he being of course George III, the colonists' legitimate King – 'is at the moment transporting large armies of foreign mercenaries to complete the works of death, desolations and tyranny already begun, with circumstances of cruelty and perfidy scarcely paralleled in the most barbarous ages, totally unworthy the head of a civilized nation.'

In the end, however, all was anticlimax. The Russian infantry never reached America, and the first clash ever between Russians and Americans, that might have changed the whole course of later and indeed of present-day history, failed to occur. If the fighting forces of what are now the two superpowers had two centuries ago come face to face, what would have been the military outcome? It is certainly – but must remain – a fascinating speculation.

The Russians failed even to reach England's shores. Catherine the Great delivered an elegant snub via the discomfited Ambassador to King George III, refusing to hire out a single Russian soldier, on grounds of principle and despite the generous money offer, 'simply to calm a rebellion which is not supported by any foreign power'. So Gibbon never saw their camp in England; and no Russian soldier has ever as yet, set foot as an invader on American soil.

Next the British government, barely daunted, tried the Dutch, hoping for more sympathy from these close allies. In particular they wanted to hire the Scots Brigade, formed over 150 years earlier and still in the service of the United Provinces. The States General, the Dutch parliament, met to consider the United Kingdom's request. Two of the Provinces were very much in favour, one – the Province of Holland itself – very much against. In the end the States General agreed to hire out the Scots Brigade – which by this time, though still Scottish-officered, was composed of mercenaries from all over Europe, a kind of Dutch Foreign Legion – 'on condition that it should not be used outside Europe'. This was therefore a disguised refusal. It was less offensive to the British government than Catherine the Great's scathingly direct comments, but it was no more helpful. So with a certain reluctance the government turned to the traditional recruiting-ground for mercenaries in Europe, the one that charged the most extortionate rates, Germany, and to Germany in late 1775 despatched Colonel Faucitt. But even in Germany his first approaches encountered only rebuffs. The Elector of Saxony refused him outright, so did all the Catholic princes. Charles Augustus of Saxe-Weimar, though only nineteen years old, rejected an open offer for the use of some of his battalions. 'Serenissimus himself', his secretary noted, 'posted the letter.'

. Finally Colonel Faucitt managed to hire a few hundred infantry from His Most Serene Highness the Hereditary Count of Hanau, 4,000 foot and 300 dragoons from His Most Serene Highness the Duke of Brunswick, a spendthrift who needed the money, and above all – his real triumph – no less than 12,000 foot, 400 Jägers armed with rifled guns, 300 dismounted dragoons, three corps of artillery and four major-generals from His Most Serene Highness the Landgrave of Hesse Cassel. The Hessian troops were the finest and best disciplined in Germany and probably in Europe; the Landgrave, a lout but a cultured lout, took a special pride in the appearance of his crack regiments, such as the Blue Hussars. The hussars were spectacularly turned out in jackets and colimens of sky-blue and white, set off by red trousers; their officers wore silver hats embellished with a bunch of heron feathers. As usual, pride in appearance was matched by pride in performance. To obtain Hessian troops was the most important part of Colonel Faucitt's mission. But negotiations were long and hard, and the mercenary contract – the treaty – with His Most Serene Highness was not signed till New Year's Eve.

Under its terms the Landgrave received 20 per cent more levy money per head than the Duke of Brunswick, a double annual subsidy for the duration of the campaign (subsidy money was an additional 'sweetener' paid to mercenary contractors, which is what rulers who hired their troops out in effect were); and the right to provide his own hospital and his own uniforms at Britain's expense. He revived a scandalous claim for £41,000 owing for hospital expenses incurred in 'the late war': the Landgraves of Hesse-Cassel had first hired troops to the British in 1702 and had continued, at more exorbitant rates, to do so ever since. Finally he insisted that British pay should be paid into the Hessian treasury rather than directly to his own troops. As the British rate of pay was higher than the Hessian rate of pay, the reason for this was only too obvious – the Landgrave intended to pocket the difference himself. Colonel Faucitt rather feebly urged that the Hessians in the field should be paid as much as the British. 'They are my fellow soldiers,' answered the Landgrave unctuously. 'Do I not mean to treat them well?'

It was agreed that the thirteen battalions of Hessian troops should march for the embarkation ports on 15 February 1776; and throughout Europe and England it was confidently expected that, with the arrival of these highly professional troops in America, the amateurish rebellion of the colonists would immediately and without further serious difficulty be crushed. Indeed the British Prime Minister, Lord North, told the House of Commons that 'in all human probability' their mere appearance on the scene would induce the Americans to submit, probably without the need to shed any further blood at all.

Rarely can such a misjudgement have been made by any British prime minister before or since, as history went on to prove. Far more astute was the reasoning of a former prime minister and in his time a far greater war-leader, the elder Pitt, now Lord Chatham. 'My Lords,' he rightly, boldly and accurately proclaimed the following year, in one of his last speeches to Parliament before his death, 'you cannot conquer America. In three campaigns we have done nothing and suffered much. You may swell every expense, accumulate every assistance you can buy or borrow, traffic and barter with every pitiful little German prince that sells and sends his subjects to the shambles

of a foreign power. Your efforts are forever vain and impotent, double
so from the mercenary aid on which you rely: for it irritates to an
incurable resentment. If I were an American as I am an Englishman,
while a foreign troop was in my country, I never would lay down my
arms; never, never, never.'

The American Attitude to Mercenaries

This brief summary of one of history's most notably unsuccessful
mercenary-hiring operations calls for several comments. First of all it
is hardly realised in Britain (and certainly never taught in the schools)
that the British relied not, in the main, on their own troops but on
hired mercenary troops, Germans, to suppress their own rebellious
compatriots, the colonists in America – a policy that incidentally,
ended in total failure with the surrender of Hessians at the battles of
Trenton and at Saratoga Springs, and with the desertion of no less
than 5,000 German mercenaries in all (they went to swell the ranks of
German settlers already established in the thirteen colonies).

Secondly the fact that Americans in their first war ever were
attacked by mercenaries (and not only by Germans but by hordes of
American Indians, also hired by the British) has left America,
consciously or subconsciously, with a permanent distaste both for the
employment of mercenary troops by their government and for the
service as mercenary troops of their own citizens. Indeed the United
States is almost the only imperial power in history that has never
employed mercenary troops directly (and only with reluctance and
secrecy indirectly). This is most exceptional. For throughout history
powers with imperial responsibilities have almost invariably employed
vast forces of mercenaries. The armies of Rome and Byzantium, of
Carthage and of Persia, of the Emperor Charles V, of Napoleon, of
countless other potentates and more recently, of both the British and
the French colonial empires – to name but a few and to ignore all the
armies of the Far East – were largely mercenary in composition.

Over two hundred years have passed since the War of Independence and American folk-memories and folk-prejudices against the
status of the mercenary soldier might be thought to have disappeared.
But it seems that on the contrary they have not been forgotten. Many
Americans admittedly dream and fantasise about becoming mercenaries – there is in the United States a flourishing sub-culture of
mercenary magazines that cater precisely to these fantasies – but
hardly any, as the chapters that follow will show, have in recent years
actually enlisted in the various mercenary forces or operations with

which this book deals. Certainly by comparison to the British and to the French their numbers are infinitesimal; and this despite the ending of the war in Vietnam which in theory ought to have thrown a vast mass of highly trained and experienced American ex-soldiers upon the mercenary market. They never materialised. The prejudice in America against mercenary soldiering is, like all prejudices, rooted in history, overwhelmingly strong.

Mercenaries in Europe

In Britain, and indeed throughout Europe, the attitude towards the employment of mercenary soldiers has always been very different. But by the time of the American War of Independence even the British, who as a rich commercial sea-power had traditionally relied on mercenaries to fight their land-wars for them, were beginning to become ashamed of this dependence. Duke after duke rose in the House of Lords to condemn what one of their number, the Duke of Richmond, described as 'a downright mercenary bargain for the taking into pay of a number of hirelings who are bought and sold like so many beasts for slaughter'. The truth of the matter was that, with the rise of nationalism, the political atmosphere was rapidly changing. In Germany itself Niebuhr wrote 'the news of the capture of German troops by Washington in 1776 excited universal joy'. Kant condemned the mercenary trade. Goethe expressed his disapproval of the Hessians. And from his exile in Holland Mirabeau, the foster-father of the French Revolution, raised his voice in protest. 'What new madness is this?' he cried. 'Germans! What brand do you suffer to be put on your foreheads?'

Until the Frence Revolution it had seemed both logical and acceptable throughout Europe that the professional soldier should fight while the ordinary citizen stayed at home. But the massacre of the Swiss Guard at the Tuileries by a Parisian mob was a sign marking the end of the days of the professional mercenary who sold his loyalties and his service to a foreign state. The French hordes rose – over a million Frenchmen took up arms in four months – and the armies of the Revolution invaded all Europe. After the French Revolution it was considered correct that every man should fight for his own country and dishonourable that a man should serve under another flag.

This principle was applied in practice in 1798. Universal conscription, unknown in Europe since the decline of feudalism, was introduced, and almost all European wars since that date have been fought by armies of conscripts rather than by armies of professional soldiers. In an army of conscripts the mercenary soldier can have no place. He is a fish out of water, for since men must have a moral basis to make unpleasant duties tolerable, the cry of patriotism excuses the burden of military service, and for the mercenary soldier the cry of patriotism is the knell of doom.

So in these last two centuries the unwritten rule that forbids the use of mercenaries in a European war has come to be thought of without any real justification as almost a moral law. In their colonial and post-colonial wars the European powers used, and still use, mercenary troops – I am thinking in particular of the Gurkhas employed by the British and the Foreign Legionaries employed by the French, both in action recently, the Gurkhas in the Falklands, the Foreign Legion in Chad. But when the battleground is in Europe itself, the use of mercenaries causes enormous resentment. In the First World War the Kaiser bitterly condemned all Britain's Indian troops as an 'army of mercenaries'; in the Second World War the Moroccans used by the Free French in Europe, the Goums, were particularly detested. In between, in the Spanish Civil War, the Republicans felt roughly the same sentiments of hatred and outrage towards General Franco's Moroccan troops as the followers of Franco felt towards the foreigners of the International Brigade. So strong has this almost instinctive feeling become that to be a mercenary is in itself immoral that it is generally forgotten how comparatively recent and illogical this sentiment is.

For throughout most of European history any such moralising attitude would have seemed ridiculous, indeed positively backward and unprogressive. The further states progressed from tribalism and the more civilised they became, the more, logically, they tended to use mercenary troops. The logic was simple and unanswerable: war being a barbaric pursuit, the citizens of a rich and flourishing state preferred to hire needy foreigners to fight for them rather than to have to interrupt their own rich and profitable lives. Thus throughout the period of the Renaissance when civilisation in Italy was flourishing but Italy itself was divided into a number of rich and cultured states, these states fought their wars against each other not with armies of their own citizens – that would have been an unthinkable waste of valuable lives – but with armies of mercenaries. These mercenaries were first foreign but, later, Italian; in time the most famous and successful of the Italian mercenary leaders, the *condottieri* as they were called, men like Francesco Sforza, founded noble houses and became themselves rulers of states. So too minor nobles from impoverished hill-towns, like Federigo da Montefeltro of Urbino, became, by the wealth they gained as *condottieri*, great patrons of the arts and of civilisation in general. There was no stigma at all attached to the *condottieri* in Italy – rather the contrary. But the very word *condotta* from which the title is derived means no more and no less than a simple mercenary contract – except insofar as very often it was a most elaborate mercenary contract (indeed with scores of clauses, in certain cases longer than this chapter) between the state that was hiring mercenary troops and the mercenary captain – a document drawn up with great care by lawyers on both sides.

It was the Swiss who in the post-Renaissance period became the most feared mercenaries in Europe. 'Bestial mountaineers' they were called; and they descended from their impoverished mountains in formidable groups of pikemen, spreading terror and panic throughout the rich plains and cities of Italy and Burgundy in search of pay and even more of loot. There is still a museum in the Federal Capital of Switzerland, Berne, devoted to *die Burgunderbeute* – 'the booty of Burgundy'. This cruel, superstitious and brutal peasantry was the first to indulge systematically in a new and ruthless form of warfare where no prisoners were taken and where the rules of war, carefully and laboriously created by medieval and Renaissance Europe, vanished in a welter of atrocities and blood.

It was the Swiss who created the system of official mercenary-hiring that had become so standardised in its German imitation by the time of the American War of Independence. That is to say, Swiss cantons such as Uri, Unterwald and Schwyz – to name the original three – would hire out their cantonal 'armies' to rulers in France and Italy only for payments made directly to the cantonal governments. These governments of the loosely linked cantons considered that they alone had the right to supply mercenaries and disapproved of freelance enlistment by their citizens. But though Switzerland was in effect a nation of mercenaries, indeed a nation whose *raison d'être* was mercenary-hiring, the cantons, being democratic, were never able to control their citizens as closely as the German princelings were later to control their subjects. By the time of Colonel Faucitt's second and even more desperate recruiting campaign for German troops to fight against the Americans, he was reduced to turning to rulers as disreputable as the Prince of Waldech, who had to escort a disarmed regiment of his own subjects with mounted Jägers to the embarkation port to prevent desertions. It was this sort of organised 'official' mercenary hiring that was felt by the end of the eighteenth century to be both inhuman and intolerable. But this total standardisation of the mercenary market, this rigid and degrading structure, was, as it were, the culmination of a long process that had begun in a much freer, more anarchic form, with the appearance in Europe long before the Swiss and the Germans, before even the *condottieri*, of their still more fascinating though lesser-known predecessors, the Free Companies.

The Free Companies

The Free Companies were vagabond bands of mercenary soldiers who as the feudal system declined, flourished in late medieval Europe for roughly a hundred and fifty years, from 1300 to 1450 approximately. They ought to be of particular interest to readers of this book in the sense that they, far more than the *condottieri*, the Swiss or the Hessians – highly organised, almost by comparison respectable mercenaries – resemble the vagabond bands of mercenary soldiers that have infested modern Africa and the Indian Ocean over the past twenty-five years, as Europe's imperial colonial system has disintegrated. Though they may not realise it, modern mercenary leaders like Hoare and Denard have emerged from almost exactly the same background and faced almost exactly the same problems as medieval mercenary leaders like Hawkwood and Moriale. In fact, if Hoare and Denard and their ilk had studied with attention the history of the Free Companies, they could have avoided many of the mistakes that they did make and have succeeded in far greater ambitions than they ever attempted. For though history in a general sense may not do so, mercenary history most certainly does repeat itself.

Indeed, to delve even further back into European mercenary history, Xenophon's *Anabasis*, his account of how a vagabond band of Ten Thousand Greeks including himself were hired to take part in a civil war in the Persian Empire, ought to be the bedside reading of every mercenary leader and of every employer of mercenaries too. It is the only memoir of more than a mere passing value ever written by a mercenary captain. In it the complex relationship between mercenary leaders, the rulers or rebels who employ them, the troops who follow them, the native allies who mistrust them, and their countries of origin which attempt to use them, are described and illustrated with the lucidity and the lack of exaggeration which were always the mark of Athenian writers. Throughout mercenary history the balance between these groups has always been delicate, and the vicissitudes tend to follow the same pattern. To take the most striking example, the treacherous killing of Clearchus the mercenary commander, the Spartan, and all his other mercenary captains bar Xenophon is the end that more often awaits mercenary leaders than death in battle or a rich old age. It illustrates the rule that no mercenary leader should separate himself even momentarily from his troops, particularly when the most difficult of all problems, that of disbanding a mercenary force, is being negotiated.

There is no such single historian as Xenophon who describes the exploits of the Free Companions, though the medieval chronicler Froissart recounts many with a mixture of both horror and admiration. As almost invariably happens in history, bands of vagabond mercenary soldiers form when peace has broken out and when they, the professional soldiers who know no other trade and wish for no other life, find themselves unemployed and unwanted. Thus the first and in many ways the most extraordinarily successful of all the Free Companies, the Grand Catalan Company, crossed from Sicily – where peace had been declared – over to Constantinople and took service, 6,500 strong, under the Byzantine Emperor against the Turks. They were light infantry, clothed only in skins and shod in brogues in an age when armour was considered almost indispensable, and recruited mainly in the mountain territories of Aragon. They were led however (as so often in mercenary history) by a German, Roger von Blum. Roger, successful, was given the title of grand duke as well as the hand of a Byzantine princess in marriage. But such favour had its dangers: he was assassinated by the Emperor's son, Michael, at Adrianople.

The Grand Catalan Company took a bloody revenge on the Byzantines, then entered the service of the French-born Duke of Athens, Walter of Brienne. Finally they turned against their employer and at the battle of Cephissus, in March 1311, killed Duke Walter and set up their own Catalan duchy in Athens. This duchy of mercenaries lasted for the almost unbelievably long period of sixty-three years until the Catalans were in their turn ousted by a Navarrese company, who however only held power for nine years. No company or band of mercenaries has ever before or after achieved such political power and held it for so long a period as the Grand Catalan Company – though many tried to. Their exploit was an inspiration to many would-be imitators, an extraordinary passage of mercenary history, illustrating in extreme form both the servitudes and the grandeurs of mercenary life.

Nearly forty years later the King of Hungary set out to invade the south of Italy, at the time Italy's wealthiest state. The signing of a peace treaty, so far from bringing relief, was once again, in the words of a Neapolitan chronicler, 'the beginning of the desire among Germans and Hungarians to prey on our Kingdom – delights which attracted soldiers from everywhere, like birds to a carcass, to the great harm of all the country, as our story will show'.

Mercenary companies after this unfortunate outbreak of peace sprang up all over southern Italy, bands of light cavalry that rode down, trapped and then ransomed for immense sums the heavily armoured southern barons. Werner of Urslingen, their most noto-rious early leader, wore on his breastplate the device: 'Lord of the Great Company, enemy of God, of pity and of mercy'. But the Great Company soon passed into the hands of a far more interesting man, a Provençal named Fra Moriale – a *Fra*, or brother, of the Order of St John – a military leader of talent and an organiser of genius. From all over Italy soldiers swarmed in to join the Great Company. It became a moving city-state, carefully administered internally and exchanging ambassadors on equal terms with the republics of central Italy. It owed loyalty to no man except Fra Moriale, and it was not so much employed as bought off by any city whose territory it approached. For two years its movements, actual or feared, dominated the politics and diplomacy of central Italy, and his contemporaries believed that Fra Moriale aimed at establishing his power over the whole peninsula. He might have done so, had he not made the mistake that was fatal to so many mercenary leaders – that of separating himself physically from his troops, as Clearchus had done. He was arrested by his ally, the dictator of Rome, Cola di Rienzi, thrown into a dungeon, tortured and beheaded. With his death the importance of the first Great Company really to deserve its name faded.

The next country to see a pullulation of Free Companies, far more numerous and far more dangerous to the established feudal order than any that had yet appeared, was France. After the defeat of France's chivalry by the English, first at Crécy, then in 1358 at Poitiers, where the Black Prince won the field, France lay open to anarchy though official warfare had stopped. English soldiers, with their Gascon and Navarrese allies, had no wish at all, however, to disband and return to their own more impoverished lands. Sir Robert Knollys formed a Great Company whose ravages in May 1359 were so terrible that the charred gables that marked his route were known as 'Knollys' mitres'. Other famous leaders of Free Companies were Sir Hugh Calveley, Sir John Hawkwood, Sir Bertrand du Guesclin, the Captal de Buch and the Archpriest – some of the most famous names of late medieval history. They hired themselves out to feudal lords and princes, grew rich on protection money and ransoms, squeezed the Pope at Avignon dry; and on one occasion – for all supporters of the established feudal order the most terrifying of all – combined to oppose a formidable feudal army sent to suppress them by the King of France, winning an unheard-of victory and killing the Constable of France himself.

They were excommunicated. They were condemned by the jurists as bandits. When captured, they were often accused of waging 'illicit war' and publicly executed after trial. But their power was so great, particularly in the mountainous regions of central France, and their military ability was so useful – they fought in all the decisive battles of the period – that the only way to be rid of them was, the feudal authorities discovered, to siphon them off elsewhere. Thus it was that – this time with the Pope's blessing – three-fifths of all the Free Companies descended on the rich and fertile plains of northern Italy, hired by the Lord of Montferrat to attack Europe's wealthiest and most populous city, Milan.

The most famous of the German, Gascon and English Free Companies that in the year 1361 crossed the Alps on this 'mission' was without a doubt the White Company, led at first by Albert Sterz, but later by Sir John Hawkwood. Each knight, heavily armoured, had one or two pages; 'and the pages' job was to keep their armour polished so that when they appeared in battle array, their arms and armour gleamed like mirrors and so were all the more frightening.' Militarily the White Company, famous for its archers, its night attacks and its general warlikeness, made short work of the remnants of Fra Moriale's Hungarian-German Great Company. The Fra's successor, Count Landau, led the Great Company in the service of the Visconti Dukes of Milan. He was defeated and stoned to death by the White Company's English mercenaries. There was no love lost between rival mercenary bands.

Nevertheless John Hawkwood – Giovanni Acuto as the Italians called him – eventually married Bernabo Visconti's illegitimate daughter Donnina amidst splendid pomp and feasting and jousting at Milan. Hawkwood appears to have been a typical English mercenary, loyal to whoever was employing him at the time, whether republic, pope or prince, and never, unlike Fra Moriale, aiming at political power for himself. (The parallels between Hawkwood and Hoare, and between Moriale and Denard or Schramme are, readers will find, very close.) Machiavelli argues that this was merely because Sir John was unsuccessful as a general, 'but everyone will admit that if he had been successful in battle, the Florentines would have been in his power'. This seems a total misconception both of Hawkwood's abilities and of his character. In fact though a vast number of mercenary leaders both then and later were ensnared and executed by their own apprehensive employers in Italy – including Albert Sterz, Hawkwood's predecessor, beheaded by the Perugians – Hawkwood himself not only died peacefully in his old age but was buried by the Florentines as a mark of their respect in the Duomo, Florence's magnificent cathedral, which his fresco still adorns.

He had always had – as later British mercenaries were to have – a rough sense of humour. In the massacre at Faenza in 1375 – he had entered papal service and rechristened the White Company, probably with his tongue in his cheek, the Holy Company – he found two of his constables quarrelling over a young nun. With Solomon-like judgement he decreed 'half each!', and cut the unfortunate (but at least still virginal) young woman in two. Earlier St Catherine of Siena, a fervent patriot, had written to her 'dearest and beloved brother in Jesus Christ, Messer Giovanni' – none other than Sir John – urging him and his followers to 'become a company of Christ and go forth against the dogs of infidels who possess our holy places'. But Hawkwood was a practical man, with nothing of the crusader in him – again resembling his compatriots and successors in this, whatever Mike Hoare – arguably a latter-day Hawkwood – may have said to me (see page xi) in the Congo.

Alberigo da Barbiano had served in the White Company as a pupil of Hawkwood's. In 1379 he formed a Company of his own on a national basis, the *Societas Italicorum Sancti Giorgii*, the Italian Company of St George, to oppose a new wave of bands of Breton mercenaries. St Catherine promised these 'new martyrs' – she cannot have been optimistic about their chances against the ferocious and war-hardened invaders – eternal life. The decisive battle took place on 30 April at Marino, twelve miles outside Rome. It lasted for five hours and to general amazement resulted in a complete victory for Alberigo. Pope Urban VI, barefoot, welcomed him back to Rome, created him a Knight of Christ, and gave him a white banner with a red cross inscribed *'Italia liberata dai Barbari'*. This battle marks the turning point of mercenary history in Italy, the beginning of the period when Italian *condottieri* took over military power from foreign captains and the Free Companies of foreigners gradually faded away.*

* A similar turning-point will, I forecast, come in modern mercenary history. See the final section of Chapter 15.

They faded away much less quickly in France where their leadership was passing from the hands of base-born professional soldiers, true 'companions', into the far more dangerous hands of minor but legitimate feudal nobles. In 1375 Enguerrand de Coucy, a cousin of the dukes of Austria, invaded Alsace at the head of no less than 40,000 mercenaries, known as Juglers from the curious conical shape of their helmets. Sixteen years later Duke Jean III of Armagnac, an over-powerful Gascon noble, led a band of mercenaries to their defeat and his death at the hands of Iacopo del Verme, a Milanese *condottiere*. As late as 1444, the 'Armagnacs', vast bands of adventurers put out of employment by the end of the Hundred Years' War (they were mostly Gascons, hence their title: this time the Duke did not lead them), were hired by the Emperor Frederick III, a Habsburg. They poured over the Jura and to their amazement were beaten by a couple of thousand rebellious peasants – in fact the Swiss peasants, outnumbered twenty-to-one, in their first international success – at the battle of St Jacob-on-Birs. Aeneas Sylvius Piccolomini, the future Pope Pius II, compared their defeat to that of the Persians by the Spartans. ('I place the Swiss above all Kings,' another Italian, Vettori, was later to write. 'I can imagine no army to oppose them.') The invaders had called themselves *Ecorcheurs* – Scorchers. The victorious peasants scornfully nicknamed them not Armagnacs but Arme-Jacken ('Poor Jackets') and Arme-Gecken ('Poor Fools').

Poor fools they may have been but they were still tens of thousands strong as they poured back in confusion over the Jura and, bootyless, an even greater threat than before to the good order of France. France's King, Charles VII, solved the problem they posed in an utterly revolutionary way. He took the bands permanently into his pay and formed from them the first regular standing army in Europe. By the Royal Ordinances of 1445 fifteen Companies, each of six hundred men, were set up. All the 'Companions' were paid not by their captains, but by royal officers, were subject to strict rules – and were sent to live, normally, a garrison life. Furthermore each captain was limited to the command of a single Company. Thus the vagabond bands that had originally sprung up as Free Companies ended as tightly-controlled and stationary Royal Companies. Thus the cause of the creation of the great glorious and renowned French Army was the desire of the King of France to free himself once and for all from the threat that mercenary bands had created. And thus too, paradoxically, feudal society, in overcoming the direct threat posed to its hierarchical principles by the egalitarian anarchy of the mercenary bands, indirectly undermined its own structure. For a regular standing army could not be fitted at all into the feudal scheme of things. In the history of the late Middle Ages the Free Companies must be given their place; just as in the history of mercenaries in general they must be given a certain pride of place. For their history exemplifies in vivid detail the treachery, the betrayals, the veerings of fortune, the national rivalries, the sudden riches and equally sudden disasters, the political considerations, the moral reproaches, the disappointed hopes, the difficulties of disbandment, the dangers of death, and perhaps above all the military competence and cunning necessary for survival that have always attended wandering mercenary bands.

The Three Categories

A history of mercenaries – it will by now have become, I hope, apparent – would be very little less than a history of warfare through the ages. There are certain categories of mercenaries, however, with which this book will only incidentally be concerned. First, the individual soldiers of fortune – the 'Wild Geese' are a typical example of these, the Irish Catholic gentry who, after the Battle of the Boyne, refused to take the oath of King William and joined armies all over Europe. There are, as will be later seen, echoes – indeed deliberate echoes – of the 'Wild Geese' in modern mercenary history, and soldiers of fortune, lone adventurers, certainly can be found here and there, in conflicts all over the world. But their presence and influence are marginal – except of course to themselves.

A second category consists of the various guards with which by tradition, or by their own initiative, heads of state have surrounded themselves – of which perhaps the two most famous examples are the Varangian Guard of Norsemen and Anglo-Saxons that protected the Byzantine Emperor, and the Swiss Guard that still serves at the Vatican. The phenomenon is as widespread as its origin is invariable – the fear of an absolute ruler who, mistrusting his relatives or his fellow countrymen, surrounds himself with a group of foreigners who owe everything to him, who are isolated by their language, by their customs and particularly by the loathing of their paymaster's subjects, in such a way that their loyalty goes to him alone.

Of these two categories of mercenaries examples will, inevitably, appear in the chapters that follow. But the third category is without a doubt the most fascinating: bands of professional soldiers, often dispersing but often temporarily united, under leaders of strong personality, fighting for pay and loot but not entirely indifferent to the claims of honour and legality or to the interests of their country of origin – these are the type of mercenaries with which this book will mainly deal. These bands reappear, as we have seen, in one form or another throughout history; usually at a time of the breakdown of empires, of political anarchy, and of civil war. Their power and influence are almost always opposed to the power and influence of the formal authorities of the time. In this they are utterly unlike what I would characterise as the semi-mercenaries that form almost a fourth category of their category of their own, a 'respectable' element hired out by major military powers to minor allies or client states which, again, this book will ignore – except where this category overlaps with that of the vagabond bands.

Precisely how to define the difference between these semi-mercenaries, such as the British officers whether seconded to or contracted to (but in both cases paid by) the Gulf States, and the vagabond mercenaries is a difficult, and ultimately a sterile, exercise. Both fall within the category of Larousse's definition: *'Soldat qui sert à prix d'argent un gouvernment étranger'*. But in this whole matter of definition the questions of both motive (money) and status (serving a foreign flag) are extraordinarily complex and become more so on examination. The idealistic young men who went out to fight for the Spanish Republic in 1936 were certainly paid: but were they therefore strictly speaking mercenaries? The mercenaries who fought in Katanga in 1960 and who were called the troops of the United Nations – volunteers, well-paid, under 'foreign' command, and certainly fighting for a cause that was no more direct concern of theirs than America was to the Hessians – *'les super-mercenaires'*: were they strictly speaking wrong? The mercenaries in the Congo were certainly mercenaries in the fullest sense, though not all of them, as Hoare makes clear in his book *Congo Mercenary* were fighting primarily for money. Is one therefore to say that the minority who fought for other reasons were not mercenaries? That would be an absurdity. The professional too – the regular army officer or NCO in any army in the world – fights for money and, as a comparison between recruiting figures and wage increases show, often mainly for money and is in that sense a mercenary himself. Indeed the only totally safe definition is a negative one: certainly neither conscripts nor tribal forces can be classed as mercenaries. That at least is clear – both in principle and by definition.

The Mark of the Mercenary

However it is not so much by principles or definition as by practice and intuition that mercenaries are judged and recognised. In Venice – to take one striking example of instantaneous recognition – can be seen a statue that is unmistakably that of a mercenary leader. Of all the equestrian statues in Italy, perhaps indeed of all the myriad equestrian statues in Europe, none has quite such an air of dominance as this statue of the *condottiere* Colleoni. Horse and rider seem to bestride not merely a piazza but a civilisation, and the bland portraits of popes and princes are obliterated by this terrible face, this harsh energy, this monstrous and potent mass of stone. Here, feels the uneasy spectator, is the brute force that lay behind the colour and the refinement of the Renaissance: a man of warfare, devoid of pity and scruples, incapable of that finesse that was the mark of the civilisation around him.

stone?
bronze.

Just as the statue of Colleoni is the visual portrait of an individual but also of a type that is recognisable throughout mercenary history, so is its verbal equivalent: Xenophon's character sketch of his own commander, Clearchus the Spartan.

> He could have lived in peace [wrote the Athenian] without incurring any reproaches but he chose to make war. He could have lived a life of ease but he preferred a hard life with warfare. He could have had money and security but he chose to make the money he had less by engaging in a war. Indeed he liked spending money on war just as one might spend it on love affairs or on any other pleasure. All this shows how devoted he was to war.

Here then is the real mark of the mercenary – a devotion to war for its own sake. By this the mercenary can be distinguished from the professional soldier whose mark is generally a devotion to the external trappings of the military profession rather than to the actual fighting. The Greeks, lacking the Christian ethos, saw nothing outrageous in this love of war. They were aware of its miseries too, they did not view the utter devotion to war of an Achilles or a Clearchus with the admiration which it would have received in traditionally warlike societies such as those of ancient Scandinavia or feudal Japan. They considered such devotion exceptional but not morally wrong. Christian society has, however, demanded that pleasure in war should be masked, often hypocritically, under the pretence of devotion to duty. This attitude still exists and it is, I believe, the unspoken reason behind the general distaste that has always been shown towards self-confessed mercenaries. The regular army officer of modern times would say he was serving his country, the conscript that he was defending his family and home; but an open devotion to war as an art and indeed as a way of life is the mark of the mercenary, and the mercenary's casting aside of a moral attitude to war that is often insincere, at best uneasy, both fascinates and repels.

2

Matrix: The Foreign Legion

Tears stood in my eyes and my voice broke as I concluded quoting:
Soldats de la Légion
De la Légion Etrangere
N'ayant pas de Nation
La France est votre Mère
P.C. Wren, *Beau Geste*

No mercenary force has ever become as well-known as the French Foreign Legion. The British had their King's German Legion, the Spanish had until very recently their own Spanish Foreign Legion, other European countries had their brigades of native or mercenary troops. Obscurity enfolds them. France alone took her mercenaries to her heart. Edith Piaf sang *Mon Légionnaire* with a catch in her voice and millions of Frenchwomen appeared to envy her personal possessive pronoun. At the annual military parades in Paris on Bastille Day, 14 July, the greatest volume of cheers and applause invariably greets the Légionnaires. The legend of the Foreign Legion has gradually grown and swelled out of all proportion until no single military unit in the world – and there were many both as picturesque and more heroic – have been as popular and as admired. Why this is so is a question that needs to be posed; and one that will, hopefully, be answered in this chapter. But, more immediately relevant, the Foreign Legion can be seen as a symbol of the continuity of mercenary history, the link between the mercenary past and the mercenary present. The link with the present will become only too obvious in the chapters that follow. The link with the past goes back in an unbroken chain to the Swiss.

The Origins of the Legion

In 1494 the French under King Charles VIII invaded Italy. Here is a description of the French army as it marched, unopposed, into Rome after having swept the Medici out of Florence. The chronicler was amazed at its size – it was 30,000 strong – its division into different corps, and its discipline.

The first to enter [he wrote] were the long columns of Swiss and Germans marching by in step to the beating of drums and under their banners, with real military dignity and unbelievable order. Their weapons were short swords and wooden lances ten feet long topped with metal blades. A quarter of them were armed with long axes from the top of which sharpened points stuck out. They would wield these deadly weapons with both hands – they call them hallebards in their language. Five thousand Gascons followed them, nearly all crossbowmen. This type of soldier seemed in their general appearance and turn-out almost deformed by comparison with the Swiss who certainly stood out the most, with their gleaming weapons and decorative headgear and their fierce looks.

All Italy quailed at the 'harshly accented voices and savage faces' of the Swiss. Thanks to these mercenaries France conquered the whole peninsula with fantastic ease. For the next fifty years whenever there was a battle in Italy the Swiss could be found fighting, though not invariably on the same side. For a brief decade they turned against their allies and employers, the Kings of France. The great warrior Pope, Julius II, formed his famous corps of Swiss Guards on 22 January 1506 and sent them as papal mercenaries against the French. The French hired from Germany *landsknecht* – lansquenets – armed and trained on the Swiss model and therefore regarded with peculiar hatred by the Swiss. In 1513 at the great battle of Novara the Swiss slaughtered 8,000 lansquenets in the service of France, though at the cost of 1,500 casualties, the greatest loss they had ever suffered. Two years later at Marignano France's new King, Francis I, took a terrible revenge on the Swiss. 'Believe me, Madame,' he wrote to his mother, 'we were twenty-eight hours in the saddle without eating or drinking. Never for two thousand years has there been so fierce and so cruel a battle.' At its end as many as 12,000 Swiss lay dead on the field. Next year, on 29 November 1516, the King imposed upon Switzerland the Perpetual Peace which regulated the relations between the two countries right up till the French Revolution. Under its terms the Swiss agreed never to supply mercenaries to France's enemies. Its result was to turn Switzerland into a mercenary recruiting ground for every French king to come.

Over a million Swiss, no less, served in the French Army from the time of Louis XI* to that of Louis XVI, till the massacre of the Swiss

* By his edict of 1481 Louis XI showed how highly he appreciated his Swiss mercenaries. He exempted them from all taxes, all garrison duties, all night guards, and all special rules. Commands were given in their own language; they could be punished only by their own officers. They were allowed to buy land and, alone of all foreigners, to make valid wills. The French envied them this privileged position and centuries later made them pay for it – at the Tuileries on 10 August 1792.

Guards at the French Revolution and Napoleon's attack on Switzerland ruined the Perpetual Peace. But at the time this seemed a mere unfortunate interlude. In 1814 when Napoleon abdicated and the *ancien régime* was restored, the Swiss too were restored to their pride of place as France's traditional mercenaries. Four Swiss Regiments of the Line and two Regiments of Swiss Guards were incorporated into the revived Royal army. All the same the idea of employing foreign mercenaries in France had become repugnant after the violent nationalism that marked the French Revolution. It could not last. The Swiss battalions were disbanded in January 1830, a year of political upheavals in France. The July revolution followed. It looked as if the long, long connection between Swiss mercenaries and the French army were finally broken.

But it was not. Within less than a year, on 9 March 1831, Marshal Soult, Minister of War, signed a decree forming 'A Legion of foreigners to be known as the Foreign Legion for service outside France'. Note the proviso 'outside France'. The privileged position of the foreign mercenaries, which had led to such resentment inside France, had gone. Seven battalions of foreigners of all sorts were enrolled. But the Swiss were still there, at the top. The first commanding officer of the Legion was a Swiss veteran, Colonel Stoffel; and the officers and NCOs of the first three battalions, German speaking, were all Swiss. It was not till the next wave of revolutionary fervour swept Europe, half a generation later, in 1848, that Switzerland prohibited all its citizens from 'service with foreign armies, and acceptance of foreign decorations and pensions', and the Confederation finally assumed its modern air of vacuous and innocuous neutrality.

The Foreign Legion at its inception was very far indeed from being considered an élite force. These first seven battalions were viewed, officers and NCOs apart, as mere extra and expendable cannon-fodder, the lowest of the low, far worse soldiers than the French themselves who still – justifiably – felt themselves to be the finest fighting men in Europe. No sooner were they formed than they were sent to Algeria. France's first colonial venture of modern times had been launched the preceding year with the landings at Sidi Ferruch. There began the long connection of the Legion with its 'home', Sidi-bel-Abbes, and with the Sahara – the visual picture that the word legionary still conjures up to most minds: with that silent *Beau Geste* fort at Zinderneuf manned by a company of dead legionaries, every man carefully propped up with his rifle at the firing position.

Life at Zinderneuf was not really life so much as the avoidance of death – death from sun-stroke, heat-stroke, monotony, madness or Adjutant Lejeune. *Cafard* was rampant; everyone was more or less abnormal and 'queer' from frayed nerves, resultant upon the terrific heat and the monotony, hardship and confinement to a little mud oven of a fort; many men were a little mad, and Adjutant Lejeune, in the hollow of whose hands were our lives and destinies, was a great deal more than a little mad.

A tradition had begun, but the Foreign Legion had not particularly distinguished itself. It was the next campaign in which the Legion fought, under the command of French rather than mercenary officers, which was decisive for its reputation.

In June 1835 Louis-Philippe of France decided to hire out the Legion to the legitimate government of Spain, embroiled as so often in the impassioned turmoil of civil war. This civil war, the first Carlist war, fought over the north and north-east of Spain, was vicious, epic and ill-organised. The Cristinos, the 'liberal' legitimists, were aided by both France and Britain. A semi-official body of British mercenaries, the British Auxiliary Legion, was raised by a British Member of Parliament, Sir de Lacy Evans, and led into Spain. They turned out to be politically embarrassing, militarily almost useless, and gradually disbanded themselves. But the French Foreign Legion virtually won the war for Queen Cristina. Her rival for the throne, Don Carlos, had in his turn raised a Carlist foreign legion. At the battle of Barbastro in June 1837, the two foreign legions, French and Carlist, almost obliterated each other while the Spaniards on both sides paused to look on.

Five thousand Foreign Legionaires had been sent to Spain; 875 fought at Barbastro; of these less than one man in five survived the battle. This was the last great battle of rival mercenary armies, equal in its ferocity if not its scale to those of the *landsknecht* and the Swiss.

Traditions

Here, properly, began the mythology of the Legion, created by its original commander in Spain, Colonel Bernelle. First the ingredients had to be stirred. Of the seven original battalions the 1st, 2nd and 3rd had been German; the 4th was Spanish; the 5th Italian; the 6th Belgian and Dutch; the 7th Polish. Bernelle decided that if national regiments were retained, national pride would subsist – at the expense of France. He mixed the nationalities by forming thoroughly heterogeneous battalions – the first and last time this has ever been consistently done in mercenary history. The experiment, against all the odds, succeeded: when Marshal Lyautey asked a soldier at an inspection in Morocco what his nationality was, the man replied, '*Légionnaire, mon Général.*'

It was at this time too that the tradition started that a recruit's past and his correct name were no concern of the Legion's. No other single rule in any army has ever become so famous and so successful. Bernelle also added those touches of eccentricity that marked the Legion out as different: he formed the platoons of bearded axe-bearing sappers that always lead the Legion parades. Above all he instituted the system of ferocious discipline that has always characterised the Legion.

> ...Colour Sergeant Lejaune, a terrible and terrifying man who had made his way in the Legion (and who made it further still) by distinguishing himself as a relentlessly harsh and meticulous disciplinarian, a savagely violent taskmaster, and a pushing non-com of tremendous ability, energy and courage; at times he was undoubtedly mad, and his madness took the form of sadistic savagery.

Bernelle's successor in Spain, Colonel Conrad, stamped the Legion with its other distinctive marks. He was a Frenchman who prided himself on that usual accomplishment among the French, an ability to speak many languages; he was known to the German legionaries as '*der alte Fritz*'. As a commander, he had the reputation of knowing only one word of command – 'Charge!' He died, suitably and heroically, at Barbastro leading a bayonet attack. From his period in command sprang the reputation of the Legion for military *élan*.

> With 100 rounds of ammunition in our pockets, joy in our hearts and a terrific load upon our backs, we swung out of the gates to the music of our magnificent band, playing the March of the Legion, never heard save when the Legion goes on active service.

The marching songs of the Legion, which all the new recruits – *les bleux* – are immediately taught, are used to bind the various nationalities together, to give them their first comprehension of French, the language in which all commands are issued, to raise morale – and above all to instil that *esprit de corps*, that pride in tradition, which is the Legion's greatest weapon.

At the evening meal, *la soupe*, the old hands showed their form and one realized fully then how new we were and how far we had to go. We were all lined up outside the *réfectoire* and on the blast of a whistle the disciplined column filed in. There were long tables laden with food, along the side of which were small square metal stools, all in straight lines – perfect precision. Each man entered, removing his *kepi* as he did so, and stood to attention in front of his stool. Complete silence, absolute order, rigid discipline. The corporal entered last and called for a song, '*La Tone*'. A single voice broke the silence with the first few bars at the end of which he yelled '*Trois*' and the old hands in silence counted four imaginary paces and then with a crash like a pistol shot in a tunnel they yelled '*Quatre*' and blasted into '*La Légion Marche*'. In the enclosed *réfectoire* it was like being in a cathedral with sixteen choirs going for their lives – deafening and fantastic, tremendously strong and impressive. The song finished and the corporal yelled '*Asseyez-vous, bon appétit*' and with a mighty roar of '*Merci Caporal*' we dived into the food.

This is not as might be thought yet another quotation from *Beau Geste* describing Legion life at the turn of the century. On the contrary it comes from the diary of a modern legionary many, many decades later. Amazingly little has changed, least of all the spirit and the traditions – nor the twenty various uniforms all of which had still to be kept in tip-top condition.

Camerone

Tiens, voilà du boudin, voilà du boudin, voilà du boudin
Pour les Alsaciens, les Suisses et les Lorrains,
Pour les Belges il n'y en a point
Pour les Belges il n'y en a point
Car ce sont des tirailleurs au flanc

Boudin is blood sausage, the Legion's traditional festive dish. Every 30 April is celebrated the Legion's great annual festival, Camerone Day. As the young English mercenary (from whose diary the above, comparatively modern, description of *les bleux* in the *réfectoire* is taken) wrote on the eve of his first 30 April: 'The Legion goes mad on Camerone Day.'

On 30 April 1864, the third company of the First Battalion of the Legion, 59 strong with three officers, Captain Danjou, Lieutenant Vilain and 2nd Lieutenant Maudet, were surrounded in a deserted farmhouse in the hamlet of Camerone near Vera Cruz by thousands of Mexican troops. Captain Danjou had a wooden hand: on such details myths are built.

From early morning until dusk the legionaries resisted all assaults and contemptuously rejected all summons to surrender. When

Captain Danjou was shot through the head, Lieutenant Vilain took over command. When Vilain was killed, 2nd Lieutenant Maudet took over command. At dusk, with only five legionaries left alive, Maudet gave the order to fix bayonets and charge – what is known in the Legion and indeed throughout the French Army as the *baroud d'honneur*. For by tradition the Legion does not surrender.

The rescue column arrived too late. A memorial stone was erected on the site:

> *Ils furent ici moins de soixante*
> *Opposés à toute une armeé*
> *Sa masse les écrasa*
> *La vie plutôt que le courage*
> *Abandonna ces soldats français.*

But the rescue column's commander detached Captain Danjou's wooden hand from his body and it was taken to the *Salle d'Honneur* in Sidi-bel-Abbes. There, every Camerone Day, it was carried onto the parade ground and 'took the salute' while an account of the battle was read to the parading legionaries by the most decorated officer present.

Camerone became the epic of the Legion. At Dien Bien Phu in 1954 legionaries noted in their diaries the gloom of a Camerone Day spent without the traditional drunken revels and blood sausage. At Bukavu in 1957 one of Schrumme's mercenary captains asked: '*Qu'est-ce que je pouvais faire avec cinq gars contre la bande qui nous encerclait? Qu'est-ce que je pouvais faire? Camerone?*'

At Bukavu the mercenaries retreated. At Dien Bien Phu seven battalions of the Legion, well over half the defenders of the doomed and isolated position, fought off General Giap's Vietminh hordes for nearly two months in the most decisive and disastrous battle in the history of France's colonial empire. When eight years of war in Indochina ended at the Geneva Conference that year 10,483 legionaries had been killed (over 1500 of them at Dien Bien Phu) – more than in the Second World War, twice as many as in the First World War. Dien Bien Phu was a Camerone on a large scale, with a less glorious ending. All that then remained for the Legion, it appeared, was a last stand, another long-drawn-out eight years of struggle, in its own homeland, Algeria. When in 1961 Algeria finally became independent and Sidi-bel-Abbes was abandoned, the Legion was not, as might logically have been expected, dissolved. Its base was transferred to Aubagne near Marseilles; and so were the famous *Monuments aux Morts* – and the wooden hand of Captain Danjou. Not only has the Foreign Legion continued to exist, it continues to serve – and to fight – in its traditional decor. At one end of Africa, at Djibuti, four thousand Legionaries continue to guarantee this 'independent' republic against both Somali and Ethiopia expansionist aims and the USSR's desires for the best of the Red Sea ports. On the other side of Africa legionaries at the moment of writing are facing the Libyan troops of Colonel Gaddafy in the Sahara desert of Chad. The Legion was a period piece, formed for colonial expansion and used in colonial battles; but as long as France continues to pursue her neo-colonialist interests and influence in Africa, as she seems determined to do, the Legion, and its legend, will continue to survive.

Myth and Reality

Here he sat on a log and absolutely thrilled us to the marrow of our bones by tales, most graphically and realistically told, of the Spahis, the Foreign Legion, the Chasseurs d'Afrique, Zouaves, Turcos and other romantical-ly named regiments.
'I'm going to join the Foreign Legion when I leave Eton,' announced Michael suddenly.
'So am I,' said Digby of course.
'And I,' I agreed.

Beau Geste was published in 1920; and since then has sold millions of copies all over the world. P.C. Wren had been a legionary and he showed in *Beau Geste* and its sequels a power of description, a mastery of slang and a touch for the ingenious plot almost equal to that of Kipling. The French authorities publicly denounced his books, furious at the powerful myth of sadistic NCOs and barely tolerable conditions. But though the heroes may be dated and conventional, the villains and their language still ring true.

'*Cré bon sang de bon dieu de dieu de sort*', swore Lejaune, 'and I'll deal with you after this *chien d'une revolte*. If you don't both die *en crapaudine*, by God, you shall live *en crapaudine*.'

Glamour and brutality are the common stuff of romantic fiction. It is in Wren's case, as it was in Kipling's, the realism of the details that establishes the myth: the 'dirty little' *Bureaux de Recrutement*: *Engagements Volontaires* in the Rue Sainte Dominique in Paris; the description of the unvarying food – *soupe*, served twice a day in tin basins called *gamelles*, no knives and forks, with unsweetened milkless coffee from a pail, the close-cropped haircut inflicted on offenders, the *boule à zéro*. The daily training routine – 05.15 reveille, 05.30 the recruit, the *bleu* – parades in white uniform, knapsack, rifle, belt and bayonets, ready for the incredibly long marches at the unvarying pace of five kilometres an hour, eighty-eight paces a minute. The continual talk of desertion – *faire la promenade*; the absolute power of the NCOs. The moral rules of the Legion: 'Theft in that collection of the poorest of poor men was the ultimate crime, infinitely worse than murder' and punished according to 'legion law' by the thief being spread-eagled on the barracks-room table and then pinned to it by a bayonet jammed through either hand. Perhaps the only peculiarity of Legion life Wren does not mention is the mobile brothel attached to each regiment of the Legion – but he was, after all, writing in a more prudish age.

In the early 1960s very little had changed, except perhaps the food. The NCOs were still brutal and slightly mad, the punishments ferocious to the point of bestial savagery, the training routine designed to break a man's spirit, the marches almost unendurable, theft still the most unspeakable of crimes, and desertions not only talked of but practised.

> We have been introduced to Sergeant Lustig, late of the German army. He has a reputation built up on a mass of stories of courage and ruthlessness and he has a total disregard for everyone and everything. He is typically Germanic in appearance, handsome if that's your taste, blond, blue eyes, looks about thirty-five, is nearer forty-five and is as tough as granite. Hesitation to Lustig is cowardice and is instantly punishable. The punishment is to stand the man to attention with his hands behind his back and then thump him with every ounce of strength deep in the solar plexus. Nobody survives. The body folds into a crumpled form, sags to the ground and is left writhing and gasping in agony with the lungs screaming for air, like a pole-axed ox. Lustig enjoys inflicting this kind of pain.

Lejaune or Lustig, the difference between myth and reality is minimal. As the English mercenary Simon Murray wrote in the introduction to his recently published diaries (from which the above passage is quoted): 'Wren had painted a picture of the Legion that was not all that inaccurate.' Even the moment of engagement (nowadays in one of 25 recruitment centres that take in 1,500 recruits a year) is much the same. After initial weeding out, and initial attempts to discourage would-be recruits:

> 'Then read this form and sign it,' he said with a distinct sigh. 'Remember, though, that as soon as you have done so, you will be a soldier of France, entirely amenable to martial law, and without any appeal whatsoever.

Your friends cannot possibly buy you out, and your Consul cannot help you for five years. Nothing but death can remove you from the Legion.'

Death or of course desertion. That was Wren; this is Murray after observing punishment meted out to 'Lefevre and Aboine' who had 'deserted this afternoon during the siesta' and been recaptured in the evening.

> There was not a man among us who had not considered desertion and there was not a man among us now who for all his feelings of revulsion and hatred against the meaningless barbarism was not also secretly afraid of what he saw – afraid at such brutality; that it could be administered by a sadist like Wissman with no control and no appeal to any authority except that of the Legion – and in the Legion there is no appeal, and the authority is in those in whom it is vested, and it starts at the rank of corporal.

The end of every war in Europe brought new recruits from the ranks, as always, of demobilised and unemployed soldiers; particularly therefore among the conquered. Hence there have always been more Germans than any other nationality among the Legion. Their behaviour by the standards of patriotic nationalism has been inexplicable. Adjudant Chef Mader, in the First World War, killed his own countrymen on the Western front and became the most decorated NCO in the history of the Legion and a Chevalier of the *Légion d'Honneur*. By all normal standards this was treason to the Reich and to the Kaiser. But by semi-mythical standards it was the acme of mercenary loyalty, fit homage paid to the overriding ideal of the Legion.

After his five years of service a legionary has the right to be naturalised as a French citizen. Those who change their nationality can be promoted to the rank of officer; indeed even those who do not become French can reach the rank of captain, though no higher. Captain Prince Amilakvari, a Georgian, rose to the rank of lieutenant colonel and commanded the second battalion of the famous 13th Demi-Brigade, the one regiment of the Legion that rallied to de Gaulle and Free France in the Second World War. He fell at the head of his troops in the Western Desert, at the age of thirty-eight. *Légionnaire Deuxième Classe* Simon Murray was promoted, before his five years of contract service were over, to *Légionnaire Première Classe*, then to *Caporal-Chef* – his salary increasing *en route* from £3 to £30 a month. He was offered a commission if he would sign on for a second term but, half-regretfully, unwilling to change his nationality, refused.

'The English appear to be held in high regard here,' he had noted at the beginning of his five years' service, 'which is welcome. I think we are thought of as something quite strange. There are very few Englishmen in the Legion and I believe the general feeling is that we are all cracked and maybe slightly dangerous. They remember the war!' He was selected to join one of the two regiments of Legion paratroops, the 2e REP, 2ème Régiment Etrangère de Parachutistes. Had he been selected – and it was, it appeared, a mere matter of vacancies and luck – for the other paratroop regiment, the 1er REP, he would have been out of the Legion well before 12 February 1965 – though without the 'colourful certificate of "good conduct" which states that we have served for five years with *"honneur et fidelité"*.

The 1er REP (Première Regiment Etrangère de Parachutistes)

Why is it that other mercenary forces have never become as well-known as the Foreign Legion? That question, posed at the beginning of this chapter, has not entirely been answered as yet. It is perhaps this matter of armies, and their traditions. The French Army has managed to keep for centuries a different sort of spirit from other armies in the West. It is not a matter of military glory or efficiency, for the French Army has known ignominious defeats by the side of its greatest victories, although even Dien Bien Phu was, like Waterloo, a triumph of a sort. Still less is it a sense of militarism, in the South American or Neo-African sense; the army of France has never become merely a passive tool in the hands of a military dictator. But what is noticeable is that its spirit, like its origins, are semi-feudal. Orders are generally but not necessarily obeyed and the criterion at a grave moment of crisis is honour – what de Vigny describes as *la conscience exalteé*. French officers are not the blind automata of a German Army obeying the High Command or even of a British Army obeying the civil power. There is and always has been a kind of anarchy of spirit about the French army, which has kept it closer than any other army in Europe to the Free Companies of medieval times, from which after all it directly derives: bold, rash, efficient but independent-minded soldiers. The French Army has always remained semi-mercenary in spirit: that is to say, it has remained sceptical and hard to control.

In that way the Foreign Legion is typical: the anarchic tradition is combined with the military virtues in war inherited from that other strand in the mercenary make-up, the Swiss tradition, and with loyalty both to an idea and to a direct commander but not to a political leader. Nowhere did this tradition make itself more melodramatically apparent in recent years than in the case of the fighting élite of the French army, the First Legion Paras, the 1er REP – the unit that was to be the direct ancestor of the Congo and other mercenaries, as succeeding chapters will make clear.

The two paratroop regiments of the Legion were formed in 1948 and quickly became what the general staff had half hoped and half feared they would become, an élite within an élite. They were formed to fight in Indochina, and in Indochina they – but in particular the 1er REP – fought as few regiments have ever fought before. In September 1950 the 1er REP was wiped out at Caobang with 90 per cent losses, including that of its first commanding officer, Commandant Segrétain, who died of his wounds in a Vietminh prison camp. Disbanded, the regiment was reformed in March 1951 only to be wiped out a second time at Dien Bien Phu where 576 of its 700 legionaries were killed – the last on 6 May after the final *baroud d'honneur* by the garrison of which they were the sole fighting survivors. Reformed again, the regiment took part in the Suez expedition before being posted to Algeria where on 7 May 1958 its commanding officer, Colonel Jeanpierre, one of the handful of officers and men to have escaped from the disaster at Caobang, was killed in action, shot down with the helicopter from which he was directing his legionaries' manoeuvres near the Tunisian border.

The war in Indochina had been a war of parachute drops. The war in Algeria was a war of helicopters over higher but more open country (and, in the vast southern desert, a war of armoured cars, with the celebrated Compagnies Saharienns Portées de Légion. of the 1er REC, the 1st Colonial Regiment of the Legion).

But it was also, more viciously, for the 1er REP a city war. The regiment, on its arrival in Algeria in 1956, was stationed outside Algiers, at Zeralda where, in the tradition of the Legion, it built its own barracks, the finest in Algeria. General Massu gave it the unpleasant task of cleaning up the Casbah, the native city of Algiers; which the regiment proceeded to do with sweeping success and ruthless brutality, largely thanks to the 'skills' of the 1er REP's intelligence officer, Captain Robert Faulques, an expert in counter-revolutionary warfare. As Légionnaire Murray of the 2e REP wrote three years later when trouble again flared up in Algiers:

> De Gaulle will not sanction the use of the methods that flattened the Casbah in the blood-bath of 1957. If the Legion is called in, this will be

tantamount to such an approval and then God help the Muslims! So we wait like Napoleon's dogs in Animal Farm; and I think I differ from my fellow soldiers, for I hope we will remain chained, whereas they strain at their leashes like panting Dobermans, desperate to be let loose amongst a Muslim crowd which they can tear apart with the fangs of their sub-machine-guns.

The reputation of the 1er REP never really recovered from the 'dirty war' of the Battle of Algiers, more suitable for secret police than for soldiers and involving many of the methods, undoubtedly including torture during interrogations, used by the most sinister of all secret polices. Out in the mountain air of the *djebels* the stained officers and men of the 1er REP cleansed themselves in 'proper' fighting; but never cleansed away the bitterness they felt towards the civilians and the government in France who had given them what they felt was an inglorious duty creditably performed but ungratefully accepted. De Gaulle's coming-to-power was first welcomed; then rejected as it became clear that he too was about to 'betray' Algérie Française for which the Legion, and in particular the 1er REP, had sacrificed so much both of its blood and its reputation. In 1960 its then Colonel, Henri Dufour, was condemned to three months' close arrest for insubordination. On 22 April next year, 1961, sudden and extraordinary news startled the whole world: a group of generals had seized power in Algiers, proclaimed their support for Algérie Française and threatened to drop their paratroop regiments on Paris unless De Gaulle gave way.

It quickly became apparent that it was the 1er REP, under its acting commander Elie De Saint Marc, that had spearheaded the *putsch*, occupying all the key government offices in Algiers and seizing the radio. The news reached the legionaries of the 2e REP, three hundred miles along the coast to the east at Philippeville, later that same day.

> By late evening [wrote Légionnaire Murray] the atmosphere was wild but we waited. The prospect of being involved in a *putsch*, a *coup d'état*, a civil war almost, has a certain fascination to say the least and is hardly an everyday occurrence. Apparently there is a possibility that we might be dropped on France. Excruciating thought to be dropped on Paris, everybody is going out of their minds with the excitement.

This was a Legion *coup*; and it quickly became apparent that the four generals who had seized power could rely in classic tradition on their mercenary troops alone. As the above extract shows, the legionaries had no loyalties to France but only to the Legion and their own officers, with excitement and possibly thoughts of booty utterly outweighing any sentiment of right or wrong. Indeed there was no question of right or wrong about it, though twenty-four hours later Murray was indignant that no officers had as yet explained to them whose side they were on. 'They assume we will just obey orders,' he noted indignantly.

They assumed correctly. By then the 2^e REP had driven through the night to Algiers where 'thousands and thousands of Europeans lined the roads madly cheering us through'. Next day his regiment occupied the airport, savagely beating back the French marines already in possession. But by the third day it was becoming clear how little support this mercenary *coup* had among the 120,000 French soldiers, mainly conscripts, already in Algeria; and even among the 30,000* Legionaries only the elite, the paratroop battalions, had taken decisive action. De Gaulle from Paris thundered over the radio, and by 25 April the *coup* had failed and the four generals, its leaders, had gone into hiding.

Next day, on the orders of the Army Minister, Pierre Messmer, himself a former officer in the Legion, the 1er REP was solemnly paraded and ignominiously disbanded. Its barracks at Zeralda were blown up. Its officers were court-martialled – as were, later, many of the officers of the 2e REP. The 2e REP was however spared the fate of its sister regiment. It continued to exist, though demoralised and losing many legionaries who deserted to the 'secret army' of *Algérie Française*, the terror groups of the OAS that later came so close to assassinating General de Gaulle. 'We have still not been paid', noted Murray on the dismal Camerone Day that followed, 'and despair is turning to disgust that could well erupt' – the classically dangerous situation with mercenary troops.

It was not till December of the following year, 1962, that General Lefort, Inspector-General of the Legion, revived morale by announcing to the assembled legionaries of the 2^e REP that the regiment would 'undergo a massive metamorphosis designed to make us a crack unit of the French Army' with specialised training in night fighting, demolition, guerilla warfare, skiing, moutaineering, underwater combat, and submarine courses. 'This is all terrific stuff', wrote Murray. 'Morale in one stroke has been given a gigantic shot in the arm. We're back in business.'

But not the 1er REP. That extraordinary regiment with its short but dramatic history, twice formally disbanded, twice annihilated, twice

* The number of mercenaries recruited by France falls drastically, of course, in times of peace. At the moment there are 8,000 men in the Legion.

having lost its commanding officer in action, and all this within the brief space of thirteen years, was never to be reformed. But in another sense many of its disbanded, embittered, experienced, professional paid fighting men, both officers and other ranks, were soon 'back in business' too, the only business they knew, the business of war – as the sequel will show.

Book One

THE CONGO AND ITS AFTERMATH

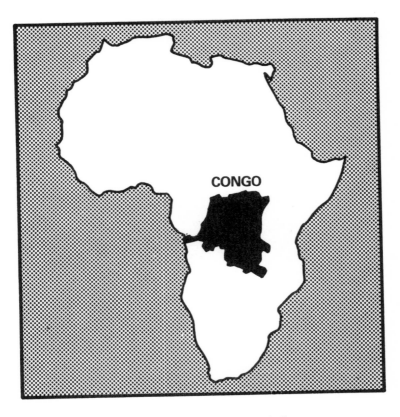

Africa: The Congo (shaded)

3

Katanga, Katanga, Katanga

'Seditious unfaithful disobedient destroyers of all places and countries whither they are drawn as being held by no other bond than their own commodity'

Sir Walter Raleigh on mercenaries, *History of the World*

Mercenaries have never had a good press. But they never had a worse press than in the year 1960 when they suddenly, and to general alarm, reappeared in the Congo, like evil genies released from some anachronistic, distastefully medieval bottle. There was little attempt to take a detached view and to see in their apparition merely a historical phenomenon reviving. Furthermore in the confusion of the Congo, in that early medley, villains and heroes were needed, both by politicians and the public. The heroes tended to change (or to die) with frightening rapidity. But the faceless villains were successfully found: the mercenaries and, ranged behind them, their backers, the sinister capitalists of Katanga.

The inevitable ranting of African leaders and newspapers – 'human vermin', 'ignoble mercenaries', 'gangsters in the service of Western imperialist capitalism' – was an understandable screech of outrage in those heady days of new-won independence that suddenly seemed threatened by the totally unexpected. It found a ready echo in the purple prose of the West's popular press.

> They are the world's last soldiers of fortune, outdated relics of the past. They are outcasts from the modern world which expelled them or from which they have fled – on the lam from an infamous past, a burnt-out adventure, a dead faith. They are all ex-something: ex-SS officers from Germany, ex-CIA pilots from Cuba, ex-students from South Africa or Southern Rhodesia. Some follow a macabre ideal of glory and adventure; some believe they are fighting a last-ditch battle against communism; some are known as *Les Affreux*, The Horrors, who just love war.

Years were to pass before mercenaries became, at least in right-wing newpapers, quasi-respectable. Little wonder that Lt. Gouhaux, an embittered French mercenary officer of the early period, told *Le Figaro*, France's equivalent of the *Daily Telegraph*: '*C'est la faute des journalistes si nous sommes si mal vus dans le monde.*' But it was not the fault of journalists, it was not the fault of African politicians or western capitalists, it was not even the fault of the mercenaries themselves. It was merely an instinctive shying away by public opinion from an unusual and little understood phenomenon – a reaction of pure bafflement. For by then people had become confused by the Congo, not merely by the actual political situation (though that was confusing enough) but by its implications: that chaos, savagery and tribalism lay just below the surface and that the former colonial masters had not really succeeded by that *annus mirabilis* of the black continent's new-found independence, 1960, in imposing their ideas and manners on these well-dressed, well-spoken, new African leaders.

The Congo Becomes Independent

The Congo is an empire rather than a nation. It is larger than Europe, inhabited by hundreds of tribes, with no common language or culture. The three principal cities are – or, to be accurate, were – Leopoldville, Elizabethville and Stanleyville. General Mobutu – Mobutu Sese Seko as he now calls himself, the President-for-life, the Saviour – changed their names in 1967; they are now Kinshasha, Lumumbashi and Kisangani. Later he also changed the name of the Congo itself to Zaire. But the history of the country will be confusing enough already without a futher confusion of names; and to save space I intend to continue to refer to the cities by their original nicknames under which I first came to know (though hardly to love) them: Leo, E'ville and Stan.

Leo, in the west almost on the shores of the Atlantic, is the capital of the country, the seat of government, held since 1960 by government forces. E'ville in the far south is the capital of the mining state of Katanga, incredibly rich in resources and dominated by the great mining capitalist conglomerate, Union Minière. Stan is an outpost in the wild territory of the northeast and has as often as not been held by rebels or breakaway leaders. No normal roads or railways join these three cities; the only real link is by air. Through the tropical forests of the Congo flows the vast river which gave the whole country its name.

On 30 June 1960, then, the Independence of what had till then

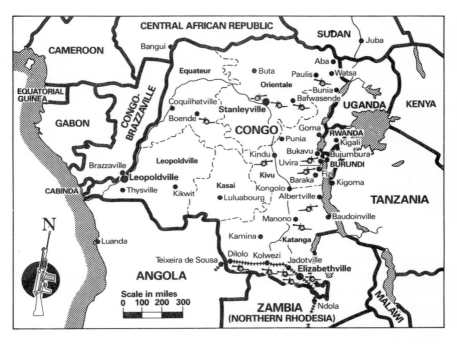

The Congo and surrounding countries

been the Belgian Congo was celebrated in the presence of King Baudovin of the Belgians in Leo and with enormous rejoicing throughout the whole country. Five days later the troops of the Force Publique – highly disciplined, smartly turned-out, 30,000 strong, the pride and joy of the colonial régime – mutinied against their Belgian officers, and the horrors began.

The Baluba War and the Coming of the Mercenaries

In the deep south of the country, in the mining province of Katanga, a large number of Belgian troops had remained behind at the enormous military base of Kamina, designed as a bastion for NATO in Africa, with barracks that could house – but never did – 30,000 men.

The *Force Publique* had been rechristened the *Armée Nationale Congolaise* – the ANC. On the night of 9/10 July the ANC at E'ville, in Camp Massart, mutinied. This was potentially the most serious mutiny of all, for not only were many civilian Belgian lives at stake in this almost garden city but also Belgium's economic control of the nearby mines and their wealth. Belgian troops moved in quickly from Kamina, suppressed the disorders and disbanded 2,500 of the original 2,800 ANC. Among the 300 retained was a former sergeant-major Norbert Muké, who was at once promoted to colonel.

The next day, 11 July, the leading black politician in the region, Moise Tshombe, proclaimed the secession of Katanga – and appointed Colonel Norbert Muké commander-in-chief of the Katangese gendarmes. For Tshombe, now President Tshombe of the breakaway, mineral-rich, Belgian-backed independent state of Katanga, a large jovial-looking figure whose name is indissolubly linked with 'his' white mercenaries, decided to form not his own army as such but his own *gendarmerie*. To all intents and purposes it was the same thing; but the Katangese troops from that day forward were always referred to as the Katangese gendarmes.

'*Katanga, Katanga, Katanga*' – they and the whites that joined them sang – '*Katanga est Notre Pays.*'

This then was the new army – a tiny one – of a new state, starting from zero.

Two days later, that is to say a fortnight only after Independence had been proclaimed, the first United Nations troops flew into the Congo and the military imbroglio began. For however much the United Nations may have tried to disguise the situation, this was not merely a life-saving or a peace-keeping force: its ultimate mission was to put an end to Tshombe's breakaway state in Katanga, and to do this it had the backing of both the Russians and the Americans, for once united. As United Nations forces took over, the last Belgian troops were pulled out.

From Tshombe's point of view, the most immediate threat came not from the United Nations troops nor from the still-demoralised ANC of the central government but from his own political and tribal rivals, the much feared Balubas who dominated North Katanga. Bands of Baluba youths, armed mainly with sharpened bicycle chains, were already forming into those gangs known as '*Jeunesse*' which later became such a title of terror. To oppose all these enemies, potential and actual, Tshombe had merely his minuscule force of gendarmes. Admittedly its officers and NCOs were (apart from their commander-in-chief and other titular leaders) regular Belgian soldiers who were, in effect, seconded to Katanga. Their *éminence grise* was Colonel Guy Weber who had arrived on 10 July with a paratroop brigade and who stayed on when the Belgian troops were recalled. He became Tshombe's military adviser, known as 'the Shadow'. but it was apparently another Belgian, Carlos Huyghe, who first suggested to the harassed president the hiring of mercenary troops and by doing so opened a whole new chapter in modern Africa's history.

Tshombe eagerly accepted the suggestion. Recruitment centres were opened in Southern Rhodesia, in Bulawayo and Salisbury, quietly at first, with discreet advertisements appearing in the local newspapers – a technique that was to become the classic method for recruiting modern mercenaries. It became known throughout the Federation of Rhodesia, Katanga's southern neighbour (then governed by the bull-like Sir Roy Welensky who was to become Tshombe's friend and supporter) that there were well-paid openings for police officers in the Katanga *gendarmerie*. The occasional English-speaking mercenary began to appear in E'ville. But it was all at this early stage very low-key, small-scale stuff.

Before the end of 1960 the war against the Balubas in North Katanga had turned savage and bitter. Meanwhile there had been constant turmoil in the Congo's capital. The Prime Minister, Patrice Lumumba, the bearded young revolutionary, whose vehement oratory had forced the pace of Independence and whose impassioned denunciations after Independence threatened what the Belgians were determined to cling onto, their economic power, was deposed by the ANC's Commander-in-Chief, the comparatively colourless but compensatingly long-lived General Mobutu, after only nine weeks in power. By the end of 1960 Lumumbist troops – ANC deserters – were invading North Katanga and helping the Balubas while isolated detachments of United Nations troops held various strongpoints throughout Katanga and attempted to keep out of trouble.

Colonel Trinquier's Mission

At this stage Tshombe took a dramatic decision. He was too agile a politician not to realise that other countries besides Belgium would be interested in Katanga. He made a move to enlist French officers and NCOs to reorganise and lead his expanding army – a secret request for aid either to the French government or directly to France's Ministry of War.

General de Gaulle was certainly by no means averse to extending France's influence into the largest French-speaking country in Africa. Colonel Trinquier, a veteran of Indochina, a specialist in 'revolutionary warfare', who had commanded the 3ᵉ Regiment de Parachutistes Coloniau, in Algeria (and who had been a leading figure in the coup of 13 May 1958 that had brought De Gaulle back to power and installed the Fifth Republic) received a letter while on leave at Nice on 5 January 1961 offering him in effect full control of the Katangese *gendarmerie*. Trinquier flew to E'ville on 25 January. With him, when he touched down in Katanga, were a handful of French officers, including Commandant Faulques of the 1ᵉʳ REP.

This was three months before the Generals' *putsch* in Algeria; where of course the simmerings of incipient rebellion had already come to the French government's notice. Faulques, like Jeanpierre, had been one of the few Legion paratroop officers to survive both the disaster of Caobang in 1950 and the Vietminh prison camps.

Colonel Trinquier's immediate mission was to write a report for President Tshombe. He presented his report in February. In it he forecast – utterly wrongly as it happened, a specialist duped by his own speciality – that the main threat to Katanga would come from subversive revolutionary cells organised in Katanga's capital, E'ville. (In fact the eventual force that overthrew Katanga was the very conventional troops of the United Nations using the most traditional techniques of warfare.) To combat this supposed threat Trinquier demanded full control of the Katangese armed forces for five years plus virtual control of the Ministries of Information and the Interior, the support of the Belgian officers of the *gendarmerie*, the full support of the President – and permission to recruit 'fifteen to twenty French officers, broken into the methods of modern warfare'. 'Alone, in fact,' he wrote, 'I will be of no use to you. It is necessary then, on this point at least, that I should obtain the aid and support of the French government.'

Tshombe accepted Trinquier's report enthusiastically, and the French colonel flew back to France to enrol his twenty officers. Back at E'ville the Belgian Colonel Weber had inevitably got word of the proposed manoeuvre – a virtual French take-over of Katanga – and was doing his best to stop French expansion into this traditional Belgian preserve. It seems that Tshombe promised both colonels, unknown to each other, his full support, and the whole idea came to an almost farcical ending, typical enough of the Congo, when Trinquier, flying back to Katanga in March with his twenty French officers, was refused permission to land at E'ville. Instead, he had to fly on to meet the sinister Godefroid Munongo, Tshombe's Minister of the Interior, at Ndola in Northern Rhodesia to continue 'negotiations'. But by then two events had occurred that completely changed, for the worse, all mercenary prospects in the Congo.

The Death of Lumumba

The first was the murder of the former Prime Minister, Patrice Lumumba. During his brief period in power Lumumba had virulently denounced the Belgians, denounced the United Nations, denounced his Congolese opponents, denounced Union Minière, and called on the Russians and Czechs for military aid. He had made any number of enemies – including of course, by his last move, the Americans. He was killed in Katanga probably on 17 January 1961 – though his death was not officially announced till 12 February. A charismatic figure, he had survived independence for only six months before he was murdered; but in death, as so often happens, he became an even more influential figure, the very symbol of anti-colonialism, than he had ever been in life.

Was it a foreign mercenary who murdered the ex-Prime Minister? It is certainly possible. Belgian mercenaries came in time to have a particularly unsavoury reputation as murderers; and by all accounts it was a Belgian mercenary named Vanne who murdered another young revolutionary African leader, President Ali Soilih in the Comores in 1976, as a later chapter will recount. Even Belgium's mercenary hero, Schramme, was arrested in June 1968, shortly after his return to Belgium, on the charge of having murdered a Belgian planter Maurice Quintin in the Congo a year before. So in February 1960 there were very strong rumours that a Belgian mercenary had administered the *coup de grâce* to Lumumba.

The mercenary was later (by a witness before the UN Commission of Enquiry) given a name, Ruys. But in any case he merely finished Lumumba off with a bullet in the head – 'mercifully', noted the chief UN official in Katanga, Conor Cruise O'Brien, no friend at all to mercenaries. But Conor Cruise's *bête noir* in every sense was the man behind the murder, Munongo. 'I should not like to encounter very often in dreams', he wrote, 'Godefroid Munongo's dark spectacles,' and he added: 'It was generally believed in E'ville that he had killed Lumumba with his own hands.'

Munongo's grandfather, the ferocious Msiri, had been paramount chief in Katanga before the Belgians came; and it had been another white mercenary of an earlier generation, Captain 'Blue Nose' Stairs, who had left conquered Katanga in 1892 taking with him Msiri's 'curiously-shaped head' in a petroleum tin. Munongo undoubtedly hated all whites. Yet

> Msiri's grandson was an adversary who compelled respect [wrote Conor Cruise]. His standards were the standards of a cruel and archaic world but at least he held to them bravely. ... Of all the Katanga politicians his was the most impressive personality. For Munongo Katanga had clearly a deep emotional significance. His voice used to shake with pride as he spoke of Bunyeka, the capital of his slave-trading ancestors; with pathos when he spoke of this or that traditional chief done to death by 'Lumumbists'.

It seems that on 17 January Patrice Lumumba was brought straight from the airport at E'ville to a villa where Tshombe and Munongo were waiting for him. After a few taunts Munongo seized a bayonet from the rifle of one of his own soldiers and drove it into Lumumba's breast. Then Ruys administered the *coup de grâce*. On 12 February Munongo announced that Lumumba had escaped and been killed by villagers; a flagrant lie that shocked all – bar one UN (Tunisian) offical in Leo. 'After all,' this representative of world opinion commented, cynically but unofficially, 'chaos has its own logic.'

In any event the scandal resulting from Lumumba's murder – news of his 'martyrdom' echoed round the world – apparently shook the desire of all or any of the French Ministries to become even semi-officially involved in the Congo imbroglio. Colonel Trinquier flew ignominiously back to Paris where his resignation from the army had been accepted. His only consolation was to sue Tshombe before the Seine tribunals for 20 million *anciens francs* for breach of contract. I do not know – but I doubt – whether he obtained more than moral satisfaction.

The Compagnie Internationale

The Trinquier débâcle however was not without results. Most of the twenty French officers who had come with him stayed on; and Faulques became their real leader, and Katanga's too, in the fighting against the United Nations. Faulques was scarred, publicity-shy, ruthless and much admired. He appeared again as a mercenary leader in the Yemen and, briefly, in Biafra. But he remains the most obscure of the well-known mercenary leaders and also the most respected by those mercenaries who fought with him.

In any case this was the beginning of the French mercenary involvement in the Congo – a failed semi-official mission. Mercenary history was repeating itself. A rich country, wracked by chaos and civil war, inevitably attracted professional fighting men from outside. France, like the Swiss Confederations, had tried to control officially the supply of her own mercenaries but had failed. Now it was the turn of the freelances. When in April, only a month later, the 1er REP was disbanded in Algeria, the inevitable occurred, as any student of mercenary history could have forecast. In dribs and drabs embittered ex-Legion paratroops found their way down to Katanga where, as an added inducement, one of their own ex-officers, the notorious Faulques, previously disgraced, was already in charge; and while in Algeria the underground army of the OAS fought their last terror campaigns against both the Algerians and de Gaulle's *barbouzes*, a continuous stream of disillusioned but hardened French ex-soldiers and policemen kept up the supply of French – or at least French-speaking – mercenary troops far to the south.

Meanwhile the English-speaking mercenaries were forming themselves into a separate group, and rivalry and mutual mistrust between the French, the English and the Belgians was already making itself felt. It was to be an odd but ever-present factor on the mercenary scene.

The first encounter between mercenaries and United Nation troops took place on 7 April 1961, near Manono – a confused skirmish rather than a battle in which the English-speaking mercenaries clashed with Ethiopian troops of the United Nations. Several Ethiopians were killed; and about thirty mercenaries, including their commander, an Englishman named Richard Browne, were captured. Intriguing echoes of mercenary history immediately appeared, not least in the nomenclature chosen.

The group of mercenaries commanded by Captain Browne had been organized in a unit called the *Compagnie Internationale* [wrote Dr Mekki Abbas of the United Nations in a subsequent report]. Although the apprehended personnel claimed different nationalities, they all enlisted for service as mercenaries while they were in South Africa, Southern Rhodesia or Katanga. Most of the personnel questioned were ex-servicemen. They were physically fit, had a soldierly bearing and showed a sense of discipline. They came from various walks of life and the motives for enlistment given ranged from financial reasons, domestic troubles and lust for adventure to a desire to serve what they considered a good cause. Most of them claimed to have been under the impression that they were enlisting for police duties and not for active warfare.

The *Compagnie Internationale* was armed and equipped by the Katangese gendarmerie and wore the same uniforms. Its present strength has been reported as approximately 200 men and other ranks. When fully operational, it would consist of 5 platoons. The unit to which the apprehended personnel belonged was used as a spearhead and fought through to Manono which its men were the first to enter. The information obtained confirmed that the non-Congolese military personnel formed the back-bone of the military operations in Katanga and were instrumental in carrying out the recent offensive of the Katangese forces. In particular the *Compagnie Internationale* commanded by Captain Browne composed of experienced and disciplined soldiers seemed to have supplied the elite necessary for this type of military operation.

Discipline: Captain Browne maintained that his unit observed throughtout the operation strict discipline and the recognized rules of military combat. He admitted inflicting casualties during the advance on Manono and while clearing a road-block but claimed that his unit fired only at military personnel opposing him, when military necessity so required.

In this connection he and some other members of his unit were sharply critical of the methods used by the Katangese gendarmerie units led by Belgians and *Les Affreux* whom they accused of burning habitations indiscriminately and firing at people who were not offering resistance. Towards the end of the operation friction appeared to be developing for this and other reasons between the *Compagnie Internationale* and other units of the Katangese forces.

This appears to be a fair and accurate report from a source naturally hostile to the mercenaries – though Dr Abbas was obviously something of an Anglophile and appears to have swallowed a certain amount of guff from Captain Browne. Browne was the brother of the Tory MP for Torrington in Devon – shades of Sir de Lacy Evans and his British Auxiliary Legion in the Carlist War – which caused embarrassment at Westminster. From other sources it seems that Browne was more often to be seen at the bars of E'ville than out in the field; he was renowned both for his drinking and for his size. The United Nations had a problem with 'their' mercenary prisoners; how were they to treat them? They had no jails, no machinery for trials – and in any case what precise offense under international law had mercenaries committed? Browne was merely expelled – but kept coming back into Katanga from Northern Rhodesia and then being expelled again.

Future Mercenary Leaders: Wicks, Puren, Hoare, Schramme, Denard

What is out of proportion, however, is the importance accorded in this report to Browne and to the other thirty mercenaries (who appear in any case not to have put up much of a show before surrendering: the remaining 170 members of the ephemeral Compagnie Internationale sound more fictional than factual.) For most of the other mercenary leaders who were later to become famous or notorious were also active in Katanga. Alastair Wicks, who had emigrated after the Second World War to Rhodesia, certainly fought in the Baluba War; he was later to become Hoare's second-in-command, a position for which he was ideally suited. ('Old Harrovian Alastair Wicks added a touch of elegance to often bloody proceedings', as the pro-mercenary press put it.) Jeremiah Puren, an obscure Afrikaner, was appointed titular Commander-in-Chief of the Katangese air force for reasons obscurer still.

Hoare was also there, though he seems to have played a comparatively minor role. He had known Katanga from pre-Independence safari expeditions; and the story goes that he was hired not as a mercenary but on a freelance basis by a South African millionaire named Anderson whose son had been reported missing in North Katanga. Sometime in 1961 Hoare led an expedition of half a dozen mercenaries out into the bush only to find that the missing son and a Scotsman had been ritually murdered by the Baluba. Thereupon Hoare sacked and burnt the village of Kalamatadi. This seems to have been his only major exploit, and he apparently left Katanga before the major battle that marked the end of the year 1961, the second battle of Katanga.

Schramme, however, took part in this battle. Jean Schramme was the son of a highly respectable Bruges lawyer; at the age of eighteen he had come out to the Congo to run a family plantation near Bafwasende to the north-east of Stan. He fled, like so many other Belgian *colons*, during the troubles following Independence and in early 1961 ended up in Katanga after having taken refuge in Uganda. There he was enrolled as a training officer at Kamina base; and, after taking part in the fighting at E'ville as one of Faulques' junior commanders, he was sent to Kansimba in North Katanga where he recruited fifteen- and seventeen-year-olds from the local tribes and formed his 'Leopard Group', officered by himself and one or two other Belgian ex-planters. In Katanga he did not cut much of a figure; he was reputed to be shy and rather nervous, though eager to please.

Denard was just the opposite – what the French call a *baroudeur*, physically large, colourfully dressed, moustachioed, and a Gascon – a contrast to Hoare and Schramme who were both small and rather precise men. 'Bob' was too flamboyant a figure for the English-speaking mercenaries to take seriously, and was viewed by the Belgians (as Schramme's later attitude indicated) with a mixture of uneasy admiration and deep suspicion. Aged thirty-two, son of a French peasant farmer, Denard had fought in Indochina as an NCO in the French marines. He later served in the security forces in Morocco and Algeria. He seems to have acted as a sort of right-hand man for Faulques, though he was never in the Legion himself. He had also apparently been involved in shadowy right-wing activities, including a plot in 1954 to assassinate Pierre Mendes-France, the left-wing Jewish intellectual and French political leader – which cost him fourteen months in prison. When Faulques left Katanga, Denard took over command of the mercenaries for the last battle against the United Nations. It was there at Kolwezi that he was to win that reputation for personal bravery and loyalty that his later activities were to do nothing to justify.

Operation 'Rumpunch'

But at the time of the capture of the Compagnie Internationale the mercenaries were still fighting the Balubas, not the United Nations forces. Captain Browne said that they had been under the impression as per their briefing by Belgian officers that there would not be any conflict between them and UN, that the only fighting would be against the 'bloody Balubas' as they were generally called. 'Sold up the river' was the phrase Captain Browne used to give vent to his feelings, and he suggested piously to his interrogators that the United Nations should take steps to warn the 'astonished' mercenaries of their true position.

Previously the Security Council had limited the UN forces in the Congo to strictly defensive police actions. A Resolution of 21

February 1961 however authorised them to go on the offensive more or less as they – or rather the Special Representative in Katanga of the Secretary-General – judged necessary. The Special Representative was a belligerent Irishman of very decided political views, Conor Cruise O'Brien; and the commander of the UN Forces in Katanga, by mid-1961 20,000 strong, was also – fortunate coincidence for Conor Cruise – an Irishman, General Sean McKeown. On 28 August the Special Representative launched what was in effect a military sweep in Katanga – the arrest, by McKeown's troops, of all the mercenaries who were still in Katanga.

There were according to the United Nations 512 'foreign military or paramilitary personnel' still in Katanga despite multiple summons to leave; about half were Belgian regular army officers on contract to the gendarmerie. As sudden sweeps went, Operation Rumpunch was a striking success. By the end of the day all but a hundred-odd of the original five hundred mercenaries in Katanga had been rounded up without a shot being fired. Conor Cruise could congratulate himself.

Those who escaped the net, however, were the fighting officers (including eleven of the French) out in the field with their units. Among those who did not escape were Wicks and Schramme. Wicks was expelled and does not appear to have returned. Schramme, according to his own account, was arrested at Kamina and was one of four mercenary officers sent up to Leo as prisoners of the ANC – if his story is true, to almost certain death. He was helped by a friendly chaplain to escape from prison, flew out from Leo to Brussels, and then took almost the first plane back to E'ville.

Paradoxically, the end of Operation Rumpunch marked the real beginning of the mercenary period in Katanga. The main result of Rumpunch was to clear out the regular Belgian army officers from Katanga – they lost a good deal of face by the rapidity with which they surrendered – and to leave the control of the Katangese gendarmerie in the hands of the three elements who formed the original freelance mercenaries: that is to say the French paratroop type, the English-speaking police officer type, and the local Belgian settler type. These hundred-odd mercenaries formed the hard core, both as types and as individuals, of all future mercenary activity in the Congo. Although the core was expanded, it never grew to any great size. I doubt whether at any one time there were ever more than five hundred mercenaries in the Congo. More likely, their strength, continually changing, wavered around the two to three hundred mark. Compared to their historical predecessors, this was a surprisingly small total.

The rest of the history of the independent state of Katanga is that of a struggle between the United Nations and Tshombe which finally ended in Tshombe's defeat but only after a series of dramatic reversals of fortune and the death of the Secretary-General of the United Nations. Three times the struggle burst into open battle between the United Nations forces and the Katangese gendarmerie led by the mercenaries.

The First Battle of Katanga: 13–21 September 1961

Following the easy success of Rumpunch, Conor Cruise O'Brien decided (with that overweening self-confidence that, as the Ancient Greeks knew, always leads to disaster) to put an end to the secession of Katanga by what was in effect a United Nations *coup d'état*. On 13 September United Nation Indian troops under Brigadier Raja seized control of key points in E'ville and throughout the state. Conor Cruise announced, unwisely: 'Katanga's secession is ended.'

Next day the Katangese gendarmerie counterattacked. Although Tshombe's airforce, nominally commanded by Jeremiah Puren, consisted only of two aged Fougas, a Dornier of First World War vintage and a helicopter from which the pilot tossed hand grenades, control of the air proved (as was almost always to be the case in Congolese battles) pretty nearly decisive. Heavy fighting followed in E'ville and elsewhere. Three days later the Irish garrison at Jadotville, 184 strong, surrendered to the Katangese led by the French mercenary Michel de Clary. Admittedly they were surrounded and their water supply had been cut off. But their position although unpleasant was not desperate; if their morale had been high, they could have fought their way out and inflicted a crushing defeat on the Katangese and the mercenaries. The least that can be said is that this surrender was hardly in the spirit of Irish history. The Swedes, the other European contingent in Katanga, won the reputation of never daring to set foot outside their armoured cars. Perhaps the morale of both Swedes and Irish was low because they had volunteered to come to the Congo and had expected to find a friendly population and be involved only in police operations; even so it was a dismal performance. The Indians at least performed respectably if cautiously; and the Ethiopians, though accused of atrocities, could never be accused of cowardice. Yet even so the mercenaries, man for man, were far superior to these well-equipped regular soldiers whom they dubbed, with some logic, '*les super-mercenaires*'.

This was the first time United Nations troops had used force in the course of their history – possibly unjustifiably, certainly unsuccessfully. On the day he heard the demoralising news of the Irish surrender at Jadotville (and following the general mess created by his two Irish subordinates on the spot) Dag Hammarskjöld, the autocratic idealistic Swede who had been for many years Secretary-General of the United Nations, resolved to fly out and meet Tshombe on neutral territory at Ndola in Northern Rhodesia. Three days later his plane crashed as it was about to land. The following day, 21 September, a ceasefire was arranged. This was a stalemate, in fact a virtual victory for the mercenaries and an extraordinary defeat for what were already overwhelming United Nations forces. The two Irishmen, Conor Cruise O'Brien and General Sean McKeown, were recalled by Hammarskjöld's successor, U Thant.

The Death of Dag Hammarskjöld

Ever since his death there have been rumours that Hammarskjöld's plane was shot down or sabotaged by mercenaries. The facts are these. Hammarskjöld flew into Leo on 13 September; when Conor Cruise's planned coup, 'Operation Morthor', began to go wrong, he was horrified and 'from his high plateau of intellectual and moral impartiality' decided on a peacemaking gesture. 'He was a very proud man,' wrote Conor Cruise later, 'who had been under intense personal strain and subject to violent personal vituperation.' At 5 pm on Sunday, 17 September a DC6 of the Swedish contract airline Transair piloted by Captain Hallonquist took off for Ndola airport in Northern Rhodesia carrying Hammarskjöld. At Ndola, Tshombe and Lord Alport, the British High Commissioner, were waiting for him. About midnight they saw the DC6 circle high over Ndola airport and head out to make a landing turn. Four minutes later it crashed nine miles away. There were no survivors.

There are theories that a bomb had been put aboard the plane before take-off by the Secretary-General's enemies; that Hammarskjöld had himself chosen a spectacular means of suicide and sabotaged his own flight; and, more realistically, that his plane had been shot down by a Vampire jet of the Rhodesian Air Force. But, as Conor Cruise points out, there was no reason for either Tshombe or Sir Roy Welensky to wish for Hammarskjöld's death. Furthermore neither they ('or even Macmillan') were, the Irishman wrote, 'murderers by disposition'. Conor Cruise himself suspected the mercenary fascists who had scores to settle with the United Nations from the days of Algeria, Suez and Tunisia. 'There was no doubt they were experienced in political assassination and would have regarded the murder of Hammarskjöld as a virtuous act.' And in particular he pointed the finger of suspicion at Katanga's Fouga pilots.

But Conor Cruise's judgement was undoubtedly prejudiced. First, because a mercenary, Lt. Delin, had strafed his own headquarters in a Fouga at midday the very next day, 18 September; and secondly, because earlier Munongo had hired 'a leathery-looking wiry' mercenary, André Cremer, precisely to form a killer group and assassinate UN officials (in particular Conor Cruise's own deputy, Michel Tombelaine) with the ghoulish instructions: '*Il me faut une victime.*' Cremer had cried off and revealed all. But, as Conor Cruise said, the flat-cheeked, heavy-under-lipped Munongo was 'the centre and symbol of the whole system'; and 'Munongo's was the one group in Katanga which would have been capable of such an act' as shooting down Hammarskjöld's plane.

These were, then, suspicions. But there was no proof at all; and both the UN and the Rhodesian Commissions of Enquiry concluded that the crash was an accident. Years later however, in 1980, some evidence began to emerge to support a new theory: that the DC6 had been attacked by a small Katangese transport plane, a mercenary-piloted Dove that had hovered above it and dropped down onto it a canister of TNT triggered by a hand-grenade. Certainly there had been reports of a flash and a bang; and some, less reliable, of a small plane seen over the larger one. The main snag with this theory was that it was put forward by Bo Virving, at the time of the crash Transair's chief engineer, who would naturally be inclined to shift the blame for the crash elsewhere. Appeals to mercenaries on Swedish television 'to ease the burden of their consciences and confess to what happened over Ndola that night' understandably met with no reponse. But I personally would be interested to hear (with the usual guarantee of complete anonymity) from anyone who has any first-hand information on this still-mysterious episode.

The Second Battle of Katanga: 5–21 December 1961

This followed only six weeks later. It was really a face-saving operation, pretty repellent whatever one's views on the rights and wrongs of an independent Katanga. The keepers of the world's conscience seemed to have no more scruples than any war-mongering nation state in seizing on the flimsiest of pretexts as an excuse for launching an attack.

The *casus belli* was a document captured by the United Nations – a plan for the defence of Katangese territory, generally attributed to

Faulques. Katanga was divided into five military zones, each to be commanded by a French mercenary: Albertville under Jacques, Kongolo under Bosquet, Manono under Protin, Kamina under Barvaux, and Kamiama under Faulques himself. In the case of a combined ANC/UN attack the mercenary plan called for 'harassing of the United Nations garrisons' with counter-attacks on the UN bases at E'ville and Kamina.

This time round the United Nations made sure that they had crushing air superiority. Sweden and Ethiopia contributed four jet fighters each; India added four jet bombers. The UN airforce opened operations on 5 December by a strike against the totaly outclassed Katangese airforce at its base of Kolwezi that virtually destroyed at a blow, on the ground, the mercenaries' main protection. In the week that followed, the UN jets bombed and strafed the centre of E'ville while mortar attacks softened up Faulques' defences. Then the Swedish armoured cars went in, followed by Brigadier Raja's highly professional Indian Army brigade consisting of a Gurkha, a Jat and a Dogra battalion commanded by Sandhurst-trained officers.

Nevertheless, in the street fighting that followed, Faulques and his men, so far from putting up a pitiful and demoralised resistance, gave the impression of being everywhere at once, always shifting and firing their mortars, knocking down walls between houses and rivalling each other in rashness. Admittedly they were supported by the local population, both black and white. But even allowing for the Belgian wives who would telephone the exact position of the United Nations troops occupying their streets or gardens, it seems incredible that this small group of only a few score mercenaries should have held out so long. On of Faulques' subalterns, Bob Denard, in charge of the mercenaries' heavy mortars showed himself to be a particularly ingenious, active and dashing commander. On 19 December, however, the Ethiopians successfully occupied Union Minière headquarters. Within forty-eight hours a ceasefire agreement was signed at Kitona.

This was a victory for the United Nations; although, given their overwhelming numbers and equipment, it had taken them far longer than it should have done to capture E'ville. Faulques and his men had fought in the best traditions of the Legion; though Faulques obviously felt he could have done better still. He left Katanga shortly afterwards, swearing that he would never again accept orders from Africans. Politically it looked like the end of Tshombe and Katanga. But Denard stayed loyally on, Puren stayed loyally on, and a year of political manoeuvring followed.

Union Minière

Were the mercenaries, as they were often accused of being, merely hired killers in the pay of large capitalist groups with African interests to defend? The *locus classicus* is certainly Katanga. But the precise relationship between the mercenaries and Union Minière is obscure. If there were any formal links, it has to be said that they have not yet been properly established.

A priori it does seem that there must have been a close working relationship: Union Minière supported Katanga's secession, Katanga's secession depended largely on the mercenaries, therefore Union Minière supported the mercenaries. Even Denard's last threat (see p. 55) can be seen as the threat of a minor employee in the happy position of being able to blackmail his undeservingly rich employer. But all is conjecture. There is no hard evidence to prove that Union Minière hired, approached or paid money to mercenary leaders – except in the indirect sense that the bulk of Katanga's financial resources, from which the mercenaries were paid and armed, came from the taxes and contributions of Union Minière.

My personal impression is that, at any rate once the euphoric initial period of Katangese Independence was over, Union Minière was continuously torn by its own internal dissensions, as is bound to happen in an amorphous, overgrown multinational conglomerate. These dissensions were further complicated by the need to reconcile the interests of all its disparate shareholders and different internal pressure groups. The result was a hesitancy and confusion of aims which made the company taken as a whole the most unreliable of allies and the feeblest of enemies.

This, let it be stressed, is merely a personal opinion. The only thing certain is that from Union Minière's point of view the mercenaries were not an unmixed blessing. But whether their leaders managed successfully to bleed Union Minière's coffers – an almost pious temptation which surely must have been ever present in their thoughts – and, if so, precisely to what extent are questions to which, unfortunately, the answers are likely to remain wrapped in indecent obscurity.

The Third Battle of Katanga: 28 December 1962 – 21 January 1963

A year passed before U Thant's military adviser, General Rikhye, delivered a final ultimatum to Tshombe, backed by the presence of

10,000 troops, demanding an end to Katanga's secession. On 28 December, the ultimatum rejected, UN troops in overwhelming numbers moved in on E'ville before dawn. This time there was virtually no resistance. E'ville fell, then in quick succession Kipushi and Kamina, Jadotville and Shinkolowbe.

Bob Denard was in command of the mercenaries at Kolwezi, half way to the Angolan border, the last bastion of Katangese resistance. Apparently, in an effort to continue the hopeless struggle, his thirty-odd mercenaries threatened to blow up the giant hydroelectric installations there, a move which would have ruined Union Minière, and only a direct appeal from Tshombe stopped them. Denard by his last stand and his loyalty to his own men (he took strong measures to force their pay arrears out of Tshombe) won in these days his laurels not merely as a fighter but also as a mercenary leader.

Schramme is reported to have set out with a large convoy from North Katanga and to have joined Denard after a dangerous journey across UN-controlled territory. Puren, of the Katangese airforce, had remained at Kolwezi till the end too; and it was no doubt now that he formed those personal links with both Schramme and Denard that were to bring him so dramatically but ineffectively back into contact with them both again at a much later date. Together the three retreated, with perhaps a hundred mercenaries and several thousand Katangese gendarmes, across the border into Angola, where they were allowed to regroup and settle – the Portuguese authorities denying, as they were always to do, that any mercenaries had so much as set foot on Portuguese soil.

In any case this marked the end of Katanga. On 21 January 1963, United Nations troops entered a deserted Kolwezi; and on 6 February Lieutenant General Norbert Muké took the oath of allegiance to the Republic of the Congo – following which he was demoted to Major.

4

The Epic of Five Commando

'That mad bloodhound Hoare'
East German Radio

Hoare came up from nowhere. Before July 1964 he was virtually unknown; sixteen months later, when he 'retired', he was the most famous mercenary leader in the world, the soldier who had swept the Congo clean of savages, the man who made modern mercenary soldiering briefly but confusingly respectable. Hoare became the *beau ideal* of the mercenary leader, quiet-spoken, quietly confident, cool, collected, charming in manner, boyish in looks, dapper in uniform, every inch the English officer and gentleman.

Which in fact, strictly speaking, Thomas Michael Bernard Hoare was not. Born in Dublin, he retained his Irish nationality and his Irish passport, plus enough sentimental attachment to his country of origin to choose as the emblem of Five Commando the symbol of the Irish soldiers of fortune of the eighteenth century, the 'Wild Geese'. But to all intents and purposes he seemed typically English – one of the many of the English middle class who came out after the war to settle in comfortable white-ruled South Africa, and by preference in or near that home-from-home for English speakers, Durban.

Hoare was an accountant by profession. He trained with the London Irish, and is said to have later served in the Far East on Mountbatten's staff; but his precise role and rank are none too clear. He emigrated to Natal in 1947, at the age of twenty-eight, married, had five children, became the sleeping partner in a used-car business, an active safari-organiser and secretary of the Royal Natal Yacht Club.

In July 1964 he flew into the Congo, to Leo; and was commissioned to raise a force of mercenaries with himself as commanding officer.

It seems, even now, an odd choice. Hoare had played only a very minor role in Katanga. I doubt he was the choice of Congolese. I would wager that behind the choice was that mysterious figure, Jeremiah Puren, who seems indeed to have guided Hoare through every phase of his mercenary career.

'A shabby figure but one of the faithful' was how a personal acquaintance described Puren to me. (It was to be many years before I was to see him in the flesh and then only at a distance, in the dock.) He was at the time in his early forties, about five years younger than Hoare, and very possibly it was the used-car business that had brought the two together. He had married a Belgian girl in Katanga, Julia. He had even learnt to fly after the collapse of Katanga, thereby justifying his former titular command. More important, he had kept in touch with Tshombe during Tshombe's exile in Spain and had flown back and forth between Jo'burg and Madrid, apparently at his own expense. It is tempting to consider him as an *éminence grise* – particularly since, according to various accounts, this was a temptation to which even the high and mighty succumbed: the South Africans considered him to be the secret emissary of Tshombe and Tshombe considered him to be the secret emissary of the South African government.

The Simba Revolt

In one of the most extraordinary twists in the extraordinary politics of the Congo, Tshombe was designated Prime Minister on 30 June 1964 – the day on which the United Nations troops finally withdrew – precisely in order to put down a seperatist movement (this time in the Eastern Congo) of the sort he had himself started in Katanga. No sooner was he appointed than he cabled Puren. Puren summoned Alastair Wicks from Rhodesia (where Wicks had in the meanwhile been an administrator with Rhodesian Air Services); and Hoare from Natal. When Hoare arrived in Leo, he found Jeremiah and Julia Puren there to greet him, plus Wicks, and, in charge of the whole country, the beaming ebullient Tshombe (and, under him, a rather more frigid General Mobutu) ready to welcome back 'his' white mercenaries, however much the black leaders in Africa might protest. Tshombe now had the backing not only of the Belgians and the mining companies but of the Americans and indeed of all the Western world. For a totally new menace was sweeping the whole country: a far more appalling revolt, in the eyes of the West at least, than that of Katanga or even the white-killing mutiny of the ANC had ever been.

'*Mai Mulele*' was the rebel war-cry – 'the Water of Mulele'. Pierre Mulele, ex-Minister of Education and the Fine Arts, had won fame as a schoolboy by forming an Anti-Immaculate Conception Society which had ramified throughout the Catholic mission schools. He now adapted Catholic doctrine by baptising his followers with his own Water, a baptism that protected them against their enemies' bullets. Shrines to the dead Lumumba were set up and '*Mai Lumumba*' alternated with '*Mai Mulele*'. Before the Lumumba monuments all the 'enemies of the revolution' – all the Congolese with any education – were sacrificed, as the movement, starting in Kwilu, spread like wildfire through many parts of the country.

The ANC, terrified by the *dawa* – the fetishes – of the rebels, fled like rabbits or joined the Simbas themselves. Simba was Swahili for 'lion', the title the Mulelist warriors chose for themselves. The most feared of all were the 'Jeunesse', the young Simbas aged from ten to fourteen, who invented some of the foulest tortures.

The Simba revolt was decolonialisation in its most extreme form, genuinely 'the African Solution', instinctive but not for all its horrors unidealistic. It spread rapidly over the eastern Congo, in particular throughout the provinces of Kivu and Orientale which had always been violently anti-European. The Chinese saw in the Simba revolt both a primitive 'cultural revolution' and the chance of increasing their own influence in central Africa. From their heavily overstaffed embassies in neighbouring Congo-Brazzaville and Burundi they arranged for aid to be sent to 'the revolution'. On 5 August 1964 the Simbas captured Stan and their leaders proclaimed His Excellency Christophe Gbenye President of the People's Republic of the Congo. The breakaway Stan government was recognised at once by most of the communist and anti-Western Arab powers. It looked as if nothing could stop the Simbas. In the east, Albertville, Baudoinville, Kindu, Uvira and Coquilhatville fell to them. Invaders from Congo-Brazzaville opened up a new front threatening Leo itself. Only at Bukavu did the ANC, led by Colonel Mulamba, fight back and finally beat off their attack.

Tshombe was the only live leader whose prestige could possibly counteract that of the dead Lumumba and the divine Mulele. Chinese action swiftly brought an American counteraction. The United States set about forming a Congolese air force; supplying planes and pilots who were generally anti-Castro Cuban exiles, and also providing the large C130 transport planes which were vital to supply and to move the ANC. From this period onward it is fair to say that Mobutu, though not precisely a puppet, was the Americans' man in the Congo; the CIA, for their part, were to support him faithfully.

But it was the Belgian military mission and Belgian 'technical advisers' who with Tshombe's return actually ran the administration of the ANC. Technically they were forbidden to take part in the actual fighting. They got round this rule by using Belgian mercenaries. Under Congolese commanding officers Belgian mercenary lieutenants were the actual combat leaders in most ANC battalions, with a Belgian regular officer as 'adviser' by the commander's side.

Schramme and the Katangese gendarmes, now swollen to over 8,000 exiles, crossed the border from Angola, re-entered Katanga and joined – at least nominally – the ANC as 'commandoes'. But Denard was not with them. He, and a handful of the French, had not waited idly in Angola; they had followed their former leader Faulques to the Yemen to train the Royalist troops of the Iman El Badr in the civil war there (of which more in Chapters 6 and 7).

But the spearhead of the ANC was to be the all-white mercenary band, Five Commando. Hoare was appointed its commander in the field, Puren the liaison and administrative officer in Leo, with Wicks as the second-in-command. Five Commando now had its skeleton structure. It only remained to flesh it out with mercenary 'volunteers'. Five Commando set about recruiting one thousand men.

The First Recruits

It was not as if those raising the force were starting from zero. They already had the Katanga experience on which to build. At that time the Belgian adviser to Katanga's Minister of Defence, Carlos Huyghe, had opened a recruiting office in Johannesburg, and a South African, Russell Cargill, one in Salisbury, the capital of Southern Rhodesia. The pattern was repeated. This time round Wicks himself opened an office in Salisbury and a fellow Old Harrovian, Patrick O'Malley, son of a former British Ambassador to Portugal, dealt with Jo'burg. Hoare himself cites the sort of slightly oblique newpaper advertisement that, as before, was used to lure recruits:

> Any fit young man looking for employment with a difference at a salary well in excess of £100 a month should telephone 838-5203 during business hours. Employment initially offered for six months. Immediate start.

This brought in an immediate rush of applicants, though the pay was no higher than that offered four years before. Hoare had in fact negotiated £140 a month minimum, at least half payable in sterling, with danger allowance, family allowance, compensation money in the case of death or injury, and so on (see Appendix 1 for details). But it was not pay, then or thereafter, that drew recruits – which was just as well from their point of view because pay, though tax-free, could not be relied on. Indeed mercenary pay can never be relied on. Nor, at that stage, was it hopes of loot, though later on loot became a prime inducement. Motives were, as always, extraordinarily mixed. But, as much as anything else, it was the saving grace of the six months' time-limit that induced men to take the risk – that, and the publicity. For O'Malley, a well-known broadcaster in South Africa, soon had his photo splashed all over the South African press, with his head clasped in his hands. 'Leave me alone chaps,' went the caption, 'I'm trying to fight a war!' In Rhodesia Wicks was interviewed on television. Furthermore in E'ville Hoare appointed as liaison officer a flamboyant figure who was also the AP correspondent there, John Latz. Hoare liked publicity. This time round, therefore, the discretion that had marked the whole Katanga affair went totally by the board; and with the discretion, the anonymity. For the Congo mercenaries very soon were portrayed, at least in Europe, as a hotch-potch of stock characters. Thus in the popular mind and the popular press any French mercenary was almost by definition involved in tortuous political intrigue. The Englishman was an officer and a gentleman, slightly distorted; the South African an illiterate tough there for the pleasure of killing kaffirs; the German a sinister former SS officer. The Belgian was less well-defined but was held to be generally despised by his fellow mercenaries. To add colour, the odd Pole or central European, usually minus teeth and invariably drunk, was thrown in.

There was enough basic truth in this to make the clichés stick. Yet very few of the stock characters were as two-dimensional as they were portrayed to be. To take one example: Siegfried Mueller, one of the very first recruits and one of the first officers too, insisted on wearing the Iron Cross (which he had won on the Russian front, with the Wehrmacht SS) at all times; he was even rumoured to wear it with his pyjamas. A few photographs were all that was needed, then, to set teeth on edge and imagination aflame. In fact Mueller, so far from being a sadistic war-criminal on the run, was part showman and part intellectual. He was not a particularly good soldier but he was a decent enough man. He was treated by the English-speaking mercenaries with a certain affection in which a note of mockery was discernible. (Having shared a villa with Siegfried Mueller in Stan, I came to know him quite well; it was, incidentally, far too swelteringly hot for the famous pyjamas to be displayed.)

The very first batch of mercenaries that arrived at Kamina were, like Mueller, mainly Germans from South West Africa – now Namibia – which had, before the First World War, been a German colony. There were only thirty-eight of them; and nine left at once when Hoare explained that they would be going into action immediately. This attempted action, Hoare's first, a lake-born attack on Albertville, ended in ignominy and the first deaths: of two German mercenaries under Siegfried Mueller's command, Nestler and Koehtler.

At first chaotic conditions reigned at Kamina base in to which the new recruits were now being flown in ever-increasing numbers. No barracks, uniforms or weapons were ready for them; no contracts were drawn up and no money appeared. A large number returned to South Africa where the press published lurid tales of their disorganisation. But gradually, with the support of a newly arrived Belgian officer, Colonel Vanderwalle, Hoare managed to get his base organised. The second large wave of 'volunteers' found themselves being trained and drilled to strict British army precedents for two or more weeks before being committed to action: as the following document, one of a number which I managed to acquire and which will follow in this chapter, indicates.

Five Commando Training Programme

Fifth day. 06.00 reveille. 06.10 to 06.30 physical training. 07.00 to 07.30 breakfast. 08.00 muster parade and inspection. 08.15 to 09.30 foot and arms drill. 09.30 to 10.00 provisional, .30 Browning. 10.00 to 10.30 tea break. 10.30 to 11.00 introduction to mine detectors. 11.00 to 12.30 introduction to field craft, judging distances, target indications, ambush drill. 12.30 to 14.00 lunch-break. 14.00 to 18.00 double march to range, firing .30 Browning and 60 mm. mortar. 18.00 guard mounting.

Not only the timetables but the skills were modelled on standard British practice.

Unit Orders: Five Commando

Two of the best lieutenants will be selected for training. Training will consist of the following items:
(a) Different formations of movement and their different positions.

(b) Exact training on fire control. Orders from officers to sergeants and from sergeants to men.

(c) If in this future operation I want a certain group of men to fire at a certain target, they must know exactly how to deliver concentrated fire on the target.

(d) Men *must* be trained in the exact methods of movement and fire.

(e) The men must be in such a state of training that when they are being fired on they act: down, crawl, observe and fire.

(f) Every man will be in such a state of training that he will inform his superiors exactly where the target is:- by reference point method; direct method; crockery method; hand degree reference method.

(g) Scouts' hand signals. Further training and instructions will be given on radio S.A.P.S.

The two 'best lieutenants' referred to would almost certainly have been Jeremy Spencer, an Old Etonian who had done his national service in the Coldstream Guards, and Gary Wilson, a South African who had served in the Household Cavalry. Hoare was fortunate in his young officers and in his NCOs, men – such as John Peters, a Yorkshireman – who had been in the British army or the British Colonial police. Five Commando's first RSM was an enormous, traditional figure: Regimental-Sergeant-Major Carton-Barber.

Hoare was less fortunate, he considered, with the thousand would-be mercenaries who were flying in to Kamina.

The general standard was alarmingly low. There was too high a proportion of alcoholics, drunks, booze artists, bums and layabouts, who were finding it difficult to get a job anywhere else and thought this was a heaven-sent opportunity to make some easy money. I discovered to my horror that there was a fair sprinkling of dagga smokers and dope addicts, many of whom were beyond recall. Perhaps the greatest surprise of all, and it was to remain so right through the three six-month contracts we served, was the incidence of homosexuals.

So Hoare wrote in his memoirs. But all this shock and horror is hardly convincing. Mercenary units do not tend to attract the most respectable elements in society; and Hoare had not even taken the precaution of advertising (as Browne had done, in Katanga) only for men who had had previous military experience. Simon Murray, when he joined the Foreign Legion in Paris on 22 February 1960, had found about forty fellow would-be recruits – 'an incredible mixture' – assembled at the Bureau de Recrutement of the Château de Vincennes. Three hours later the forty had been whittled down to seven – and this for a mercenary unit that knew that it could, by its ferocious discipline, turn even the poorest material into professional soldiers. A little knowledge of mercenary history would have helped Hoare, and subsequent mercenary leaders, to be more realistic.

Hoare too had of course to reduce his numbers, though by nothing like so drastic a ratio as was common in the Legion. The thousand fell to three hundred; and Five Commando was never to number much more than two to three hundred men. Hoare divided it into small units of approximately thirty men and two officers, known as 51, 52, 53, 54, 55, 56, 57 and eventually (these last were anti-Castro Cubans) 58 Commandos. Each of these units could and did operate separately as a completely independent command. When they were operating at a distance, Hoare's control over them was remote and occasionally non-existent, to such an extent that some of his men claimed that he got undue credit for military successes which he had nothing to do with. However there seemed to be a general respect for 'the Major' (or 'the Colonel' as he later became) and the various attempts at mutiny, almost all started by mercenaries finding out that no money had been paid into their bank accounts at home, tended to die down when Hoare appeared. There was much less respect for Jeremiah Puren, universally known as a '10-per-cent man'. His position as administrative officer at Leo was not unrewarding; he is reliably estimated to have made nearly £100,000 during his time there. Inevitably there were bitter recriminations from the mercenaries in the field against all the administrative officers, Belgian or other wise, who were accused of embezzling pay and equipment. More than one Five Commando paymaster disappeared, unwisely, I would think, in view of the far from empty threats that such behaviour evoked.

Military Tactics

Five Commando's first success was the recapture of Albertville by Lieutenant Gary Wilson and 51 Commando. The tactics that the mercenaries used so successfully were those that had been developed in the Baluba War. Basically they relied on speed and firepower. A mercenary attack would be a lightning affair: the commando in jeeps would drive at full speed into an enemy position or village and open up with heavy machine guns and automatic rifles. These tactics were the reverse of conventional European tactics, for, according to the rule book, advances along a road into enemy territory must be made by 'bounds' – one vehicle advances while the other covers it – and in no circumstances must a column go speeding down a road.

The unorthodox tactics of the mercenaries nearly always paid off, though the Congo with its dense bush and jungle was an ideal terrain for ambushes. Once too a mercenary commando in a group of jeeps came speeding round a corner and almost crashed into a group of Simba lorries heading in the opposite direction. For the mercenaries stuck to the roads and to their jeeps; they rarely ventured into the bush and never put in a traditional infantry extended-line attack on foot. Their tactics, though limited, succeeded and kept succeeding, first because of the speed of their attacks which almost always gave them the advantage of surprise, and secondly because of their firepower – not so much of the firepower directly as of the enormous noise which the weapons of even a handful of mercenaries could create and which demoralised and panicked their opponents. Five Commando was almost certainly more successful in the circumstances than a similar British Regiment would have been; for regular armies are tied down by rules, traditions and handbooks, and the mercenaries were freer to experiment. One unit of Five Commando used a repentant Simba who would dress up as a woman and scout forward whenever they suspected an ambush, and certainly part of the mercenaries' superiority was due to this sort of ability to improvise.

After 51's victory at Albertville the various commandos were flown all over the Congo and invariably succeeded in recapturing towns held by the Simbas. Admittedly the mass of the Simbas were not formidable opponents. Their leaders and their commander, General Olenga, genuinely believed that the discovery of the *dawa* had given them a weapon as important as the atomic bomb. The *dawa*, the *Mai Mulele* (see page 58) would protect the lives of the Simbas and make bullets harmless provided the Simbas observed certain rules – for instance, never to look backwards when going into battle. The failure of the *dawa* could therefore in any given case be explained away logically. Certainly belief in it, combined with *chanvre*, the drug with which almost all Congolese – Simbas, ANC, Katangese gendarmes – primed themselves for battle, gave the Simbas extraordinary powers and the ability to go on living and fighting for minutes even when riddled with machine-gun bullets and technically dead.

But the Simbas were fanatically brave, often armed with automatic weapons (unlike the Balubas who had hardly had a modern weapon among them), and there were hordes of them. They were not negligible as enemies; and though I was given detailed accounts, horrifying enough, of mercenaries mowing down with their machine guns hundreds of spear-carrying Simbas pressing around the slowly moving jeeps, many mercenaries of Five Commando were killed. Atrocities too were common. But there were so many atrocities committed on all sides in the Congo that even the most macabre enquirers would soon have their fill of atrocity accounts. What can be said for the mercenaries is that they shot rather than tortured prisoners – unlike their opponents or their 'brothers-in arms' of the ANC.

In this summer of 1964 51 Commando captured Bumba but was accused of looting and recalled in disgrace to Kamina. 52 Commando ran loose around Boende till Hoare replaced Siegfried Mueller as its commander by Lieutenant Ben Louw. 53 Commando was commanded by Jack Maiden with, under him, 2nd Lt. George Schroeder who had been in the South African Defence Force – South Africa's army. They seem to have been the most successful of the scattered units. Based on Bukavu (which had been – an astonishing thing – recaptured by the ANC under their only good commander, Colonel Mulamba), they dominated the surrounding territory. 54 Commando achieved little. The remainder, 55, 56 and 57, now assembled at Kongolo for the most important move yet in the war: the recapture of Stan.

North to Stanleyville

Colonel Vanderwalle had drawn up a masterplan for the attack on the Simba capital. Five Commando was to form the spearhead of the main motorised column, Lima One, that was to advance directly from Bukavu northwards. A second column, Lima Two, under a fellow Belgian, Colonel Liegois (late of the Force Publique), was to support this advance. As spearhead of Lima Two, Vanderwalle assembled a group of French-speaking mercenaries to whom he gave the title of Six Commando. Six Commando was placed under the orders of yet another Belgian regular army colonel, Lamouline, assisted by a mercenary as combat commander, Commandant Protin. But Six Commando never formed an all-white mercenary unit like Five Commando: at this stage its members were spread out in small groups among ANC companies and battalions. 'Frenchie' Delamichel, an ex-Katangese mercenary with enormous handlebar moustaches, commanded the 'armour' – three Swedish armoured cars, paradoxically enough abandoned by the Swedish UN Forces, 'Frenchie's' ex-, and much despised, opponents.

What follows is an extract from the unit diary of 56 Commando kept by its commander Lieutenant Jeremy Spencer. (57 was commanded by Ian Gordon, of Winchester and the Rifle Brigade, a very hard man with Sergeant John Peters, a noticeably violent character, under him. 55 was to be taken over by the RSM, in the first of what was to become a series of promotions from NCO to officer that eventually changed the whole complexion of Five Commando.)

As always with these extracts from documents, which were acquired on the understanding, express or implied, that I would observe the rules of reticence and discretion, I have been obliged to substitute initials for names and occasionally to change points of reference by which ex-mercenaries now living normal lives might be embarrassed. As a general rule the only names left unchanged are those of mercenary leaders already well-publicised or of the dead who can no longer be harmed. These constraints, though annoying, are compensated by the vividness of documents never intended for publication.

29 October 2/Lt S. and Vol.* L. sent to Kongolo to guard supplies sent from Kamina base same day.

30 October 56 Commando consisting of thirty-one all told left Kamina base for Congola.

31 October Still at Congola. Very dull day. Fired the men's rifles to check gas regulators but unfortunately not allowed to fire our 75mm. Recoilless Rifle, which we were all very keen to see firing, because the Belgians were scared we would hit one of their planes.

1 November Left Congola for Manono and spent night there.

2 November Left Manono for Samba (194 kms from Congola). On arrival did Recce Patrol down to Lualaba River (29 kms) to discover whereabouts of ferry. Fired a few shots on way but did not kill anyone. Took Sgt R. with me as well who, when we discovered the Barque was the other side of the River, volunteered to go over in a prow and bring it back. Would like to have let him do so, plus myself, but luckily realised it was not vital – and secondly I'm not a very good swimmer!

3 November Left Samba 10.00 hrs and camped 3 kms other side of Lafote River. Not a very safe crossing as we also had a jeep in front of us on the pontoon containing RSM Carton-Barber – everybody egging our driver on to slip his clutch and push him in. At 07.45 hrs Sgt., S. and Vol. B. detonated 48 Energa grenades and approx. 1,000 rounds of bad ammo. Very impressive bang and also blew the building to pieces in which they had placed the charge.

4 November Left Lafote river at 11.00 hrs and arrived Kibombo at 15.30 hrs and drove straight in. Then we did a recce patrol to Lualaba river (8 kms) where everybody had a swim and fired their rifles at a sniper across the river. Left Kibombo at 20.00 hrs for Kindu. About 5 kms outside Kibombo the leading Ferret met a rebel armoured car coming towards us, which opened fire with a .50 Browning at the leading Ferret armoured car. Terrific bombardment and nobody knew what the hell was going on.

* Abbreviation for 'Volunteer' – official title of ordinary mercenary soldier.

Lot of tracer flying about which luckily did no damage and then eventually we managed to kill the chap on the rebel armoured car and all was peace.

5 November Arrived Kindu (2nd largest rebel-held town) where we had a terrific shooting match at nothing in particular, everybody blazing as we drove through the centre of the town. We then drove down to ferry (56) where Vol. Patience killed General Olenga.* We also managed to sink a barge with about 50 rebels on board. At 18.00 hrs we drove 3 kms out to the airport (3 kms) – 56 only – (with myself on bonnet of leading jeep expecting to be fired on any moment by .30 Browning machine-gun and very scared too!). We met one guard at Airport who fired on us but everybody opened fire on him and he was very quickly polished off. I opened fire with my Vigneron and loosed off 25 rounds but don't think I hit him! Luckily someone else did.

6 November Left airport at 10.00 hrs and returned to Kindu. Went over to the other side of the river and spent night there preparatory to leaving for Kalina next day to rescue 70 Europeans.

7 November Left Kindu at 05.45 hrs for Kalina. Arrived Kalina 10.00 hrs and once again drove straight in to discover the rebels had left at 23.00 hrs the previous night. Rescued Europeans from Mission where I had a very refreshing gin and drove back to Kindu (100 kms).

8 November Found ourselves a house to sleep in and managed to acquire a fridge to keep our champagne in (which we acquired at Kalina) plus a few other goodies. T.B.H. [Hoare] jumped on 2/Lt S. and Sgt R. when he found them in town driving around in a V/W and as he said looking like ragamuffins. Asked them where they had been and what they were doing and they said testing the car but they were, I suspect, looking for more interesting things!!

9 November Was going to be a show-the-flag parade round Kindu but luckily it poured with rain so it was cancelled. At 9.30 we crossed over the river to hold the position the other side. Fixed up two machine-gun posts with boxes and sandbags to the accompaniment of groans from all concerned. Nothing doing late at night so most people had a good night's sleep.

10 November Reveille at 9.0, so we could get a bit of sleep in. Did nothing all day – fired at a couple of rebels and shot one in chest but he escaped; were issued with 48 Primus beers which were welcomed by all – also received a bottle of Cinzano off Ian [Ian Gordon, O.C. 57 Commando] which went down well.

11 November Left Kindu at 12.00 hrs for the Elela river to hold the bridge against rebels crossing from Stan. A nasty pile of bloated bodies greeted us when we arrived which one of our men Vol. R. proceeded to sort through! Managed to fix our jeep up with machine-gun mounting

---

* Olenga was the commander-in-chief of the Simbas. He was continually being reported killed but always survived.

today which gives me a bit more confidence – though not very nice for the man sitting behind it.

12 November Another quiet day at Elela. Rained all morning but stopped about 10.00 hrs. A very miserable morning which the majority spent in bed as there was nothing else to do. Tried to get P. to fix a seat on the back of the jeep but rather like trying to get a Clydeside to pull a plough when it doesn't want to.

Friday, 13 November A nervous early morning for superstitious people like myself. Having heard 9 trucks had left Stan 3 days ago to attack us I was fully expecting some sort of attack but as usual nothing materialised.

The entry for the following day is written in a different hand.

14 November This morning at 07.00 hrs Lt Spencer killed by enemy fire which opened up on us at 05.35 hrs. Jeremy was hit in the head and died without regaining consciousness at 07.15 hrs. It is my unpleasant duty as 2 I/C of the unit to take over temporary command and continue this diary. Jeremy sadly missed, a good officer and friend. Having opened fire with mortar and .50 machine-gun contacted HQ at 07.00 hrs. 57 Commando sent to reinforce. Constant enemy fire. Air support requested. Air support arrived at 10.15 hrs and opened fire with rockets and machine-guns on the enemy. 10.15 hrs 57 Commando arrived with the Commandant [Alastair Wicks – Commandant is a Belgian military title] and after brief assessment of position and after heavy mortar support led the attack over river. 57 dug in other side. 56 left to maintain position defending bridge. The men are rather shaken up but not too bad, morale still good.

Jeremy Spencer was the first but by no means the last officer of Five Commando to be killed. This diary – indeed the very fact of keeping a unit diary at all – shows how Hoare tried to make a typical British army unit of his men and how far he succeeded or failed. As regards discipline it was an impossible task – of which more shortly. Hoare had been on compassionate leave in Durban where his wife Phyllis was expecting a difficult birth. Back in Leo, a father once more, he no sooner heard of Spencer's death than he cabled his wife to call the new-born boy Jeremy. He reached Kindu on 18 November, in time for Spencer's funeral celebrated by the Bishop of Kindu with a High Mass in the Cathedral. He had now lost his two best officers – for Gary Wilson had shot his thumb off by accident – and 51 Commando, up to join the column, had to be commanded like the bereaved 56 by a comparative nonentity. Meanwhile events at Stan precipitated the culmination of the 'march' north.

With the approach of the apparently unstoppable mercenaries the government of the Popular Republic of the Congo panicked. All the

whites still alive in Simba territory, mainly missionaries, were rounded up and held as hostages. President Gbenye wildly appealed for
help to all African leaders of goodwill and announced: 'We will make
our fetishes out of the hearts of Belgians and Americans and clothe
ourselves in the skins of Belgians and Americans.' As Lima One
advanced from Bukavu, the Belgian government, supported by the
British and the United States governments, decided to drop paratroops on Stan and Paulis in an attempt to rescue the white hostages.
Despite Hoare's rule, never to move by night, Lima One moved out
for Stan at full speed shortly before dusk on 23 November.

Wicks described that night to me as the most nerve-wracking
experience he had ever had. The column was held up by a series of
ambushes. Among those killed was George Clay, a CBS Radio
correspondent, hit by a burst of machine-gun fire that just missed
Alastair Wicks and John Latz. 2nd Lt. Hans von Lieres, one of the
more courageous mercenaries and leader of the twenty-odd Germans
with Five Commando, was twice badly wounded. Several 'volunteers'
were killed. When the column reached Stan next day, it found the city
almost totally in the hands of the Belgian paratroops – though many
of the hostages had been massacred in front of the Lumumba
memorial. After dropping on Paulis shortly afterwards the paratroops
were flown back to Belgium amid furious protests from the Afro-
Asian world at this neo-colonialist intervention; and Stan became the
headquarters of the white mercenaries of Five Commando.

Discipline and Looting

In the eyes of at least the Western world the white mercenaries were
now almost totally acceptable; and as in the months that followed,
Hoares's commandos scoured the towns and villages of Orientale
Province rescuing missionaries and nuns literally by the score they
became almost heroes. It was hardly possible at one time to open a
Western magazine without coming across technicolour photographs
of such a scene; for nuns and mercenaries together were irresistibly
photogenic. The admiration always remained a little uneasy, however,
because the whole situation seemed a hundred years out of date. For
here was a handful of white men routing thousands of black savages
and rescuing white missionaries from appalling tortures. It was
happening but it hardly seemed, in the mid-Sixties, either possible or
appropriate. Furthermore, the colour issue complicated attitudes,
except of course in Rhodesia and South Africa where it merely
reinforced prejudices. The mercenaries were white; their enemies

were black. Praise of the mercenaries, then, appeared to be racist. The line was: undesirables possibly but almost despite themselves defenders of Western civilisation and values.

Of course there was another, darker side to the story. Hoare tells, with a touch of self-congratulation, how he and three of his officers held a summary court-martial of a white mercenary who during the sack of Stan had first raped a Congolese girl, then frogmarched her down to the river's edge and shot her. The four 'just men' heard the case by guttering candlelight; then, finding no extenuating circumst-ances, each wrote down on a piece of paper the punishment they considered suitable. One was for immediate execution, another for giving the man a loaded revolver and the chance to shoot himself, a third for the cat-of nine-tails and expulsion. Much later, on British television, Hoare gave his own version of what had then happened: as there was no agreement and as the man was a professional footballer he, Hoare, decided to make the punishment fit the criminal. There-fore, taking the loaded revolver, he blew both the man's big toes off. To many this punishment seemed in itself an atrocity, and it was particularly repugnant to the two regular British Army officers who were confronted with Hoare on the programme. One of them, Brigadier Peter Young, described the act as 'orthopaedically unjus-tifiable'. But their main objection to Hoare himself, interestingly enough, was not that he had served in a foreign army (indeed Young had been in the Arab Legion and the other officer, General Alexander, had commanded Nkrumah's army – it would have been a case of the pots calling the kettle black) but rather that Hoare had not stuck to the British military code of behaviour and justice.

Of course these regular officers totally misunderstood the prob-lems of discipline in a mercenary band. Any acts of punishment generally have to have the agreement, at least tacit, of the majority; for at heart all mercenaries feel themselves to be equal and equally engaged for pay or loot. There is therefore none of the respect for each other or even for their officers that the tradition of a regular army creates. In that sense discipline is tribal; for the authority of mercenary commanders is not backed by the majestic authority of an impersonal state. To take one example: it would have been unthink-able for an officer of Five Commando to have had one of his own men shot for a major crime; even rape and murder could, as recounted above, only be dealt with hurriedly, almost clandestinely, and compa-ratively mildly, and then only when the crime had excited general indignation. As for desertion, that for a mercenary is no crime at all, merely a way of breaking a contract. The authority of the mercenary leader, the tribal chief, had to impose itself more by personality and abrupt violence than by formal rules. Hoare for instance crushed an incipient mutiny very early on by smashing the man to the ground with his revolver butt. His successors had more difficulty; for when immediate danger fades, discipline becomes almost impossible to maintain. By the end of Five Commando's existence serious brawls even between officers were common, and on at least two occasions officers will killed. One RSM had a particularly vicious reputation; he killed an American in Albertville who was probably a CIA agent and therefore himself finished up in a military jail in Leo – where he was probably killed in the massacre of the mercenaries in July 1967.

But all this was under Hoare's successors, who were as leaders less respected. Hoare himself generally managed to make his authority felt, though, as Jeremy Spencer's unit diary entry for 8 November indicates, even Hoare was unable to prevent looting. Years later, in Johannesburg, an ex-NCO of Five Commando described to me with glee and, I would say, almost without exaggeration how he had commandeered a C130 to transport all his personal loot from Stan to Leo to be sold there to Indian traders – refrigerators, prams, cameras, furniture and several cars. Two South Africans are said to have found $65,000 in the safe of a private house during the sack of Stan; whereupon they bribed a medical orderly to certify that they were ill and disappeared for good. On the other hand nine mercenaries of 53 Commando, when their long-delayed mail eventually reached them in Stan four months later, wrote out letters of resignation on the spot because their banks in South Africa had not received that proportion of their pay due in hard currency (see the contract in the Appendix to this book, Article 32, Clause A). They told me that the only way they could raise a little cash was, when given bottles of whisky by rescued and grateful missionaries, to open a bar and sell the whisky off in tots to the Belgian technical assistance officers in Stan, thereby making a little profit.

But this heartbreaking tale of woe (followed by temporary arrest for attempted mutiny – the letters of resignation were thereupon withdrawn) was not exactly the full story. The same group had earlier taken half a million Congolese francs off a rebel paymaster's truck and had also blown up the governor's safe at Balemba when they 'liberated' that town. Indeed no sooner was any town 'liberated' than Five Commando's jeeps would immediately race for the banks – following which business premises and private houses would be toured by small groups of determined and dynamite-carrying mercenaries in search of safes to blow. Looting was therefore much more resented by the Belgian settlers and businessmen, who had naively imagined that, thanks to the brave and devoted white mercenaries, they would recover their homes and offices intact, than by the Congolese whose premises for obvious reasons attracted far less mercenary attention.

Most mercenary officers, like Hoare, soon gave up the struggle and turned a blind eye to this type of looting, for reasons that are only too clear. Commandant Protin of Six Commando once ordered a group of his mercenaries, who had captured a rebel paymaster's suitcase holding a million francs, to hand it over intact to the local Congolese police commissioner: thereupon the police commissioner and the suitcase disappeared without trace. What the mercenaries left the ANC looted. The only armed bands that showed any restraint seem, surprisingly enough, to have been the Simbas. There are well-attested and convincing stories of systematic plundering even by the United Nations troops in Katanga.

Morally, therefore, it seems difficult to adopt too rigid an attitude. And in any case all the money gained by looting seems to have gone very quickly. Siegfried Mueller, for instance, within a year of leaving the Congo was apparently back where he had started, as a barman in South West Africa. Few of the mercenaries had the strength of character of that South African who came to the Congo for six months, determined to take back with him enough money to satisfy his ambition to open a garage, and succeeded. Hoare was recognised as being very comfortably off afterwards. On the other hand he probably made a considerable part of his money from the serial rights of his story, which were sold to newspapers all over the world and brought him in a small fortune.

The motives of the senior mercenary officers were in any case far more difficult to disentangle than the comparatively simple explanations for the enrolment of the 'ordinary volunteers' or NCOs. 'We shall show them', Hoare is reported to have said, 'what a small group of determined white men can do.' No doubt this was a partial explanation for his presence in the Congo; but he and others such as Wicks were skilled in proferring with every appearance of sincerity what can at best have been only half-truths. Much more frank was one of Hoare's – and indeed Tshombe's – favourites, a Rumanian mercenary named Ferdinand Calistrat, who had served in the Spanish Foreign Legion at Rio Muni and Ifni and who later became a captain in Five Commando. 'Ah,' he said longingly as he drove slowly through Leo at about this time, gazing at the pavement cafés on the main avenue which were crowded with prosperous Belgian businessmen and well-paid UN officials, 'if only it was the rebels who held this town!'

Hoare's Last Months

After the fall of Stan another 150 mercenaries (including a pipe major, Sandy King) were recruited by Darby de Jaeger in Johannesburg to fill the gaps left by the dead, the wounded and (though Hoare avoids mentioning this) by deserters. By January 1965 almost all the original members of Five Commando had left. To have survived six months in the Congo was enough for most, though many later came back again as the following exchange of letters indicates:

Col Sir,
How is things still up there. I hope you are still having a nice time up there. Sir, I would like to be with you again because you are Five Commando. Sir, if it is possible for me to come up again and if you want me back, please let me know when I can come up. I believe maybe there would be another contract. If so, do let me know please. Well, Sir, I hope I will be with you in Five Commando soon.
Always yours faithfully
D.E.

Dear Sir,
I acknowledge your letter of November 8, instant. You may return to the Congo and rejoin Five Commando. I suggest that you report to the liaison officer whose address appears below, with this letter at the earliest opportunity.

Many of course had not survived, as the moving letter that follows from a mother in Southern Rhodesia shows only too well; and the realisation of the real possiblity of death gave would-be 'volunteers' in South Africa and Rhodesia pause.

Dear Sir,
I wrote some time ago about my son P.F.'s belongings. The tape recorder has been returned to me but what has happened to the clothes, passport, private papers, and any letters? He had with him a black leather jacket, a pair of expensive dark glasses, a black railway fireman's cap, a light leather jacket which he wore when he left Umtali on that awful Saturday. I shall always remember him wearing it. He had on a pair of dark trousers. He took lots of hankies; they were marked with his name. He also had a very old pair of blue jeans, a pair of yellow boots. These things may not be of great value but they are of great sentimental value to me because when I lost my beloved child I lost everything. He was my life. Please help if you can ...

Hoare himself very nearly left when his six-months contract expired. He was due to be replaced as commanding officer by the very tough and very unpleasant Ian Gordon (who put me under arrest for twenty-four hours in Stan – so I may be prejudiced), a man ten years younger. But in the end it was Gordon who left, and Hoare who stayed on, apparently at Tshombe's insistence.

At first it had looked as if the fall of Stan meant the end of the rebellion. But the Egyptians and the Algerians reacted by sending modern arms and weapons down to the Simbas mainly through the Sudan, and there were continual rumours (never substantiated) of Arab and even Chinese 'advisers' leading the rebel forces. The Simbas' new arms and improved tactics certainly made them more formidable enemies; a column of forty vehicles commanded by Siegfried Mueller was ambushed near Bafwasende and most of the vehicles destroyed. On another occasion two Ferret scout cars of Five Commando were destroyed by falling into a sort of elephant pit dug into the road. Even the decisive air support was not invulnerable – the most famous of the Cuban pilots, 'El Toro', was shot down and his mutilated body found by a group of Five Commando (which led to reprisals on their part). But in spite of defeat and deaths which at times lowered the morale of the 'white giants' (the local nickname for the mercenaries, discovered much to his delight by Hans Germani, a paunchy, rusty doctor who had attached himself to Five Commando), Hoare succeeded in defeating the rebellion in the northeast. Watsa was 'liberated' in March 1965, and with Watsa the fabled gold mines of Kilo-Moto. All other tales of loot pale into financial insignificance beside the legends that float around the gold bars of Kilo Moto; possibly – but I have been unable to discover by whom and to whose precise benefit – smuggled out through neighbouring Uganda.

One rebel redoubt remained – the wild Fizi–Baraka region to the east of the province of Maniema where Schramme, back from Angola, was pacifying the area in which he owned plantations. His 'Leopard group' was now dignified with the name of 'Ten Commando'.

The Fizi–Baraka region was inhabited mainly by the robber Wabembe tribe, aided at this time by bands of roving Watutsi warriors, the giant exiles from nearby Rwanda. By the time Hoare was ready to tackle the task, the second contract had ended and there was a shortage of 'volunteers' for this unglamorous and certainly dangerous expedition. For Fizi–Baraka was a mountainous plateau, and the only road approach led up the Lulimba escarpment, an absolutely impregnable position. Worried, Hoare wrote to the C in C of the

ANC, General Bobozo, to propose an extraordinary solution for the shortage of recruits.

> Sir,
> Further to my letter of July 22, 65.
> 1. 2/Lt. Von Lieres has just returned from our office in Johannesburg. He confirms my fears that we will be unable to raise 300 men in South Africa in the next few weeks.
> 2. I therefore intend sending Captain S.B. to Leo to await your further instructions in the event that you should instruct him to raise men in England.
> 3. A third possibility has occurred to me since writing to you yesterday. It may be possible to persuade the South African Defence Force to let us have 200 regular serving soldiers expressly for this campaign who would be sent back immediately it was over. These men could be given special leave from their units. From our point of view this would be entirely to our benefit but I would point out that if complete secrecy were not maintained the political reaction might be disastrous. However, if so decided, I feel confident that I could arrange such a force on a short term engagement.
>
> T.M.B. Hoare

This last solution was never put into practice. But Hoare's 'confidence' does prove that he had very close links with the South African military – though not necessarily with the South African government; as events in the Seychelles many years later were to show.

As for the point about raising men in England, this was never done on a systematic scale if only because there was no permanent recruiting office or liaison officer in Europe. The Zambezi Club in Earls Court, the *Bar Renaissance* in Brussels and the *Chat Noir* in Pigalle eventually became known as informal contact points. But by this period, as the following exchange shows, what recruiting there was of Englishmen was done by correspondence – a laborious process.

> Sir,
> I would be most grateful if you could tell me how to become a member of your Commando, together with details of pay, etc. I am at present serving in the —— Regiment and have been in England for almost two years on an E.R.E. job, and have now decided to purchase my discharge, as an alternative to wasting my time in B.A.O.R. My present rank is Sergeant; age 26 years; seven years service. Active service Brunei revolt, Sarawak. I am married, luckily to a woman who understands that I am not a nine to five man. It is very difficult to find out anything about your

Commando here in England, but I would like to point out that I am willing to do whatever necessary in order to enlist under you. I am not a glory hunter or an idiot; I just want more out of life than I can get at present. I hope that you can find time to give this letter your consideration and let me know one way or the other as soon as it's convenient to you.

Yours sincerely,

X.Y.

Dear Mr Y,

Thank you for your letter dated September 12, received here today. Unfortunately Five Commando does not have a recruiting agency in England; our only office being in Johannesburg. The liaison officer there is Lt D.L.S. at Rooms 112–3, Sheffield House, 29 Cruit Street, Johannesburg.

Due to restrictions imposed by the Congolese government, we cannot offer you a paid passage to the Congo from England. However, if you would make your own way to Johannesburg or alternatively direct to Kinshasha, Leopoldville (carnet de route may be obtained from the Congolese Embassy in London), I would be glad to accept you at Five Commando. In view of your military experience, I am prepared to offer you the rank of sergeant which carries a basic salary of £182 per month. Half this amount may be transferred at the official rate of exchange, 504 Congolese francs to £1 sterling, to any bank in the world, and the other half will be paid in cash in Congolese francs. In addition to this a family allowance which is transferred in its entirety in hard currency is paid: £19 16s per month for the volunteer's wife, £11 18s per month for the first child, and slightly more for each subsequent child. Marriage and birth certificates must be produced. Whilst in a danger area, although not necessarily in combat, a danger-pay premium of £144 per month is paid. Again half of this is transferred in hard currency and the other half is paid in Congolese francs. Upon completion of the six months contract, a volunteer may transfer at the official rate of exchange one half of the cash received in the Congo. So, in fact, three quarters of the gross pay and danger pay is paid in hard currency in a foreign country.

In conclusion, I may add that there are ample opportunities for promotion, providing a recruit exhibits capability. Also in exceptional cases, upon my discretion, paid leave and free return passage to England may be granted. If there is any further information that you may require, do not hesitate to write.

Eventually the ranks were filled; and, on 27 September, the attack on Fizi Baraka was launched. Hoare had prepared with great care a 'combined operation' on land and water, with air support. Peters, now promoted to commandant and commanding 'Force John John', particularly distinguished himself by his efficiency and cool courage till he was wounded by a hand grenade and had to be evacuated.

George Schroeder, now a captain, took over from him – 'a military machine' Hoare called Schroeder. Wicks led the land group and blocked the road out at the foot of the Lulimba escarpment. In the water-borne night assault from Lake Fizi, Hans von Lieres, the Beachmaster, was killed; and so was a Jewish mercenary lieutenant, Ron Columbic. The mercenaries suffered heavy casualties. But resistance faded away once they had captured the lakeside town of Baraka and by October 1965 the Simba revolt was virtually over. It had been militarily the finest, and properly speaking was to be militarily the last, of Five Commando's operations. In any case it was Hoare's swansong in the Congo. On 5 November Tshombe, who had also outlived his usefulness, was overthrown and once again went into exile. On 25 November General Mobutu once again seized power in a bloodless *coup*, but this time for good. And on the very next day, 26 November, Hoare received an elegant letter of dismissal and thanks, from the new '*President de la Republique*, Mobutu, J.D., *Lieutenant-général*', addressed very firmly '*Au Colonel Hoare*, Durban, *Afrique Du Sud*'. With Hoare went Wicks and Puren; and of the Belgians Colonel Vaunderwalle, Colonel Lamouline and Commandant Protin. Protin was replaced at the head of Six Commando by Bob Denard. And Commandant Peters was appointed commanding officer of Five Commando in Hoare's place.

Peters In Command

Hoare had commanded Five Commando from July 1964 to November 1965; Peters was to command it from November 1965 to February 1967, almost exactly the same length of time: fifteen months. But this was for the mercenaries a far less glorious period; they were static, garrison troops. The publicity disappeared, the glamour faded, and only boredom and brutality – plus, it must be said, a certain sense of service – survived.

Unit Orders: Five Commando

1. Upon receipt of tools and equipment for road and bridge building you will start immediately with this project. Use your own men and the assistance of the civilians in that area.
2. The roads between villages will be divided in half and each respective village will be responsible for the clearing and fixing of the road in that area.
3. Keep up the good work and the good name of Five Commando.

But there was another side to the picture, as the following message (sent probably to the exhibitionistic Hans Germani – Starlight is normal British army code for the medical officer) shows.

Colliers' Signal Sent to Starlight from C.O.

My instructions to you were quite clear, that you must stay at Cheta's position and that you will, I repeat will, return to Cheta's position after receiving this message. You will get medical treatment from Starlight Minor and he will put a report in about this matter and apply plaster of paris if necessary. Furthermore my instructions were that you would clear the small-pox epidemic, and until this is done you will not leave Cheta's position. Any medical staff can be trained in the field while they are doing nothing. Why was the rebel 2 I.C. not sent here with the Kookoracha today, and why was I not informed of this capture or surrender? You are paid to do your duty in the field and not to lay about in Albertville where there is nothing to do. Now this is final. In connection with this matter I do not want to hear any more of this nonsense. If Cook's case were not so urgent you could have treated him there. You have all the necessary medical equipment and if there was anything you were short of you could have sent a message. Furthermore I do not want you to interfere with the orders of my field officers. Your orders to them will be confined to the line of medical treatment in requirement. In the future if you want to transfer yourself from one position to another, you will firstly get confirmation from me, excluding the area where you are treating small-pox. Stop this childish acting of yours. You are making a fool of yourself in front of all officers and men of Five Commando and I will not allow any officer of mine to behave like that. Furthermore I want a full statement from you regarding the sinking of the P boat, also where you obtained permission to use same. I want acknowledgement of this letter. A.S.A.P.

And fighting did continue against the remnants of the rebels, often with horrifying results.

A Military Report

To: Commanding Officer
   5 Commando ANC
   Fort Baraka

re Tiger Patrol of 13.3.66

Sir,

It is with regret that I must inform you of the death of six of my men who were killed instantly while on patrol some eleven kilometres from this position.

Below is a fully detailed account of the patrol's progress and actions until they returned to this position.

Leaving Baraka at 20.00 hours 13.3.66 we made the top of the escarpment in good time and reached a commanding position approximately 5–6 kilometres from this position by 00.30 hours where we rested for some 45 minutes. We were very wet and cold due to the heavy downpour of rain which lasted until approximately 14.15 hours.

Leaving our resting position we moved on in a NNW direction, skirting the highest points of the range in order to locate any smoke from enemy fires that may have been present. We however neither saw nor heard anything until nigh on 05.45 hours when Lt M. and his group of scouts reported having seen what appeared to be two fires some 3 kilometres from the 12.7 position captured four days ago.

I briefed the men and scouts on what to do. The plan was to approach the indicated position with extreme care avoiding all tracks and paths until we were within 600 yards of the fires. I would then creep forward with the scouts, make observations and return to my patrol to formulate an attack plan. On reaching our planned position we heard a number of voices. I estimated there to be about twenty persons present in what appeared to be a small camp. Suddenly a rebel appeared, walking up a path directly towards us. He saw us and opened fire. We returned the fire, killing him. This warned the remainder of the camp-dwellers, so we rushed forward until we reached a small bivouac area consisting of some eleven huts. There was some firing from the trees and we managed to kill one more fleeing rebel. I formed a perimeter and searched the camp area but found nothing of value.

We burnt the hut and then retraced our route up the path to the first dead rebel. Not 30 yards past him was a small well-used track running off to the right which we followed with Lt M. and his scouts some 400 yards ahead of us. We had not gone far when one of the scouts returned saying they had found a large ammo dump, but could not tell me what was inside as there was a makeshift door on the underground dump, but they had seen boxes inside with the use of a torch whilst peering through a crack. He had not yet finished his report when there was terrific explosion which virtually shook the ground we stood on. We rushed forward and found to our horror an enormous crater in the ground which had been created by the blast. Of the scouts there was no sign. The nearby trees had been stripped of their branches, leaves and bark. We called and searched for the scouts but did not have to look far. I found a ribcage and tattoed left arm belonging to what was once Vol. X. On further searching we found the grisly remains of the men. Hands, bits of body, twisted legs, etc. One man vomited and another began crying, it was a terrible scene. Myself and four others collected what we could find and buried them in a shallow grave nearby. We did not search too deep in the trees for fear of mines. The morale of the men had dropped to zero, so I returned to base immediately.

I can only assume, sir, that the ammo dump judging by the size of the crater was an extremely large one and it had been booby-trapped, the trap being connected to the door for any intruders i.e. 5 Cdo. Either Lt M. or one of his men must have been attempting to open the door when the explosion took place. Possibly the trap was badly placed or the detonation set off the whole dump. A few pieces of anti-tank mines and mortar shrapnel were found, that is judging by the colour of the metal pieces.

The names of the dead are 2/Lt M., Vols ...[*Five names follow*]

Sir, may I request that I take my force on another patrol ASAP for I feel that whilst they sit around and brood over this tragic occurrence, their nerves may fail them on any patrol they may be sent on at a later date. I myself feel somewhat un-nerved by this shattering experience.

Witness: Adj-chef M.   Captain P.R.
Witness: Adjudant C.   O.C. Force Tiger

However Mobutu's main purpose in continuing to keep Five Commando in existence was not so much to damp down the dying embers of the Simba revolt as to have a force at his disposition thoroughly loyal to him in a dangerous and potentially turbulent situation. That was why he had immediately on taking power rid himself of the pro-Tshombe mercenary commanders, Hoare, Wicks and Puren – and substituted the French mercenary Denard (much despised by Hoare) for Belgians like Protin and Lamouline.

Peters was a very different type indeed from his predecessor. He had served in the British Army as an NCO but deserted from a West Yorkshire regiment and emigrated to South Africa. He had a reputation as a killer and as a very cold man; he was however equally respected and even more feared.

There had been very little love lost between Peters and Hoare. Peters had a fanatical prejudice against the British officer-class, and there is a revealing passage in Hoare's generally anodine memoirs in which he describes Peters as being 'mad as a snake' when a rebel was executed who alone knew where the dead Belgians in Watsa had hidden their money and jewellery. Furthermore Hoare had once had to cashier Peters for being involved, indirectly, in a brawl that led to the violent death of a Katangese Adjudant.

One result of this murder was that Peters was detested by all the Katangese; indeed this must have been one of his major virtues in the eyes of Mobutu. For the military situation in the northeast of the Congo was this: 4,000-odd Katangese gendarmes, the Baka Regiment, under the Katangese Colonel Tshipolo were, since the fall of their leader Tshombe, glowering with increasing hatred at their old enemies the ANC, and in particular at Colonel Tshatshi, military commander of the Stan area and leader of the élite Israeli-trained ANC paratroops.

The Baka Regiment was divided into four battalions, 11th Commando, 12th Commando, 13th Commando and 14th Commando – each commanded by mercenary officers, French, Belgian and German. In addition Schramme's Leopard Group, now Ten Commando, was virtually in independent control of Maniema province. Mobutu could not dissolve or dismiss these Katangese, who both loathed and mistrusted him. His counterweight, his balancing forces, were the two white mercenary units, on whose loyalty he now believed, rightly, he could count: Peters' Five Commando and Denard's Six Commando.

In Belgium a group of plotters, Tshombe's old 'advisers' from the Katanga days, planned – almost certainly with the tacit connivance of the Belgian government – to oust Mobutu, in their eyes the CIA's puppet, and restore their old favourite. They approached Hoare in Durban to ask him to lead the revolt. Theoretically he was the obvious military commander, the only man with enough prestige to act speedily and successfully, and notoriously loyal to Tshombe. But apparently the South African government showed no interest. Hoare, for reasons that are none too clear, telephoned Peters who was on leave in Rhodesia, to warn him that the conspirators planned to approach him next – possibly indeed not so much to warn him as to induce him to turn his coat.

The conspirators made the approach. Peters was offered £15,000 in cash if he would lead Five Commando swiftly south, seize E'ville and raise Katanga for Tshombe. He refused. This is where the story gets very confused and even more murky. Peters had not been a success as commanding officer of Five Commando. As an ex-NCO he did not have the officer-like qualities needed to administer and control a restless unit, though in action he was unrivalled. His second-in-command Captain Hugh van Oppens was (despite his name) a tall, authoritative, moustachioed British officer, ex-regular army, who had fought in Korea and had joined Five Commando shortly before the Fixi-Baraka operation. Van Oppens was due to take over from Peters in July. But on 13 May Van Oppens was killed – and an extraordinary amount of mystery surrounds his death. At a guess I would say that he had been approached by the conspirators directly or indirectly in Peters' absence; and had either agreed (or, which would have been equally fatal, was suspected of having agreed) to lead the planned revolt. Peters meanwhile had hurriedly left Rhodesia, fearing that he would be kidnapped and disposed of for refusing to join the conspiracy. He flew to London for the World Cup finals, then back to Leo where he told Mobutu as much as he knew about the conspirators' plans. Alastair Wicks meanwhile, also like Hoare back in southern Africa, had also been approached by the conspirators. He first accepted their offer to lead the pro-Tshombe revolt but then, after making contact with both Hoare and Peters, backed down. The chronology is confused here; as is the sequence of events. All that is absolutely clear is that by July 1966 Peters was totally in charge of Five Commando, loyal to Mobutu, and after Van Oppens' death backed largely by young Afrikaner officers of the type of George Schroeder who were politically naive and could be relied upon loyally to obey straightforward orders.

The First Revolt

On Saturday, 23 July the Katangese gendarmes rose in revolt, killed Colonel Tshatshi in Stan, occupied the airport and then the radio station. They had planned to wipe out all the other ANC paratroop officers at a christening party; but this macabre *coup de main* failed. The situation, as Denard immediately reported by phone to Mobutu at Leo, was 'confused'. In the weeks that followed it was to become even more confused and bloody.

It seems as if, at first, Denard sat on the fence. Six Commando, the unit he commanded, was based in Stan and could have swung the pendulum one way or the other. Instead Denard ordered his white mercenaries to seize the post office and the bank and to remain neutral. Probably he was waiting to see exactly how much support there was for the revolt among his fellow-mercenaries.

The answer is: a certain amount but not enough. Commandant Wauthier of 11th Commando was by now the lynchpin of the plot, the compatriot the Belgian conspirators had turned to after failing with Hoare, Peters, Wicks and possibly Van Oppens. He attempted to move on Stan, telling the mercenaries with him that a *coup* had taken place in the capital. His subordinates did not believe him. In the ensuing quarrel Wauthier was shot by his own lieutenants. One of them, Piret, then suggested flying Wauthier's body to Leo as a sign of good faith. He did so and was rewarded for his pains by being interned in Camp Kokolo – a move that cured him of loyalty to Mobutu as his later 'career' was to prove.

The other unit definitely involved was 14th Commando, under a Bavarian mercenary named Wilhelm. Wilhelm came to an equally messy and violent, though rather less dishonourable, end. The Katangese of 14th Commando had worked closely for the previous year with the white mercenaries of Five Commando and had been much praised by Hoare. They descended on Paulis, captured it in a quarter of an hour, sacked and fired the town, and then set out for

Stan. En route however they were unexpectedly ambushed by a well-armed party of Simbas. Sixty out of the six hundred Katangese were killed, and ten out of the twenty-one mercenaries were wounded. Wilhelm either died of his wounds afterwards or was caught and killed by the ANC. In any case the rest of 14th Commando, now under 'Frenchie' Delamichel, did not reach Stan till 15 August, three weeks too late.

Possibly because of their emotional links with 14th Commando Peters and his men took no action against the 'mutineers' then or later. But units of Five Commando blocked the escape route south when, after tortuous and confused negotiations that dragged on for two months, 3,000 Katangese of the Baka Regiment at last broke away from Stan. They fled towards Punia in Maniema, the area controlled by Schramme. Schramme's role is obscure; he too had been sitting on the fence, avoiding taking sides. According to his own account he acted as peacemaker and protected the Katangese until a truce was arranged. But according to other accounts he was preparing to attack them himself.

The Katangese were promised an amnesty, and surrendered. Their reward was death. They were all, incredible though it seems, massacred. The precise manner of the massacre is obscure. Did it follow a surprise attack by Denard on the disarmed Katangese? Or was it the direct responsibility of Mobutu and the ANC? Questions that will probably never be answered ...

In any case in all this nightmare of treachery, bloodshed, murder, massacre and sudden death one thing is clear: the plot had failed, largely due to the conspirators' error in under-estimating the importance of Six Commando, actually in Stan, and therefore the attitude of its leader, Denard. As Radio Leopoldville announced: 'Most of the mercenaries grouped around Colonel Bob Denard at Stan have remained loyal to the Republic.' For the time being at any rate. The year 1966 ended with, for the Congo, an unusual but at the same time an uneasy calm. In late December Denard visited his dying mother in France. It was later rumoured that he also very secretly met Tshombe in Madrid.

The Disbanding of Five Commando

In early 1967 the following letters were exchanged between a would-be American mercenary and Five Commando:

Sir,
    I make application to join your unit in the capacity of private mercenary

soldier. In support of my application. I submit the following particulars: I am 22 years of age, born November –, 1944 in Dakota, and I am a United States citizen by birth. I am white. I am in good health and have not had any serious illness since I was a child. I stand six foot tall and weigh 13 stone. This I know is overweight by about 10 lbs but it can be easily corrected. I have completed 2½ of the required 4 years of the A.B. course at the X— University. I am presently employed as a debt-collector in the credit department of the Y— Co. in Cleveland. I lack prior military experience but I submit that this is an asset since I would adapt more readily to your training in irregular warfare. My savings are about 200 dollars and will no doubt increase. Also I own moderately valuable items of personal property which I can sell in aid of raising passage over, if need be. My salary is 68 dollars a week – after taxes, 55 dollars. I am free of debt. However, I would like to discuss by subsequent correspondence borrowing passage money from the unit and repaying it by payroll deduction from my first contract, unless you provide passage to the Congo as a condition of service. If formal amplification of this application is necessary, I request you send the relevant forms to me at your earliest convenience. I will answer such questions as you think necessary in further support of this application. If transportation to the theater of operations is your unit's policy and in pursuit of this you send me an airline ticket, I will give security to the limit of my ability to do so, to any agents in the United States you specify, that I will use the tickets only for passage over and will not convert it to other use. The same for passage assistance loan or any other aid.

I have a legally clear background and have never been arrested nor cited for anything more serious than a parking violation. I hold a valid United States passport and driving license. I request you instruct me as to the type of visa I should secure when you answer this application and also about import licensing requirements for my weapons. I am going into this with my eyes open. A year ago I researched the Congo mercenaries to the limit of the Cleveland Public Library, and I will review and update my research while awaiting your reply. I realize the possibility that I may be killed in action and I accept it. I also realize the sureity that I will forfeit United States citizenship by taking service with you. This also I accept. I can in good conscience give a note of loyalty and obedience to the mercenary commander, and determined upon this I will whole-heartedly commit myself to this course of action, with your help and participation in this.

I am,
Faithfully yours,
P.R.

Five Commando replied:

Dear Sir,
   In reply to your letter of 25th instant, we regret to advise you that we do not take persons of American nationality. This is in accordance with the wishes of the American Government, who have requested that we employ no American citizens.*

Yours faithfully, etc.

But P. R. was persistent:

Sir,
   The United States Department of state has reiterated this advice to me, to the effect that enlistment in a foreign military force operates as an immediate and automatic revocation of United States citizenship and nationality. It would seem, therefore, that if I did join Five Commando, as I fully intend to do so if given permission to do so, the automatic loss of United States citizenship and nationality that I would thereby incur, would render the State Department's objection to American mercenaries irrelevant to me. I would no longer be American, etc. etc.

His logic, though unanswerable, was unavailing. Five Commando replied:

   I would like to bring to your attention again that we are *not* taking persons of American nationality. Secondly, Five Commando will cease to exist as from between June and July ...

So Five Commando was coming to its end, though not without regrets on many sides:

Unit Report
10.4.67 from O.C. Cheta to O.C. Paradise; info CO Five Commando; Subject, Civilian Report. Chiefs and local Chiefs from surrounding area have been informed that Five Commando is vacating this area. Big deputation has just informed me that themselves and all their people intend moving at the same time we move. They will not stay in the area under any command other than Five Commando. A large party of women

---

* To a New York doctor who, earlier, had wanted to join Five Commando as an orthopaedic surgeon the reply was more explicit.

   Unfortunately Five Commando has an agreement with the United States Embassy not to accept American citizens. It is the law of your country that upon enlistment in a foreign army you will lose your American citizenship. We thank you for your application and regret that we cannot assist you ...

and children on their way to this position so that they can plead with us. All villages will be vacated and will follow Five Commando.

Peters had in fact left two months before this report, in February 1967. George Schroeder, aged twenty-four, took over for the last three months of Five Commando's existence till it was finally disbanded without incident towards the end of May. Peters had planned to go back to South Africa but the South African government refused him the right to reside there and he was forced instead to return to England. One of his officers wrote an indignant letter from Albertville to the South African Ministry of the Interior pleading against the decision:

February 1967.
    I would like to bring to your attention that I have already been in contact with your department as well as the S.A. police and the Department of Defence in connection with the above person. I would like to reiterate the following points. More than 90% of the present members of Fifth Commando are South Africans. These men fight for the unit with the ultimate idea being the suppression of communism.
    1) Under the excellent leadership of Lt Col J. Peters, a terrific amount of success has been achieved and the rebel forces have almost completely been destroyed. The remaining rebels now moving in small groups – they are, too, diminishing.
    2) In the past I can assure you South Africans have at times found themselves in most undesirable circumstances. Lt Col Peters was the only man who fully assisted these men and refused to hand these men over to black authorities for trial.*
    3) On various occasions did men of the Fifth Commando, including myself, hand rebel weapons and ammunition to the S.A. police and the Department of Defence in order to assist their study of communist weapons. This was insisted upon by Lt Col Peters.
    4) Since Lt Col Peters has been appointed Commanding Officer of Fifth Commando there has been no warranted complaints of wages not being paid.
    5) Under the command of Lt Col Hoare this was not the case. The men were never sure of receiving their pay.†
    6) In excess of 90% of the Fifth Commando officers are not only South Africans but actually Afrikaans speaking, which again proves that Lt Col Peters promotes his men on merit only, regardless of the language

---

* Perennial problem for mercenary leaders. For the formal position see Appendix (Article 3). A similar clause is always to be found in Italian *condottas*.

† True, but in Hoare's defence it can be said that Puren, not he, was responsible for this side of the administration, and that Hoare was, unlike Peters, fighting a war of movement in conditions unfavourable to efficient paper work.

they speak. The following are the names of some of the Afrikaans speaking officers in this Commando: Major G. Schroeder, 2 I/C, Captains B. B., S. A., B. S., Lieutenants A., S. G., L. C., Captain Q. S., M.B., C.H.B., University, Cape Town, served as intern at Groote Schuur Hospital, Cape Town. In the past these men were not even considered by Lt Col Hoare.

7) The relatives of all men who die in the Congo receive an amount of Rand 14,000. When Lt Col Peters took command of this unit more than 80% of these claims were outstanding, but have now been settled. This again proves the negligence of Lt Col Hoare, compared to the efficiency of Lt Col Peters who immediately took steps to have these claims settled.

8) As far as discipline is concerned we endeavour to uphold the good name of Five Commando, but as usual the individual can do a lot of harm; a problem also encountered by the authorities in R.S.A. The men applying in our recruiting office can be divided into the following groups:

a) The man with domestic problems, viz. the recently divorced;

b) The fortune-seeker;

c) The man who wants experience;

d) The man who wishes to dodge the law;

e) There are also those who arrive here with disreputable pasts who wrongly imagine he can continue with his criminal career.

With the above types we have to maintain our good reputation. On the last flight, for example, a number of men were sent back after being found in possession of 'dagga'. This is the type who usually goes back to S.A. with untrue stories to blacken our name. These are normally the people who cannot submit themselves to discipline. The most prominent excuses for their sudden return are given as—

a) Not being paid;

b) Murder is being committed;

c) Looting;

d) The non-existence of apartheid.

With regards to the latter, the latest order from Lt Col Peters read in part, as follows:

a) If found guilty imprisonment for the balance of the contract.

b) No further wages to be paid.

This proves once again how strongly Lt Col Peters supports apartheid.

9) The authorities are aware that Lt Col Peters invested all his money in the Republic of South Africa with a view to settling there. Due to something in his past he was banned. I do believe that if a person has the desire to start anew he should be given the chance.

10) I am aware that the honourable late Dr Verwoerd was assassinated by undesired immigrants and can assure you that we fully supported the late Dr Verwoerd, as we now do Minister Vorster. I do beg that should it meet with your approval, Lt Col Peters be permitted a reasonable period of time in order to present his case to the authorities, even if this period is for three days only. Whatever his plea is I do not know, but I am

convinced that he is better equipped to present his case than any of us or even his counsel.

11) I am also aware that the S.A. Police and Department of Defence desires an interview with Lt Col Peters, even though they are not prepared to submit this request to you in writing.

12) With reference to a report in some English newspapers, I can only repeat what I always say to the officers here, that during the time of Lt Col Hoare he never had the well-being of his men at heart. He was more interested in publicity as his name did appear on the front pages of newspapers. This was mainly due to evidence of success on the side of Lt Col Peters who at that time served as a Sub Lt in command of force John John.

13) In the past we also experienced shortage of medical supplies. Thanks to the efforts of the present Commanding Officer of Five Commando, we now have sufficient. Most of the supplies, however, were bought in South Africa out of his personal funds.

14) He also supplemented all shortages of uniforms. This again was also from South Africa and paid for with his own money. Our present uniform compares favourably with that of any army in the world, unlike the past when every member wore a different style or colour of uniform.

It is most certainly not my intention to glorify this man's past but I do feel that people's newspapers are victimising him for actions he was not responsible for. It is my honest opinion that what Five Commando is doing here is also indirectly done for South Africa; perhaps not now but certainly in the future and all this is due to the Commanding Officer of Five Commando.

I have stated the above facts to impress upon you the type of person Lt Col Peters really is. I again respectfully request that you grant him the opportunity to visit South Africa and put his case personally to another departmental head. I do appreciate your co-operation and interest in this case. A reply from your department by return of post will be esteemed a favour to me and many other fine South African officers serving under a man who is respected by Great Britain.

Not everything in this extraordinary *apologia* needs to be taken *au pied de la lettre*. The word *apartheid* in paragraph 8 is enigmatic, probably a euphemism referring to sexual intercourse with black women, a crime under South Africa's apartheid laws. It seems unlikely that Peters could have controlled this; one of the pleasures of mercenary life was the solace derived from 'jungle bunnies'. As regards the reference in the next paragraph to the honourable late Dr Verwoerd, this is even more obscure. Can the letter-writer seriously have believed that Peters was banned for fear he might assassinate Vorster? Or is there an echo here and in paragraph 11 of the mystery surrounding Van Oppens' death?

Peters' version of events apparently was that Van Oppens attempted to murder him and, on failing, committed suicide.

As for the list of the motives which pushed men to join the mercenaries, it is rather too black to be convincing. But what is convincing is the deep-seated rancour felt against Hoare by a correspondent who was obviously not a literate member of the British officer class, and of the ever-present tensions between Afrikaners and English-speaking South Africans inside Five Commando – as indeed inside South Africa itself.

A final document follows: a report sent by Colonel Schroeder, as he had now become, to General Bobozo, titular head of the ANC, in the spring of 1967, about six weeks after he had taken over command and six weeks before disbandment. If this is the report of even a portential pro-Tshombe conspirator, it would be a Machiavellian work of art. In my opinion it shows the political naiveté of the youthful Afrikaners now in control – a naiveté balanced by an obvious loyalty to their immediate employer:

Mon Générale,

First I would like to assure you of my co-operation and sincerity towards the Congolese government and yourself and extremely appreciative of the confidence you have shown in appointing me as Commander of Fifth Commando unit and will strive to give you the type of security and strength that is so badly needed to rebuild the Congo.

My initial orders to this unit were based on the obvious need for reconstruction and resettlement, as well as the security necessary for the local population to settle back into a productive way of life. We have embarked on projects lying close to the roads: rebuild bridges, repair schools and many other things essential to regain normality in the Republic.

The areas not clear of rebels, small patrols are harassing them continually so that the native population is spared the atrocities so common to rebel occupation. After the rainy season is finished, we shall progress much more rapidly in opening the Nmoya Nakalitza Enemendi complex to the normal civil adminstration.

I have assigned certain of my best qualified men to establish an intelligence unit designed to detect any form of opposition that might be detrimental to the best interest of the Central Government. It is my good intention to provide you with an intelligence report periodically in the near future.

The following points have come to my attention which shall be pointed out to you at this time.

1) Arms and ammunition are coming in approximately three kilometres south of the C.L.F. harbour. This fact was confirmed from information received from several civilians.

2) The arms and ammunition are brought in by local fishing fleets from the Tanzania side of the lake. The arms and ammunition are being carried in fishing nets under the water. When our naval force investigated these fishing boats they cut the ropes with the result that no proof can be produced.

3) The amount of arms and ammunitions already in Albertville is unknown to us but I do know it is quite a substantial amount.

4) A Greek by the name of Sporof went to fetch these arms and ammunitions on a number of occasions.

5) A local shop-owner by the name of Klanthonides Leonadis came approximately ten minutes after the beach droppings into the harbour. Furthermore we suspect that a house in the village contains a very strong radio set but we cannot do anything until we have more proof. We do know further that four ex-rebels are having a meeting in this house every second or third night.

We also suspect that arms and ammunition are coming in in bags and in foodstuffs to the docks. We do know furthermore that there are between three hundred and four hundred here possibly originating from Somalia. They are here without permissary documents. We checked on this point with the local police saying that we are looking for a certain Arab we had met before and that we now believed he is in Albertville. We requested them to go through their records to confirm this and supply us with his residential address. They informed us that this would be impossible owing to the fact that few of them have legal documents. We have checked with different civilians and they agree that there are quite a lot of Arabs in Albertville.

6) I suspect that they are here for one of the following reasons (a) starting a new rebellion, (b) mutiny in the army and police, (c) preparation for Tshombe.

On 16.3.67 one of my officers was doing investigation work and came across a group of fifteen men with rifles having a meeting. Unfortunately he could not understand much, due to the fact that they were speaking Arabic but he could follow that there was an argument in the group. The name of General Mobutu was used, as well as my own name and that of one of my officers who was working in this intelligence force. While listening in on this discussion, two armed guards attacked him and tried to overpower him. Only through fast reaction and good capability he managed to get away, with only cuts on his hands. The report of this incident immediately reached me. If I may give my opinion I suspect that it starts the local rebellion on the shrewd movement of the Tshombe group. We all know that President Mobutu is arriving at my position tomorrow, 17.3.67. [Mobutu cancelled his visit]

If I could inform you I suspect it would be a great opportunity for opposition forces to start off with an assassination of the President, which I would like to prevent as far as possible from my side. At the same time they will attempt to knock off other high authorities which will leave the

Congo without leading men. They will also attempt to eliminate me and my officers. This would leave Five Commando for a short time in a position where they cannot act to protect Albertville properly. After this it would be easy for a ship to enter the harbour with arms and ammunition, since our navy could only operate for a certain time, and then have to return to harbour for re-fuelling and re-loading purposes. Should the navy stores be taken by rebels it would be impossible for them to carry on with operations.

I have only a few men in the position. You will appreciate that if you would give me orders to withdraw some of my men from the field to protect Albertville from what could well be a very serious situation.

I would like you to send immediately a special security force to investigate these matters of arms and men coming into Albertville. I do think this matter is more serious than what anyone would like to believe at this stage.

Furthermore, we know that Tshombe is supposed to be in jail in Southern Arabia for high treason. This could be a bluff and these Arabs could be working in conjunction with him. This information about him could only be to take us off the hook.

Once again, Generale, I wish to thank you for your confidence and I hope you do believe and trust my motives. I can assure you my duties are only to serve you and the President. Rest assured that the Fifth Commando will be loyal to the Republic of the Congo as long as I am in command.

5

The Mercenaries' Revolt

'Ils ne ressemblent en rien à la Légion Etrangère avec ses traditions de discipline et d'obéissance aux chefs ... Ce sont plûtot des bandes operant à la façon des Grandes Compagnies et fort chatouilleuses sur le point d'honneur'.
Max Clos, in *Le Figaro*

The story that follows is perhaps the most extraordinary of all. If the mercenaries' revolt had succeeded, the consequences would have been incalculable. The pale-eyed Schramme could have become the Sforza of black Africa. But it failed – though the margin between failure and success was, at times, narrow indeed.

In certain conditions it is almost inevitable that mercenaries will revolt against their employer. The moment of danger for both sides comes when the employer decides that he no longer needs the services of these always-dangerous troops. In rare cases both sides will trust each other, and, as happened with Five Commando, will be demobilised without incident. But when an atmosphere of suspicion already exists, it is only natural for mercenaries to fear that, once disarmed, they will not be paid off and dismissed with honour but killed out of hand. On the other side the employer will see in every tergiversation of the mercenaries the first signs of revolt. In the Congo in 1967 an atmosphere of suspicion already existed. The mercenaries had seen and noted how the disarmed Katangese of the previous summer's revolt had been massacred despite promises of pardon and safety. On his side Mobutu knew that the whole country was seething with plots. He was particularly suspicious of Schramme and Ten Commando – Kansimbas from North Katanga.

'Black Jack' Schramme

In Maniema Schramme had succeeded in forming almost a state

within a state. He had, with other Belgian planters of the area, rebuilt roads and bridges, reorganised trade and education, sent on his own initiative to Europe for technicians and missionaries, and used gangs of captured Simbas as forced labour. It was a notable achievement, though directly in the old colonial pattern.

Schramme's base was his own plantation, complete with airstrip, at Yumbi in the heart of Maniema. His reputation and his power were spreading rapidly, and ever since the massacre of the Katangese the summer before he had been discreetly preparing the defence of Maniema against a possible attack by central government forces. However discreet his preparations were, no doubt reports of them had come to the ears of Mobutu.

The second general situation in which mercenaries are likely to revolt arises when they calculate that they have a good chance of being taken onto the payroll of a rival to their employer. When the rival has a more attractive personality and a reputation for being loyal to his mercenaries, a sudden switch of allegiance and an armed revolt is even more likely to occur.

The third situation arises when a mercenary leader sees an opportunity to seize power himself and to take his employer's place.

None of these situations, none of the three guiding motives – fear, avarice and ambition – is mutually exclusive. When all three conditions and all three motives co-exist, a revolt is inevitable. Such was the case in the Congo in 1967.

It would be hard to say how and when Schramme's ambition grew. Probably he acted at first out of a mere instinct of self-preservation. But no doubt, too, he had always felt that the way to solve the Congo's problems was to apply everywhere the methods he had so succesfully used in Maniema.

It seems that the actual thought of an uprising rather than of defensive action did not enter Schramme's head till early December 1966. Then he was summoned to Leo for an interview with the new President. Mobutu told him of his intention to disarm the Kansimbas and to replace them with ANC recruits: Schramme and the other white officers would still remain in command of the 'renovated' Ten Commando.

To this Schramme retorted that he was willing for both himself and his men to be demobilised – he and his officers to be sent back to Belgium, the Kansimbas to North Katanga – but that he wuld resist any attempt at 'disarming' his men. The tone of the conversation must have been remarkably like that of a feudal overlord confronting a powerful and semi-independent vassal. During that interview

another powerful vassal, on whose loyalty the overlord counted, sat
silently by without a word – Bob Denard.

From Schramme's point of view Denard was a mere mercenary
and adventurer. He himself was a planter and administrator, in
uniform only through force of circumstances. There was never any
love lost between the French and the Belgians in the Congo. From
the days of Katanga any intruding Frenchmen were looked upon with
suspicion. Denard's silent presence at the interview was an implied
threat to Schramme. Indeed in my opinion Schramme was lucky to
leave the capital alive.

The interview nonetheless ended in an outwardly friendly atmosphere with Mobutu letting the talk of disarmament drop. Schramme
flew back to Yumbi apparently reassured. By March 1967 it became
known throughout the northeast that Five Commando would soon be
disbanded. In April Denard and Six Commando received orders to
disarm Schramme. But Denard made no move to do so. Instead, he
paid a secret visit to Yumbi, told Schramme of the orders, but added
that he had no intention of obeying them. He may have known or
suspected that Mobutu had Six Commando next on the list for
disarmament. He may simply have been placed in a dilemma where
he had either to take up arms against a fellow white mercenary,
French-speaking at that – a drastic move that might have resulted in a
mutiny among his own men and for himself the fate of Wauthier the
year before – or else to join in orgainising a revolt himself. He may
just have been preparing plans for every eventuality, including double
and triple crosses. Of all the mercenary leaders, Denard's history is
the most controversial and his motives the most confusing. Official
French diplomats were very scathing in private about Denard's
character, activities and attempted intrigues. But less official French
'services' have a tradition of using this sort of rough but ready tool. I
would hazard the guess myself that Denard was by now part of a vast
conspiracy for Tshombe's return, backed at least unofficially by
certain sections of the French government, and at this particular
conjuncture supported by the Belgian government too.

The 'Kyrellis Plan'

For official relations between Brussels and Leo were at a particularly
low point. The continual squabble between Union Minière and the
Congolese government had once again touched off a crisis. Schramme later claimed, unconvincingly, that the 'Kyrellis Plan' was an
ingenious smokescreen personally thought up by him in order to

mislead Mobutu. Admittedly the Belgians who had plotted Mobutu's overthrow the previous year had been once bitten and may have been twice shy. But there was every economic reason for the Belgians and every political reason for the French to attempt to halt the growing American influence that Mobutu symbolised. What had been missing the year before had been the masterstroke: the reappearance on the scene of Tshombe in person. This was now to be the hinge on which the whole plan turned. There are strong rumours that Schramme was at a later stage directly approached by the Belgian government and covered by Belgium's Foreign Minister, M. Harmel. As for Denard, no plot involving directly or indirectly Jacques Foccart, de Gaulle's *éminence grise* for African affairs and Denard's probable puppet-master, can be dismissed as non-existent or improbable simply on the grounds of complexity.

In May a Belgian planter, Maurice Quintin, had called on Schramme in Yumbi to propose a pro-Tshombe revolt. At the time Schramme had refused to discuss it, suspecting that Quintin might be an 'agent provocateur'. It seems more likely that Quintin was the first Kyrellis contact – and a very clumsy one. He threatened to inform Mobutu that Schramme had agreed. 'I could not run the risk of reprisals against my men and myself,' Schramme declared at his eventual trial for murder in Belgium. 'It was my duty to prevent Quintin from putting his plan into action. I shot him and ordered Rodrigues (a mercenary barman, accused together with Schramme) to finish him off and throw his body into the Lowa.'

But by early June the situation had changed dramatically. First Mobutu had horrified world opinion by the public hanging in Leo of the 'Pentecost Conspirators' – four eminent politicians including a former Prime Minister Evariste Kimba. Then he had horrified all white mercenaries by condemning three of them to twelve years' penal servitude (they had 'liberated' a bank in Goma, claiming that they had not been paid). Finally he had horrified all Belgian planters still in the Congo by having the fingers and ears cut off one of their number in Katanga, for alleged participation in the blowing up of the Lubudi bridge. This act of sabotage in itself threw the whole country's economy into chaos, for it effectively cut off copper exports. On 22 June Denard once again visited Yumbi.

This time the moment was ripe, the atmosphere was right. The two mercenary leaders agreed on a coordinated revolt. Schramme was to arrange the initial assault, and seize Stan. There Denard – whose forces were dispersed – would join him with the hundred-odd whites of Six Commando and eight hundred Katangese under command.

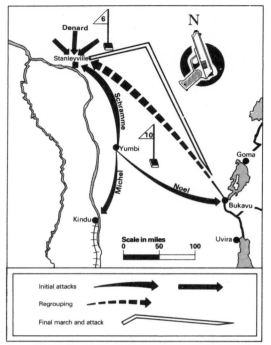

The Mercenaries' Revolt – in theory

Meanwhile two more of Schramme's Belgian officers would lead out assault columns of Ten Commando: Noel to seize Bukavu and Michel to seize Kindu. Schramme and Noel would then regroup at Yumbi; move to captured Kindu, Ten Commando's new base, ready to head south; and then strike south deep into Katanga. Denard's role in all this was to give the order for revolt to the surviving Katangese commandoes, the 7th and the 9th, and to hold Stan and the North-East.

The second phase of the planned operation was even more ambitious. Schramme and his men would rendezvous at Kongolo with two thousand Katangese ex-gendarmes, already warned. The combined force would then assault Kamina base. E'ville would fall, Tshombe would be flown in from Spain, the rest of Katanga and the province of Kasai would rise; and then the 'rebels' would pause, and demand Mobutu's abdication. All was fixed except the date for the uprising. Next day, 23 June, Jeremiah Puren landed at Yumbi in a DC4 bringing arms, ammunition and nine South African mercenaries whom he left with Schramme as guarantees of his good faith and indication of greater reinforcements to come. Or that at least is

Schramme's story; and on all these events the only full account we have is Schramme's. What is clear is that Puren was involved, and was based in Angola – which means that the Portuguese colonial authorities also connived at the revolt. (Whether the South African government ever knew about it is far more doubtful.) But then came almost literally, a bolt from the blue that threw the whole complicated conspiracy into confusion. On 30 June, only a week later, Tshombe was kidnapped – hijacked on a flight off the coast of Spain between Ibiza and Majorca.

Tshombe's Kidnapping

One thing is certain. Whether the 'Kyrellis Plan' did or did not exist in all its ramifications, there had certainly been a very carefully planned and executed counter-plot to dispose of Tshombe. The hijacked plane was flown to Algeria where Tshombe was imprisoned. It is still not clear who precisely was behind the plot. It was not organised by Mobutu; that at least is certain. Had it been, Tshombe would have been flown directly to Leo and hanged, for he had already been condemned to death *in absentia* with the 'Pentecost Conspirators'. It is unlikely that it was organised by the Algerians, who appear to have been taken by surprise and to have had no advantage to gain. The most probable explanation is that it was organised by the CIA. The CIA's duty and policy was to keep Mobutu in power. Any plot, actual or potential, to restore Tshombe would be foiled by Tshombe's imprisonment in Algiers, and yet this imprisonment would not leave bloodstained consciences behind it.

François Bodenan, the hijacker, was a thirty-three-year-old Frenchman with a semi-criminal past, living in Spain. Some say he knew of, and had reported to his 'masters', the secret meeting between Tshombe and Denard in Madrid the previous December. At any rate he was obviously a 'bodyguard' in whom, on 30 June on take-off, Tshombe still had confidence. He held up the five passengers at pistol point and forced the two pilots to alter course for Algeria. In the sense that he had disposed of plenty of money at the time, he was of the mercenary class himself. Fifteen years later, I am happy to say, he was tried before a Spanish court martial at Palma de Majorca, accused of infringing Tshombe's civil rights; for which the prosecutor demanded a twenty-year-prison sentence. Hijacking, as the last major episode to be recounted in this book will show, is one offence that mercenaries would be very wise to steer clear of. But even Bodenan's 1982 trial failed to reveal – it was, of course, irrelevant to the offence – who had paid him, who were his 'masters'.

It was more than Tshombe's 'civil rights' that were at stake, however. It was his life. Moise Tshombe died in that prison in Algiers, a sad ending for a flamboyant character, not unlike that of the also-betrayed Duke Ludovico il Moro in a French dungeon centuries earlier. His death was announced on 30 June 1969 – two years to the day after his kidnapping, five years to the day after his appointment as Prime Minister, nine years to the day after the Congo's Independence. The Algerian authorities collected a batch of doctors to certify that his death was due to natural causes. But scepticism is almost unavoidable; and, if it should ever be proved that there was a mercenary-led rescue attempt on his prison, would become entirely justified.

For there was every logic, from the mercenary point of view, in liberating Tshombe. An extraordinary figure named Colonel Hubert Fauntleroy Julian, the 'Black Eagle' of Harlem, claimed, shortly after Tshombe's death, to have been involved in precisely such an attempt. This aged adventurer had flown for Haile Selassie against the Italians (a curious coincidence here with the Swedish Count Carl Gustav Von Rosen, of whom more in the next chapter), and thereafter led a suitably rocambolesque life. He eventually became part of the wide variety of fauna attracted to Katanga where, apparently, he would boast of multi-million arms deals one moment and casually request the price of a taxi-fare the next.

The details of 'his' Tshombe rescue saga were not unbreathtaking. Originally it was to cost Tshombe's backers six million dollars, mainly in bribes to Algerian officals. But then at the end of May 1969 – that is to say, one month before Tshombe's death was announced – an independent and quite separate attempt at a rescue was made by a group of mercenaries unknown to the Black Eagle (and, it must be added, unheard of, before or after, by anyone else). This raid ended in failure and the death of several mercenaries; but as a result the price demanded for bribes and flight organisation rose to $15 million. Nevertheless the Black Eagle had everything arranged and set up, only to be foiled once again by the news of Tshombe's death.

This melodramatic farrago may just possibly have some basis of truth – at least in the not-improbable report of a failed mercenary raid, which bears the Denard touch. But at the time, when on 30 June 1967, news of the kidnapping reached Schramme at Yumbi and Denard near Stan, the two mercenary leaders and their backers must have been thrown into total confusion. For without the figurehead how could the revolt go ahead?

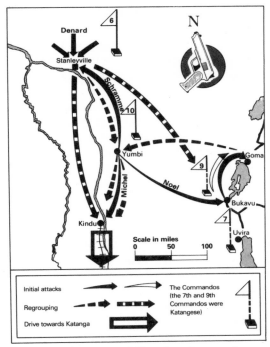

The Mercenaries' Revolt – in practice

The Revolt Breaks Out

On 3 July Denard radioed Schramme to arrange an urgent meeting. They met half-way between Yumbi and Lubutu. The news Denard brought was decisive. The 3rd Paratroop Regiment of the ANC, Israeli-trained, was due to arrive by boat in forty-eight hours time at Stan – and Denard's orders were, with the 3rd Para, to disarm Schramme and his men. Figurehead or no figurehead, Tshombe or no Tshombe, this was the crunch. The two mercenary leaders took the decision to launch the uprising immediately.

Schramme's detachments rolled out from Yumbi next day and at dawn on the morning of 5 July Ten Commando went into action, launching surprise attacks as planned on Stan, Kindu and Bukavu. Schramme himself occupied Stan almost without difficulty, fifteen jeeps careering, guns blazing, through the city's centre. The ANC fled before his captain, Noel, at Bukavu. But at Kindu the tiny detachment under Michel soon found themselves defending the airport against a counterattack by two or three thousand ANC. This was the first disaster. Most of the mercenaries in this group including their leader Michel escaped into the bush and eventually made their way back to Yumbi by foot, an extraordinary achievement.

Then things began to go very wrong at Bukavu. Neither Denard's promised relieving column under one of his officers, Nodyn, nor the 7th or 9th (Katangese) Commandos appeared. Later that day Noel got a radio message either sent or received – stories differ – by a drunken radio operator which he interpreted as an order to pull out of Bukavu and fall back on Stan. Less than twenty-four hours after its capture, therefore, Schrammes's mercenaries abandoned Bukavu, leaving its considerable white population at the mercy of a returning and vindictive ANC. Many white settlers were killed or tortured as a punishment for 'collaboration'.

Schramme later blamed the failure of Phase A on Denard. Denard according to him had not warned the outlying patrols of Six Commando in time, and it took these men a week to assemble at Stan. Therefore Schramme was forced to stay in Stan, defending the city against the fierce attacks of the 3rd Para and was unable to relieve Kindu quickly or to regroup at Yumbi as planned. However, this does not square with other accounts. The cause of the failure was probably muddle, confusion and ill-luck rather than the sinister motives which Schramme later insinuated were behind Denard's actions.

Leo: The Killing of the Mercenaries

What Denard did do is fail to warn the thirty-odd mercenaries of Six Commando in Leo. Possibly he thought that these men, mainly occupied in liaison and administrative work, would not be harmed. Possibly he feared that to warn them would risk leaking information. Possibly he attempted to warn them and failed. But most probably he shrugged his shoulders and left them to take their chance. One of them, an Algerian who had taken French nationality, had been enlisted by Denard in Paris and was employed by Mobutu as a personal bodyguard. He eventually (thanks to the colour of his skin) managed to escape. He was probably the only survivor of the thirty (who included two mercenaries of British origin) and his subsequent account of how these unsuspecting mercenaries in the capital were rounded up on 5 July and led like sheep to the slaughterhouse is both vivid and terrifying. This was the first group of mercenaries in the modern age to suffer the traditional fate of being massacred treacherously by their employer. For the horrifying position in which they found themselves and for their pitiful, unexpected, totally unmerited deaths Denard must bear to his own grave the responsibility.

Schramme's AnaBasis

On the day the revolt broke out Mobutu decreed a state of emergency, general mobilisation – and appealed to the Security Council for aid. The Congolese Radio announced, falsely, that two plane-loads of foreign mercenaries had landed in Stan. Two days later the radio reported, also falsely but more convincingly, 'a great victory'. On 10 July twelve wounded mercenaries including Denard flew to Rhodesia in a stolen DC3. It looked as if the insurrection was over. The Congolese Radio announced that the horde of *affreux* had taken flight. On President Johnson's initiative the United States despatched three giant C130s to the Congo to transport ANC troops to Stan. *Le Monde*, France's most informed and reliable daily paper, announced categorically, '*La rébellion des mercenaires serait terminée.*'

In fact what had happened was that the mercenaries in Stan were left in much the same sort of position as Xenophon's Greeks had been after the loss of Cyrus, their employer, claimant to the Persian throne, and the treacherous killing of their general Clearchus. Their hopes of surprise and a quick success were gone. The native 'pretender' in whose name they were fighting, Tshombe, had been eliminated. The enemy was assembling large forces. Their position was untenable, their escape looked difficult, and their future uncertain. In addition the most renowned of their two leaders had been lost. Denard had eventually arrived in Stan, with the scattered groups of Six Commando, only to be wounded in the leg by (probably) a stray ANC bullet from the far bank of the Congo, and, as reported, evacuated with other casualties.

After a week in Stan Schramme and his men moved out – though not in fact till 12 July. To have stayed would have been purposeless. The surrounding population, still largely Simba, was hostile and Stan was neither a possible centre for spreading revolt nor near enough to a frontier to offer a way of escape. There were several alternatives open to Schramme. The first was to fall back defensively onto his own fortified region of Maniema, though this would have been almost pointless both tactically and strategically. The second was to go ahead with the revolt despite the loss of surprise, to plunge south, and to attempt to raise Katanga. The third was to give up and to try and save his skin and that of his men by heading towards a frontier.

That, at first, is what seemed to have happened. For three weeks the 'fleeing mercenaries' with their 'white hostages' (for whose safety the Red Cross expressed great fears) disappeared into the wilds. At first they were reported to be heading north-east, towards the Central African Republic. Then, three weeks later, Radio Congo reported clashes near Bukavu. This implied a total change of direction. The two-thousand-strong European population of Bukavu started fleeing across the Shangugu river into the small, safe, neighbouring country of Rwanda. On 7 August Radio Congo announced that Mobutu had stationed ANC troops all along the Rwanda border with orders to 'annihilate' the mercenaries should they attempt to flee across to safety and refuge inside Rwanda.

Then, two days later, on 9 August, came a sudden reversal of fortune, a 'bombshell' that shook the whole expectant and curious world. Schramme's column, 1,500 strong, descended on Bukavu, led by an 'armoured' bulldozer and captured the lakeside city with conspicuous, nonchalant ease. It was the ANC due to 'annihilate' them who, instead, fled across the Shangugu to take refuge in Rwanda, handing in their weapons to the frontier guards under the gaze of astonished television cameras. Subsequently *Le Monde*, no doubt smarting a little at its unusual failure to supply accurate news, asked (under the heading *'À la gloire des Mercenaires*) whether it was really necessary to present them on television as *'de sympatiques héros menant un juste combat'*. But in fact, if only because their enemies always appeared to be fleeing in the opposite direction when direct action sequences were shown, it would have been difficult to present them visually in any other way.

Before 9 August Schramme had been virtually unknown. By 10 August he had become a figure of enormous importance, a white mercenary leader who seemed to hold the whole future of the Congo in his hands. On the day following his descent on Bukavu he gave interviews galore to press and television. There was no question of fleeing mercenaries or white hostages now. Indeed it turned out that the 'hostages' with Schramme's column were white civilians from the North who of their own free will had chosen to be escorted by Schramme to the Rwanda frontier and safety rather than face Mobutu's rampaging ANC.

As for Schramme, he showed all the self-confidence of a man totally in charge of events. So far from being about to flee into Rwanda, he announced that his column had defeated the ANC in two pitched battles en route to Bukavu (which was, in terms of Congolese warfare, true enough); and that he and his men intended to stay. Not only did he intend to stay but he would, he announced, invade Katanga or move directly on the capital, Leo, if Mobutu did not negotiate. Ten days to negotiate – that was the mercenary colonel's ultimatum to his former employer. By Schramme's side a new figure appeared, also hitherto unknown: Colonel Leonard Monga of the

Katangese. Monga announced the formation of a Provisional Government of Public Safety – no less – at Bukavu. In his 'Presidential Proclamation', issued that same day, Monga made an impassioned appeal to General Moshe Dayan, urging 'the conquerors of the Arab demagogues to cease their aid to the demagogues of Mobutu' and to 'recall to Israel the Israeli instructors who are in the Congo'. World television and press publicised this appeal, as well as Monga, the new 'government' and Schramme's presumptuous but appealing ultimatum, with glee.

World opinion was, indeed extraordinarily confused by these totally unexpected events. On the one hand it seemed ridiculous that a handful of white mercenaries backed by a few hundred Katangese gendarmes (150 of the one, approximately, and 800 of the other) should attempt to dictate the course of history in the richest and largest country in black Africa. On the other hand the precedent set by Hoare and his men was remembered. The ANC were not the Simbas, but they seemed, though better armed and equipped, to have even less fighting spirit or ability. Furthermore throughout the previous month the Congolese Radio had clearly been feeding the world a pack of lies, in what now seemed to be a disastrous attempt to boost Mobutu's weak position. Even American support for him appeared to be waning: in the face of angry reactions both from Congressmen and Senators the administration quietly withdrew its plans to put more C130s at his disposition.

Lull at Bukavu

Five days before the ultimatum issued to him expired, Mobutu released his own ultimatum, giving the 'ignoble mercenaries' ten days, in their turn, to quit Bukavu. Next day Schramme issued yet another ultimatum – this time directed at the President of Burundi, Rwanda's southern neighbour. If Burundi continued to allow free passage to ANC troops, he, Schramme, would, he threatened, cut off all that little country's electricity – which depended on Bukavu's hydroelectric works. Burundi, like Rwanda an ex-colony of Belgium, in its turn issued an ultimatum to the Belgium government demanding that Belgium 'assume its responsibilities'. The only result of this 'war of the ultimatums' was that Brussels obligingly 'disowned' the mercenaries and Colonel Schramme. Schramme then announced that he would never be satisfied by anything less than the fall of Mobutu. Mobutu for his part retorted that 'there never has been and never will be negotiations between Schramme and the Congolese government'. Two days later a forty-eight hour truce was proclaimed, giving the lie to Mobutu's statement, followed by a strange pause in almost all military activity. The radio battles continued unabated, however, with the Congolese Radio claiming, heatedly but none too convincingly, a record of objectivity.

One of Schramme's reasons for seizing Bukavu had been precisely because Bukavu had a radio station; and in the weeks that followed Radio Bukavu beamed insults against Mobutu, appeals to the besieging ANC, and false news of the success of the rebellion all over the east of the Congo. The 'official' reason Schramme gave for choosing to head towards Bukavu rather than strike deep into Katanga was that it was his responsibility to escort the white refugees to safety and that therefore he had been forced to head for a border city. Unofficially there were rumours of Schramme's refurbished 'treasure-chest' and much controversy about the Bukavu banks. Were the guards whom Schramme ostentatiously placed outside these banks really there to protect the deposits of this rich trading city or to deceive observers? Were millions transported by Schramme across to Rwanda, and if so, where are they now?

Militarily there were, all the same, good reasons for Schramme's decision. Bukavu was stocked with huge supplies of food, drink and ammunition and it was tactically defensible by Schramme's small army. On the other hand its very proximity to the border was a psychological disadvantage; the temptation for deserters was great, and indeed twenty mercenaries deserted immediately after the capture of the city. An even greater disadvantage was that Bukavu lacked an airstrip, unlike Goma to its north. Clearly, though, the question of an airstrip was only important if Schramme expected aid from outside.

He did expect it; and he did, though only to a minimal extent, receive it. In the twelve weeks that Schramme had his men held Bukavu three planes landed or attempted to land there. The first was a twin-engined Piper, flown by a former Katanga mercenary, Bracco. He crashlanded it on the lake, where it sank, but not before the two passengers had had time to inflate a canoe. One was Captain Nawej, a Katangese who had been Tshombe's head of security. The other, almost inevitably, was Jeremiah Puren.

But where Puren came from, and what news he brought, and exactly why he had come is obscure. Almost certainly he would have been in touch with Denard who, discharged from hospital in Rhodesia (though limping, and with a cane), had made his way to Angola. Schramme was apparently in radio contact daily with Denard in Angola and possibly with more mysterious allies elsewhere. For two more planes followed; the first a DC3, loaded with arms and ammunition, for which Schramme had built an improvised airstrip and the second a DC4, which circled overhead and in the end parachuted its supplies rather than attempt a landing.

Meanwhile nobody knew what Schramme had in mind; and few could understand why he did not break through the encircling cordon of the ANC and strike south towards Katanga before it was too late. For the ANC was rapidly tightening its grip around Bukavu. Mobutu had sent no less than half his total force – 15,000 troops – to besiege the city. It was a mild enough siege, limited to skirmishes and occasional mortaring on both sides, with the white mercenaries living a reasonably relaxed and indeed luxurious life in the deserted city, more bothered by the occasional rocket attacks of T28s than by the overwhelming numbers of their besiegers on the ground.

Three of these T28s were shot down by one of the handful of ex-Legionaries with Schramme, a tiny German known as 'mini Schmidt'. Mobutu then replaced his own inexperienced Congolese pilots with anti-Castro Cubans officially employed by WIGMO – an air outfit fronting for the CIA. But the Cubans were reluctant to do serious damage to the 'enemy' – partly through a sense of mercenary solidarity but also because too dramatic a success would immediately have put an end to their own contracts. Suspecting this, Mobutu reinstated his own pilots once again. They flew too high but their almost daily strafing had in the long term a demoralising effect on Schramme's men. To the onlookers, to those of us watching from the opposite shores of Lake Kivu, the little planes wheeling above Bukavu against the hot sky of the Congo, with the distant crackling of machine-gun fire and the occasional puff of smoke, gave, I remember, the impression of a graceful aerial ballet laid on almost for our entertainment.

As for the Katangese gendarmes, they camped with their women and children in a different part of the city. Whereas Five Commando had been openly racist (even its batmen and barmen were white), Schramme and the Belgians, on the other hand, made great play of their devotion to 'their' Leopards. But it was noticeable at Bukavu that the mercenary officers lived a strictly segregated life; even 'President' Monga was only rarely admitted to the white officers' mess where French and Belgians uneasily co-existed. For all that, the atmosphere inside Bukavu seemed relaxed and confident enough. By mid-October, eight weeks after Bukavu's dramatic capture, it looked as if Schramme were prepared to hold out indefinitely in the hopes that Mobutu's ever-weakening position inside the Congo would get worse and worse. The general economic situation was rapidly deteriorating. There were reports of food riots in Katanga.

The Raid on Bula-Bemba

At this point Denard took a hand. To rescue Tshombe from Algeria was beyond Denard's limited resources. But Denard, always ingenious, had decided to attempt the next best thing. By early September he was back in Angola from Brussels. Godefroid Munongo, Tshombe's former minister of the interior and a tribal leader of great importance in Katanga, was one of the few opponents of Mobutu to have escaped hanging, shooting or assassination. He was mildly imprisoned on an island in the Congo estuary. Denard from his coordinating centre in Luanda, Angola's capital, set about organising his rescue. In mid-September one of Denard's assistants, a mercenary recruiter named Moreau, began hiring men in Paris. Eventually, on the night of 28/29 October a commando of thirteen mercenaries, six of whom were French, set out from their base in Angola and attempted a canoe-borne landing. They should have been more superstitious. The raid ended in a farcical failure. But, for all that, the basic idea behind the raid showed Denard's political good sense. Munongo would have been a leader of a totally different calibre from the obscure Monga.

The 'Second Front'

Meanwhile all had been prepared to take advantage of Munongo's rescue. In the north of Angola near the border with Katanga Denard had assembled a 'strike force' of 110 white mercenaries and 50 Katangese. Arms were issued to them on the 28th; and presumably if Munongo had been rescued they would have gone in, with him at their head, on the 29th. As it was, Denard must sorely have been tempted to abandon his proposed – and long-awaited – opening of the Katanga front. First Tshombe kidnapped; then the fiasco with Munongo. What induced him to go ahead were hopes of success, of course – for Schramme had over half the ANC 'fixed' around Bukavu – but also, I suspect, a sense of honour. For on the morning of the 29th, on Mobutu's orders and no doubt in direct response to the failed raid on Bula Bemba, the ANC at last launched a violent assault on Bukavu.

Schramme had established eight strongpoints on the outskirts of Bukavu, covering a perimeter of 25 kilometres – a Dien Bien Phu in miniature. But he seems to have underestimated his opponents. The 7th and 9th Commandos, which had been meant to join in the revolt, were among the troops besieging Bukavu and continual appeals over Radio Bukavu for them to desert and change sides had had no effect. The élite of the ANC, the 2nd and 3rd Paras, were well-organised and disciplined troops with the will to attack. They – and the Commandos – attacked. Nevertheless Schramme's men, with their mortars and their jeep-mounted heavy machine guns, with their strong points and their mobility, successfully beat back an attacking force fifteen times their own strength. Battle raged for two days, 29 October and 30 October, around the Bukavu perimeter till, sullen and temporarily exhausted, the ANC withdrew. Bus Schramme must have known he could not beat back another major assault. His ammunition supplies, particularly for the mortars and heavy machine-guns, were almost exhausted. The only hope of success, indeed even perhaps of survival, now lay in Denard's promised 'Second Front', which would raise Katanga and relieve the pressure on Bukavu. And sure enough on 1 November, two hours before dawn, Denard's invading column crossed the frontier, Denard himself commanding, with 'Frenchie' Delamichel as second-in-command.

They crossed on bicycles. The Portuguese had been co-operative only to a certain extent. They had transported Denard's men to the frontier but had refused to supply him with any vehicles. However the 'bicycle invasion', as one of the mercenaries involved later put it, may have sounded farcical but was not so stupid as all that. It gave the column the advantages of silence and mobility. They seized the border village of Luashi without difficulty – the two ANC soldiers defending it understandably took to their heels – and then Piret (the mercenary who had flown Commandant Wauthier's body to Leo the year before) pedalled off with fifteen men to nearby Kisenge, the centre of a manganese mining company. There his men routed a platoon of the ANC and seized six lorries and two jeeps. A day was wasted, however, largely owing to Piret's reluctance to 'requisition' European-owned lorries, and surprise was lost. On the other hand the Denard column was now motorised and capable of making a rapid attack.

Next day, 2 November, Denard shifted his operational headquar-ters a few miles north to Kasagi on the railway line, a town deserted by its garrison. It was not deserted long. Katangese came flocking in from all around, eager to support the mercenaries and aid the uprising. By the end of the day Denard had an 'army' of two to three thousand 'gendarmes', but with only twenty aged Mauser rifles to

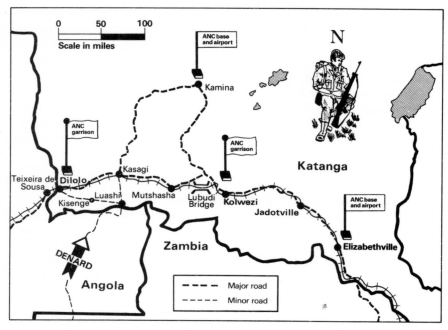

The Mercenaries' Revolt – Denard's Invasion of Katanga

distribute among them. It was now vital to capture an ANC barracks and, with the barracks, an armoury. To the west, back towards the frontier with Angola, was Dilolo garrisoned by 600 ANC; to the east lay Denard's old base in the Katanga days, Kolwezi. But that day and the next were wasted in contradictory feints, first towards one target, then towards the other. On the Saturday, the fourth day of the invasion, the decisive engagement took place. A decision had been taken. An attacking convoy had been moving through the night towards Dilolo – its rear protected by an ambush set up by Frenchie Delamichel and twenty men at Mutshasha. At dawn the convoy itself ran into an ANC ambush. They dealt with that successfully. Then came an attack by two T28 Congolese jets from Kamina base. That too they dealt with successfully. They had tapped the telephone wires from Dilolo to Kamina and had the lorries off the road and camouflaged by the time the T28s appeared overhead. But then came the third and this time the decisive and disastrous enemy initiative. Just outside Dilolo the column ran into a second and much more efficient ANC ambush, with crossfire, mortars and a Ferret Scout car. The column commander panicked and ordered his men to abandon their lorries and escape through the bush to Angola. However a lieutenant took charge, turned the lorries round even though under fire, and retreated pell-mell back to HQ at Kasagi. Though the engagement had lasted two hours, the only casualties were three wounded. Frenchie Delamichel had meanwhile also pulled back (without orders) to Kasagi.

There the whole mercenary force reunited that evening and furious discussions began. 'Denard was arguing like a women', reported a mercenary afterwards. The Congolese Radio announced that Mobutu had flown down his crack 1st Para Regiment from Leo to Katanga and that the ANC were about to put in a triple attack from Kamina, Dilolo and Kolwezi. In an atmosphere of near panic the mercenaries pulled back that night to Luashi on the border. They suffered their first and last casualties in that retreat. Three of them were killed, as they drove back, by another group of mercenaries who had set up a rearguard ambush and mistook them for ANC. A fourth was crushed to death when his lorry overturned at a river crossing.

In any case their presence was now of very little use. For that same day, Saturday, 4 November, Bukavu was falling.

The Fall of Bukavu

The turn of events in the south of the Congo had immediately influenced what was happening in the north. If Denard's invasion had not obviously run out of steam by the Friday, Mobutu would hardly have dared risk the all-out assault on the Bukavu perimeter that followed the next day. As it was, however, Mobutu (and his American advisers) no doubt felt, quite justifiably, that they had Denard's mercenaries on the run in Katanga; and that now was the moment to finish with Schramme's mercenaries in Bukavu. The ANC launched an all-out assault. In the final battles on the perimeter two of the mercenary officers commanding the eight defensive posts were killed – a young and courageous Belgian of twenty-five, a settlers' son, much admired, Guy Leleup, and an older man named Vanderveuken. Schramme later blamed for their cowardice on that final day of battle two of the other post commanders, Laboudigue and Captain Gilbert Martin, a former Adjudant-Chef of the Legion, of the 1er REP. Both of them were Frenchmen, both members of Six Commando. If there was one subsidiary underlying reason for the failure of the revolt, it was the never-ceasing mistrust and suspicion felt by the Belgians for the French, and vice-versa. In just the same way Xenophon's Ten Thousand Greeks had been torn by rivalries between Athenians,

Spartans, Corinthians and the rest which were only patched over in moments of great danger. Yet, that said, there was solidarity between the different nationalities too. The Cuban pilots were back in the air that last day. Schramme's men tuned in to their wavelength and were warned a few minutes in advance which of the various targets was due to be rocketed, to allow them to take evasive action.

After day-long combats the mercenaries and the Katangese fell back towards the bridge leading across the Shangugu to Rwanda. There were confirmed reports of truckloads of banknotes passing, that last night, clandestinely across Lake Kivu. The next morning, a Sunday, Schramme and the rearguard retreated across the bridge. 'His people' – 130 surviving mercenaries, 800-odd Katangese, and 1,500 odd women and children (including one white woman and her daughter) – were disarmed and interned by the Rwandese authorities. Just before his final retreat Schramme sent a last bitter message over the radio to Denard:

'ICI SCHRAMME EN PERSONNE – STOP – SITUATION SANS ISSUE – STOP – N'AVONS PLUS DE MUNITIONS – STOP – NE SAVONS PAS ENCORE COMMENT CELA VA FINIR – STOP – REGLERONS COMPTES PLUS TARD – STOP – VOUS ETES DES ASSASSINS – STOP ET FIN'.

['This is Schramme in person. Situation hopeless. Ammunition exhausted. No idea how things will end. Will deal with you later. You are murderers. Ends.']

Possibly Denard received it at the time. It might explain why his men held on at Luashi though all hopes of success was lost till the Tuesday following when they were fiercely attacked and mortared. Denard by then was already across the border, having demonstrated, arguably, that he had more staying power than Schramme. At dusk Piret and the rest of the mercenaries (less those who had already deserted) followed him, and were disarmed by the Portuguese. The Mercenaries' Revolt was over.

The Reasons for the Failure

The whole 'Second Front' episode is a classic example of the disadvantages of a mercenary force. Mercenaries are easily discouraged by setbacks and by very slight casualties. Mercenary officers tend not to obey orders and to take their own decisions. In defeat furious arguments rage and accusations of treachery are hurled about. A mercenary leader has to show personal courage and to lead his men in attacks; otherwise, he is quickly despised. There is no way to prevent desertions, particularly when a frontier is near. Denard's 'invasion' was ruined by bad leadership, time-wasting, inefficiency, lack of administrative planning and of clearly defined strategic aims. It was not untypical of the mercenaries in the Congo. All their groups and all their operations suffered, in varying degrees, from the same inevitable weaknesses. Their command was never united, their administration never efficient, their courage never superhuman. It is all the more extraordinary that, apart from this episode, they either won, or, if they lost, lost with distinction.

Was Schramme justified in this case in blaming Denard? He himself was blamed for sitting inactive in Bukavu rather than heading south to Albertville. According to some reports he had had every intention, in August, of breaking away towards Albertville, possibly via Lake Bukavu; but Denard pleaded with him to stay and promised him, over the radio, a flying-boat loaded with arms and ammunition.

Naturally enough there was talk of treachery and suspicions that Denard had been playing a double game. However this seems a less likely explanation for the failure of the 'bicycle invasion' than muddle and confusion. Admittedly Denard had not led his men into the attack personally. On the other hand he had to stay at Kasagi, between Dilolo and Kolwezi in order to maintain radio contact with Schramme at Bukavu and contact of some sort with the Portuguese. Denard in his turn blamed the Portuguese. He later claimed that the Portuguese had promised him 2,000 rifles to arm the Katangese; and even if this was not true (or if, as seems more probable, the Portuguese had made Munongo's rescue and presence a condition of their help), Denard obviously hoped for arms and supplies from Angola once the Katanga uprising was well and truly launched. As for the flying-boat with the vital arms and ammunition, possibly this was Jeremiah Puren's responsibility rather than Denard's – Puren was normally the liaison and administrative man, particularly where airborne operations were concerned. He had been lying very low in Bukavu – doing, one wonders, what?

The Belgian and French press, largely favourable to both the mercenary leaders, blamed the eventual failure of the mercenaries' revolt almost entirely on the Americans.* There were reports of American pressure on both Portugal and South Africa to prevent aid

* Unlike the British press. 'No Orchids for Colonel Schramme' was the heading of a leading article in *The Guardian*. 'The mercenaries are being ignominiously stripped of what spurious glamour they have,' noted the leader-writer. 'Their plight will cause relief far beyond the Congo – for mercenaries have become a symbol of chaos and neo-colonialist meddling wherever trouble brews in Africa.'

reaching Schramme and reports of American 'advisers' with the ANC besieging Bukavu – though even the mercenaries did not believe the current tall tales of American negroes leading the ANC against them. On the other hand they did suspect that Israeli instructors were directing the unusually accurate mortar fire. And clearly American support, particularly in the air, was decisive – not only with the T28s but even more with the C130s which gave Mobutu the ability to shift his three Para Regiments rapidly from point to point.

The fundamental reason for the failure of the revolt was, however, neither treachery nor bad strategy nor cowardice nor inefficiency. It was quite simply that the revolt was a revolt of mercenaries, and almost by definition mercenaries' revolts cannot succeed except by speed and surprise. However discontented the subjects of a tyrannous ruler are, they will normally prefer to be ruled by a tyrant of their own race rather than by a group of rebellious foreigners formerly in the service of a tyrant.

Yet even so, if Tshombe had been freed and if Tshombe had himself appeared at Bukavu, then the revolt would probably have succeeded. Schramme's political ineptitude was shown by his choice of Colonel Mongo as a figurehead; possibly any black leader was better than none but Mongo's 'Government of Public Safety' was a farcical failure. Without Tshombe (or possibly Munongo) the revolt was doomed.

The End of the Affair

When the revolt broke out there were, according to the Congolese Radio, 189 mercenaries in the Congo. A score or so had deserted; 30 were massacred in Leo; in the actual fighting only about 20 mercenaries were killed, eight at Bukavu.

They – and the Katangese – had been evacuated under the auspices of the International Committee of the Red Cross, the Swiss body that intervenes in the case of armed conflicts. Understandably, Mobutu wanted his revenge. First he demanded a monetary indemnity from the governments of the mercenaries' countries of origin for the damage caused by the revolt. Next he demanded their extradition and announced that they would be tried in Leo for war crimes. Finally, in January, he broke off diplomatic relations with Rwanda, 'the protector of assassins'. The OAU leaders who had guaranteed the Red Cross their support in all this affair did not keep their word; and it was not till 23 April 1968, that two Dutch DC6 jets hired by the Red Cross took off from Rwanda with the 123 remaining mercenaries aboard. Their only 'punishment' (in addition of course to five months' internment and the general uncertainty as to their fate) was this: their passports were stamped 'Not Valid for Africa'.

One of the Dutch planes stopped off at Pisa, Zurich and Paris. At Pisa seventeen mercenaries including three Greeks and one Israeli plus several of their African 'wives' and children got off; at Zurich Jeremiah Puren, plus three other South Africans (who all immediately caught a connecting flight back to South Africa) and one Swiss, who was at once arrested; and in Paris twenty-five Frenchmen, two Germans and four Britons, including a twenty-eight-year-old Glaswegian, Alexander Gay.

The other plane flew directly to a military airport near Brussels. The Belgian authorities took extraordinary precautions to keep the time and place of the arrival secret because they feared a hero's welcome for Schramme. Sixty-one mercenaries (all Belgian bar six Portuguese and two Spaniards) disembarked, of whom two were immediately arrested for past crimes. Eleven women and eleven children followed.

Schramme returned to his family mansion at Bruges, apparently having been warned by the authorities to make only the briefest of declarations to the press. Two months later, on 27 June, shortly after a private visit paid by Mobutu to Brussels, Schramme was arrested on the charge of murdering Maurice Quentin at Yumbi the year before.

The charge, and Schramme's admission that he had ordered Quentin's 'execution', ruined his reputation as an idealist and a hero. Not even the fairly convincing account he gives in his book of the reasons and formal justification for the killing could justify him in the eyes of his own compatriots. Furthermore, it had by then become clear that in spite of his much-vaunted attachment to 'his' Katangese he had in fact abandoned them despicably to their fate.

Once Schramme's aura had been destroyed, the Belgian judicial authorities showed no particular haste to press the charge against him. In August he was released pending trial. In the spring of 1969 he was still out on bail; he applied for authorisation to visit Brazil in order to investigate buying a plantation there. 'Consideration having been given to the state of the investigation', went the official Belgian communiqué, 'the competent judicial authorities gave him this permission.' And so this presumptive murderer had his passport restored.

The 'competent authorities' then learnt with amazement that Schramme had never arrived in Brazil but had assumed a false name and had flown elsewhere, in all probability to Angola. A minor diplomatic incident between Belgium and Portugal blew up and as quickly blew over. Schramme disappeared from the scene on which he had made so sudden, dramatic and ambitious an appearance. For the past fifteen years he has not been heard of. There were rumours earlier this decade that he had in fact ended up in South America, though not as a planter, and not in Brazil. He was said to be working in Bolivia for the state security police.

For a failed mercenary leader Schramme had escaped lightly; as had his white followers. There were others who were not so fortunate. Mobutu had offered the Katangese under Schramme's command 'amnesty' and 'resettlement'. The Red Cross, sceptical of this bloc offer, had said that they were ready to provide help in transporting the Katangese back to the Congo 'on the condition that the free choice of individuals should be verified under their control and on a new basis guaranteeing the interested parties effective freedom of choice'. But in mid-November a special mission of the OAU visited the internment camp and persuaded the Katangese, including Colonel Mongo, to accept Mobutu's offer. How Mongo, who had publicly proclaimed Mobutu a bloodstained thief and a traitor, could have hoped to survive passes all comprehension. According to a reliable eyewitness he left with the first planeload for the Congo and then returned to the camp in Rwanda to persuade the rest of the Katangese to follow. Then, of his own free will, he went back himself. 'Thus', said the annual report of the International Committee of the Red Cross (who had little option but to wash their hands of the affair), 'at the end of the month of November began the repatriation of the Katangese gendarmes to the Congo – organized by the Congolese authorities alone and without the Red Cross having been invited to lend its assistance.'

The Katangese departed, singing mournful songs expressing the desire to die in their country. No more was heard of them for several months. Intermittent attempts by the Red Cross to obtain, all the same, some information met with vague but reassuring replies. Then on 25 April 1969 a brief official statement announced that Monga, Nawej and six other Katangese officers had been shot a fortnight previously at Camp Kokolo in Leo.

A few days later Monga's widow held a press conference in Brussels. She claimed that her husband and the other officers had been tortured for thirty-four hours before being killed and also that over six hundred of the Katangese gendarmes who had been officially 'resettled' had also been killed. She accused the secretary-general of the OAU, Diallo Telli, of breaking the OAU guarantee that the terms of Mobutu's amnesty would be respected. Though her allegations were treated with a certain scepticism by the Red Cross, no more has ever been heard of these wretched Katangese – vicims, very probably, of yet another treacherous massacre by the bloodstained Mobutu.

Tailpiece

The story of mercenaries in the Congo ends here. But, at least as regards Katanga – since rechristened Shaba – there is an ironic epilogue. Of the original eight thousand-odd Katangese gendarmes who had taken refuge in Northern Angola with Denard, Schramme and Puren in January 1963, probably a good half had remained there – reinforced no doubt (if these had any instinct for self-preservation) by the 2–3,000 who had pressed around Denard at the time of the 'bicycle invasion' demanding rifles. The exiled Katangese subsequently played a role as black mercenaries fighting for the Portuguese in the long war against Angola's 'liberation armies'; and, more marginally, in the civil war that followed the departure of the Portuguese and Angola's own Independence in the autumn of 1975.

But by 1977, with the Angolan civil war over (at least in the north) they wanted to go home. The first 'Shaba rebellion' in April that year was a ragged affair, though sufficient to frighten Mobutu. He appealed to King Hassan of Morocco for support, and 1,500 Moroccan troops pushed the 'rebels' back into Angola.

Next year they tried again. Imitating Denard's plan, but with greater success and drive, five hundred Katangese gendarmes 'invaded' and seized Kolwezi at dawn on 13 May 1978. But by this time France, Belgium and America had reconciled their respective roles in the Congo, and were all openly and officially backing Mobutu, that bulwark of the West. The Katangese were described in the Western press as a cross between the Simbas and Balubas, a bizarre reversal of viewpoint. And on 19 May French paratroopers, transported by US C130s to 'rescue' Belgian civilians, dropped on Kolwezi and in a day of fierce fighting, for the price of three dead, restored 'order' and ended what was grandiosely described as the Second Shaba War.

The irony was this: that the four hundred French paratroops were men of the 2^e REP, the surviving regiment of paras in the Foreign Legion, now based at Calvi in Corsica. Colonel Erulin, their commander, was greeted as a hero when he and his legionaries returned glowing with victory and pride to the 'shrine' of the Legion, at Aubagne outside Marseilles. So by their action the Second Regiment, France's official mercenary élite, destroyed the last hopes of men whom other Legionaries, ex-officers of the disbanded First Regiment, had so brilliantly led in battle against the '*supermercenaires*' of the United Nations a decade and a half earlier. One wonders whether the Katangese appreciated the paradox – which resulted in three hundred of them being killed, many brutalities committed, and the rest driven back once more into exile across the border. A bizarre ending indeed to the bloodstained history of Katanga.

6

Biafra: The Myth – And The Men

Se inicio tanto la localizacion de veteranos; de Robert Denard, Jacques Schramme, Charles Rous, Carlo Shannon y otros que, al iqual los 'gansos salvages' de Hoare, habian influido decisamente en el curso de las guerras de Biafra, Sudan, Congo etc.

Raul Valdes Vivo, Member of the Cuban Central Committee,
Angola: Fin del Mito de Los Mercenarios

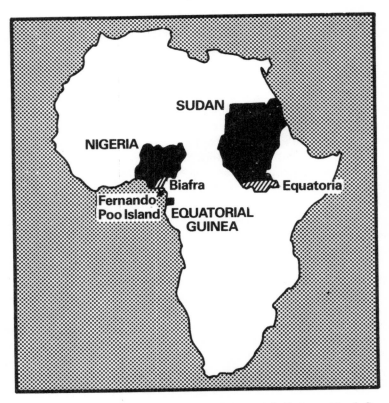

Africa – Nigeria, the Sudan and Equatorial Guinea (shaded)

Three men, three mercenaries, dominate this chapter. One, Count Carl Gustav Von Rosen, was a genuinely legendary figure, both in his life and in his death. The second, Rolf Steiner, span a legend around himself and became almost fatally entwined in a myth of his own making. The third, Taffy Williams, was, rather, the raw material of fantasy, on the borderline between the dross of fact and the gold of fiction – if, at least, the extraordinary story that has his Doppelganger as its central figure is itself true.

The stories of these figures are set against the background of the Nigerian civil war, and in particular of Biafra for which all three fought. But they did not appear upon the scene till the conflict was well under way, almost indeed into its second year. In the early months it was the 'old guard' of the mercenary movement who appeared likely to dominate the scene.

The Old Guard

Hoare was in Durban, Wicks in Rhodesia, Schroeder in Johannesburg and Peters in London when, on 30 May 1967, Colonel Ojukwu announced the secession of Biafra, homeland of the Ibos, from the Federation of Nigeria. Almost immediately rumours of mercenary involvement began to circulate. Five Commando had only just been disbanded, and in Johannesburg George Schroeder was running a travel agency in cooperation with several other ex-mercenaries. A travel agency is an ideal cover for mercenary activities and Schroeder had a list of two thousand ex-members of Five Commando on his books. He waited for a summons that, even when the first serious fighting started five weeks later, never came.

On the ground in the months that followed, July, August and September, battle swayed dramatically to and fro with neither side gaining the decisive advantage. Hoare visited first the Biafrans, then the Nigerians to offer his services. But at this early stage of the war both sides were accusing each other violently and often of employing white mercenaries while denying that their own side was doing so. There were numerous accounts of journalists, businessmen and even missionaries being arrested, particularly in Biafra, on suspicion of being an 'enemy' mercenary. Walter Schwarz, *The Guardian* correspondent, was kept incommunicado for several weeks in a remote Biafran jail and appears lucky to have escaped with his life. It was therefore a very dangerous business for would-be mercenaries to arrive in Nigeria or Biafra hoping to enlist on the spot. It was also difficult for either side to admit openly, after this initial furore, that they were in the market for white 'volunteers' *à la* Tshombe. So Hoare departed empty-handed, consoling himself by writing, for the centre page of *The Times*, an article in the role of the elder-statesman of the mercenary movement sagely condemning the use of mercenaries at all in this most regrettable and deplorable 'Commonwealth' affair. He himself, he added, had decided, despite offers by both sides, to steer clear of the whole business. (Jeremiah Puren, it must be noted, was at the time Hoare wrote the article – 1 December 1967 – in the internment camp in Rwanda and due to be kept there for another four months. If he had been free and at Hoare's side, 'Mad Mike' would in my view have been singing a very different song.)

In any case by no means all of Hoare's once-faithful stable accepted the views of their former leader. Alastair Wicks, apparently without Hoare's knowledge, approached the Officers' Association at 28 Belgrave Square in London with a request for 'responsible ex-officers who need not have any business experience but must have had a previous administrative experience'. He needed, he informed the Secretary, 'junior executives' up to the age of thirty-five, at a salary of about £2,000 a year, and (as was quite usual) 'did not at this stage wish to divulge further details'.

But in London Wicks, who was recruiting for the Biafrans, came up against Peters. Peters, since handing over Five Commando to Schroeder that February, had set up in the British capital, ostensibly as a property dealer. The temptation for any former mercenary leader to keep an organisation going at his own expense in the hopes that opportunity will knock once more is strong, though potentially ruinous. Peters is said to have had liaison officers in Europe, a hundred men permanently on standby in furnished flats, equipment ranging from mugs to machine-guns stashed ready – all this in addition to the extra expense of a beautiful young wife. It is my impression that he was losing a considerable amount of his accumulated fortune in yielding to this perennial temptation. No wonder, if so, that he seized on the Nigerian civil war as a godsend and warned Wicks off. 'I will do all in my power to stop recruiting for Biafra,' he is reported to have said; and to Wicks directly on the phone, 'Don't recruit for Biafra. I don't want my boys fighting yours.'

Rivalry between the two was particularly vicious because by this time they were both concentrating on the air, on pilots. Peters had visited Lagos, the capital of Nigeria, in July, only weeks after Biafra's breakaway, in the ill-defined role of 'military adviser'. He was accompanied by a former bodyguard of Tshombe, by name Schrot, and was in contact with the French mercenary Michel de Clary who had forced the Irish to surrender at Jadotville in the Katanga days. (Irish missionaries – this may or may not be totally irrelevant to Clary's involvement – practically administered Biafra.) Peters' attempts to achieve a position of influence on the spot failed, though he did become briefly involved with 'military security'. He left Lagos, however, with a contract to hire British, Rhodesian and South African pilots at £1,000 a month, paid directly into a Swiss bank account – all living expenses, including drinks and women, to be covered by the Federal government.

Biafra had begun the war with a lone B26 bomber piloted by a Pole known as Kamikaze Brown and six Alouette helicopters under the command of a young Biafran named Augustus Opke. Blockaded by the Nigerian navy, Biafra even at this early stage was forced to rely for its supplies of arms and ammunition on an air bridge. Wicks' Air Transport Africa had planned to operate the supply route direct from Lisbon; but with Peters' twelve or so pilots flying converted DC3s and DC4s for the Nigerians, Wicks virtually cried off. His place was taken by a freelance American gun-runner, by name Hank Wharton, who flew direct flights from Lisbon into Biafra with his three Super Constellations.

The Biafrans, however, were faced not merely with the problems of getting arms in but also with the difficulty of getting the money to pay for them out; and Alastair Wicks managed to take charge of what by then had become a drastically urgent affair. What had happened was this. The Biafrans' aim had been to unload their banknotes on the European market as quickly as possible – before the Federal Government should tumble to their operation, change the design of the notes, and declare the old currency null and void. The Banque Rothschild in Paris offered them a credit of £5 million a week, at the exchange rate of 12s.6d in British currency for each Nigerian pound. But the Biafrans, with foolish greed, held out for a higher price. In January 1968, six months after secession, the Federal authorities announced their decision to change the currency, a move which would of course reduce the Biafran reserves to so much worthless paper. And so in a last-minute panic-stricken rush the Biafrans loaded all the planes they could hire with millions of pounds worth of banknotes to be flown out of the country.

One former Congo mercenary was due to land on a December night at Geneva airport with no less than eleven tons of banknotes on board. Waiting to meet him on the tarmac were the Biafran representative in Switzerland, a bank official, a former French mercenary and, curiously enough, a member of the French consular staff. They waited – and waited – and waited. The mercenary in question had diverted to Lausanne, landed, unloaded, and had then very rapidly visited a number of banks where he had, presumably, opened various numbered bank accounts for his own personal benefit. He caught a flight to South Africa and thereafter disappeared from view – a dream-ending for any mercenary.

Possibly once bitten, twice shy. Possibly that is why Wicks' mercenary career came to an unfortunate end the following month. He and a Rhodesian pilot, Jack Malloch, flew out with another cargo of banknotes, and landed in Togo to refuel. There Wicks was arrested. In April, after eighty-four days' detention, his relatives received 'despondent letters' from him. Understandably: the interior of a Togo jail must have been unpleasantly primitive for a man of Wicks' stamp. He was released shortly afterwards; but, like Peters, then disappeared, presumably for ever, from the mercenary scene. The banknotes were 'confiscated' – possibly to Biafra's eventual benefit. For Malloch was working hand-in-glove with the French 'services'; and the tiny country of Togo was, though independent, like so many other black countries in West Africa, watched over by the beady eye of Jacques Foccart, De Gaulle's *Secrétaire d'Etat pour les Affaires Africaines et Malgaches*. And France, even more than Portugal, was supporting Biafra's breakaway. '*Brave petit people*,' De Gaulle is reported to have said. '*Foccart, il faudrait faire quelque chose pour eux.*'

It was indeed time to do something for the Biafrans; for by the beginning of 1968 the Nigerian army, with its far superior strength, was advancing and the 'invasion' of Biafra had begun in earnest. On 6 January 1968, *The Times* carried a report of: 'Biafra Mercenary Force Massing'. According to their Africa Correspondent: 'Major Bob Denard, the French mercenary leader, has arrived in Biafra with a force of about 100 men.' According to unconfirmed reports, *The Times* Correspondent, fortunately for his reputation, added.

Faulques into the Breach

In fact it was not Denard who was in command of the French intervention but his old commander in Katanga, Robert Faulques. Denard had got wind from Paris that there would be clandestine but official support for a mercenary venture in Biafra; but despite his intrigues he was rejected as its potential leader. Reputation – a reputation at least for efficiency and bravery – is absolutely necessary for mercenary leaders, and the Dilolo affair, the failed invasion of

Katanga, had ruined at least for the moment Denard's reputation. The choice in Paris therefore fell upon Faulques.

Faulques on leaving Katanga had made his way straight to the Yemen where the civil war, sparked off in 1962 by the death of the aged Iman, overlapped with the end of the Katanga secession. Faulques was the first to join the Imam's successor, El Badr, the leader of the Royalist guerillas. A number of the Katangese mercenaries followed in due course. Denard was certainly there for a spell, Laboudigue of Six Commando too and also the Flemish mercenary Goosens who was to die in Biafra. From time to time there were rumours that the whole of Five Commando was about to go out. Certainly Schroeder had the idea of leading a group from South Africa into the Yemen. But it was a far-fetched scheme that was never really taken seriously.

Though almost all the mercenaries in the Yemen seem to have been French, it is hard to see what French interests, actual or potential, were at stake there, and it seems that for once the French government had nothing to do with what was purely private initiative. In any case there were never more than forty-five mercenaries there at any given time, and all were officers or NCOs. That is to say, the mercenaries in the Yemen never exercised the sort of decisive influence that they did in the Congo. They were specialists whose job it was to train the Royalist forces in the use of modern weapons, much in the way of an ordinary military mission – though indeed such military missions do not usually make their appearance at the height of a civil war. Politically the presence of this small group of mercenaries had no direct effect. Militarily they were probably fairly successful in training the tribesman – though, when weighed in the balance against the 50,000 Egyptian troops that Nasser sent to aid the Republicans, their influence was obviously infinitesimal.

From their own point of view it was a very different sort of war from that which most of them had been used to in the Congo. The main advantage was the lack of danger; during the four-odd years that the 'operation' lasted – approximately from 1963 to 1967 – only one mercenary was killed, Tony de Saint Paul, hit by the shrapnel from an Egyptian bomb at Christmas 1963. On the other hand it was a roving, mountainous, uncomfortable guerrilla-type life; drink, women, glory and loot were in that poor and puritanical land unobtainable. The whole affair finally fizzled out when King Feisal of Saudi Arabia withdrew his financial support (funnelled apparently through a small group of British ex-army officers) and pay began to become irregular.

But Roger Faulques had emerged from the whole episode with his reputation intact, though his body was badly scarred and his old wounds troublesome. That at least is one explanation for what followed. He was in Angola at the Hotel Katekero in Luanda at the time when Denard retreated from Katanga. There were rumours that Denard had been diverting some of the arms and equipment destined for the 'bicycle invasion', selling them off more profitably to be transported to the Yemen; but in my view these were unfounded and Faulques was already, in that November of 1967, in charge of the Biafra operation. His task was 'to form a black army equipped and trained by Europeans', and a contract was signed with the Biafran government which stipulated that 100 mercenaries would be recruited, that they would be paid six months' wages in advance, and that they would be provided with modern weapons and equipment. Ojukwu had been disappointed over Hoare – he had apparently flown 'Mad Mike' out at his own expense from South Africa, and did not much appreciate his subsequent visit to the other side ('to resolve my doubts', as Hoare somewhat pompously put it in his article in *The Times*) – but he may have been convinced by Hoare's military analysis in the same article.

> From a purely military viewpoint I was convinced that a small well-led force of white soldiers – ghurka type, not *les affreux* such as have been making a spectacle of themselves recently in Bukavu and Katanga – would have little difficulty in pushing the Federal troops back over the Biafran frontiers.

So the hundred men were not, as *The Times* had reported, Denard's but Faulques'; and indeed they were still at this stage a phantom army.

Faulques spent only a week in Biafra, in late November – time enough to sign the contract and set up camp near Port Harcourt – before flying back to Paris, apparently on an arms-buying mission. He left in charge of the camp a former colleague, an ex-Legion officer named Picot, and in charge of operations a paratroop lieutenant. Both these officers were bitterly criticised afterwards by the men under their command for their regular-army approach and their addiction to the bottle, two factors which were viewed as equally responsible for the events which followed.

For the venture ended in yet another mercenary disaster. It got off to a bad start, with only fifty-three mercenaries (of whom forty-seven were combatants) arriving instead of the hundred stipulated. The Nigerians meanwhile had on October 18 made a daring seaborne landing at Calabar near Port Harcourt, and the French decided to 'clean up' this incursion rather than to train Biafran units, the task for which Ojukwu had originally hired them. Nine however preferred to fulfil their original role, and Picot gave them permission to go off and form their own units in various parts of Biafra. The remainder made a frontal assault against Calabar in the classic Congo mercenary tradition, found Nigerian fire-control alarmingly unlike the Congolese variant, fell back, formed an unprotected front, were outflanked by Colonel Adekunle, the so-called Black Scorpion, commander of the Federal Army's Third Division, and suffered a stinging defeat. Five mercenaries were killed in one day. This is the sort of loss that inevitably demoralises a small mercenary force.

Faulques was informed, flew out from Paris, and decided to wind up the operation. His critics have said that though in his day he had been an efficient officer and an inspiring leader, his day was over, his leadership – from an armchair in Paris – was to say the very least uninspiring, and his one intention was to risk as little and to gain as much as he could. This he apparently did, having collected six months' advance pay for forty-seven non-existent mercenaries, a total (according to a not-too-reliable source) of 110 million *anciens francs* or close on £90,000 at the time. As a pretext for their withdrawal after roughly two months only out of their six months' contract, Faulques' mercenaries alleged that they had never received the modern armament stipulated in the contract. Though disarmed and therefore justifiably apprehensive, they were allowed to depart without difficulty. They flew out on 2 February 1968. Nothing more has been heard of Faulques either as a personage or as a mercenary leader. His 'career' ended in unexpected ignominy – though from another point of view it might be said that he had wisely and realistically set about obtaining what most mercenary leaders never achieve, a sizeable nest-egg for his retirement and old age.

However of 'his' nine mercenaries scattered over the bush four decided to stay on. These were Rolf Steiner, a German and a former NCO in the Legion, in Faulques' 1er REP; Giorgio Norbiatto, an Italian frogman who had taken part in the unsuccessful raid on the island of Bula Bemba the previous September; 'Taffy' Williams, a Welshman living in South Africa who had served in the Congo; and an anonymous Englishman who left shortly afterwards. Norbiatto was killed, in a lone stand, in the first week of May. It was at this stage, with only two mercenaries left, that Ojukwu decided to form the Fourth Commando Brigade, a unit of mercenary-led raiders with Steiner in command.

The Gabon Connection

By May the situation had become fairly desperate for the Biafrans. Fourteen million of them were opposed by the rest of Nigeria, 41 million strong. The Biafrans had in their favour their cohesiveness – they were mainly Ibo – their intelligence and 'progressiveness', and indeed their Catholicism which won them the instinctive sympathy of much of Western Europe. But the weight of numbers and the fighting qualities of the Northerners, the Muslim Hausa and Fulani, were inevitably beginning, by the end of the first year of civil war, to tell. One after another the towns and provisional capitals of the Biafran enclave fell to the three Divisions of the advancing Federal Army – Onitsha in the north to Colonel Mohammed's First Division, then Abakaliki, then (to Colonel Adekunle's Third Division) Afikpo and finally at the end of March the great prize, Biafra's only port and major remaining city, Port Harcourt. Only foreign intervention on a far more massive scale than before could save Biafra; but in May 1968, as defeat loomed, that foreign intervention became more than just a gleam of hope in the eye of the stout, bearded Biafran leader, the genial and ever optimistic Chukwuemeka Ojukwu.

It was Felix Houphouet-Boigny, known as *'Le Vieux'*, the black president of the Ivory Coast, who first formally recognised Biafra as an independent and sovereign state on 4 May; but it was the youngest and newest president in French-speaking West Africa who actually provided the assistance Biafra so desperately needed. This was Omar Bongo, at the age of thirty-two the youngest head of state indeed in the whole world. The country which he ruled, Gabon, just north of the Congo, was about the size of Biafra but populated by only half a million backward and diseased inhabitants.* Gabon, known in the 1890s as the White Man's Grave, had been the wildest part of West Africa, with its mangrove swamps, its cannibal Fangs, its snakes, its leopards, its lepers, its multiple diseases and dangers – and even three-quarters of a century later its tiny, dilapidated capital, Libreville, retained something of that air of a Wild West frontier town that it must have had in the days of the 'palm oil ruffians', the white settlers and hunters who had earlier dominated the Coast. It was not yet rich (riches were to come suddenly at the end of 1973 when oil prices quadrupled), and indeed, compared to the immensely prosperous and populous Côte d'Ivoire, *'Le Vieux's'* fief, was very much a poor relation. But that made Gabon, with its tiny population, its youthful but ambitious ruler, and its lack of resources, all the easier to control. For though Gabon had been independent since 1960, real power, as

* For the relative positions of the Ivory Coast and Gabon see the map on page 238.

in so many of France's former African colonies, was exercised by the French authorities based in the country and above all by Jacques Foccart in Paris, and by Foccart's *reseaux*, his networks. Foccart was hand in glove with the wily Houphouet-Boigny, a devoted Francophile and indeed a former French senator; and right from the start of the Biafra secession Foccart had installed in the Ivory Coast, at Abidjan, his link-man with Biafra, 'Monsieur Jean' – Jean Moricheau-Beaufre, a Gaullist, a member of the Resistance, a former journalist on *Paris Match* and an experienced conspirator. From Abidjan 'Monsieur Jean' controlled the purse-strings, hiring and firing mercenaries (and incidentally, sending Denard back to Paris where in May 1968 the student revolt – later backed by the workers – nearly toppled De Gaulle's government; certain Gaullist elements felt the need for strong-arm squad organisers of Denard's calibre back in mainland France at the time).

But right on the spot in Libreville Foccart also had his man: the Ambassador of France, in effect the proconsul, Maurice Delauney, an ex-colonial administrator but also very much a Gaullist and a soldier, a cavalry officer in 1940, a *maquisard* in 1944, harassing the SS division, *Das Reich*. As for President Bongo, his power – or rather his retention of power – depended almost entirely on the Presidential Guard, composed largely of ex-legionaries and commanded by a legendary French officer, once again formerly of the 1er REP, Colonel Le Braz.

Brave, gay, charming, Le Braz commanded a mini-army of 1,200 men, with its own tanks and helicopters, capable of anything, responsible to no-one but Bongo and, more importantly, to Foccart. Le Braz – like his second-in-command and eventual successor, the much-loved and admired 'Loulou' Martin who was also of the 1er REP, but a simpler man, a Breton – had fought at Dien Bien Phu. To put it in a nutshell, the armed forces of both Gabon and to some extent of Biafra were run by a mercenary mafia, almost all ex-members of the Legion paratroop regiment dissolved in dishonour eight years earlier. As starvation and mass killings in Biafra began, that summer, to arouse world-wide alarm and the war, therefore, world-wide interest, it became clear that Rolf Steiner, who had been merely a corporal in the Legion, now that he was promoted Colonel in the Biafran army, had allowed Legion mythology to go to his head. His commandos wore the green beret, carried as their colours the green and red of the Legion, and displayed as their device 'Honour and Fidelity'. The Legion's first standard, presented, by Louis Philippe, had borne the legend *'Honneur et Fidelité'*). 'The Marseillaise' alternated with the Biafran national anthem at the training parades near Umuahia, Colonel Ojukwu's capital; and in August Steiner was joined by yet another *ancien* of the 1er REP, who became his second-in-command, Armand Ianarelli. At this stage the Fourth Commando Bridgade (which had still never seen united action) was divided into three battalions, each roughly a thousand strong: Ahoada Strike Force under Ianarelli; Abaliki Strike Force under another newcomer, a Rhodesian named Johnny Erasmus recruited by 'Taffy' Williams; and 'The Guards' led by Williams himself, with, as his assistant, yet another 'new' mercenary also recruited in July, Alexander Gay, the stocky Glaswegian who had fought under Schramme at Bukavu.*

By this time, that is to say by the summer of 1968, the 'air bridge' from Libreville to Biafra's one remaining airstrip at Uli was functioning – and was to continue to function to the very end. 'Monsieur Jean' had hired Jack Malloch, the ex-Spitfire ace from Rhodesia, at the time forty-nine years old, to organise the first of these dangerous missions. The first plane loaded with arms and ammunition landed at Uli on 13 July; and thereafter every night arms and ammunition were flown in from Libreville by an assortment of semi-mercenary pilots hired for the occasion. But not only arms and ammunition; ever greater quantities of food and . supplies were flown in, as the conscience of the world became smitten by pictures of starving Biafran children.

And not only from Libreville. In August, at the height of the famine crisis, Nordchurchaid, a group of Scandinavian Protestant churches, hired the Swedish charter company Transair to fly in food supplies from the Portuguese island colony off the coast of Gabon, Sao Tomé. Their Swedish pilot, Von Rosen, a grandfather approaching the age of sixty, the retiring age for civil airline pilots, was a large, sympathetic, rather tired-looking man, who had spent a lifetime flying and who had worked for Transair from 1957. He had been employed for two years (1960–62) flying in supplies for the United Nations in the Congo, so he knew very well what he was doing. From Sao Tomé he broke the Nigerian blockade with a wave-hopping, hedge-hopping flight in a DC7. 'But I soon realised,' he said, 'that every priest, every doctor, every black and white man in Biafra was praying for arms and ammunition before food, because the idea of feeding children only to have them massacred later by cannon fire from Saladins or Migs doesn't make sense.' It seems that he then took the law into his own hands and flew in a cargo of arms and ammunition – exactly the crime of which the Nigerians were accusing the Church relief organisations.

* So much for passports stamped 'Not Valid in Africa'. Several of the French had also been at Bukavu.

He was therefore encouraged to resign, and he resigned. But he had not faded from the history of Biafra: far from it. He spent the next few months preparing a most ingenious scheme for which his adventurous past – of which more later – had inspired him.

When Port Harcourt had fallen four months earlier, the Biafran airforce, such as it was, had been destroyed on the ground, and the only substitute had been a lone B25 flown by a former Luftwaffe pilot Fred Herz – not much of an opposition to the Nigerian airforce which, almost from the beginning, dominated the skies. It is said that it was Hank Wharton who first supplied the Nigerians with Ilyushin bombers and Mig fighters. He had earlier been hired by the charitable organisations and the Red Cross to ferry food and relief supplies into Biafra direct from Portugal – until they managed to discover the landing codes which his pilots had been attempting to keep secret, break his monopoly and organise their own flights. In perhaps understandable pique he had sold his services to the other side. At any rate the autumn of 1968 saw a vast increase in the number of these modern planes threatening Biafra's lifeline, though at first they were manned mainly by ineffectual Egyptian pilots who never flew low or at night. It was at this stage therefore that the blockade-runners from Libreville flew in only at night in almost perfect safety. By October they were flying in twenty tons of arms and ammunition every twenty-four hours in a sort of night-time aerial waltz. As Colonel Ojukwu put it, 'more aeroplanes are landing at Uli than at any other airport in Africa, with the one exception of Johannesburg'.

The Second French Intervention

Maurice Lucien-Brun, a young handsome French ex-cavalry officer who had served in Algeria, had in 1964 sailed his 38 foot ketch *Sinbad* from Brittany via the Seychelles to Durban where he had presented himself to Mike Hoare, then on Christmas leave in his Natal home. Hoare found him charming – 'he spoke English like Charles Boyer' – and was no doubt impressed as much by his yachting exploits as by his accent or indeed military qualifications. For Hoare's passion was yachting; and as a much younger man Hoare had himself sailed in the Seychelles. In any case Hoare had enlisted him on the spot, taken him up to the area north of Stanleyville, and put him in command of 53 Commando. There, near Aru, early in 1965 he had survived a bullet wound over the right eye, only half an inch away from death, and was later to become effective 'district commissioner' of Niangouru district. Apparently he refused to serve under Peters (or possibly was dismissed by Peters as being too much Hoare's man), moved over to Denard and Six Commando and at the time of the 1966 Katangese revolt had played a role as a would-be intermediary which had aroused the suspicions of Five Commando. In any case he left the Congo in May that year; and next reappeared as one of Faulques' fifty-three mercenaries in the attack on Calabar in early 1968 where he was wounded and honourably evacuated. In July Lucien-Brun showed up briefly again in Biafra using the alias of Paul Leroy. He left in mid-August. But he was back in West Africa two weeks later, on 1 September with a group of fifteen French mercenaries, ready to fly in to Biafra from Libreville.

It seems that the French felt that the situation was slipping out of their control. Steiner was quite obviously suffering from delusions of grandeur and in any case was in very close contact with West German reporters and relief groups, and the presence of Welshmen and Scotsmen like Williams and Gay was not found reassuring in Paris.

But by then the military situation had sharply deteriorated. Aba, the one large city remaining in Biafran hands, fell on 4 September. This heralded in the eyes of the world – wrongly as it proved – the final collapse of Biafra. Steiner's Fourth Commando Bridgade was blooded in the fighting around the city and suffered a bloody defeat. Of its 3,742 men only 922 remained alive and unwounded by the time it was pulled back from the lost battle. Steiner himself fought his way out of the doomed city with a posse of cooks armed with machine guns. Maurice Lucien-Brun's group flew in to restore the situation. But a dispute about pay arose and they decamped on 2 October with two months' pay – which they had earned for three weeks sitting in Libreville and one week inactive in Biafra. The second semi-official French intervention had ended in an even greater fiasco than the first. Lucien-Brun was by all accounts an intelligent and politically sophisticated man – too sophisticated perhaps for such a rough venture.

Steiner too was back in Libreville at the end of September, a disastrous month for the Biafrans marked by the fall of Oguta, Obinza, Okikwi and finally of Owerri. But Steiner whatever his other faults was not, voluntarily, a quitter. Apparently he had persuaded some charitable West German groups to support a project for a seaborne commando raid on Nigeria. This involved the purchase of expensive Zodiac canoes. In Libreville Steiner banked the 25,000-odd dollars he had received for the financing of this venture, announced that it was impossible, recruited instead a dozen whites from the bars of Libreville and reappeared in Biafra as commander of Fourth Commando Brigade, which was raised to the dignity (and nominal strength) of a division in early October and of which great things were now expected.

> I command 8,500 men [Steiner told Christian Brincourt of the *Nouvel Observateur*] that I have formed into commandoes. We only have 1000 rifles for 10,000 men, so we can only attack the enemy when they are on the roads. The plan is to kill the maximum number of Nigerians in order to get hold of their arms. The Nigerians are advancing every day but I will not leave my men. Here we have only one choice, to defend ourselves or to die: they don't take prisoners, nor do we.

Steiner's illusions by this time appear to have been almost Napoleonic. He was being driven around in a white Mercedes decorated with Legion colours and, as a personal pennant, the death's head (shades here of the Hitler Youth in which he had served as a boy of fourteen) which he chose as the emblem of his division. There was a touch of Grand Guignol about the whole affair suitably expressed in its tragic-comic ending.

Steiner planned not only to recapture Onitsha on the Biafra-Nigerian frontier (in two hours!) but by an outflanking movement to seize the Nigerian base of Asaba on the far side of the River Niger. Then, amidst the total Federal confusion, he would lead a mobile column in a swift dash upon the Nigerian capital, Lagos. Had the attempt succeeded it would no doubt have been hailed as a feat worthy indeed of a Bonaparte. As it was, disorganisation reigned and the Fourth Commando Division was, once again, decimated. A few days later, on 10 November, Steiner burst into State House at Umuahia, bottle of beer in hand, and insulted Ojukwu to his face. The melodramatic scene that followed ended with the arrest and expulsion of Steiner and all but six of the remaining mercenaries. Steiner arrived in Libreville still handcuffed. In his defence it can be said that he had been living longer in Biafra than any other mercenary, and under conditions of great strain. But he was extraordinarily lucky to escape with his life. In all his dealings with 'his' mercenaries Ojukwu showed astounding restraint, and perhaps a sort of paternal pity. He appears to have won the total devotion of those who remained.

Two days later the remnants of Fourth Commando Division, now commanded by Taffy Williams, made yet another attempt to recapture Onitsha. A French television camera team, there on the spot, filmed the initial attack led by the Flemish Marc Goosens and his

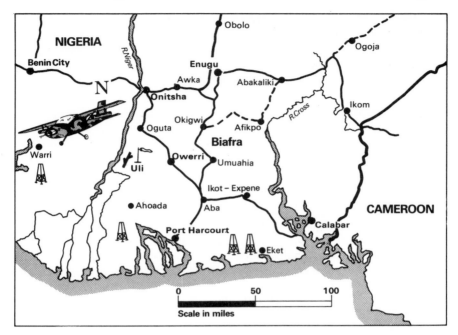

Biafra

grisly death – a sequence which must have given pause to a number of
would-be mercenaries in France.

  *(An interview with one of the minor French mercenaries in Biafra
gives a significant idea of how important publicity and photographs
were in inducing some men to enlist. This was a twenty-seven
year-old builder. He was far from being the only young Frenchman
who had 'always dreamed' of such a future. A bizarre episode had
occurred earlier that year in May when Paris students occupied the
Sorbonne. A band of young things calling themselves 'Les Katangais'
and describing themselves – a total fantasy – as ex-mercenaries had
'policed' the Sorbonne till they were thrown out in a 'pitched battle'
by the students themselves. The Congolese Ambassador in Paris
protested solemnly against the misuse of the name of the inhabitants
of a peaceful Congolese province!)

---

* 'One day in the Ardennes a friend approached me. He proposed I came to Biafra: 1000
dollars a month. Mind you, I think that for even half that I would have come to Africa. I like
taking risks. I liked the idea. I had always dreamed of becoming a mercenary. Why? I don't
know. It attracted me because I had seen some stuff on the mercenaries in the Congo, photos
and things in *Paris March*.'

'Major Mark is dead', noted the eloquent unit diarist of Ahoada Strike Force, Armand Ianarelli's command, 'after having destroyed a reservoir of enemies. The fossil is being taken to his native land without delay. It is very pitiful the death of the Major. His death has saddened all the commandos of the Republic of Biafra.' And Goosens was not the only casualty nor the Nigerians the only danger; for, as (without comment) the diarist added, 'Captain Armand has been bitten by a snake during the attack.'

Next day, 13 November, saw the final attack against Onitsha. There is an extraordinarily unpleasant account of Taffy Williams executing by revolver at least six Biafrans who refused to go forward in this hopeless assault on fortified positions. Once again the unit diarist gives a vivid, almost Homeric picture of the battle:

> The Abaliki striking force which should be the reinforcement, they have not been able to. They withdraw backwards. So do the Guards. All the troops of Captain Armand, that is to say Ahoada Strike Force, are almost finished. The enemies are content to say: 'Charge them, charge them! Those commandos of the red scarf of Ahoada Strike Force!' The enemies also say: 'These are the ones who have killed our four mercenaries and wounded our six mercenaries the last time.'* The enemies also say: 'These commandos of the red scarf are the most dangerous. Take them alive, these assassins, these commandos of Ahoada Strike Force!'
>
> Towards six o'clock in the evening nobody knows anything about the commandos of Captain Armand. We hear the enemy say: 'Ahoada Strike Force is finished, they are all finished.' When Captain Armand has heard this, it saddens him. He has had the wounded brought back and he has departed in misery.

This indeed was the miserable end of the Fourth Commando Division. Ianarelli, Williams and Gay stayed on till the first months of 1969; but these last weeks were spent as training officers rather than as field commanders, and when their contracts expired they were not renewed. From that time onwards it seems that Ojukwu for understandable reasons employed no more mercenaries on the ground. His attitude had in any case been almost unexampled in the annals of mercenary employers – pay forthcoming even when no services had been rendered, and, as reprisal for open mutiny, merely handcuffs and expulsion.

★   ★   ★

* Were there white mercenaries fighting with the Nigerian ground troops? If so, they were probably British Army 'technicians' who kept very much in the background. None were reported killed – whatever the Biafrans might have thought.]

The mercenary experience cost Biafra dear both in lives and money, and was a total failure throughout. Their major mistake had been their obstinacy in attempting to fight an orthodox war on a fixed front and in launching direct frontal attacks with inferior armament upon strongly fortified positions. The one Biafran military success of note was gained after the departure of the mercenaries when Owerri was recaptured in May 1969 – not by a frontal assault but by the use of guerilla-style encircling tactics.

In Biafra white mercenaries were for the first time in Africa faced with an enemy whose armament was vastly superior to their own. If one single factor can account for the on-rush of Federal military victories, it is the Saladin armoured cars and Ferret scout cars supplied by the British government. The mercenaries failed to develop any tactics capable of stopping this armour. They never ceased to complain of their lack of grenades, mortars and bazookas, and of the First World War equipment issued to their troops – the single-round Mausers, and the cannon on two wheels. They seemed incapable – surprisingly so, in view of their success against the United Nations eight years before – of adapting themselves to difficult circumstances and of improvising to make up for the lack of orthodox equipment. This was not to be the case with the next mercenary to appear on the scene who found precisely in these difficulties his opportunity and at one moment seemed on the point of saving Biafra, almost single-handed, from the brink of defeat: the ageing Swedish pilot Von Rosen.

The War in the Air

Count Carl Gustav Von Rosen had 'resigned' from Transair in September. Christmas 1968 found him back in Biafra with a letter to Ojukwu from his old friend and former employer, the Emperor Haile Selassie of Ethiopia. It also found him in tears after seeing the results of Nigerian bombing – dead women and children everywhere, killed by the Egyptian-piloted Ilyushin bombers. For the Federal forces had undisputed air control, the Biafran air force having long since ceased to exist.

Five months later, however, this nonexistent airforce according to a Biafran communiqué attacked the Nigerian airbase at Port Harcourt, and in quick succession raids against Benin, Enugu and Calabar followed. The first announcement, on 22 May 1969, was greeted with some hilarity, which quickly vanished as eyewitness reports on the raids came in. It appeared that at least eleven Federal planes (including two Migs, three Iluyshins, a Canberra and a Heron) had been rocketed to pieces on the ground by a group of five twin-seater light aircraft that looked more fitting for the dogfights of the First World War than for effective air attacks in the nuclear age; and the Swedish magazine *Expressen* revealed that this group was led by Von Rosen, a name forgotten by the world at large. The romantic side of these exploits, the first touch of the heroic in this barbaric war, at once appealed to the popular and embarassed the official mind. On 28 May the Swedish government officially informed the Federal government that they disowned Count Von Rosen's actions entirely and explained apologetically that the five aircraft, bought from the firm Malmö Flygindustrie, were listed as 'light sporting aircraft' for which no export licence was required.

On 24 July the Swedish government held a special cabinet meeting and decided, ridiculously and tardily, to classify these light MCI-9Bs, or Minicons, as 'war material', and to instigate official enquiries into Von Rosen's legal position *vis-à-vis* recruiting Swedish citizens for foreign mercenary service. But by this time Von Rosen had left Biafra (on 6 June, less than two weeks after his first raid) and had in any case become a national hero; the court of enquiry acquitted him and the MFI firm of any possible charges. 'There are no Swedish pilots there now,' he said shortly after his return. 'But we will be happy to go back if they call us. I think that half Sweden would stand up and go down there.'

He was probably right. The worst mistake the Nigerians ever made was to reduce this elderly idealist to tears. Admittedly they could hardly have been expected to know how this scion of a family of aristocratic adventurers had risked much the same sort of foolhardy escapade almost exactly thirty years earlier in the winter of 1939. Then, indignant at the Soviet invasion of Finland, he had 'borrowed' a DC2 from the Dutch airline, KLM, for which at the time he had been working, converted it into a fighter-bomber and attacked to their vast surprise (for Finland, like Biafra, had at this time no airforce) the Russian positions. Marshal Mannerheim, Finland's leader, had personally to forbid his attempting a single-handed raid on the Kremlin. But in Finland from then onwards Von Rosen was a national hero.

What a life Von Rosen had had! His most famous ancestor had been a distinguished officer and personal friend of the great Swedish Warrior king, Charles XII; another had fought with Byron and married a Greek princess; his father, Count Eric, a well-known explorer, had in 1911 traversed Africa from Cairo to the Cape. The fourth of seven children, he had been reared at the family castle and educated at Lundsberg, Sweden's Eton, where his best friend was Prince Bertil Bernadotte, the present King's uncle. Expelled, he had at the age of nineteen bought an old Sopwith Camel and lived from then on a life of flying and adventure. He had been the first pilot ever to fly a Red Cross plane, in Ethiopia at the time of the Italian invasion in 1935–36; when Ethiopia fell and Haile Selassie fled, he continued as a freelance to fly in messages and emissaries from the exiled Emperor to the guerrillas still fighting on near the Sudanese border. Goering, another flier, had married his aunt, the beautiful Karin von Rosen before the Second World War; and built in her memory his famous palace, Karin-Hall. Back in Holland in 1940, again working for KLM, Von Rosen was arrested by the Gestapo as a spy and only released thanks to Goering's personal intervention. For the rest of the war he flew a courier service between Berlin and neutral Stockholm, and at the same time aided members of the Dutch Resistance. He had spent ten years after the war back in Ethiopia, helping Haile Selassie build up both the Royal Ethiopian Air Force and Imperial Ethiopian Airlines – for which he was rewarded (one of the few foreigners ever to be allowed to own land in Ethiopia) with a coffee plantation. But the Count was a man dominated by an inherited love for adventure, a passion for flying, and a genuine devotion to the underdogs in any war. At sixty he was not too old to repeat what had become the regular pattern of his life.

> When I thought of Biafra [said Von Rosen later] I realised they would never be able to buy or fly in a jet fighter. Maintenance and fuel would pose an unsurmountable problem anyway. The Minicon has many advantages. It cannot easily be hit by anti-aircraft fire or detected by radar because it flies too low. It's easy to fly and simple to service. It's a new weapon of war.

In Biafra at that time was a virtually unknown Englishman of thirty named Frederick Forsyth. He had come out to Nigeria in the summer of 1967 as one of the BBC's group of diplomatic correspondents covering the early stages of the civil war. But, disgusted by the partiality which both the British government and the BBC's Africa Service were showing towards Nigeria, he had left after three months, then resigned from the BBC to return in early 1968 to Biafra where he worked technically as a freelance reporter but in fact largely as a member of Ojukwu's public relations team. It was at his caravan in Umuahia that the old Swedish flier had broken down in tears that Christmas, and had started rambling on about the need for small planes painted blue underneath (to blend with the sky when seen from below) and green above (to blend in with the jungle when seen from above) that could challenge Nigerian control of the air and halt the merciless bombings. At the time Forsyth thought nothing of it – just one of those pipedreams which he knew only too well from his contacts with Steiner and the other whites working in or passing through Biafra.

But Von Rosen's pipedreams were very different from those of other men. He worked out a complex plan, and on that same visit persuaded Ojukwu to put it into effect. Early in 1969 the situation became even more menacing for Biafra; the Nigerians imported new and far more effective pilots (a mixture of British, Australians and South Africans) to replace the ineffectual Egyptians, installed radar, and purchased far more sophisticated aircraft including six Canberra bombers and MIG 21 night flyers. This gave them complete command of the air. All the same they refrained from attacking the night flights of the Red Cross and Nordchurchaid which were bringing in 400 tons of relief supplies every night to Uli airstrip. These planes were buzzed by a South African mercenary pilot flying a Dakota who sat on their tails and tuned into their radio sets. He gave himself the call-sign 'Genocide' but limited his mission to checking by radio that the incoming flights were carrying food and medical supplies, not arms and ammunition. A sort of complicity grew up between 'Genocide' and the pilots flying the aid in – though his taunts and threats drove one of the aid pilots to christen himself 'Homicide' and promise 'Genocide' his comeuppance one day. But black humour broke no bones.

Meanwhile Von Rosen was back in Sweden. And early in 1969 the Tanzanian embassy in Stockholm (Tanzania had been one of the four African states to recognise Biafra) approached Malmö Flygindustrie and announced that their government was interested in establishing a small flying school. The 'cover story' was carefully prepared; to make the request more convincing, word was let out that Tanzania was also looking for pilot instructors. The Tanzanian government then purchased the five Minicons for $60,000 (a very cheap price for an airforce, though refitting plus the pay of the Swedish pilots and technicians cost Biafra a further $140,000). The Minicons, now the property of the Tanzanian government, were on its orders flown by MFI technicians to France and landed, somewhat to their surprise, at a military airport. There the French technicians measured them for rocket fittings, switched over the electrical system, and addded an extra fuel tank. This done, the aircraft were dismantled, crated, loaded secretly into a couple of Super Constellations and flown off to Africa, there to be reassembled under the supervision of the one remaining MFI technician who accompanied them, Per Hazelius. To his bewilderment he and his cargo were landed not in Tanzania as he had expected but on completely the opposite side of Africa, at — where else? — Libreville. Von Rosen met him at Libreville airport, to tell him (one cannot suppose Hazelius believed him, or that at this stage Von Rosen — whose plans were now maturing — much cared whether his isolated compatriot believed him or not) that the flying school had been 'temporarily' transferred to Gabon.

At Libreville the Minicons were off-loaded and assembled. Then they were flown by Von Rosen, two other Swedish pilots whom he had recruited, and two Biafrans (one of whom was Augustus Opke) to a small airstrip in the Gabon bush. There the Swedish markings were painted out, the blue and green were (as planned) painted on, and twelve rockets were fitted to each plane, six to a wing. This was in early May 1969. Several days were spent in Gabon training the pilots and testing the rockets. When Von Rosen was satisfied with the results, the five Minicons were flown north by night across the sea to a secret landing strip in Biafra; and on the 22nd the first, startling raid was carried out.

Von Rosen's extraordinary tactics proved astoundingly successful. The Nigerian airforce suffered heavy and expensive losses (among the planes destroyed on the ground by the Minicon rockets was 'Genocide's' Dakota), its supremacy in the air was challenged, the oil companies whose rigs were also rocketed were made to realise that the war was not yet won nor their profits safe, and Biafran morale received an enormous boost. In the five raids Von Rosen personally led none of the Minicons was damaged — though apparently it was a very close thing in his third raid on Port Harcourt. It was after this that he was reported to be ill and overwrought; his return to Sweden soon followed. Ill-health apart, he felt that he had given the Biafrans the necessary impetus and that he would be more useful as a propagandist for Biafra in Europe than as a pilot for Biafra in Africa.

> I had no intention [he explained] of getting mixed up with this war or the fighting in any way. I had flown for the United Nations in the Congo and after that fiasco I resolved never to get involved in the affairs of new African states again. But when I understood the Biafrans were a people, a united people headed by a legal government and a very honest and brave man whom the people could dismiss if they wanted to, then I went all out to try and stop this terrible killing of innocent women and children. The idea was not to add fuel to the war but to keep the sophisticated war

machine that the Nigerians have at their command – the Saladin armoured cars, the Migs and the Ilyushins – away from the little children . . . . And so in the end if you are an honest man and you have gone to fight for Finland because it was close to your own country and because they are white people, there is no excuse for backing out of a similar situation because it is further away and because the people are black.

There are those who reject out of hand the label of 'mercenary' when applied to Carl Gustav von Rosen. Let them, however, consider the problems of definition discussed in the first chapter of this book. By his situation Von Rosen was a mercenary, even if his motives were exceptionally pure. That he was of a different class from a Hoare or a Denard is only too clear. Yet even if for every hundred self-serving mercenaries there is only one Von Rosen, perhaps that hundred may be worth enduring precisely for the one that emerges. It is arguable after all that Von Rosen, by his efforts and by his efforts alone, postponed – though he failed to prevent – the eventual collapse of Biafra. If so, there is a certain saving grace illuminating the sordid tale of treachery, intrigues and bloodshed of which most of the history of mercenaries in modern Africa – as in particular the next chapters will show – is compounded.

The Nigerians reacted quickly. More modern MIG 19s, piloted by East Germans, appeared in the skies. On 5 June a MIG shot down an International Red Cross Plane, clearly marked – a DC6 piloted by a US veteran, Captain David Brown. (In fact it later emerged that this atrocity was committed by an Australian mercenary pilot, not by an East German.) Thereafter Uli's landing lights were only switched on for a few seconds at a time, for each incoming flight. Fighting, as always, died down during the rainy season; at the end of the rains in October the Nigerians launched their fifth 'final assault' on the Biafran redoubt. But the East Germans strafed and bombed by mistake the Nigerian columns, and the Minicons, Biafran-piloted, rocketed the serried columns of supply lorries. The attack petered out. Biafran morale rose again.

On 2 November two single-engined Harvards, monoplanes that could carry bombs and machine-guns as well as rockets, flew in to Biafra to join the Minicons; one was piloted by the West German, Herz, who previously had flown Biafra's solitary B25. It seems that at the time Von Rosen was back for a short time, not flying himself but masterminding 'his' flyers' tactics. On 9 November the Biafrans for the first time lost a Minicon, shot down by a Mig on a raid over Benue. Nothing daunted, on 13 November both Harvards and three

Minicons raided Port Harcourt, and claimed eight planes destroyed on the ground. On 19 November they strafed an American cargo boat and a Norwegian ship near Warri, only 200 miles fom Lagos – interspersing these with attacks on oil rigs. It is difficult not to see Von Rosen's driving force behind bold tactics of this sort .

However, the long struggle against both famine and overwhelming odds had taken their toll; and in the second week of January 1970 Biafra suddenly collapsed. Nigerian Saladins rolled forward to find no opposition. On 10 January after a last cabinet meeting Ojukwu and a few colleagues boarded Biafra's Super Constellation, the 'Grey Ghost' and took off for exile in the Ivory Coast. The secession – independent black Africa's second major secession – was, after very nearly three years of civil war, over. Biafra, like Katanga before it, had passed into history – and legend of a sort.

Steiner in the Sudan

By the time Biafra crumbled Rolf Steiner had already found other mercenary employment. He was in the Sudan, deep in its rebel south, the Field Commander of the Conventional Army of the Anya-Nya. He had been given that grandiose title the previous November, that is to say in November 1969, one year exactly after his ignominious handcuffed expulsion from Biafra to Gabon.

From Libreville he had returned to Germany. February 1969 found him in Rome, at the Vatican, pleading Biafra's cause with anyone who would listen. A strange man, Steiner. He was only twelve years old when the Second World War ended, and at the time his mother Anni had wanted him to be a priest.Though he had later signed up with the Foreign Legion at a recruiting post in West Germany's French Zone, his period in a seminary had marked him for ever. In Rome Father Agostini of the Verona Fathers awakened his interest in a country whose problems were very similar to those of Biafra and Nigeria: the Sudan. And so by June he was in the Sudan, an emissary for half a dozen charitable Catholic societies based in West Germany, with a brief to investigate the aid that was needed and how it should be controlled. He stayed there six weeks, came back to Germany, appeared on television, reported to the Human Rights Society in Bonn and then flew out again to Kampala, capital of Uganda, Sudan's southern neighbour. On his first visit he had been in contact with the veteran Anya-Nya guerrilla fighter, 'General' Emilio Tafeng. Back again as Field Commander in November he was given the task of organising a conventional army of eight infantry

brigades, two artillery brigades, one commando brigade plus supporting units, to step up the struggle against the central government of the
Sudan and its regular army.

These figures were pure fantasy: an attempt by Tafeng to bluff his
way into continued control of the Anya-Nya guerillas, split eighteen
months earlier by the secession of their eastern commander, Joseph
Lagu who had set up his own Anya-Nya National Organisation. The
blacks of the Southern Sudan, though all oppressed by the Arab and
Muslim Northerners who ruled them from Khartoum, were themselves riven by complex tribal and religious differences: Christians
against animists, Nuer against Dinka, the older generation like
Tafeng (who had helped form the Anya-Nya in the first rising against
the Northerners seven years earlier) against young and ambitious
successors.

In the sweltering almost roadless marshlands of Equatoria Province, the southernmost of Sudan's nine provinces, bordering Uganda, all Steiner could count on were a few hundreds of Tafeng's
followers, mostly his fellow Latuka tribesmen. Two Englishmen,
Anthony Dival and Beverly Bernard, backed him up: they ran a small
charter airline from Uganda, and Dival at least was reported to work
for British Intelligence. They suggested he call in Alexander Gay to
assist him; and there is some evidence that both Gay and Armand
Ianarelli turned up for short spells in the southern Sudan to work
with their former commander. But for most of the eleven months he
was in the field Steiner was undoubtedly on his own, training
Tafeng's guerrillas and working increasingly for an agreement with
the gifted ex-Sudan Army Captain, Joseph Lagu. Lagu was receiving
Israeli help, his fighters were the best trained and equipped, and in
April 1970 Tafeng, pressed by Steiner, agreed to accept the younger
man's orders. Their accord was celebrated after the rainy season with
an attack led by Steiner on a northern garrison at Kajo-Kaji. That
was in October 1970. It was a disaster. Steiner's men were dispersed,
he himself was wounded, and evacuated to Kampala. There on the
orders of the President Dr Milton Obote (political attitudes change
quickly in black Africa) he was arrested; and the following January he
was handed over – it was Obote's personal decision – to the Sudanese
authorities.

On the OAU's urging Steiner was arraigned and tried in Khartoum that summer. The trial lasted almost all the month of August.
Steiner was arraigned before a military tribunal on five counts –
which ranged from 'waging war on the government of the Sudan'
(Count 2) to 'smuggling medical drugs into the Sudan without a

licence and distributing them without being a pharmacist, doctor or a person licensed to distribute medicine or dispose of it in any way' (Count 5). The prosecution was conducted by the Advocate General, Sayed Khalafalla El Rashid, who called six witnesses. The brain behind it was Dr Mohammed Omar Bashir of the Ministry of Foreign Affairs. The defence was conducted, skilfully, by Dr Salim Eisa, a Christian, a Copt, married to a German. Steiner made his own statement to the tribunal on 13 August, claiming humanitarian motives and criticising the East German technical advisers of the Sudan Police for having falsified his declarations. He appeared in court with his head shaved – the *boule à zero* which must have reminded him of his service in the Legion. The last public session of the trial (conducted very much on British lines) was held on 12 September. The prosecution had called for the death sentence; and when judgment was delivered on 20 September the death sentence was indeed pronounced – the first death sentence to be passed by any court on any white mercenary in Africa.

But Steiner's was not a show trial. It was managed very discreetly, very quietly, almost without publicity. Fifty-two days after sentence of death had been passed Sudan's ruler, President Nimeiry, commuted it to twenty years' imprisonment. Less than three years later Steiner was quietly released, technically on the grounds of ill-health but in fact following pressure from the West German government who supplied the Sudan with large sums in aid. He retired to West Germany, wrote a weak book, instigated a hopeless lawsuit for false imprisonment against Nimeiry, and faded from the mercenary scene, all his high hopes of glory and fortune disappointed.

'The Dogs of War'

The story that follows is, if true, one of the most bizarre sequels to the Biafra war imaginable. I do not guarantee its truth, particularly as it has been (understandably) denied by the main participant. But it has been told, there is both internal and external evidence to support it, and personally I believe it to be more likely than not.

In 1974, that is to say four years after the collapse of Biafra, Frederick Forsyth, the ex-BBC correspondent who had since become a world-famous best-selling novelist, published his third thriller: a mercenary adventure entitled *The Dogs of War*. It tells the story of a successful coup by a handful of mercenaries who land by sea and in a swift night-attack storm the presidential palace of a dingy, corrupt, minor and imaginary West African republic called 'Zangaro'. The disappointing thing for many readers is that of the four hundred-odd pages only the last forty or so deal with the actual attack and battle. Elsewhere in the book there is very little blood and thunder. Indeed the whole central section, almost half the book, deals in meticulous detail and almost exclusively with the administrative side of setting up a mercenary coup. If you want to know how to obtain an end-user certificate for the purchase of arms, how to open a numbered bank account in Switzerland, how to set up a holding company in Luxembourg in order to disguise your vessel ownership, if you are vague about the uses of certified bank cheques, the techniques of freight clearance, or the habits of French customs officers, here you will find, astonishingly authentic in tone, all the information you may need. It seems, on reading it, almost as if the author has been through the process step by step himself and is far more interested in these mechanics than in the rather cursory sub-plots of Russian interference, rivalry between English and French mercenaries, and sex (a minimum) that are thrown in almost as a sop. For a best-selling thriller it is, if extremely authentic, almost rebarbatively technical.

Frederick Forsyth left Biafra in February 1969 after a year's stay, with almost all of a non-fiction book on Biafra written: *The Biafra Story*. Back in Europe he finished it, adding an Afterword in April, and it was published in June as a Penguin Special (priced 30p or 6s!) very quickly. Here, quoted from it, is his general view of white mercenaries in this period:

> Most have been revealed as little more than thugs in uniform and the riff-raff of the Congo did not even bother to come out to Biafra at all. Those who did fight at all fought with slightly greater technical know-how but no more courage or ferocity than the Biafran officers. The lack of contrast between the two is underlined by Major Williams, the one man who stuck by the Biafrans for twelve months of combat, and the only one who emerges as a figure really worth employing . . . . His assessment of most of the mercenaries, and notably the French, is unprintable.* [And Forsyth concludes:] Ironically the Biafran war story, far from consolidating the position of the mercenary in Africa, has completely exploded the myth of the Congo's 'White Giants'.

By the time he came to write *The Dogs of War* Forsyth's views had clearly changed. The book is dedicated:

---

* The fictional French mercenary in *The Dogs of War*, Charles Roux (not Rous, as Raul Valdes Vivo, compounding his errors, had it) is a pretty unprintable character too.

For Giorgio, and Christian and Schlee
And Big Marc and Black Johnny
And the others in the unmarked graves.
At least we tried.

in a fashion that suggests that the author now identifies himself with the 'White Giants'. Giorgio is clearly the Italian Giorgio Norbiatto, Big Marc the Flamand Marc Goosens, Black Johnny might be the Southern Rhodesian Johnny Eramus (though I am not sure that he was killed: Norbiatto and Goosens certainly were); Christian and Schlee are unknown to me. But in the thriller 'Tiny Marc' Vlaminck (who is killed in the final assault) is clearly modelled on Goosens; and the Corsican Jean-Baptiste Langarotti (who survives) is equally clearly modelled on Armand Ianarelli. The more fascinating question of course follows: who is the hero, the mercenary leader, Cat Shannon, modelled on?

> Carlo Shannon [goes his imaginary file]. British. Served under Hoare in 5th, 1964. Declined to serve under Peters. Transferred to Denard 1966, joined the 6th. Served under Schramme in Bukavu. Fought throughout the siege. Repatriated among the last in April 1968. Volunteered for Nigerian civil war, served under Steiner. Took over remnants after Steiner's dismissal November 1968. Commanded till the end. Believed staying in Paris.

Shannon, though Anglo-Irish in Forsyth's thriller, is clearly modelled on 'Taffy' Williams, the 'lean Welsh-born South African' whom Forsyth had so admired. In Forsyth's non-fiction book Williams, 'cheerfully admitting he was half-mad', emerges as the hero, in April 1968, of the battle for the Cross River where his 'redoubtable presence' with 'a hundred of his personally trained Commandos' held the Nigerians of Adekunle's Third Division on the riverline for twelve weeks till he was called back by Steiner. And that August Williams with a thousand young Biafrans and the Rhodesian Johnny Erasmus with his weird Biafran-invented mines, the *'ogbungigwes'*, had held the 24,000 Federal troops of Third Division outside Aba till they ran out of ammunition. The real hero of *The Biafra Story* however, is Colonel Ojukwu, to whom Forsyth became – and remained – devoted; but if there is a white hero, it is 'Taffy' Williams.

Forsyth did not make much money with *The Biafra Story*, though the first printing sold out, as did a later updated version. He had by his idealistic, indignant resignation burnt his boats with the BBC; Biafra had collapsed and there was no place for him in Africa; he was jobless and almost penniless. Before joining the BBC in 1965 he had worked for Reuters in Paris, and he decided to take a chance: to use his knowledge of France to write a novel, a thriller based on an (only partly fictional) attempt to assassinate De Gaulle ordered by the OAS. The result was *The Day of the Jackal*, a long novel refused by many British publishers. Finally accepted, it became almost instantly a world-wide best-seller. With this, and with his next German based thriller *The Odessa File*, Forsyth made a great deal of money. For a period he went to live in Ireland (where writers pay no income tax), so he had even more at his disposal. But he had not forgotten Biafra – as *The Dogs of War* proves. Its prologue vividly describes Ojukwu's last flight out from Biafra on the Super Constellation and his farewells to 'his' faithful mercenaries led by the fictional Cat Shannon. And the story ends with Shannon double-crossing his capitalist employers and proposing to put Ojukwu (never named, merely described as 'the general') in power in imaginary Zangaro and with a long heartfelt tirade by Shannon (in this instance clearly the author's mouthpiece) against British capitalists and the British Foreign Office and against the suffering and starvation they had without conscience condoned in Biafra. There can be absolutely no doubt where, in Africa, the author's heart and sympathies continued to lie.

That is why I do not find it difficult to believe that *The Dogs of War* is not so much fiction as 'faction'; indeed very possibly the thinly disguised account of a real mercenary *coup* planned and financed by Forsyth himself.

It seems that Frederick Forsyth had kept in touch with one of the Biafran mercenaries to whom he refers but discreetly never names in *The Biafra Story* – the Scotsman Alexander Gay. Forsyth made his fortune with *The Day of the Jackal*; and together the two of them allegedly began to plan a mercenary coup against the shabbiest, most obscure and most corrupt of all West Africa's tiny independent states, Equatorial Guinea. Equatorial Guinea, a former Spanish colony, lies north of Gabon, well to the south of Biafra with, on the mainland, 200,000 inhabitants only. The island of Fernando Poo with under half as many inhabitants was also granted independence, as part of Equatorial Guinea, on 14 November 1968; and the new government infuriated Forsyth and the mercenaries and Ojukwu almost immediately by creating difficulties for the Red Cross aid flights from Fernando Poo into Biafra. 'This change of policy', Forsyth wrote in *The Biafra Story*, 'originated, apparently, on the night the Guinean Interior Minister turned up drunk at the airport with the Nigerian Consul.' Forsyth had therefore his reasons for detesting the independent government; and under its dictator Francesco Nguema Macias it became utterly detestable in every way. Nguema's cruelties, his farcical tyranny, were worse even than Idi Amin's were to become in Uganda; with the difference that in this tiny unimportant enclave on West Africa's coast they attracted hardly any publicity or interest.

In *The Dogs of War* Shannon visits the capital of Zangaro, Clarence, as a tourist and spends three nights there, in personal reconnaissance, before making his assault plans. It seems probable that Forsyth or Gay or both flew to Gabon, obtained a visa there, and then went in to Fernando Poo – their target – on a similar mission. They planned their assault for January 1973. Undoubtedly (if there is any truth in this story at all) they bought arms, set up bank accounts, and holding companies, and leased or purchased a ship that would transport the assault team, the *Albatross*. (In *The Dogs of War* the ship was named the *Toscana*.)

But Forsyth's coup, in which he had invested over £100,000, aborted. Spanish security headquarters in Madrid had wind of the affair, and the mercenaries on the *Albatross* were arrested in the Canary Islands before they could sail south towards their target. (In *The Dogs of War* Colonel Antonio Salazar, head of the exporting office of the Spanish Army Ministry (Foreign Arms Sales), is intensely suspicious of the 9mm ammunition he is asked to authorise for delivery to the ship: possibly in the actual event the colonel, or his real-life equivalent, was the man who blew the whistle on the Forsyth/Gay operation).

So the planned mercenary coup aborted, unfortunately for the wretched population of Equatorial Guinea whose sufferings continued for another six years till the 'Freedom coup' of 1979 finally put an end to Nguema's bloodthirsty tyranny. But Frederick Forsyth wove from his experiences in allegedly planning and financing it another most successful thriller, published the following year, that more than repaid him for his initial investment. Real life was the blueprint for *The Dogs of War*, and the fact that the assault never took place in real life explains too the structure of the fictional thriller.

None of this would have come out at all if a man called Alan Murphy had not shot himself in 1978 in an East London room after opening fire on the police. The police then discovered his diary; Murphy, who had been for fifteen years apparently on the margins of the mercenary business, was one of the men allegedly involved in Forsyth's plotted coup. There seems no reason for the police to have forged or for Murphy to have invented the 'facts', recounted above, contained in the diary. But there are a score of fascinating questions that remain. For instance, was 'Taffy' Williams personally involved as well as Alexander Gay? Where are they now and what have been their real careers after leaving Biafra? Above all, perhaps, did Ojukwu in exile know anything of the proposed plan to restore him from his exile in the Ivory Coast to an independent power base? If so, did he approve?

Only Frederick Forsyth can answer these questions. But as he has always denied that there is anything to answer, it seems most doubtful whether he will ever do so.

The Death of Count Von Rosen

Carl Gustav Von Rosen took no part in the various post-Biafran ventures, not even in neighbouring Sudan. He returned to his coffee plantation in Ethiopia, which he ran with his son Eric, fourth of his five children by three marriages. Even the overthrow of the age-old Empire in the summer of 1974 did not affect him though the deposition of the Emperor himself, the aged Haile Selassie, by the left-wing military junta on 12 September, must have struck a pang. But it is not true that he was killed, as rumoured, attempting an air rescue of the Ethiopian princesses from the gaol in which some have died and some still pine away. The famine in Wollo that the Emperor's government tried to cover up or gloss over and which led almost directly to the Revolution, had shocked him; and he accepted the new, uncorrupt (though bloodstained) regime. In the summer of 1977 he was at Gode in the Ogaden, at the house of Bellete Ergete, an Ethiopian married to a Swedish wife, making plans to implement a Nordchurchaid-type programme for 'bombing' famished villages with sacks of wheat. During the night of 12 July the house was attacked by Somali guerrillas. Eight of its twenty inhabitants were killed. The dead included the sixty-eight-year-old Count – a tragic but somehow not entirely unsuitable ending for a man whom it would never have befitted to die of illness or of old age, peacefully, in his bed.

Book Two

ANGOLA

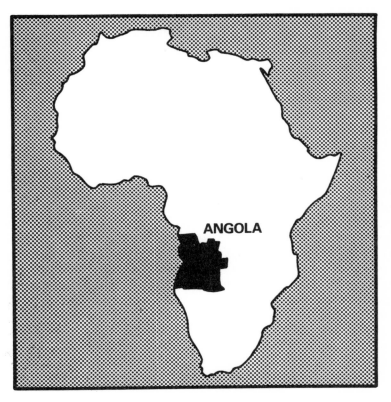

Africa: Angola (shaded)

7

The Mercenary Market

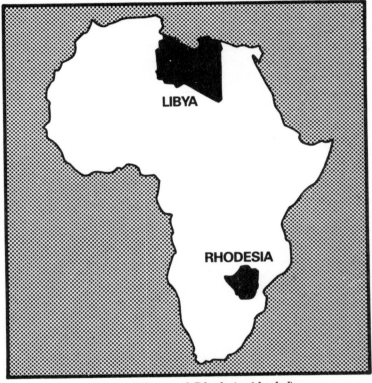

Africa: Libya and Rhodesia (shaded)

It was David Stirling, a young second lieutenant in the Scots Guards, endowed with great height, a vivid imagination and a forceful personality, who in 1941 inspired and founded what was years later to become perhaps Britain's most famous military unit, the SAS. It was Stirling who in January 1942 after the first disastrous raid behind Rommel's lines, the Gazala Raid that almost wiped out the original SAS (of sixty men who took part twenty-two survived), undiscouraged, reconstituted the unit and chose for it those outward marks which have since become legendary: the winged dagger worn as a cap badge, the motto '*Who Dares Wins*', and the sand-coloured beret.

Stirling disappeared into a prisoner-of-war camp a year later, waking up from a catnap in the Grand Ergh Sand Sea to find himself surrounded by five hundred German soldiers; and the history of the SAS continued without him. But though Paddy Mayne, George Jellicoe and Dare Newell became as famous for their exploits in the SAS, none was ever quite as admired and respected as its legendary founder.

In 1967, then in his fifties, Colonel David Stirling (retired), founded an organisation named Watchguard which John Banks once described, not inaccurately, as 'the civilian branch of the SAS'. Ex-SAS soldiers were in demand all over the world but particularly in the small newly independent states of Africa and the Gulf, and Watchguard placed them. In a sense the SAS were at the time the cream skimmed from the top of the British Army. There was only one full-time battalion, the 22nd SAS, stationed at Hereford on the Welsh border; therefore at any one time there would only be about six hundred SAS soldiers – each a rare and precious commodity, chosen (for it is impossible to join the SAS directly) from a mass of would-be volunteers who were already, officers and men alike, members of other British Army regiments. Furthermore an air of intriguing mystery surrounded – and still surrounds – the SAS. The names of its serving members are never, as a matter of policy, revealed; its activities are still shrouded in a certain secrecy. Its detachments are discovered in the oddest places, from the jungles of Malaysia to the icebound wastes of the Baltic shores. No wonder that to have a bodyguard formed of or trained by ex-members of the SAS became almost a mark of prestige for presidents or prime ministers of black African countries that had formerly been ruled by the British and for the emirs of the Gulf States that had formerly been protected by the British.

In the late Sixties all this semi-official semi-mercenary activity concentrated on the periphery of the Arabian peninsula where the knowledge that British troops were due to be totally withdrawn from a region rich in oil and in strategic importance concentrated minds wonderfully. The SAS had fought in Aden and in the Radfan mountains; but not only the SAS were involved. To take one example among many: in the autumn of 1969 Major David Neal, a regular British Army officer serving with the Trucial Oman Scouts, left the British Army and entered the service of Sheikh Saqr Bin Mohammed Al-Quassimi, ruler of the Gulf state of Ras-Al-Khainah, as head of his three-hundred-man 'mobile striking force'. As for the out-and-out mercenaries, they too attempted to take a hand in the new game. George Schroeder had the far-fetched idea of leading a group of former members of Five Commando from South Africa to the Yemen; Mike Hoare, less nebulously, was in contact with various regular British army officers, with plans to raise a mercenary force to replace the British troops in the Gulf. But this too came to nothing. Meanwhile, in that same autumn of 1969, on the shores of North Africa another crippling blow was struck at British influence in the Arab world. Britain's old friend and ally, the Emir Mohammed Idris Al-Senussi, whom after the war the British had imposed as the independent ruler of the desert where Stirling and the SAS had cut their military teeth, was suddenly unexpectedly and ungratefully, on 1 September, deposed by a young group of 'Free Officers'.

The Libyan Contract

Ten months later, on 28 July 1970, a South African businessman appeared at Watchguard's offices at 22 Sloane Street, with an intriguing proposition. He was, he announced, the emissary of an immensely rich exiled Libyan named Umar-al-Shalhi, whose family had been almost the Viziers of the deposed King, Idris I. Umar-al-Shalhi was planning (from Geneva) a counter-coup to restore the monarchy and, with the monarchy, British influence – as well of course as his own position as the power behind the Senussi throne, a position which had brought his family a fortune estimated as at least $25 million. As an essential element in his proposed coup, Umar-al-Shalhi wished to hire a team of twenty-five British, preferably ex-SAS, mercenaries for one night's work. That was why he had sent his emissary to the offices of Watchguard, the SAS specialists.

The man whom the South African intermediary saw at Sloane Street was not Stirling himself but one of Stirling's younger associates, a former regular army officer named (or at least giving his name as) James Kent. Kent must have been relieved when it was explained to him that the small team of British mercenaries were not expected to attack the presidential palace and kill or overthrow Libya's new leader, Gaddafy, and his 'Free Officers' themselves. On the contrary all they would have to do was to raid the main jail outside Libya's capital, Tripoli, release the hundreds of political prisoners held there and disappear into the night. Umar-al-Shalhi would then arm the prisoners, his supporters, and carry out the actual coup in nearby Tripoli without outside support. It did not seem an impossible assignment.

The problem was, though, that Watchguard was in the business of providing protection and training *against* coups, not of organising or helping *in* coups. On the other hand Gaddafy was an enemy of the West, the Senussi had helped the SAS in their early raids, Libya's newly discovered oil had transformed the country from one of the poorest in Africa to one of the richest in the world, and Watchguard was also in the business of making money. Stirling, who had been in a bad car crash, was convalescing on his Scottish estates, at Keir by the Bridge of Allan. James Kent flew up to Scotland to see him next day; and they settled on a compromise solution. The contract would be accepted but the operation would be run independently from Watchguard, as a one-off from a 'headquarters' in Montpellier Street, Knightsbridge, where Stirling would instal himself semi-clandestinely. Kent would liaise with the backers. The 'strike' was due to take place in a month's time. The team leader would be an ex-SAS major, John Brooke Miller, supported by an ex-warrant officer, in his thirties, Jeff Thompson. Both would also work from Montpellier Street.

There, in late August, twenty-five British mercenaries, mainly ex-SAS, recruited by word of mouth, turned up to be briefed by Brooke-Miller. They were told they were needed for a total of two weeks, for a short sharp affair, and that on being given the signal they would assemble at Glasgow. They were told that $5,000 had already been deposited on account for each of them, which would be released after the operation. They were not told the precise objective nor that Brooke-Miller and Thompson had already flown out to Libya as tourists, recced the jail, the nearby beach, and the lonely road linking the two, and had drawn up a precise plan for the military assault; nor that Kent had flown out to Malta and set up an operational base for the 'team' there; but there was a general impression of efficiency and smoothness as might be expected from a Watchguard-run operation. They left, confident and ready to go.

They never went. The SIS (the British Secret Intelligence Service – not to be confused with the SAS) got wind of the proposed coup, and reported to the Foreign Office. The Foreign Office vetoed it: British nationals were not to be used in any attempt that might go wrong and that would inevitably be blamed on the British government. Anthony Royle, Parliamentary Under Secretary at the Foreign Office and himself a former SAS Territorial Army officer, broke the news to David Stirling. Stirling, whose whole life had been ruled by the code of patriotism and loyalty, and who in any case was venturing into unknown waters far outside his original conception of Watchguard, at once accepted the Conservative government's veto. The team were informed and paid off (how generously is not clear). The Libyan assignment appeared to have ended before it had properly begun.

Not for James Kent, however. Though he accepted the British government's veto on the use of British nationals, he did not accept – he had more of the autonomous mercenary spirit – their right to forbid the whole operation. And this is where the whole story becomes very confused and to my mind very dubious. According to the account published by two reputable journalists, Patrick Seale and Maureen McConville of *The Observer* – the only full account of the whole affair (entitled *The Hilton Assignment*: the Tripoli jail was jokingly referred to as the local Hilton) – for the next nine months James Kent supported only by Jeff Thompson of the original British contingent attempted again and again, on Umar-al-Shalhi's behalf, to get the raid operational, hiring a team of French mercenaries to replace the British. But one damned thing after another kept going wrong. First in late 1970 the boat and the arms, the responsibility of the South African intermediary Steve Reynolds, failed to appear. Then in early February 1971 when all was apparently ready Jeff Thompson's nerve broke. And finally a month later, when the boat purchased by Kent, the *Conquistador XIII*, was about to sail to Plöce in Yugoslavia to pick up the fifty-five crates of arms ordered from the Czech arms export agency Omnipol, the Italian *carabinieri* pounced, impounded the *Conquistador* at Trieste and arrested its crew – acting on information supplied by the CIA to Italy's secret service, the SID.

I am not sure how much of this very rocambolesque story is fact, and how much is fiction. It is certainly true that no mercenary operation of any size can be kept hidden from the official authorities of the West and that most, to have any chance of being launched, need at least the tacit approval of Western governments and very often the active support (as the next pages will show) of the Western secret services. But I have never heard, before or after, of 'Leon', the leader of the French mercenaries, who is said to have been one of Denard's subordinates in the Congo. And the account given in *The Hilton Assignment* does not mesh, in several of its details, with the account given by John Banks in his own 'autobiographical' book, *The Wages of War*. Not that John Banks (who claims he was arrested on the *Conquistador* at Trieste and jailed for a week by the Italian police) is to be trusted in this or any other accounts that he has given of his own experiences. But nor are the accounts of the mercenaries, on whose information the authors of *The Hilton Assignment* must have based their work – information which could not reasonably be checked, and which they would have had therefore to take largely on trust. It is difficult enough to arrive at the truth about actual mercenary operations that have taken place; but it is almost impossible to separate the nucleus of truth from the mass of embroidery that surrounds planned mercenary operations that have aborted. Which is why I am dubious too about the truth of many of the details of the next episode, again an aborted operation, that I intend to recount. However, like the Libyan contract, the Rhodesian contract certainly contains a nucleus of fact; and is in any case the prelude to the real subject of this and the following chapters, the disastrous mercenary experience in Angola.

The Rhodesian Contract

The SAS had begun as paratroops – hence their official name the Special Air Service. But their first raid, the Gazala Raid of November 1941, had ended in so many deaths precisely because of the difficulties of parachuting accurately onto the target area; and thereafter, though they retained their original title and continued to practise 'jumps', parachuting became only one of their ways (and generally speaking, the least important) of reaching their targets. By way of contrast the soldiers of the Parachute Regiment have always concentrated on this particular skill.

Like the SAS, the Parachute Regiment was formed in the Second World War, in this case as a belated British response to Hitler's airborne divisions. Like the SAS, the Parachute Regiment prides itself on its training and its toughness. But the Paras are very much more of a rough, tough mob than the SAS. Intelligence is not a requirement, nor indeed much sought after, in the Parachute Regiment. Its troops, with their famous red berets, have a kind of brawling swagger that makes them much disliked by other regiments in the British Army and that has rendered the red beret an object of dread to bar and brothel owners both east and west of Suez. That they are efficient and effective fighting soldiers when kept under control none can deny (and most recently the Falklands War has proved this once again); but that the Parachute Regiment with its three regular battalions – close to two thousand men in all – comes closer to being a killing machine than any other unit in the British Army is also undeniable.

John Banks, a wiry little man with a long hatchet face, was in the

2nd Paras from 2 September 1962 when he took the oath at the recruiting office in Reading, till 10 June 1969 when at the age of twenty-four he was dishonourably discharged, having been sentenced to a year in prison by a civil court for the comparatively minor offences of driving a car while disqualified and without insurance – a car moreover that he had bought with a bouncing cheque. 'Comparatively minor' these offences certainly were when compared to those of many of the ex-Paratroopers who were to appear as mercenaries in Angola. And very definitely minor when compared to the offences of Banks' main associate in his subsequent 'business affairs', Dave Tomkins. Tomkins, five years Banks' senior, had spent eight years of his life behind bars as compared to Banks' solitary one. He was a professional criminal, a tall, prematurely grey, rather good-looking safe-robber, one of the few of Banks' 'friends' who had never been in the Army himself. A curious relationship seems to have developed between the two: they were continually to quarrel, continually to betray each other, occasionally to set each other up, and yet were always apparently ready to be reconciled and to try their hand together at another quick-riches scheme. It is impossible to say whether they really liked one another; it is impossible to say whether any of Banks' 'friends' ever had any real affection for him. But, like Pavlov's rats, Banks and his associates cohabited, occasionally snarling and baring their teeth at each other, in the caged world of Camberley and Aldershot, 'Home of the British Army', from which so many of them had been dishonourably discharged but to whose womb so many of them rather pathetically continued to adhere.

Banks tried, on his release, to join the Australian Army but 'they were not interested in my military experience, just whether I had a clean record and the reason for my discharge from the British Army. Having had enough of the modern British Army because of their "holier than thou" attitude', he gave up this attempt – just as, when a teenager, he had given up an attempt to train as a navigation officer at the Royal Navy boarding school because 'everyone spoke with a plum in their mouth and were the sons of Captains and Admirals'. Banks and his associates had a dominating prejudice: against the British officer class (whose hallmark was honesty) which they both resented and envied. When the time came they would give themselves the outward trappings of that class, ranks of lieutenant, captain, major, even colonel; but under stress any veneer of polish vanished and they would revert to the behaviour of the primitive, murderous animals they basically were by nature – a nature reinforced, it must be said by the training that they had received in the Parachute Regiment.

Banks, according to his own account, then ran refugees across the East German border for US Military Intelligence, spent a year in Vietnam training anti-Vietcong tribesmen, met Colonel Stirling and James Kent and Leon when he was hired as a radio operator for the Libyan Contract, went as one of two British mercenaries to fight in Kurdistan, set up his own bodyguard agency of ex-Paras, worked on building sites, and drove trucks through Turkey as a long-distance lorry driver. All this, plus a year in jail, between June 1969 and November 1974: quite a schedule – one to be taken, therefore, with a large pinch of salt. In November 1974 he and Dave Tomkins set up their own long-distance haulage business, Trans-Asian Express. It boomed briefly – and here Banks' story has the ring of truth – overexpanded, and went bankrupt, with debts of over £200,000. In May the following year Banks, Tomkins and a couple of other associates gathered despondently in TAE's offices above a 'washeteria' in Yorktown Road, Camberley to consider new money-making schemes; and Banks came up with the idea of running a mercenary agency.

As business ideas went, it was not a bad one at all. Banks had the imagination to visualise himself doing for ex-Paratroopers what David Stirling and Watchguard had been doing for ex-members of the SAS – without, of course, any of the self-imposed restraints of discretion or patriotism that had limited Stirling's scope. Trans-Asian Express had recruited long-distance lorry owner-drivers by inserting small advertisements in the *Daily Mail* and *Daily Mirror* employment columns, and Banks used the same method, merely changing the requirement:

> Ex-Commandos, paratroopers, SAS troopers, wanted for interesting work abroad. Ring Camberley 33451.

TAE's switchboard was deluged with phone calls. Inevitably when a large number of ex-soldiers are unemployed as an imperial epoch comes to an end, a call for mercenaries brings – as this call brought – an enormous response. Within a day Banks and Tomkins were up at Company House in London to register the name of their new company – International Security Organisation Ltd. All callers were asked to send in details of their military experience, and within forty-eight hours hundreds of would-be recruits were being processed. The difficulty of course (as 'John-John' Peters had found during his stay in England) is not in forming a mercenary army on paper but in finding an employer for that army once formed. Here too Banks, if his own account and that of Tomkins is to be believed, was (as it first seemed) luckier than most.

Almost immediately he was phoned by a 'Charles Grange', in the market for a large number of mercenaries. Banks flew secretly, he later reported to his partners, from Blackbushe Flying Club to a spacious country house near Hereford, guarded by hard-faced men in civilian clothes carrying machine guns, where he was interviewed by a tall aristocratic ex-colonel and two ex-SAS majors whom he recognised from the Libyan Contract. Two new contracts, the ex-colonel told him, were on offer: one to overthrow General Gowon, the Nigerian leader, Biafra's conqueror; the other for a thousand white men – no less – to attack in small SAS-style groups across the Zambezi: that is to say, from a base in what had previously been Northern Rhodesia, now the independent black state of Zambia, to attack white-ruled Southern Rhodesia. Rhodesia had, since Ian Smith's UDI almost nine years earlier, been technically in a state of rebellion against the British Crown. It had been decided, Banks was told, to accept the Rhodesian rather than the Nigerian contract; and the ex-colonel, unwilling to implicate himself and his organisation, was ready to use this sudden new apparition springing fully armed from Camberley. Money, it was added, would not be lacking.

This whole scenario sounds like a farrago of imaginative nonsense, complete with heavily scored hints (tall aristocratic ex-colonel, country house near SAS headquarters, heavily patrolled; no marks for guessing who this figure – thereafter referred to merely as 'the Paymaster' – might be). I am inclined to believe that this was the story Banks spun Tomkins to impress the partners with his own top-level contacts and importance, and to imply that behind their own venture would be the reassuring, solidly established presence of Watchguard. But I am also inclined to accept that Banks and another of his partners, Frank Perren, an ex-sergeant in the Royal Marine Commandos, were contacted and did subsequently meet in a London hotel the two ex-SAS majors, Duggan and Varley – and that, whatever smokescreen might have been thrown up about Nigeria, an apparently genuine proposition was put before them, apparently by Watchguard (or so at least it would have been hinted); and that it did involve, incredible though it may seem, a proposed attack by white mercenaries on Rhodesia.

I must admit my own interest here. I had previously published a book on mercenary history in 1970 (now out of print) and at its very end, discussing the possible future employment of mercenaries, I had written:

It would no doubt seem frivolous to suggest that the government of Great Britain should enlist mercenaries in order to crush the Rhodesian rebellion by force ... On the other hand, if white mercenary officers were to appear training and leading the 'terrorists' or 'freedom fighters' of the black Rhodesian and South African groups in Zambia, this would be no more than the natural development of a situation in which British national policy and international mercenary tradition temporarily coincide.

It is always flattering to a writer to think that his suggestions have been noted by governments, filed away and, as in this case, subsequently resurrected and acted upon – even though only in an ultra-machiavellian fashion, as the sequel will show. Certainly by the spring of 1975 Her Majesty's Government had every reason to be infuriated with the devious white Rhodesian leader, Ian Smith. He had seemed the previous December to be making concessions that would be bound to lead to a peaceful settlement and 'majority rule'. But in March, with the arrest of a prominent black leader, Sithole, all had been thrown into confusion once again. The 'kith and kin' argument prevented the British authorities from using their own troops directly against the 'rebellious' white minority. But, exasperated, they might – just might – have decided to risk using mercenaries; who could always, however hypocritically, be disowned.

At any rate Banks and Perren were instructed to raise three SAS-type squadrons of 110 men each, plus one logistical squadron, with unit support, to be ready for service within one month. They were told that £2 million had been deposited in the bank by the operation's backers; that the pay would be £150 per week for each 'trooper', rising to £500 per week for the 'officers'; that a £25,000 insurance policy would be taken out on each mercenary; and that bonuses would be generous. Highly and understandably excited, the directors of International Security Organisation Ltd sent out cables to the best of the would-be recruits summoning them to a series of briefing and selection meetings at a London hotel. Banks and Tomkins at the same time set about enlisting their own personal acquaintances.

As commander of the first of his three 'SAS-type squadrons', A Squadron, Banks selected on Perren's recommendation a reliable, cheerful man aged thirty-seven, formerly both a sergeant in the Commandos and a warrant oficer in the Foreign Legion – Mike Johnson, 'a quieter, more decent man', wrote Banks later, 'you could not hope to meet.' And certainly, apart from his propensity for calmly grinding out cigarette ends on the cheekbones of his detractors (admittedly only after considerable provocation), no-one ever appears to have had a word to say against Mike Johnson. Ex-Royal Marine Commandos generally seem to have been better behaved and disciplined than ex-paratroopers, and less neurotic than the ex-SAS. The second-in-command, selected by Banks, was a very different kettle of fish; an ex-SAS combat instructor, also an ex-sergeant, a thick-set aggressive Scot named Pete McAleese, whom Banks claimed to have met on the Libyan Contract. (It is certainly possible that McAleese and his sidekick – also an ex-SAS sergeant, Barry Maddison – were two of the original team of twenty-five stood down by Stirling.) Dave Tomkins for his part recruited an old mate of his with whom he had once worked on a road-repairing job, Chris Dempster. Tomkins was due to come up on an eight-robberies conspiracy charge at the Old Bailey on 1 July, so he was understandably eager to get out of the United Kingdom whatever the risks. Chris Dempster had been in the Army but only in the Gunners; he had applied to join the SAS but had been rejected. Subsequently he had as an army cook hit an officer in the face with a frying-pan, been sentenced to fifty-six days' detention in the 'glass-house', gone AWOL and been dishonourably charged. Thereafter he had had a variety of short-lived jobs – *Death Before Employment* was tattooed on his right arm. But though tempted by the idea of action, he had no desire to fight for blacks against whites: having been blown up by a Mau Mau mine in Kenya, his sympathies were all with the Rhodesian settlers. Nevertheless he agreed to take charge of the security arrangements at the planned recruitment meetings.

The first of these was held in the banqueting hall of the Regent Centre Hotel on 27 May, a Saturday. Instructions had been cabled to 120 would-be mercenaries to attend at 5 pm; among those who also tried to attend were Tony Geraghty, the Defence Correspondent of the *Sunday Times* (he was wired for sound: Chris Dempster broke the microphone hidden up his sleeve before expelling him) and 'a furtive looking man in a leather jacket who gave his name as Leslie Aspin'.

At 7 pm four men filed in and took their places at the top table: John Banks and Frank Perren, the organisers, Mike Johnson and Pete McAleese, the potential commanders. 'Good evening, gentlemen,' said Banks at once. 'Anyone who has any scruples about fighting white settlers or soldiers on the side of black guerillas, please leave the room now.' Duggan and Varley, the ex-SAS majors, also present, must have been fascinated to see how very few left: between three and fifteen (depending on whose version is the more accurate). In any case it seemed conclusive proof that British mercenaries were theoretically prepared to fight anywhere for any cause in the world, even against their own 'kith and kin', provided the money was right. The meeting was certainly well and carefully organised, and one sees behind the organisation the experienced hand of Watchguard rather than the rough and ready methods of Banks and his inexperienced partners. Each would-be mercenary was asked, when the general briefing was over, to step up with his papers: passport, vaccination certificates, army discharge papers; and was reminded to make, if selected, a will. Group life insurance forms were issued for completion. After the meeting broke up, the 'furtive-looking' Leslie Aspin, who had been waiting in the bar, introduced himself to John Banks: a thirty-two-year-old ex-RAF corporal, he seems to have out-Walter-Mittyed Banks with his tales of working for the Secret Service against the IRA, the Mafia and Gaddafy's own secret police, the GID. Banks was impressed and promised to keep in contact with this man whose story had been published by the *Sunday People* under the title/pseudonym 'I, Kovacs: The Spy They Could Not Kill'. Banks can hardly therefore have been too surprised when next morning, a Sunday, the story of the recruitment meeting broke in the same paper.

Despite this theoretically unwelcome publicity however, the plans – and more recruitment meetings – went ahead. By mid-June two hundred mercenaries had been selected and 'A' Squadron had been formed; fifteen platoons, each consisting of the traditional SAS four-man team trained to operate behind enemy lines, with as commanding officer 'Major' Mike Johnson and as squadron sergeant major, his right-hand man, a new figure to appear on the mercenary scene, a big bulbous-faced boisterous twenty-nine-year-old ex-Para sergeant, 'Sammy' Copeland. Copeland had been courtmartialled in 1971 for illegal possession of firearms, and dishonourably discharged. He was rumoured to have gone berserk long before that, in British Guiana with a machine gun. The best that can be said for Copeland is that he was a soldier with more experience than most; the worst that that experience had bred in him a real and unsatisfied lust for killing.

A month's lull followed: a lull that led the press to dub ISO's mercenaries the 'farce force'. Then in mid-July came a minor but encouraging change of plan. The 'Paymaster' sent instructions for the fourteen 'officers' of the first two 'squadrons' formed on paper to fly to Zambia in advance of their men and set about establishing a good working relationship with the black guerilla commanders there – in effect with Joshua Nkomo's men. Banks cabled the fourteen: they were to report to the Skyline Hotel at Heathrow Airport at 1500 hours on 25 July, a Friday. On the Saturday the 'Paymaster' would arrive. On the Sunday they would fly out. Food and drink would be chargeable to ISO.

Banks and the two ex-SAS majors checked their 'officers' in, then departed for a series of meetings leaving 'Major' Mike Johnson in charge. Among his subordinates were two close friends, both older than him: the so-called 'Siamese twins' (because inseparable), Jamie McCandless and Tony Boddy. 'Lieutenant' McCandless was a powerful man who had served eighteen years in the Army, many as a trooper in the SAS. As the Saturday wore on without any sign of the mysterious 'Paymaster', the situation began, understandably and inevitably, to deteriorate. As Banks later vividly put it, 'The men went wild. They ate like Henry VIII, drank like fishes, and screwed like Casanova.' The second was certainly true. McCandless complained to Johnson that he, the official commander, was unable to keep his men under control. A scuffle followed. McCandless threw a punch at Johnson; the 'Major' retaliated by grinding his cigarette out on his 'Lieutenant's' cheekbone. As Tomkins puts it, 'an ugly fight ensued'. Ugly it may have been, but it was a mere precursor, a mere warning sign of the ugliness that was to develop later in Angola among these brutal, officer-less men.

As ISO's so-called 'officers' threatened to tear the hotel apart, the manager contacted the police; Special Branch contacted Banks; Banks assured them that his men would have flown out by that night, Sunday night. But the 'Paymaster' heard of the disturbance while travelling down from Scotland: his reaction was frigid and immediate. The mission was cancelled. The mercenaries were dismissed. Or at least that is the story that Banks told his abashed employees when he reached the Skyline Hotel that Sunday, complaining bitterly that they had cost him £4,000 in drinks and damage alone. The Rhodesian contract was over.

Later Banks and Tomkins and their associates began to suspect that the 'mission' had never been intended to take place at all. The intention had been to prove to Ian Smith and the white Rhodesians that there were British soldiers, albeit unofficial ones, ready if necessary to fight on the side of the black 'terrorists' against their own 'kith and kin'. It had been as it were a warning shot fired across rebel Rhodesia's bows. This seems to me very probable; for even if the details of this shadowy 'assignment' are in many cases obviously invented and the witnesses highly unreliable, yet it is certain that the recruitment meetings did take place at the Regent Centre Hotel in May and that, in July, there was an assembly of mercenaries at the Skyline Hotel: and that all this cost money that certainly did not come from Banks' own empty pockets. Whether David Stirling and Watchguard were in any way involved and, if so, whether the 'Colonel' was totally aware of the deception due to be practised, or only partially aware, is very much another question. In any case ISO, its credibility totally destroyed, was wound up. Unabashed, John Banks decided on yet another money-making plan, combining his Agency Bodyguards project with his mercenary-hiring idea – a Watchguard-style venture offering 'a sophisticated counter-coup capability' as well as a bodyguard service at home and overseas. He had, after all, a potential army on file already. He asked Dave Tomkins to come up with a name; and Tomkins, who had no respect for the British Army or its traditions, came up with what, to others, might have seemed a title reeking of an impertinence that bordered on *lèse-majesté*: Security Advisory Services – SAS Ltd for short.

The only trouble was that for a long period afterwards, despite all efforts, despite Banks concealing his own discredited identity under a false name, SAS Ltd could find no clients. It began to look like yet another fiasco. Peter McAleese and Barry Maddison stayed on in Camberley for a time sleeping in one of the offices over the 'washeteria' that had been first TAE's, then ISO's and were now SAS's; but within weeks even they gave up and moved back to Hereford closer to old friends in the real SAS. In near desperation Banks and Tomkins (who had, incidentally been tried and acquitted at the Old Bailey meanwhile) drove out to Zurich on a potential assignment only to be arrested as suspected terrorists and hit-men by the Swiss police, held for two days in jail, and banned for life from Switzerland. That was in December. In the first days of January came an approach from, and meetings with, black Africans of a rebel group in Angola; but Banks had the impression that this group, UNITA, though ambitious had no money. It was not till ten days later, on the evening of 16 January that he was approached again on behalf of quite a different Angolan group, this time by a white man and one who, though Banks at the time was not aware of it, was like himself an ex-paratrooper and had, like himself but for far more sinister offences, been dishonourably discharged. That man called himself 'Major' Hall.

The Four Friends

Nick Hall had served in the 1st Paras, the notorious battalion that had been sent to Northern Ireland to 'keep the peace' between Catholics and Protestants in the Sixties. His political views – he had political views – were extreme right-wing, his sympathies were with the Protestant extremists, and he sold army weapons to the banned semi-terrorist Ulster Volunteer Force. Nick Hall was cocksure and self-confident, an extremely nasty piece of work. He was caught, courtmartialled, sent to prison for two years and dishonourably discharged.

His friend Costas Georgiou, born in Cyprus in 1951, had emigrated with his parents to North London at the age of twelve, and had later joined the British Army where Hall met him in the 1st Paras. Though he never lost his Greek accent, Costas Georgiou was rather surprisingly a success even in a regiment as racist as, basically, the Parachute Regiment inevitably was. But in the case of efficient soldiers colour prejudice vanished, and the Cypriot proved himself both highly ambitious and highly skilled, the best machine-gunner, the best self-loading-rifle shot, the best all-round recruit in the battalion. That is until, with a fellow paratrooper, Mick Wainhouse, he carried out an armed raid on a Northern Irish post office. At the subsequent courtmartial Costas Georgiou swaggered defiantly, even at one stage threatening to kill the officer who was prosecuting him. He was sentenced to five years' jail and dishonourably discharged; as was his companion-in-arms Mick Wainhouse. The pair, with Nick Hall, formed an even more disagreeable and dangerous trio than Banks and his associates – or rather not a trio, but a quartet. The fourth member, also an ex-para but in his case (for once!) honourably discharged, was another Greek Cypriot, Charley Christodoulou whose cousin, Rona Angelo, Costas Georgiou was taking out. Charley lived in Birmingham; the other three were working together as occasional builders in London. It was not much of a life; indeed it was not much of a life for any of these ex-paratroopers in an England where unemployment was already rising sharply and where in so many cases their own criminal pasts effectively barred possibilities open to others. It seems that it was Nick Hall who in November 1975 took the initiative and again by way of a newspaper advertisement offered the four ex-paratroopers' services overseas. It also seems very probable that earlier Costas Georgiou had applied to join John Banks' ISO force but had been one of those turned down for the Rhodesian contract without even an interview: a fact that rankled. In order to make head or tail out of what is to follow, it must be grasped that this little gang of four, the 1st Para quartet, always mistrusted (when they later came into direct contact with them) the slightly more sophisticated operators from the 2nd Paras, like John Banks himself, and from the SAS and the Marine Commandos; and that even though the

Banks' group were themselves riven by intense rivalries, they were to close ranks, suspiciously, against the 1st Para quartet – except indeed in the case of one of their members who was to find in Costas Georgiou an aggressively similar spirit.

But that is to jump somewhat ahead of the narrative. At the same time as John Banks was trying desperately but unsuccessfully to find work for SAS Ltd, Nick Hall quite independently received an encouraging reply to his virtual offer of four mercenaries for hire ready to serve anywhere in the world from, of all unexpected sources, a British doctor living in Leeds.

Holden Roberto and the FNLA

Doctor Donald Belford was not a bad man or a scoundrel but he was not, as it turned out, a genuine qualified doctor either. He was an ex-Army PT instructor who had worked as a medical orderly in Leeds and who had gone out to Africa as a volunteer with a medical-aid mission five years earlier. The 'doctor' was an honorary title bestowed on him by grateful black patients in northern Angola. While there he had been contacted by, and agreed to treat, guerillas fighting for the liberation movement in that part of the country against its Portuguese rulers – rather a brave and idealistic thing to do. Since then, since 1970, he had been back several times, had become friendly with the leader of that particular liberation movement, Holden Roberto, and had indeed become such a passionate partisan of the FNLA, as the movement was called (the initials stood for *Frente National por el Liberacao de Angola*), as to be appointed its 'official representative' in Britain. A fairly meaningless title normally; but for once, rather tentatively, 'Dr' Belford had been given a job to do for the organisation which he 'officially' represented. For Angola had, after four hundred years of Portuguese rule, become independent. But on the very eve of Independence the FNLA had lost a battle against one of the rival movements, the MPLA, the biggest battle yet, fought only twenty-five miles outside the capital Luanda.

That had been on 10 November. Holden Roberto had hoped to enter Luanda triumphantly at the head of his victorious troops on Independence Day, 11 November. Instead, as the last Portuguese governor Admiral Cardoso lowered the Portuguese flag and slunk almost surreptitiously away with the few remaining Portuguese troops to a troopship waiting in Luanda's harbour, the rival MPLA had joyously proclaimed Independence in the capital, firing thousands of rounds into the air to celebrate both the departure of the Portuguese

and their own victory the previous day over the FNLA. Holden
Roberto had for his part been reduced to proclaiming Independence
rather less joyously a hundred miles up the coast at the small town of
Ambriz. Meanwhile, way down in the south of the country, the third
liberation movement, UNITA, led by the bearded and bumptious
guerilla fighter Jonas Savimbi (who had once been Holden Roberto's
lieutenant) also proclaimed and celebrated Independence. It was, in
other words, an extremely complicated and confused situation in this
vast new country on Africa's eastern seaboard. But one thing was
clear: the Portuguese were, at last, out; and the struggle for power
between the three rival liberation movements, the FNLA, UNITA
and the MPLA, was definitely, on.

The other thing that was clear was that Holden Roberto and the
FNLA, who had once been in a position of relative strength and had
looked like winning, were now in a position of relative weakness and
had begun to look very much like losers. For the two other
movements were backed by efficient foreign support but Holden
Roberto and the FNLA were not. In the vast under-populated
plateaux of the south of Angola, the South Africans were discreetly
helping Jonas Savimbi and UNITA with helicopters, armoured cars,
artillery and – even more discreetly – white troops of the SADF, the
South African Defence Force, South Africa's army. This was not
because they had any particular sympathy for bearded and boisterous
black guerilla fighters but because, in their eyes, now that their white
Portuguese allies had 'scuttled', Savimbi's UNITA was very much
the lesser of two evils. Its rival the MPLA had struck fear into the
heart of South Africa – though not indeed the MPLA itself so much
as its allies and backers, the Russians and the Cubans. The Russians
had supplied the Marxist-orientated MPLA with impressive armaments and weapons: AK 47s, the efficient Czech-made modern
sub-machine guns, T34 and T54 tanks, and the 122 mm Katyusha
rockets fired from multi-barrelled 'Stalin's organs', with their terrifying wailing sound that had sent Holden Roberto's FNLA troops
running at the battle of 10 November. But all over Africa the
Russians had supplied leftist 'liberation movements' with armaments
before: there was nothing particularly new or unexpected in that.
What was totally, utterly, unexpected and what had thrown the South
African government into a state of near panic was the sudden arrival
of Cuban troops in Africa: first a handful of commandos and
instructors, but soon hundreds and then literally thousands of
Castro's men. These were largely black Cubans (and so outwardly
indistinguishable from their MPLA allies, who aped their uniforms

and their berets and beards) but they were, though inexperienced, far more disciplined and better trained than the MPLA troops they were supporting, and above all far more capable of wielding the Russian weapons. The South African government feared that they might be merely the first wave of a revolutionary Cuban human tide designed, once successful in Angola, to sweep away white rule in South Africa itself. Hence their support for UNITA. Which was fine for Jonas Savimbi and UNITA (whose columns in the days after Independence began rapidly recapturing towns they had previously lost south of the capital). But it was not so fine at all for Holden Roberto and the FNLA in the more heavily populated north of the country where their forces, lacking South African support, were rapidly disintegrating in the face of the Cubans and their Russian weapons.

What Holden Roberto did have, however, was two assets: backing and a safe base. Holden Roberto's birthplace in the north of Angola, Sao Salvador, had in the days before the coming of the Portuguese been the 'capital' of the Bakongo empire that spread all over the lower Congo basin; Holden Roberto, himself a Bakongo, had lived most of his life in what had since become by far the greatest Bakongo city and centre of Bakongo power, Leopoldville. Leopoldville was renamed Kinshasha by President Mobutu (and the Congo rechristened Zaire); but I will continue to call it, as in the earlier part of this book, Leo and the country of which it is the capital the Congo, both to save space and to avoid confusion. Holden Roberto, rather a stiff dour figure like many of the Bakongo, had set up and had always maintained the FNLA's headquarters in Leo, in a rather shabby villa-compound in its outskirts. For, though he was not only a Bakongo but President Mobutu's brother-in-law, he had not always been generously supported (though he had always been tolerated) by Mobutu. Indeed, in the early Sixties, when I was there, his 'organisation' had seemed seedy, run-down and above all very, very short of cash.

All that had changed most dramatically in the spring of 1975 when the first Cubans landed south of Luanda, to launch a successful seaborne assault on the UNITA-held port of Lobito. If South Africa was horrified, America was appalled. The Cubans were America's bugbears, Castro America's Frankenstein monster. It was bad enough having Cubans on the United States' own doorstep, off the coast of Florida, without their being permitted to spread their infectious poison to other continents. There could be no question, after Vietnam, of countering a Cuban presence with American troops or even with American military advisers: public opinion in the United States would never have stood for such a move. But Dr Henry

Kissinger, in charge of America's foreign policy, was perfectly determined that neither the Russians nor the Cubans should be able to boast of another foreign policy success. He persuaded President Ford to set aside nearly $32 million to keep Angola safely in the hands of the West, and by July 1975 in response to his wishes the CIA had set up an Angolan Task Force to administer and distribute their funds, under the control of an experienced CIA operative, John Stockwell.

The Hiring of the Mercenaries

The CIA operated almost entirely through the Congo (where their headquarters in Leo were only a few hundred yards from the FNLA villa-compound) and almost entirely through Mobutu. The plan was for Mobutu to distribute arms and aid both to the FNLA and UNITA and to use the CIA's money to replace the arms he was distributing – not a very satisfactory system, open as it was to abuse by Mobutu's venality.

At first there had been no thought of hiring mercenaries – after all Mobutu was the last man in the world to want to see white mercenaries based in his country once again, afer his own bitter experiences of their treachery in the Mercenary Revolt of 1967. It seems, though, that Mike Hoare was hawking for a contract almost as soon as the first Cubans arrived in Angola, offering 350 white mercenaries, ex-Five Commando, to oppose them: but even Hoare did not dare set foot in the Congo. He was reported to be in Gabon that spring. But the price he was asking seemed at the time excessive, he had been inactive for almost ten years, and in any case at that stage neither the FNLA nor UNITA nor the CIA were much interested in hiring white mercenaries, with all the doubtful propaganda that would inevitably result, when it seemed the game might in any case well go their way without. It was very different by the summer when John Stockwell took charge. The cry then was for French mercenaries; the CIA's Paris bureau contacted the French Secret Service, the SDECE. The SDECE cannily demanded $25,000 as a 'proof of good faith' – and then told the CIA (expensive information at the price!) how to contact Bob Denard.

Denard was at the time based in Libreville – heaven knows if he and Mike Hoare met there and, if so, who warned the other off what – and he had apparently already been supplying a handful of mercenaries to the FLEC in Cabinda. Cabinda was a tiny enclave, Portuguese, officially part of Angola but separated from Angola by the estuary of the Congo – and therefore by Mobutu's territory. Its importance was oil: it was oil-rich. None of the three liberation movements of Angola was therefore willing for it to go its own way; all claimed it as an 'integral' part of Angola. But Cabinda had spawned its own independence movement, the FLEC – confusingly split into four factions, which in the summer of 1975 hired their own white mercenaries to fight the Portuguese, the MPLA and each other. A freelance French mercenary, Jean Kay, a loner famous for his activities in the Middle East and the Caribbean, was rumoured to be active there; as also (though this seems less likely) was François Bodenan, Tshombe's kidnapper. Possibly Denard went there himself; certainly he supplied, from Gabon, a handful of French mercenaries. But it was a brief venture, swiftly over. On 1 November FLEC declared Cabinda an independent nation. On 2 November a three-column Cuban-led MPLA invasion put an end to the 'independent state'; and the French mercenaries, unharmed, beat a hasty well-timed strategic retreat to Gabon.

From there almost simultaneously Denard was summoned to Paris to negotiate with, for the CIA, a retired US Marines lieutenant-colonel. It was a very tough negotiation and when agreement was finally reached, on 24 November, Denard had obtained what he wanted: a guarantee of no less than $350,000 payable in advance to recruit twenty French mercenaries for a contract of five months; these mercenaries to be based in Leo, trained there on SAM 7 missiles and then to be sent south to join Jonas Savimbi and UNITA as both instructors and, if necessary, operatives – particularly against the two squadrons of Russian MIGs that were reported to be based in Brazzaville, ready – it seemed – to intervene in Angola. But this, though expensive for the CIA (in the end it cost them $425,000 including life insurance), was in numerical terms a very minor and discreet mercenary operation. For Jonas Savimbi did not want, then or thereafter, to win the reputation of relying on white mercenaries.

Nor, at first, did Holden Roberto. In any case he had at that time little money of his own – control of his finances was firmly in the hands of his brother-in-law Mobutu. In Leeds 'Doctor' Belford informed the four ex-paratroopers that he could at the time – it was towards the end of the disastrous month of November – afford to fly only one of the four out to Angola, and in any case that that one would be acting not as a soldier but, under himself, as an unpaid medical orderly. Costas Georgiou had been set a test by Donald Belford's bodyguard, another unsavoury character, a loud-mouthed Londoner named Colin Taylor, who called himself the FNLA's 'European

Security Officer'. This test was to set fire to the Soho offices in London of the MPLA's 'front', the Angolan Solidarity Committee; and Costas Georgiou with two gallons of petrol showed his initiative by obeying instructions. Costas Georgiou was therefore the first 'mercenary' selected by the FNLA to fly out from London – an odd sort of mercenary at that, unpaid and medical. He and 'Dr' Belford and Colin Taylor arrived in Leo on 2 December; Costas Georgiou had chosen – and thereafter always used in the brief months of life remaining to him – a name that was to become notorious in the annals of modern mercenary history, an anglicised pseudonym, Callan.

8

Callan in Angola

Callan's was a complex personality. In many ways he was a primitive murderous lout, like so many of the EOKA terrorists whose struggle, in Cyprus, he had been too young to share. But like many of them too he had a certain heroic stature, a certain almost ancestral courage with, in his particular case, a strong instinct, a near Homeric urge, as Homer's own murderous hero, Achilles, had had:

αἰὲν ἀριστένειν καὶ ὑπειροχον εμμεναι ἀλλων.
("Always to be the best and to be outstanding above all others."
Homer, *The Iliad*, 2088 VI.)

He was impulsive, he was on occasions inspiring, he was dominant, he was contradictory, he was pitiless. But that was not the side of his personality that first emerged in Angola. On the contrary he worked hard, well and responsibly in a subordinate position under 'Dr' Belford, cleaning up the FNLA military hospital at Carmona, scrubbing out the wards, acting as an assistant during surgical operations, and driving an ambulance to the 'front' to pick up wounded, whereby he saved many lives. He even helped at the premature birth of a baby whose mother he had picked up to rush to hospital.

Donald Belford and his bodyguard Taylor left northern Angola to return home for Christmas. Callan stayed on. Two days after Christmas Day he woke to find that the FNLA had abandoned Carmona overnight; and that only 50 yards from his bungalow a Russian T34 tank was standing. That marked the end of Callan's medical, and the beginning of his military, career in Angola. Enraged at the ease with which the enemy had been able to capture one of the few remaining important towns in FNLA hands, he decided on his own initiative to organise a counterattack. And when a few days later on 5 January his three friends Nick Hall, Charley Christodoulou and Mick Wainhouse, finally arrived at Leo (escorted in by Colin Taylor), it was to be welcomed on their arrival at the airport by Callan and a man of his own age who much resembled him, stocky, swarthy, brave

– one of the handful of Portuguese still fighting for the FNLA, an ex-boxer, known only as Madeira.

Callan's First Battle

Madeira and Callan had a proud tale to tell. They, and one other Portuguese, had attacked and routed – just the three of them – an MPLA column advancing from Carmona onto Negege (the FNLA's military airport) six hundred strong, leaving sixty dead (mainly Cubans) and destroying four Russian T34 tanks and four truck-mounted 'Stalin's organs'. It sounded – and sounds – a tall tale but, allowing for some exaggeration in numbers, I am inclined to believe it. For it bore the hallmark of Callan's future, authenticated exploits: an almost suicidal frontal assault relying entirely on speed and surprise upon far superior and more heavily armed enemy columns.

Admittedly Callan, Madeira and Lopez had caught the enemy column in camp, resting and entirely off their guard. While the Portuguese sprayed the six hundred with their sub-machine guns, Callan, armed with a 66 mm portable anti-tank rocket launcher, had – recklessly ignoring his own safety – dashed around picking off from close range the enemy armour. The explosion of the 'Stalin's organs' had caused an understandable panic; and by the time the MPLA had recovered from their horror, their assailants had vanished into the surrounding jungle.

It had been – in terms of the Angolan war – a great victory, proving that the 'invincible' Russian tanks were not unstoppable, the superior MPLA weaponry not decisive, and the feared Cubans immune neither to death nor to defeat. It shook the MPLA (though they went on to capture Negege); and above all it gave the CIA Bureau in Leo furiously to think. Mobutu's two Zairois battalions, sullen and ineffective, had spent more time looting the villages of northern Angola than supporting their nominal allies; and the 'Zorrens', bands of thugs released from Mobutu's jails to swell the FNLA ranks, had turned into marauding raiders who preyed on the FNLA rather than on the mutual enemy. But if one British ex-paratrooper, plus a couple of Portuguese, could halt and hurt an MPLA column at odds of 200 to 1 against, then what might not a group of ex-paratroopers be expected to achieve? The CIA immediately loosened the purse-strings and from that time on, from the beginning of the year 1975, Holden Roberto had dollars almost literally in sackfuls at his disposition. Important – and immediate – results followed.

The first was the paying of Callan's three comrades' air fares out to

Angola by Dr Belford, who now had the funds to do so. The second, much more striking, consequence was the sudden appointment on the CIA's 'suggestion' of Callan as Field Commander of the FNLA 'army'. The third result was the handing by Holden Roberto of $25,000 in cash to his newly promoted 'Major', Nick Hall, with instructions to return to England and to recruit within a week another twenty-five British mercenaries: $500 would be needed for the air fare, Hall had calculated, and $500 per head for initial expenses (the extra $600 were for his own expenses). 'So for a million dollars,' Holden Roberto said, 'you can buy me a whole British Parachute battalion?'

It did not, of course, in the end come to that. The whole drama in Angola was over before anything like a thousand British ex-paratroopers could be recruited. But if – if! – such a force had been hired, and if – an even bigger if! – it had been properly officered, then there seems little doubt that the eventual outcome of the Angolan civil war would have been changed. In real life, however, the mercenaries dribbled in in small packets, too few and too late. Even then if they had all been ex-paratroopers (or ex-SAS or ex-Marine Commandos or indeed ex-fighting soldiers of the British Army), they might have turned the tide; but they were not. And even given their small numbers and – in the case of the later recruits – their dubious and in some cases positively unmilitary backgrounds, they might have held the MPLA if they had been properly officered. But not one ex-officer of the British Army was ever in a position of authority over them; all the lieutenants, captains, and majors in the FNLA's white mercenary army from 'Colonel' Callan downwards were former troopers and corporals, or at best sergeants and warrant-officers. There was not a Hoare or a Wicks, a Jeremy Spencer or even an Ian Gordon among them. This was what in the end caused the whole force to dissolve in a welter of bloodshed. Not that they needed the British officer class to lead them into battle: Callan with his fierce pride (and others of the early comers inspired by Callan's example) proved themselves perfectly capable of doing that. It was off the battlefield that the calm authority of a Hoare, supported by others of his class and type, was needed to impose discipline, mutual loyalty and in moments of crisis a sense of restraint. As it was, ex-paratroopers and jailbirds like Hall and Callan sporadically attempted to emulate the attitudes and behaviour of the officer class they had known in the Parachute Regiment. But it was not natural to them; it ran contrary to their training and to their instincts; when emergencies occurred the unsteady mask slipped and they reverted to the primitive behaviour that was their natural bent. Mick Wainhouse was, according to other mercenaries, 'a tall Englishman with a moustache, looking every inch an officer in the British Army'. But when he finally finished off Sammy Copeland with three shots in the back of the head, it was with the casually chilling phrase coming more naturally to the lips of the gangster he was than the officer and gentleman that he half-aspired to be: 'That's him finished, then.'

Hall, Wainhouse and Charley had reached Leo on 5 January 1976. On 9 January Callan was installed as Field Commander at the FNLA's 'captial' of Sao Salvador, with 'Captain' Wainhouse and 'Captain' Christodoulou, his old friends and comrade-in-arms under his orders; while, by 11 January, Hall was back at Heathrow Airport, wondering how and where to find the twenty-five new recruits that Callan and his 'army' so desperately required. For, with the fall of Carmona and Negege, the FNLA forces, such as they were, held only a small band of territory along the border with the Congo. In this enclave three towns were important (and I would urge readers to look at the map (see p.174) and fix their names and positions firmly in mind): first San Antonio on the coast, with its back to the River Congo; secondly, further inland, the 'city' of Sao Salvador, the historic capital of the Bakongo people, Holden Roberto's birthplace and the FNLA's military headquarters; and finally on the eastern flank, towards the interior, the little town of Maquela that was to become Callan's base and the main setting – Maquela and its surroundings – for the melodramatic events that were to follow. It is important to bear in mind how close these towns were not only to the Congolese border but to Leo itself. It was only somewhat over 250 miles by road from Sao Salvador to Leo and the distance could be driven in a few hours. Holden Roberto – 'my President' as the mercenaries were instructed to address him, adapting the French formula of '*mon President*' – would often be driven to and fro overnight, or even by day, in his presidential Range Rover between his villa-compound in Leo and the FNLA's military headquarters, the two-storey colonial 'palace' in Sao Salvador; or be flown out in a far shorter time in the FNLA's Portuguese-piloted Cessna. The coaches and the twin-engined Fokker Friendship that transported the mercenaries to and fro were only marginally slower.

It is also important to realise that black soldiers of the FNLA still existed as organised units – scattered, a few hundred here and there, as garrisons in the three towns and in a handful of barracks or semi-fortified positions outside them. And there were, with the black troops, a handful of Portuguese (who were of course the only ones

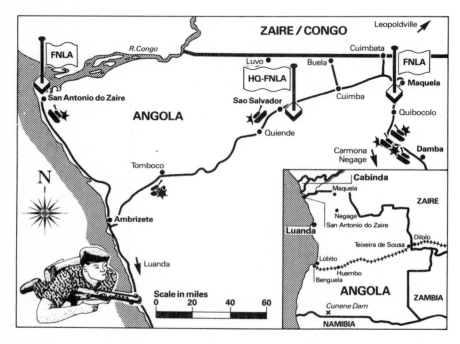

Northern Angola and inset of the whole country.

who could communicate with black troops directly, for neither Callan nor any of the British mercenaries could speak Portuguese). But in general these black troops were, as the events at Carmona had shown, demoralised and ineffective since their 10 November defeat outside Luanda. On the other side, with the MPLA, were not only Cubans but other left-wingers, Portuguese ('mercenaries' too, technically) and, an extra boon for the MPLA, hundreds if not thousands of the Katangese gendarmes. In effect these last were black mercenaries, who had switched allegiance from their previous employers and protectors, the Portuguese Army, to the new power that appeared to control the country and certainly controlled the capital: the Russian-equipped, Cuban-backed government of Dr Agostinho Neto, the MPLA President. No wonder that Callan, Wainhouse and Charley, the three ex-paratroopers, waited nervily in Sao Salvador for the reinforcements that the fourth of their little group, Hall, had flown to England so urgently to recruit and bring back to their aid.

Banks Becomes Involved

On arrival in England, Hall had little or no notion of how to set about recruiting the twenty-five men he had promised within the week. He travelled to Leeds to report to Donald Belford, pursued a possible contact in Scotland that came to nothing, then returned to London, to the Regent Palace Hotel. Apparently he then remembered an article he had read in *The Sunday Times* the previous August, at the time of the Rhodesian contract. He rang *The Sunday Times* offices and made contact with Tony Geraghty, the paper's Defence Correspondent and the author of the article in question. Geraghty, no doubt scenting an exclusive story, put Hall in touch with the man whom he, Geraghty, knew to have a mercenary army already lined up, specimens of which Geraghty had seen in the flesh: John Banks of Camberley. Provided this account is true – and there seems no reason to doubt it – that is how Hall, late of the 1st Paras, came to contact Banks, late of the 2nd Paras: via a highly respected British newspaper and via one of its most highly respected reporters. For, contrary to the popular image, journalists, who as a matter of right insist on demanding information from others, are not – British journalists at least – chary of giving out information generously when requested, even to unknown voices over the telephone. Whether in this rather special case it was moral to do so is another matter: for indeed, if Geraghty and *The Sunday Times* had not passed on the information, then the contact between would-be hirer and would-be provider of mercenaries would very probably never have been made; and many men's lives, black and white alike, would have been saved. But in any case Geraghty, though he did not know it at the time, was to risk paying – again if the mercenaries' account is true – with his own.

From London Hall had contacted Banks in Camberley on 16 January, a Friday. It was important that it was a Friday, for ISO's files (with the names and addresses of all the potential recruits for the Rhodesian contract) were locked away in the insurer's offices, unavailable till the following Monday morning; and Hall had strict instructions to be back within the week. So it followed that, with no time at all to lose, John Banks attempted via his personal contacts to raise twenty-five men, ready to drop everything and fly out to Angola immediately.

All this meant a confused weekend of telephoning, travelling and meetings, the whole based at the Tower Hotel — to which Hall had moved in an attempt to throw Tony Geraghty and *The Sunday Times* off the trail. There Banks' associates, old and new, hastily gathered: Frank Perren and Dave Tomkins, but also Leslie Aspin who had, since the previous August, elbowed his way into the inner circle. A telephone call from Aspin to *The Sunday Times* quickly revealed that Geraghty had not been thrown off the scent; but was prepared to hold back the story provided that he was allowed to accompany the twenty-five mercenaries to Angola in person. Thereupon this gang, who after all had been brought together by Geraghty's information in the first place, proceeded to sit down and coldbloodedly plan Geraghty's murder. The appalling Nick Hall offered $6,000 to anyone who would have the Defence Correspondent of *The Sunday Times* 'rubbed out'; and according to his own account Dave Tomkins (who, as far as I know, had never committed murder or even been jailed for grievous bodily harm) 'found the money tempting'. One is left with the impression that these were the real scum of the mercenary criminal underworld, prepared to kill or to arrange a killing coldly and casually, with no regard for human life at all, restrained (and even that erratically) only by a sense of self-preservation. In the end self-preservation dictated that Geraghty should not be murdered in London; instead, they decided to take him along to Angola as their comrade and there out in the bush treacherously shoot him. Geraghty of course knew nothing at the time of his 'future having been decided'; and, as the whole recruiting story was blown in *The Sunday People* next day by one of Les Aspin's contacts, he lost – fortunately for him – his means of pressure on the mercenary gang and never accompanied them to Angola, the bush, and to death in a casual ditch. Some may think I am making over-heavy weather of what was arguably only late-Saturday-night drinking talk. I do not think so. Even if these men only half meant at the time what they were saying, even if Tony Geraghty, once out in Angola at their side, might have established friendships and survived, all this casual and unscrupulous talk of murder, and almost motiveless murder at that, is symptomatic. It demonstrates only too clearly the lack of any human decency that would become so horrifyingly apparent out in Angola when the restraints of civilisation – such as they were – had been removed.

Tony Geraghty the outsider was not the only man threatened with death that weekend. As Hall, Banks and Aspin juggled for control of the operation and for authority over each other, taunts and menaces rained down on all sides. In the end it was Hall and nineteen men only who caught the flight that Sunday night from London to Brussels. Those nineteen men did not include John Banks himself; he had been persuaded, very forcefully and despite his wishes, to stay behind in England and recruit many more men. Perren and Aspin also remained behind. But Dave Tomkins went out as 'explosives officer' and his old friend Chris Dempster with him as 'vehicle maintenance officer'. The rest of the group were mainly those who had been involved in the aborted Rhodesia contract, with the difference that Mike Johnson, the then commander (who had proved incapable of exercising control at the Skyline Hotel) was demoted to a mere minor officer's rank and Peter McAleese, then second-in-command, the tough ex-SAS sergeant, was now appointed commanding officer in his place. The other 'officers' were Jamie McCandless, Mike Johnson's antagonist, and an old acquaintance of Banks, 'Brummie' Barker. Barker was yet another dishonourably discharged ex-paratrooper, a thug who had once worked – most violently – for Banks' Agency Bodyguards venture and who had since become notorious in and around Aldershot and Camberley for pub brawls. Finally in the ranks of the 'officers' (each of whom were handed $500 in advance by Nick Hall) there was the ex-Squadron Sergeant Major of ISO's paper 'A' Squadron, the twenty-nine-year-old bulbous Sammy Copeland.

Jamie McCandless brought with him his 'Siamese twin', Tony Boddy; the other eleven mercenaries in this initial draft were Andy MacKenzie, Barry Freeman, Mick Rennie, 'Fuzz' Hussey, Paul Aves, Dougie Saunders, 'Stars' Griffiths, John Tilsey, Bryan Lewis and the easily confused Pat MacPhearson and Stuart McPherson. These men had this in common; they were all unemployed or casually employed, they had – most of them – at least a nodding acquaintance with each other, and they had all been professional soldiers. It would be exaggerating to say that they knew what was waiting for them in Angola – 'Major' Hall had painted a rosy picture of FNLA strength, weapons, and even of FNLA medical facilities and a corresponding picture of Cuban weakness – but they did realise very well that they would be going into combat and they did know very well all that that implied. Meanwhile, as their Sabena flight winged its way from Brussels to Leo that Monday, John Banks and his associates set about recruiting, from their Camberley offices and with files to hand, far greater numbers: another hundred mercenaries, to follow within ten days and a further 250 within a week after that. At a recruiting fee of £200 per head – the sum promised by Nick Hall – it would not do, John Banks obviously decided, to pick and choose too carefully. The rush and pressure, to be fair to him, must have been enormous; and the strain on the virtually nonexistent 'organisation' of Security Advisory Services Ltd overwhelming. What Banks was after was bodies: if he had to tell potential recruits that they would only be used in training and administrative duties, that they would have a period of acclimatisation on arrival, that they would be stationed at the FNLA bases and training camps in the safety of the Congo, not (in all probability) ever to set foot in the war-zone of northern Angola, then he was prepared to tell them this and salve his conscience by marking their trades and designations formally on the recruiting papers that would accompany each man. For what was essential was speed. And, again to give John Banks his due, he did – at great profit admittedly to himself – get together (and it cannot have been an easy task) the required number of men in the few days he had been given to assemble and expedite them. The following Friday, that is to say 23 January, accompanied by his own best friend from his own 2nd Para days, 'Satch' Fortuin, a man of mixed white and coloured blood who acted as a bodyguard, John Banks went to the Park Court Hotel to pick up the equivalent of no less than £60,000 in new dollar bills. These were handed over by two well-dressed black men who, Fortuin later testified, spoke together in a foreign language. The two, therefore, whatever else they may have been, were clearly not black Americans – for Americans, white or black, would of course have spoken together in English.

The American Connection

There was one, but only one, North American mercenary/adventurer in Leo at the time and he was in any case not from the United States but from Canada, Douglas Newby. The British mercenaries suspected him of being a CIA agent; Newby merely laughed. For the CIA had distanced themselves from the FNLA mercenary operation in a very noticeable way. They channelled the funds, certainly, but they channelled them either in comparatively minor sums to Holden Roberto himself or via Mobutu; the two well-dressed black men in the London hotel were almost certainly Congolese diplomats, Mobutu's men. But the CIA did not deal directly with Hall or Banks or even Callan – the FNLA mercenary recruiters and their mercenary commander. This was in complete contrast to their direct negotiations with, and direct paying of, the French mercenaries for UNITA – eleven of whom had reached Leo on 10 January.

Why the contrast? In my view it was simply because the FNLA operation was English-speaking, and the CIA were therefore extremely worried that it would inevitably attract American mercenaries; whereas the UNITA operation being both French-speaking and more discreet would not. One would-be American mercenary of a distinctly superior sort, George Bacon III, a graduate in Political Science from Georgetown University and an ex-Green Beret who had fought in Vietnam, had earlier flown at his own expense to Zambia and there tried to enlist with UNITA. It was probably the CIA's doing that he had not been accepted. For there was certainly at this time both a fear and a hope – fear by the authorities, hope by others – that the United States would become the major mercenary recruiting ground of the future. As Major Robert K. Brown, also a former Green Beret, of Boulder, Colorado, put it: 'The Vietnam War has left the U.S. with the largest number of unemployed combat-trained soldiers in the world. That's why I foresee most of the new mercenaries coming from here in the next few years.'

It never happened; but that was certainly not the fault of Major Robert K. Brown. He had, on retirement, produced an information sheet on possible openings for ex-Vietnam combatants in Oman that grew into a fully fledged magazine entitled *Soldier of Fortune* and subtitled *The Journal of Professional Adventurers*. In one sense *Soldier of Fortune* was – and is – nothing more than yet another glossy vehicle for the advertisements of guns, weapons, and semi-military paraphernalia that the United States seems to spawn in such quantities. But, formally at least, it was the first magazine specifically aimed at would-be mercenaries from the States, ready to serve anywhere in the world; and as such its appearance on the newstands in 1975 must have appalled the United States authorities. By the turn of the year it was well-established; but on the other hand splash advertisements such as that announcing 'Mercenaries Needed Now!' (all applicants had to send $25 'processing fee' to El Kamas Enterprises; and heard no more of the process, their application or of course the fee) had somewhat destroyed its 'recruiting' credibility. The truth seems to be that many, many Americans are tempted by the fantasy life of a mercenary; many were even prepared to pay several thousand dollars to such people as 'General' Mitchell Livingstone Werbell IV of Powder Springs, Georgia, for a short, intensive combat training course at his Cobray International War School; many will have read with close attention the booklet of Larry D. Loper *So You Want to Be a Mercenary?* (published in Sugarland, Texas) with its emphasis on the need for obtaining a passport, speaking a second language, medical care, practising tactics and strategy on playboard war games, preparing a proper curriculum vitae and studying the US Army Area Handbook for the 'target' country or countries involved – but almost all are aware of the fact (never mentioned in these mercenary magazines or guides) that in real life they risk on joining any foreign army the loss of that most precious possession, their US citizenship. Prudence and circumspection therefore usually prevail over dreams. But not in all cases. Daniel Gearhart, a thirty-six-year-old married man crippled by medical debts for his family's health bills, inserted the following advertisement in the winter 1975 issue of *Soldier of Fortune*:

> Wanted: Employment as mercenary on full-time or job contract basis. Preferably in South or Central America but anywhere in the world, if you pay transportation. Contact Gearhart, Box 1457, Wheaton, MD 20902.

In that same issue there was a feature article about another would-be mercenary recruiter, David Bufkin. Bufkin, a cropduster from Kerman, California, had been bitten by the fantasy bug and had been placing small advertisements in local papers such as the *Fresno Bee* offering work to ex-Marines and ex-Green Berets. He had of course no 'work' to propose; it was merely his attempt to build up his own paper mercenary army. By the time *Soldier of Fortune* interviewed him, he was claiming to be able to offer a six-months' contract at $8,000 a month and already to have had a hundred applications, of which he had accepted only seventeen. For where? Why, for Angola of course, the country then in the news. All this was baseless; but in a sense Bufkin was thereby hoisted on the petard of his own invention. A number of would-be mercenaries contacted him, eager to serve in Angola. George Bacon III, back in America, gave him a call – to be told that there were already 150–200 US veterans already in Angola, with the FNLA – obvious nonsense, which Bacon knew to be such. Tom Oates, an ex-Los Angeles police-sergeant, invalided out of the force, was both more gullible and more pressing. Another, a twenty-five-year-old named Lobo do Sol, was taken on by Bufkin to keep his files and seems to have become the brains behind this 'operation'.

The CIA's fears were justified. There was an upsurge of interest in the mercenary 'career' in the United States and the presence of English-speaking mercenaries in Angola was acting, inevitably, as a magnet for that interest. American mercenaries despite all the difficulties, would appear with the FNLA forces; but in such small numbers and so marginally that the CIA itself could not seriously be accused even by its most rabid opponent of having recruited them, and the US government could justifiably and convincingly disclaim all responsibility.

The First Nineteen

In any case there were no American mercenaries yet on the scene, only 'Canada' Newby, when Hall and his nineteen new recruits flew into Leo on Monday, 20 January. They were given no time to acclimatise themselves. Fed, and hastily equipped, they were driven overnight to Sao Salvador, which they reached on Tuesday morning, little suspecting that the whole war would be over in exactly four weeks' time, little thinking that six of their own number were destined to die in a country of whose existence they had barely been aware three days earlier.

McAleese drew his men up and presented them for inspection to their new Commanding Officer, Colonel Callan. A certain antagonism immediately developed between the two groups – that is to say between the new arrivals, experienced and in many cases older men, almost entirely English or Scots, and the swarthier group of Cypriots and Portuguese, already in place, among whom Mick Wainhouse was the only Englishman. Admittedly 'Shotgun Charley' (as Christodoulou soon became nicknamed – his favourite weapon was an ornate Spanish double-barrelled shotgun) spoke with a strong Birmingham accent; but Callan was an obvious foreigner and, for a 'Colonel', at twenty-four years old ridiculously young. On the other hand the twelve days during which he had been Field Commander of the FNLA forces had given him an aura of both authority and experience. From Callan's point of view these new recruits were the first batch of hundreds promised to him by Holden Roberto – not enough to counter the MPLA columns (which, fortunately for him, had made no move forward in the past few days) but enough at least to impose discipline on his own troops. For the FNLA black soldiers at Quiende barracks a few miles south of Sao Salvador were in a state of semi-mutiny. Callan gave his new recruits a day to sort themselves out; then, on the Wednesday, they saw for themselves the brutality of his methods. Twenty of the ring leaders of the mutineers – overawed by the appearance of the band of whites – were shot by Callan and Charley personally; and a suspected spy was later in the day executed and dumped into the river from Quiende bridge, apparently a very usual process. Already on the evening of their arrival at Sao Salvador the new recruits had heard the screams of another suspected spy whom Callan and Wainhouse were 'interrogating' in a room in the Sao Salvador 'palace' , the FNLA's military headquarters. This had clearly been the rhythm of the previous twelve days, and this was to be the rhythm of the days to come – casual executions of suspected spies, mutineers, deserters or traitors, 'toppings' which soon ceased to shock and began to stimulate the newcomers.

Callan's first move after the suppression of the Quiende mutiny – and a very wise move too from his point of view – was to send over a third of the new recruits, seven mercenaries, to the coast, to hold and garrison the town of San Antonio on his right flank. This removed at a stroke the two potential challengers to his own authority: Pete McAleese and the former ISO 'commander', Mike Johnson. 'Brummy' Barker, another 'officer', another possible threat, went with them too (the other four were Rennie, Tilsey, Saunders and McPherson). These seven therefore remained for the next two weeks totally detached from, and ignorant of, the dramas that were to follow, leading a rather pleasant existence in San Antonio, unthreatened by the enemy, and above all detached from the realities of life, or rather the realities of death, that clung to Callan like a sort of disease and that began to infect all those around him. For the man who was now the senior 'officer' of the twelve newcomers remaining in Sao Salvador, Sammy Copeland, seems to have felt an almost instinctive affinity for Callan. He became Callan's admirer, imitator and, as RSM (for Callan was chary of distributing officer-rank to the new recruits), Callan's right-hand man. Indeed he became Callan's executioner, killing on Callan's word when Callan was too preoccupied or busy to carry out yet another execution himself. Power seems to have gone to Copeland's head from the moment when he was put in charge of the ex-mutineers at Quiende where he was seen firing volleys into the air to emphasise his orders and drilling the black FNLA troops to shout, as they marched, '*Viva la Sammy*!'

That same evening of the Quiende killings, within, that is to say, only forty-eight hours of their arrival in Sao Salvador, morale had deteriorated so fast that Dave Tomkins and Chris Dempster, the remaining pair of Banks-appointed 'officers', were planning to kill Callan and his comrades, and 'leg it' to the border. Fortunately (from the point of view of the unity of the little mercenary group) the enemy at long last made a move; and in the face of the enemy, as often happens in times of war, treachery and plots were at least temporarily forgotten. For on the Thursday news came that an enemy column, led by five tanks, had taken Damba and was threatening the left flank of the FNLA enclave; on the Friday – the day on which John Banks in London was receiving the £60,000 to cover the airfares and down payments for the next batch of recruits – a column of vehicles was hastily repaired and prepared in Sao Salvador; and on the Saturday morning, three hours before dawn, the column led by Callan, his Portuguese driver Uzio, and Dave Tomkins – 'Explosives' to Callan who had taken a liking to him, little knowing the plans the former safe-breaker had been making for his future only a short time earlier – set out for Maquela.

★   ★   ★

Maquela was a small once-prosperous Portuguese colonial town, about a mile square, single-storey houses and villas now looted and semi-destroyed by Mobutu's bands of marauding ex-prisoners, the Zorrens. It took the tail end of Callan's column the whole of the day to reach Maquela over the appalling roads and tracks that linked it with Sao Salvador; by the time the last vehicle was in, Tomkins had, on Callan's orders, blown the Rio Zandi bridge to the north of Maquela by which the advancing MPLA might have attempted a turning movement. Callan was no fool as a military commander; he had (as a psychiatrist who gave evidence at his trial for armed robbery in Ulster had attested) 'very ambitious leadership qualities', and he certainly inspired his men with his energy, his power of decision and his drive. Even those who hated him admitted afterwards, however reluctantly, that Callan was a fine soldier. By midnight the following night, that is to say, Sunday, 25 January, Callan had occupied the large village of Quibocolo forward of Maquela on the road to Damba, established a base camp behind Quibocolo, six miles south of Maquela, and personally supervised the placing of a five-man-strong 'killer group' in ambush only ten miles outside Damba from where the enemy might at any moment be expected to debouch.

The Cubans and MPLA column did advance from Damba that Monday morning, having cleared the road ahead – as they thought – by a barrage of 122 mm rockets. They were caught, therefore by surprise; and in this their first action the unblooded mercenaries (all five – Dempster, Boddy, Aves, McKenzie and Griffiths – were of the new group) were amazingly and encouragingly successful. According to his own account Chris Dempster scared the three leading Russian T34 tanks into beating a hasty retreat with his shoulder-fired 66 mm rocket launcher; and without firing a shot in reply the rest of the column turned tail and scuttled for Damba, leaving twenty-one dead on the road.

This little action had, as so often occurs in war, disproportionate results. First, it gave the newly arrived mercenaries confidence in themselves and in their leader; no more was seriously heard of killing Callan, even though on the following day one of his two initial comrades-in-arms, Wainhouse, had to be evacuated to Leo with dysentery. On the contrary the eleven – 'Fuzz' Hussey had remained behind alone in Sao Salvador, in charge of wireless communications – were now almost Callan's men too, of Callan's mind certainly that the MPLA and Cubans were, despite their superiority in arms and weapons, despicable adversaries, easily routed by professional soldiers such as Britain could produce. Secondly, it gave Callan the breathing space he desperately needed: for the enemy had been shaken and for the rest of the week, most fortunately for the thin white line of the FNLA 'army', made no attempt at all to advance. Callan was not strong enough yet to counterattack; but all his instincts were clearly that way, and he calculated that he would be strong enough when the promised reinforcements, the next batch of mercenaries, arrived from England. Meanwhile he continued to set up ambushes, arrange supplies, liaise with the President, and execute deserters. According to Dempster (whom Callan appointed commandant of Maquela itself) he even tested Charley's double-barrelled shotgun by calling over the nearest FNLA soldier, standing him to attention, inserting the shotgun in his mouth, and blowing his head apart like a mango – that after having at dawn the same day executed six FNLA whom he believed to be planning to desert on the slimmest of evidence. But by then, as Dempster put it, they were all used to the daily 'toppings'. Tomkins for his part made a special trip to study the 'man without a head' – of which 'the only recognizable part that remained was the jawbone, resting on the twisted neck like one half of a mangled pair of false teeth'. By then, in his own words, the safe blower had 'developed a ghoulish interest in the physical processes of death'.

Bufkin's Mission

On the Tuesday, the day following the ambush, Denard's remaining nine French mercenaries arrived in Leo for the UNITA assignment; and so, more significantly (for the French, true professionals, kept themselves very much to themselves) did two would-be American mercenaries. Bufkin had finally been persuaded to come out to Africa by Tom Oates, who had had to pay the air fare for both of them. 'Major' Nick Hall interviewed them on Holden Roberto's behalf, approved them both, appointed them captains in the FNLA army, and within a day Bufkin was flying back to the USA, with talk of recruiting a thousand Vietnam veterans within the week. Holden Roberto had virtually no funds to give him though – a few thousand dollars for expenses and salary – and of course in view of CIA dissaproval there would be no Congolese diplomats in Washington with suitcases full of dollar bills to back him up. Bufkin had to persuade the recruits he did find to pay their own air fares out; one of the few prepared to do so (despite the proviso in his initial advertise-ment in *Soldier of Fortune*) was the desperate, rather naive Daniel Gearhart. George Bacon III was neither naive nor desperate; but when he heard that Bufkin had actually been out to Leo and had met Holden Roberto, he determined to join Bufkin's 'army' if only as a means of winning an introduction to the FNLA President and presenting him with his own plans – for Bacon was a committed and idealistic anti-communist – for setting up a non-profit-making but efficient mercenary recruiting operation in the United States.

Meanwhile, however, pending Bufkin's return, the only American mercenary in central Africa – and he stayed in Leo – was 'Captain' Tom Oates, the former Los Angeles police sergeant. But Holden Roberto had on the Wednesday promised his Field Commander another hundred white soldiers; and, sure enough, on Thursday the 29th, news reached Sao Salvador that ninety-six new recruits, with John Banks in person 'in command', had landed safely at Leo aboard Sabena Flight 10288 from Brussels.

9

Friday, 30 January to
Tuesday, 17 February

Banks had in his way done wonders. He had raised and delivered, as promised and within a very tight time limit, almost exactly a hundred men – admittedly with the stimulus of £20,000 in 'recruiting fees' to urge him on. But even so, allowing for all the hesitations, waverings and backings-down inevitable in any rushed recruiting operation, it was an undeniable organisational feat. The only trouble was that the men Banks had recruited were by no means all fighting soldiers; there were, for instance, non-combatant medical orderlies among them, plus pilots, truck drivers, cooks, Banks' own two personal bodyguards 'Satch' Fortuin and Barry Maddison, PT instructors, and even a middle-aged Russian-speaking Scotsman whose job, he was told, would be to interrogate Russian prisoners; on his recruiting papers Banks had marked *Fluent Russian: Definite.*

For a conventional army, or even for a long-established mercenary operation, these men would, most of them, have been acceptable, fulfilling needed roles. But they were not what Callan wanted and they were not what Callan was expecting. Callan wanted fighting soldiers, with military experience, of the calibre of the first nineteen whom Banks had supplied; and understandably he expected that this second batch would be very much the same type. He waited impatiently at the 'palace' at Sao Salvador for them to arrive.

Instead, on the Friday morning 'Major' John Banks (as he had overnight become) arrived at Sao Salvador with an escort of ten of 'his' mercenaries, an advance guard. Banks, it seemed, was understandably uneasy. He had, after all, never set foot in Angola or the Congo before, he had no news of the progress or otherwise of 'his' first contingent, he had promised his new recruits a period of acclimatisation that they were obviously not going to be allowed to enjoy, and he had been told, in Leo, by his fellow 'Major', Nick Hall, that the mysterious Callan – whom he did not know, or knew at best only in his files under the name of Costas Georgiou – bore a grudge against him, having been rejected for the Rhodesian contract. The confrontation between Callan and Banks on the steps of the Sao

Salvador 'palace', with sub-machine guns cocked and ready on both sides, was therefore tense. But even more significant, minutes later when initial tension had fallen, was the encounter between Banks and his old friend and business partner, Dave Tomkins. According to Tomkins' own account, he realised at that moment that he would willingly kill Banks if Callan gave the order. As for Sammy Copeland, also once Banks' man, he – again according to Tomkins' account – warned Banks at one point that, 'if the supplies you promised don't turn up, I'm *personally* going to kill you'.

In the short ten days that had elapsed since they had set foot in Angola, the first group of Banks' recruits (bar McAleese and the other six shunted aside to San Antonio) had in other words definitely shifted allegiance: they were now Callan's men, even more so than Hall and Wainhouse, both now back in Leo, and neither of whom had actually engaged the enemy under Callan's orders. How far Callan's style had influenced those under his command is shown by what was happening that same day, that Friday, back in Maquela. There Chris Dempster as local commandant had decided on his first execution, and ordered up a firing squad to shoot a wretched Zorrens found in possession of some minor items of loot. The Zorrens was rescued at the very last moment by Jamie McCandless, who ordered his release – regardless of the fact that he, McCandless, had twenty four hours earlier executed two FNLA soldiers himself on Callan's orders. What had been words, possibly idle words, in London a fortnight early were becoming almost routine acts in Maquela. Just before leaving there for Sao Salvador, Callan and Copeland had tortured and gruesomely mutilated another suspected spy, and Copeland and McCandless had (on Callan's orders) shot dead – after allowing them to make a run for it – the two headmen who had captured the spy, watched with indifference by Chris Dempster and 'Canada' Newby. It is horrifying how quickly these men accustomed themselves to what had by now become almost mindless killing, killing for killing's sake.

Then McCandless himself was killed, the first white mercenary to die in Angola. With Callan absent in Sao Salvador, and no-one very clearly in command, he – the oldest and most experienced soldier on the spot – took it upon himself to commandeer a Landrover and drive out from the forward ambush position near Damba on a 'snatch'. He took Bryan Lewis and two FNLA soldiers with him. They managed the 'snatch' skilfully enough – two MPLA soldiers were spotted, surprised, disarmed and captured on foot in a village – but on the return journey the Landrover suddenly came under heavy machine-gun fire. All were killed, prisoners and escort alike; all bar Lewis who, though wounded, managed eventually to escape his pursuers and make his way back through the bush to Maquela where other and more murderous scenes were meanwhile being enacted.

John Banks, wisely, spent only an hour in Sao Salvador, returning with Holden Roberto – but without his abandoned and forgotten bodyguards – in the presidential Range Rover to the comparative safety of Leo. From there he flew back almost immediately to Heathrow, with instructions to recruit and despatch within the week another two hundred mercenaries on a formal six months' contract. Hall followed, with, apparently, $76,000 in cash, to pay initial expenses and also to charter an aeroplane for the flight – a more economic way of bringing out such large numbers and one that would avoid, also, the need for an overnight stop in Brussels. Banks was never to set foot in Angola or the Congo again. His associates in Camberley, Perren, Aspin and a newcomer introduced by Aspin, Donald Bishop, had meanwhile been busy with advertisements, interviewing and processing; and there seemed every likelihood that Security Advisory Services Ltd would be richer by a further £40,000 in recruiting fees before the week was out. But the vast sums of cash now floating around posed both a large problem in control to 'Dr' Belford in distant Leeds, and, it seems, an irresistible temptation to Aspin, who was given the task of chartering a plane from Dan Air – and, according to Banks, £49,000 to do this with – ready to fly out the following Friday with the third and by far the largest batch of mercenary recruits yet.

The New Recruits

Meanwhile, the second batch, still over ninety strong, had finally, after two nights of travelling, reached Maquela. They paraded before Callan early on the morning of Saturday, 31 January. The scene was being set for the most sanguinary and tragic episode of the whole Angolan affair. At first all seemed to go reasonably well. Callan had grown in stature as a leader of men. He welcomed the new recruits, he briefed them and he made it very clear what they could expect: the same rules of discipline as in the British Army (with the difference that any serious breach of these rules would be punished by death); and immediate entry into action in small mobile 'killer groups' to be infiltrated behind enemy lines and to concentrate on sudden attacks and ambushes, particularly against the Cuban-manned Russian tanks.

It seems that it was the mention of Russian tanks that was the last straw. The new recruits had been on the move since the previous Wednesday, never quite sure where they were heading or why, and once in Africa abandoned by the man they had imagined would continue to command them, the only 'leader' they knew, John Banks. Many of them had not only no fighting experience, they had never served in the British Army at all. Others, who had, had expected to be training black troops, not themselves to be thrown into the fray – and against far superior forces and weaponry. Murmuring arose, they broke ranks; and heated discussions ensued. Callan became, understandably, almost incoherent with rage. In the end he sorted out twenty-three non-combatants, men who were either unwilling to fight or who, he decided on interrogation, had no military experience at all. They were all told to strip to their underwear – the usual prelude to a Callan execution as Chris Dempster and Barry Freeman, two of the 'old hands' watching idly and cynically from a safe distance noted – but were then issued with fatigues, put under the charge of two stout middle-aged men. Ken Aitken and Brian Butcher, and handed over to Dempster for non-combatant duties behind the lines in Maquela. The rest, seventy-odd, were divided into three 'killer groups' one under Callan's personal command, one under Copeland and one under Shotgun Charlie.

By now it was believed that both McCandless and Lewis were dead. Dave Tomkins had been wounded in the buttocks by one of his own explosives and evacuated to Leo, as had Wainhouse with dysentery and Griffiths with a nervous breakdown. With Hussey in Sao Salvador and Dempster in Maquela, this left Callan with only six experienced mercenaries of the first intake, most of whom were out in ambush positions on the Damba road. The FNLA's invaluable Cessna, Portuguese piloted, brought news that the Cubans and their tanks, the proposed target of all three 'killer groups' were dug in further down the Damba road. But then came more news, by radio, that immediately diverted Callan: the town of Tomboco (see map p. 174) was reported to have fallen to another advancing tank-supported enemy column, and both San Antonio and Sao Salvador itself were thereby threatened. It looked as if the new intake had arived only just in time to save the situation for the FNLA. Callan assembled the twenty-odd men of his own 'killer group' and at once set out for Tomboco. Copeland, left in charge at Maquela – this time there was no failure by Callan to make it quite clear who was to command in his absence – was infected by Callan's own daring spirit. He decided on a frontal attack on the Cuban-MPLA position outside Damba, with two columns – one led by Chris Dempster, the other by 'Spider' Kelly, seemingly the most experienced of the new recruits – assaulting by night.

The 'killer groups' assembled for training on 66 mm rocket-launchers and for target practice at Quibocolo south of Maquela. Rain was falling, some of the new recruits were in tears, provoking sneers from the handful of Portuguese mercenaries and the fury of wounded national pride from the few hardened men of the first intake.

But at Maquela, meanwhile, morale was even lower. The non-combatants were shakily discussing their rights, their duties and their position, only too aware of their new Colonel's raging temper and his threat to shoot men for any serious breach of discipline. Their morale was not raised when Dempster and Freeman returned in search of more vehicles for the night attack. This was the first they had heard of a night attack; and to the two more experienced older men, 'CSM' Aitken and 'CQSM' Butcher, it sounded very much as if this apparently suicidal manoeuvre would end in the annihilation of Copeland's 'killer groups' and the descent of the Russian tanks upon Maquela and upon themselves by dawn the next day – at the latest. Night attacks are notoriously difficult to manage, even for experienced troops who have trained together – and the 'killer groups', so-called, were neither experienced nor trained nor practised. Dempster, despising what he later called 'their gutless attitude', advised the twenty-five non-combatants (that is, the twenty-three new recruits and the two 'fat men' Aitken and Butcher) to change into camouflage gear, equip themselves with FN rifles and be ready to move out that night and join in the attack. He and Freeman would be back after dark to pick up the Toyota, and he would hope – if they seriously wanted to avoid the Colonel's displeasure – to find them equipped and ready for action then.

Darkness fell. Stories of Cuban atrocities, much exaggerated, were told and repeated. Dempster did not reappear in a 'couple of hours' as he had promised. The non-combatants all the same changed from fatigue gear into camouflage uniform and then, armed with FN rifles and rocket-launchers, prepared for the worst. 'Non-combatants' they may have been but many were experienced soldiers, like James Marczynski, a former Coldstream Guardsman, and Kevin Whirity, an ex-sergeant in the 3rd Paras whose refusal to fight Callan had found almost inexplicable. 'If anyone dies, you'll be one of the first, okay?' Callan had screamed at him on the parade ground at Maquela that morning. Towards ten o'clock at night a small armed group set up a roadblock and ambush a hundred yards outside the bungalow they had been assigned as sleeping quarters. The remainder of the twenty-five (including the older men, Aitken and Butcher, and apparently under their directions) loaded supplies – all the food and ammunition they could find, also petrol and diesel oil – onto three trucks and clambered aboard, ready to dash north towards safety and the border if the terrifying Cubans broke through. It must have been almost midnight when a vehicle appeared, lights doused, heading towards the now-deserted bungalow. The group in ambush – on the orders of Aitken and Butcher according to one account – immediately opened fire.

But the vehicle they had raked was not the advance guard of the Cuban column. They may genuinely have believed it to be; but it seems far more likely that in their general jitteriness and state of near-panic they were ready to open up on anything that moved. One of them, Phil Davies, a twenty-two-year-old ex-soldier from Birmingham, fired a rocket that shattered the front of the vehicle, a Landrover. But, miraculously, none of the four men in the Landrover were killed or even wounded. It was of course Chris Dempster and Barry Freeman, returning as promised, bringing with them Tony Boddy and a new-intake mercenary they knew only as Max. 'Don't shoot,' yelled Dempster in the lull that followed, 'it's Commandant Chris! Stop, you crazy bastards . . . It's us, we're English!' The only reply, according to Dempster, was another hail of bullets that sent the four racing away from the Landrover to take cover; and from cover, as fast as their legs could carry them, out of Maquela. For they were now convinced, understandably, that an enemy column had outflanked them by night and that the Cubans had captured, and now held, Maquela. It must have been a Cuban ambush that had opened fire on them! Dempster and Freeman crawled through the bush to the safety of a village. Boddy and 'Max' found the Damba road and walked through the night to Quibocolo to report to their commanding officer, Copeland, that he was now cut off. They found Copeland there – he had postponed his night assault till the three of his six most experienced men returned – and he listened with growing fury and alarm to their story.

Meanwhile from Maquela the three trucks filled with non-combatants and supplies had taken the road north towards the Congo immediately after the 'successful' midnight ambush. None of those who had opened fire delayed to examine the consequences. Possibly none of them had heard Dempster cry out in English in the pause between the two bursts of firing. If indeed it had been a Cuban jeep, they would have had no alternative but to clear out before reprisals followed. On the other hand if they now suspected that it was one of Callan's lieutenants whom they had ambushed and very possibly killed, to stay would have been even more suicidal. They took the road west heading for Sao Salvador; then, a few miles outside Maquela, they branched off to the north, towards the little post of Cuimbata that marked the Congolese border. It may have been a near-spontaneous confused flight but this turn north began to make it look much more like a carefully-planned and well-organised desertion. Admittedly, once across the Congolese border the fugitives were not necessarily totally out of danger; but they would be only a few hours' drive from Leo, which they could hope to reach by first light: and in the capital of the Congo they would find, if not civilisation exactly, at least a refuge from the Cubans and from their Colonel, plus the longer-term security of a British Embassy and an international airport to see them safely home.

What they were not to know, though – and how their hearts must have sunk when they discovered it – was that at Cuimbata on the frontier Callan had, en route to Tomboco that morning, detached and posted a group of FNLA soldiers under the command of one of his 'killer group', an ex-SAS trooper named Terry Wilson. Wilson, as per orders, halted any traffic: in this case two northbound trucks (the third had been accidentally ditched and abandoned). In the darkness, at 2.00 in the morning, the fugitives now therefore found themselves surrounded by an unknown number of black soldiers nervously fingering their weapons. They might have attempted to shoot their way through; but it would have been neither wise nor in character. Instead, they tried to bluff. They told Wilson that Maquela had been overrun by a column of at least twenty Russian tanks; that they, despite being taken by surprise, had managed to knock out at least two tanks and kill a score of Cubans before beating a retreat. As for Copeland and his 'killer groups', they must all, alas, have been lost in the night attack on Damba. There was nothing to do but to flee across the border before the Cuban columns arrived.

Wilson did not agree. He was in radio contact with 'the Colonel'; and Callan, from Sao Salvador, on hearing his report, ordered Wilson to demolish a nearby bridge and thus halt the Cuban advance from captured (as he believed) Maquela. He himself would set out at once from Sao Salvador. As for the non-combatants, they were to be congratulated on having shown at least some fight – and sent back to meet him on the Sao Salvador-Maquela road. Wilson obeyed instructions.

Callan had found the 'enemy column' that had captured Tomboco to be a comparatively small affair. He had run headlong into it – a tank, a troop carrier and some MPLA infantry – with his 'killer group'. According to Tom Chambers, a member of Callan's group who claimed to have fought previously for the Nigerians in Biafra, Callan had reacted more quickly. The group had routed the enemy, killing twenty; and then Callan personally to Chambers' horror had shot eight prisoners. Leaving a small detachment in possession of Tomboco, they had made their way back to the 'palace' at Sao Salvador for the night. It says something for Callan's nerve that he reacted so aggressively to the reported fall of Maquela (coming, as it did, in the small hours when so many men's morale is at its lowest ebb) and to the apparent loss of two-thirds of his forces, including almost all his best men.

As for the twenty-five would-be fugitives, a certain understandable lassitude after the strains and stresses of the past day and night seems to have overtaken them. They did what they were told. They drove back to the Sao Salvador – Maquela road, as ordered, turned right towards Sao Salvador rather than left towards Maquela, as ordered, were met by Callan a few miles past the turn, told him the same story as they had told Wilson and were at once set to digging a defensive position on a hillside covering the road, in anticipation of the expected Cuban advance. Callan went forward with an armoured personnel carrier, a Dodge, and his Portuguese mercenaries to reconnoitre a possible ambush site.

The Massacre of the Deserters

It must have been already dawn when, to his amazement the 'Colonel' saw a Landrover careering towards him from the direction of Maquela carrying the men he believed to be dead, men who in hot pursuit of the non-combatants had already been to Cuimbata and had heard from Wilson the lies the fugitives had been spinning. Copeland, Dempster, Freeman, Aves, Boddy and Andy MacKenzie piled out of the vehicle – Copeland to be embraced by Callan with tears in his eyes. They poured out their story excitedly: the ambush that had almost killed three of them, the certainty that the Cubans must have taken Maquela, the discovery by an enraged Copeland hours later that Maquela was not only deserted and unoccupied but emptied of all reserves of fuel and ammunition; and, the final insult added to injury, the reported boasting by the twenty-five murderous and cowardly liars that they had destroyed Russian tanks and killed Cuban soldiers. 'So you're not dead in Maquela, eh?' Callan repeated several

times with a grim smile when he had finally taken in the story; and, as
he moved down towards the foxholes being dug in the hillside, he
added: 'I want to see those two fat men get it. I want to see them with
their guts hanging out.'

The twenty-four* were still fully armed; it was their last chance to
act as a group and reverse the situation. But they were, unlike Callan
and his six and the Portuguese, unused to killing; they clearly lacked a
leader; and Callan showed self-control enough to approach them with
apparent calm and good humour. Within the hour, disarmed and
under arrest, they were back once again in Maquela, parading on the
square where they had first paraded on arrival only twenty-four hours
earlier. This time, however, the rest of the second intake, the other
seventy, were drawn up not side by side with, but facing them. And at
every corner of the square were armoured vehicles or jeeps, manned
by Portuguese mercenaries – Uzio, Madeira and Sergeanaro, another
of Callan's first followers – with their machine-guns and sub-
machine guns trained not only on the prisoners but also, just in case
of trouble, on all the new intake.

There was no trouble. The only 'trouble' was that the two fat men,
Aitken and Butcher, had somehow managed to slip off the trucks on
their drive back into Maquela, and thereby had preserved their guts
intact. Two more younger men in the confusion of the arrival and the
parade had also, at least for the moment, escaped from the line-up.
There were therefore twenty deserters on parade. As Callan haran-
gued them with understandably incoherent fury – 'These were no
Cubans, you bastards. You tried to cover murder up and leave
everybody with no fuel, no ammo, no food. . . . My ten men been here
for two weeks, no sleep or food, holding the Cubans in Damba and
you bastards tried to kill them. . . .' – one or two had the temerity to
grin. The 'Colonel' pulled himself tightly together.

'Who fired the rocket at my men last night?' he asked.

'Me, Sir,' replied Phil Davies.

Davies stepped forward with a half-apologetic smile on his face.
Callan flourished his pistol.

'This is the only law here,' he said.

He then shot Davies in the head three times.

According to Dempster, it was Dempster who then, for pity's sake,
suggested to Callan that he should offer the rest at least one more
chance to fight. Five men stepped forward: Kevin Whirity, the ex-3rd
Para sergeant whom Callan had earlier threatened with death, Dave

---

* The twenty-fifth, Malcolm Mott, a nineteen-year-old mechanic, had been (fortunately for
him) a little earlier sent off to Sao Salvador – with Shotgun Charlie as his driver.

Paden, Mike McKeown, Colin Evans and – on Callan's call for a driver for himself – Kevin Marchant. Freeman saved another, whose name is not known, by claiming to have fought with him in Northern Ireland.

As for the rest, the remaining thirteen now stripped to their underpants and standing, dazed, against a wall, it must be doubtful whether they were able to take in the awful finality of what had happened to Davies or what was about to happen to themselves.

'Take them away, Sergeant Major', said Callan to Copeland. 'You know what to do with them.'

The prisoners were loaded into the Dodge troop carrier. Uzio drove it out of Maquela, with Dempster sitting armed at his side. Behind it came a Landrover carrying not only an almost hysterically excited Sammy Copeland and the other two men, who, with Dempster, had nearly been killed the midnight before in the deserters' ambush – Barry Freeman and Tony Boddy – but also, to round out the numbers and on Callan's orders, Paul Aves and Andy MacKenzie. About three miles outside Maquela, Copeland gave the order to halt by a gently sloping grass valley. Some of the deserters were crying. They were ordered out; and told to turn and face the valley. The five-man squad was lined up at attention behind them. Copeland then ordered the wretched thirteen to make a run for it. Most did so. As they ran, Copeland opened fire with his sub-machine gun. On his orders, the other five also fired. It must have been a nightmarish scene, especially in that pastoral, pleasant setting. The fifty-two-year-old Scotsman, Jock McCartney, who had signed on as an interrogator in Russian, refused to run and pleaded for his life. Copeland smiled and shot him in the belly. Dempster finished him off with a bullet in the head. Several of the remaining twelve had been terribly wounded but not killed. The execution squad moved forward into the grass valley to adminster the *coups-de-grâce*. Dempster killed one more man, Boddy and Freeman one each. Copeland finished off at least three. In what Dempster describes as a 'stunned silence' the executioners, themselves perhaps barely aware of what they had done, drove back to Maquela.

It is Dempster's account of the massacre that I have followed here. It appears to be accurate, insofar as it can be checked against other accounts, except for the curious and inexplicable fact that Dempster insists that there were only eleven deserters executed outside Maquela, not thirteen. In his account he tends slightly to whitewash the only three members of the execution squad still living: himself, Barry Freeman and Paul Aves. The *coups-de-grâce* were, he insists, just that, an act of mercy. He blames all on the taunting, jeering Copeland and (to a lesser extent) on the exultant Tony Boddy, avenging – as it were – his own best friend, Jamie McCandless' death. Dempster says he deliberately arranged – as did Freeman – for his gun to jam, and stresses that they were all themselves covered by Uzio with his machine-gun. In other words they were only obeying orders; and that without relish – this despite the fact that they were (in the case of Dempster, Freeman and Boddy) executing men who only a few hours earlier had, as they certainly believed, treacherously ambushed and deliberately tried to kill them. I have my doubts about their later report of their own feelings and restraint.

What is quite undeniable, however, is that Callan took no direct part in the mass execution. He ordered it and he killed, under considerable provocation, one man. Were the killings justified? It is for the readers to judge. Certainly there was no court martial, and no formalities. On the other hand a similar episode in the British Army – desertion in the face of the enemy in time of war, aggravated by the stealing of all the unit's remaining stocks of fuel and ammunition – would almost certainly have led to a similar, though more formalised, result. Of course in another sense the men who should have been shot were John Banks and his associates, for sending out untrained recruits instead of fighting men, and this purely for personal profit. That was the root cause of the whole tragedy. But even in John Banks' case it is impossible to be certain that he acted with culpable dishonesty. What seems, in the end, almost more shocking than the executions themselves is the eerily haphazard manner in which of the twenty-five deserters the fourteen who died were selected. They were probably the least guilty. For Aitken and Butcher, who were almost certainly the brains behind the planned desertion and if so deserved to die more than the rest, were casually pardoned by Callan the following day and placed in charge of the stores at Maquela. Similarly, it seems more than likely that it was Kevin Whirity, the fighting soldier with most experience, who set up the ambush that nearly killed Dempster and his companions – yet Whirity had, at the last moment, saved his own skin. It was as if the bloodletting had been necessary to assuage Callan's wrath, and as if, instinctive and changeable as an animal, tigerish, he cared nothing at all about the rights and wrongs, the life or death, of individual beings. But, his wrath once assuaged, he was ready to put the whole episode behind him and concentrate only on future action. He and Copeland decided to launch immediately the attack that Copeland had planned for the previous night on the Cuban position outside Damba – the 'redeem-ing attack' as Callan now christened it.

Callan's Last Battle

It is hard not to feel at least a twinge of admiration for the brutal energy of these two men, Callan and Copeland. They were murder-ous towards their own side but they were not personal cowards, not armchair warriors who let others take the risks for them while remaining careful not to risk their own lives. On the contrary: they led from the front. They set out that afternoon from the base camp outside Maquela with sixty men in eight heavily armed Landrovers. At Quibocolo one of the Landrovers, slightly off course, was blown up by an FNLA minefield and another badly damaged: three of the new intake were killed and eight wounded, a fearsome 'own goal', yet still Callan did not call off or delay the attack. A third Landrover, piled high with bodies both alive and dead, was detached and sent back to Maquela; and with less than fifty men now crammed into five Landrovers Callan drove at dusk, quite deliberately and at top speed, straight into the enemy's ambush position. These totally suicidal tactics amazingly paid off. Even the appearance of four apparently indestructible Russian T54 tanks, with much heavier armour than the T34s, did not rout the mercenaries, now on foot and spraying the enemy's roadside bivouacs. Two of their remaining Landrovers were destroyed; but Callan alone accounted for two tanks, Copeland for one, and the new recruits finally, after nine hits, for the fourth – which 'brewed up' and exploded. Its flying debris severely wounded two of the attackers.

Nine more mercenaries were slightly wounded. But in the whole action, that had lasted only a few minutes and had for the second time sent the enemy scuttling back in panic and dismay to the safety of Damba, these were Callan's only casualties – as opposed to the two hundred enemy dead that Callan claimed. The 'accidental' casualties had been far more serious – bringing the total of the 'new intake' killed that day to seventeen in all, with nineteen more wounded: not far short of half the total force now left to defend Maquela. Back in Maquela that night Callan slept for the last time a victor's deep – but possibly far from dreamless – sleep.

Next day, Tuesday, 3 February, Bryan Lewis, long given up for dead, appeared at Maquela – and on hearing of what had been happening, promptly deserted with two more of the 'old hands', Barry Freeman and Pat MacPhearson. They commandeered the Fokker

Friendship that had brought the American 'Captain' Tom Oates on his first visit to Angola, persuading the Portuguese pilot that they needed urgent medical treatment in Leo. Up to the moment of take-off Freeman stood in the plane's doorway with his gun cocked, ready to shoot Callan or Copeland if either should appear on the scene.

Neither did. Callan was far less concerned about his original band now that the new intake had been so successfully blooded in the 'redeeming attack' of dusk on Monday. He and Copeland, and Shotgun Charley with them, back from Sao Salvador on Monday night, had been up and out on the rampage again since well before dawn on Tuesday, determined to follow up their successful blow of the eve with another crippling attack. This time it was a smaller 'killer group' that Callan and Copeland took with them; but they were still twenty-four strong in all, over half the remaining surviving and unwounded men.

This time there was no headlong attack. Astutely Callan varied his tactics. Several miles outside Damba he dismounted his men and they advanced stealthily on foot – their one casualty being 'Satch' Fortuin, who sprained his ankle. Before dawn they had set up a carefully sited ambush on high ground and there settled in to wait for the tank-led column to debouch from Damba once again. That day, Tuesday, was mainly passed in waiting. Two enemy Landrovers went by. Callan held his fire. Several truckloads of MPLA troops went by. Callan still held his fire. But by late afternoon his natural impatience proved stronger than his now-skilful tactical sense. He led his men forward. On the road ahead they saw a cluster of tanks, trucks and Landrovers, plus an armoured bulldozer – the sharp end (though they were not at once aware of it, for the rest of the convoy was out of sight) of a vast straggling mile-long column of 1,600 troops under the joint command of high-ranking Cuban officers and a Russian adviser known as 'General Yuri'. The MPLA and their allies had called up strong reinforcements to put an end, once and for all, to the impertinent FNLA counterattacks from Maquela that were robbing them of their expected victory. The convoy had halted. Ahead of it – and it was just as well that Callan had instinctively abandoned his wheeled transport – a helicopter was scanning the Damba-Maquela road for any sign of FNLA activity.

Callan's men crawled close to the head of the column and then, suddenly, attacked. Within seconds they had crippled three tanks and Callan, 'laughing and shouting', was seen 'mowing down the Cubans scrambling to escape from the burning wrecks'. They took to the bush again, then attacked again, in roughly the centre of the column, wiping out two truckloads of MPLA troops and another tank. They took to the bush again and, still closer to Damba, set up an ambush on a temporarily empty stretch of road. This time three Russian-built armoured cars and two more truckloads of troops, driving forwards, were halted and largely mown down. Callan 'with a total disregard for his own safety ran laughing into the road' – a sort of latter-day berserker.

The Cuban commanders must have thought that there were enemy ambushes in position and springing to life all up and down the road. They seem to have had little idea of who or what was hitting them, or from where, and certainly not the least idea of how to deal with these short sudden attacks, three of which had decimated their column in the space of an hour and a half. Dusk was now falling and Callan beat a retreat through the bush. But he decided, being the man he was, on one last attack before he and his exhausted but elated little band sought the safety of their own transport a few miles back – an attack on the feared bulldozer which they found still where it had been originally, stationary at the head of the column. But this time Nemesis struck. An ammunition truck, hit probably by Callan's own rocket, exploded. It was carrying several tons of ammunition, and it blew apart scores of men on both sides, mercenaries and MPLA alike.

Copeland survived unwounded; and, according to Copeland, in the exchange of fire that followed as through the smoke and the dark Cuban troops moved forward to counter attack, Tony Boddy was shot dead – but shot through the back of the head, by, that is, a fellow-mercenary. (But Dempster, to whom Copeland recounted this story, believes that Boddy died later. His shooting in the back of the head had of course, if true, highly unpleasant implications for Dempster – that the new intake of mercenaries were out to 'get' members of the execution squad.) Nine other mercenaries died or disappeared. A mercenary known only as 'Ginger' had his leg blown off. Callan himself, the invincible Callan, was struck by shell casing below the knee and lamed. He and 'Ginger' had to be carried away. Thirteen of the mercenaries, who survived the explosion, carried them under Copeland's orders from the scene of that almost infernal noise and carnage. During the night they spent in the open bush 'Ginger' died and Callan became delirious with fever. At dawn – the dawn of Wednesday, 4 February – two of the survivors were sent out on a recce. Both were ambushed by the MPLA troops now combing the whole area, and killed. There were now twelve men left including Callan, exactly half the original 'killer group' that had set out from

Maquela forty-eight hours earlier. Malcolm McIntyre, recruited as a
medical orderly carried Callan on a rough stretcher, helped – suitably
– by Kevin Marchant, the mercenary who had saved his own life by
volunteering as Callan's driver.

That day they stumbled across the isolated hut of a peasant, Joao
Antonio, and his wife Sende Isabel, whom they held hostage, inside
the hut, for fear of betrayal. There seemed to be food enough there
for several days. Copeland and one of the new intake, John Malone
from Glasgow, set off through the surrounding swampland to fetch
help. Later Shotgun Charley and Sergeanaro (Madeira, Callan's very
first fellow-fighter, had been killed in the final attack) followed;
leaving seven men and the wounded Callan in the hut of the
apprehensive Angolans; Copeland, and later Shotgun Charley, each
with their companion, appeared safely, though dazed, in Maquela
twenty-four hours later – to give Dempster and the rest the news that
the 'killer group' had been eliminated and to insist that Callan,
wounded and abandoned, must be rescued. They felt a loyalty to
Callan that Dempster, understandably, did not share. He set out for
Sao Salvador, theoretically to fetch fuel for the proposed 'rescue
column' but in fact with the intention of deserting. 'Fuzz' Hussey, in
Sao Salvador, decided to join him.* They drove north next day, 'all
along the road looking anxiously behind them in case Copeland,
Charley or even Callan was on their tail'. That was on Thursday, 5
February, the day on which the news reached Leo in garbled form
that many of the mercenaries had been killed by their own comrades,
apparently on Callan's own orders. News followed that Callan himself
had been missing for three days.

The Third Batch

In England, meanwhile, far from – and totally unaware of – the
troubles that had befallen the ninety-plus men he had left behind only
a few short days before, John Banks had succeeded in assembling
another two hundred men. The scale of the operation had now
become so great, however, that the press – all the press – was
inevitably hot on the story; for this was the first ever major recruiting
campaign of mercenaries in Britain to be conducted almost publicly.

* Of the first intake of nineteen, therefore, only Sammy Copeland was still in Maquela. A third,
Andy MacKenzie, was with Callan in the hut. Two were dead: the 'Siamese twins', Jamie
McCandless and Tony Boddy; one, Paul Aves, was missing, and the rest had 'deserted' to Leo;
bar of course the seven in San Antonio who still knew nothing of what had been going on.

Banks' main problem was to assemble the new recruits, and then to hold them together, keeping the press at bay, till the charter aircraft was ready for take-off. An odd sort of paperchase, all around London and its outskirts, followed. The new recruits were bedded down on the night of Monday, 2 February in the crypt of an East End church, St George's – which made a great story for the popular press when they discovered it, as they did. Next night Banks switched them, as 'the Innsbruck Ski Club', to the Park Court Hotel in Lancaster Gate. By the following night their numbers had almost halved, as many, more frightened by the publicity than attracted by the pay, cried off. They were scattered around hotels in Gatwick. But the Dan-Air charter, promised by Aspin for the Wednesday, was not ready on the Thursday either; and on the Friday – 6 February – Banks, presumably faced with hotel bills he was unwilling and possibly unable to continue to pay, dismissed his men. About half of them were promptly re-recruited by one of Aspin's associates, John Chownes; for in the quarrels viciously raging about money and responsibilities Aspin, by laying his hands on most of the cash brought over by Nick Hall, had virtually succeeded in making himself the piper that called the tune. On the night of Sunday, 8 February, fifty new recruits, the third 'intake', were finally winging their way out to the Congo in two separate groups: twenty-four aboard a Sabena flight from Brussels, twenty-six aboard a Swiss Air flight from Zurich. But on that very Sunday night, as they were in the air, the story of the 'massacre of the mercenaries' at last broke, garbled and inaccurate in detail but true enough in its gist, and for the first time listeners to radio and, later, spectators on television heard the name – though they knew nothing of the personality – of 'Colonel Callan'. The sensation was immediate, and so was the outcry. What had seemed to be a farcical affair earlier that week in London was turning out to be a macabre and bewildering tragedy out in Africa. The Foreign Office had instantly requested the Congolese government to put an end to the use of their country as a base for British mercenaries. In immediate reaction not so much to the Foreign Office as to the worldwide uproar Mobutu ordered the Swissair flight turned back. The Sabena flight was allowed to land at 10.30 that Monday morning; but the twenty-four mercenaries aboard were escorted into the airport by armed guards and locked into a room, without explanation – a prelude, apparently, to their expulsion on the same plane when it flew out on its return journey later that night. It would have been better for many of them if they had calmly accepted their sweltering 'detention'. They did not. They broke out early that afternoon through a baggage hatch, commandeered a fleet of taxis, and managed to make their way successfully, though pursued, to the FNLA villa-compound. There they reported to the new Field Commander of the FNLA, 'Colonel' Peter McAleese.

The Killing of Sammy Copeland

McAleese had been appointed to fill the post of the missing Callan four days earlier, on the morning of Thursday, 5 February. That must have been a day that will remain engraved on McAleese's memory for as long as he lives: the day that saw the final act in what was becoming almost the Shakespearian tragedy of Maquela. Holden Roberto flew down to San Antonio early that morning and there he informed the astounded mercenaries that Callan (whom they hardly knew) and Copeland (whom they knew comparatively well) had murdered fourteen British recruits – whom they knew not at all. By midday McAleese, with Rennie at this side, was in Leo, at the Mama Yemo hospital, questioning there the members of their own intake, such as Dave Tomkins (who knew little) and the semi-deserter Barry Freeman (who knew much more) about the events in Maquela. Holden Roberto, who had had both McAleese and Rennie flown back with himself in his plane, allowed them to conduct their own enquiries. Then the President held a council of war, with McAleese, Rennie, the American Tom Oates (the only one there to have set foot in Maquela since the killings and since Callan's last foray) and with two of Callan's own original companions, 'Major' Nick Hall and 'Captain' Mick Wainhouse. Of them all Wainhouse, his partner in the Ulster post office robbery, knew Callan best: and it seems that Wainhouse offered to go back to Maquela alone and there try to liquidate the unsuspecting Callan. (Clearly all who knew him were convinced of Callan's near-invincibility and expected him to be by then safely back in Maquela, as both Copeland and Shotgun Charley were, and once again in command.) McAleese, now Field Commander in Callan's place, was in a difficult position. It was hard to imagine how violently Callan might react to the news of his own dimissal. Nevertheless, McAleese decided, Callan should be court martialled, not murdered. The whole group of them, therefore, with the President – five white mercenaries and their employer – flew down to Maquela.

At the airport they were met not by Callan but by Charley with his shotgun much in evidence but, though apprehensive, easily put at ease till he was disarmed. McAleese, who hardly knew the Cypriot, hit him several times in the face with the butt of his own shotgun. 'I wasn't even effing there,' shouted Charley. Sammy Copeland, found at the base camp, was equally easily induced by this group of 'superior officers' to relax and to be parted from his Uzi sub-machine gun.

A drumhead courtmartial of the two was held on the spot, then and there, that Thursday afternoon in the base camp outside Maquela, with a stream of witnesses from the surviving recruits of the second intake – who had witnessed of course not the mass execution itself but the parade of the deserters and the killing of Phil Davies in front of them. Callan, Davies' murderer, was as much on trial in his absence as the two formally present and accused; but by this stage it seemed obvious that Callan (and the other seven mercenaries still missing) must have been tracked down and killed by the MPLA. Holden Roberto held himself unhappily apart from the trial; in view of the language barrier his presence would have been useless. He vested his authority in Major Nicholas Hall who presided – Hall whose only experience of courtmartials, as it was later pointed out, had been that of his own, in Ulster, in the 1st Paras, for selling weapons to the Protestant extremists. The five judges reached their verdict in half an hour. Shotgun Charley was acquitted of mass murder; Sammy Copeland was convicted. He was sentenced to immediate execution and a firing squad was detailed. But even here, even in this comparatively clear-cut situation, the old initial rivalry and mistrust between the first group, the group of four, and the second group, the group of nineteen, flared once again. McAleese, incredibly, demanded that Copeland, whom he knew, should be spared and Shotgun Charley, 'that wog', whom he did not know, should be executed in his place. Hall hastily appealed to Holden Roberto; who confirmed the original sentence. It was rough and ready justice but no-one could – or can – deny that it was justice of a sort.

As the argument was continuing, outside in the open where the execution was to be held, Copeland made a surprise move. He was not the sort of man to wait passively to be shot down as his own victims had done. He broke away, dashing for the bush and for cover. If the firing squad had not been standing by, ready, he might have made a temporary escape. As it was, he ran swerving from side to side, and over twenty shots were fired before one hit him in the body and brought him down before he could reach the corner of the building and safety. He lay curled on the ground, still alive. Wainhouse, Callan's partner, whom in a sense Copeland had replaced, walked over with his pistol and fired three shots into the back of Copeland's head. 'That's him finished then,' he said, a banal and casual verdict on a man who had been more dangerous and dynamic than himself. As for McAleese, possibly as a sort of counterstroke, an assertion of his own new authority in face of Wainhouse and Hall, he ordered that Callan, if by any chance he should reappear, should be shot on sight.

Callan did not reappear at Maquela, staggering out of the bush, nor did any of his comrades. If he had done so, would those formerly under his command have had the pitiless courage to shoot him, as ordered, on sight? Even if he had been on a stretcher, I doubt it. Particularly as their new commanding officer did not stay to enforce his orders. He left Wainhouse in charge, though, Callan's would-be executioner-by-treachery. McAleese, Hall and Rennie flew back to Leo, to interrogate Dempster, whom many had witnessed on his return to Maquela after the executions, pumping bullets into Phil Davies' body which, according to Dempster, had still been breathing. Within twenty-four hours the remaining mercenaries at Maquela – basically 'Spider' Kelly and his men – had followed them. Maquela, for which so much blood had been spilt, was abandoned to the enemy without anything in the nature of a last stand. Neither Wainhouse nor McAleese were remotely of Callan's or even Copeland's calibre as leaders or fighting men.

The Fall of San Antonio

Maquela 'fell' on the Friday. On the Saturday, at the other extremity of what was left of the FNLA enclave, at San Antonio, panicky black sentries ran to McAleese's 'military headquarters', a large white house close to the Congo River. McAleese of course was no longer there; in his absence 'Brummie' Barker had been put in command. The five remaining mercenaries had been roused the day before on what had turned out to be a false alarm. They took therefore little notice of the reports that the enemy were in the town's outskirts, particularly as there were no gunshots. But when they saw their Angolan cook hurriedly put on his overcoat – it was a rainy day, breakfast time – and dubiously gathered at the doorway, guns cocked, it was to face a Russian-built armoured car from which heavily armed men were debouching and scattering for cover.

They ran for it. In preparation for this very eventuality McAleese, no Callan, had had a motor-boat moored and ready at the nearby jetty. With them was an American journalist, a young woman named Robin Wright, who had arrived with Holden Roberto on one of his earlier trips and had stayed on. She ran for the jetty too, and made the boat in time, along with sixteen Angolans and three of the five mercenaries. But Mike Johnson was killed as he ran, the ex-legionary, the ex-Marine Commando, the man whom John Banks had appointed 'commander' of his 150 'army' for the non-existent Rhodesian contract. And 'Brummy' Barker, who had been trying to organise the 'evacuation', was left behind on the shore (for which he later blamed John Tilsey's panic) in his underpants, stripped to swim but not daring to dive into the bullet-torn water as the motorboat headed fast across the Congo estuary for the far shore, Mobutu's territory, and safety. Possibly it was the presence of Robin Wright that inspired him, moments later, to tell his captors that he was not a mercenary but a *Daily Mirror* reporter and thus avoid immediate execution.

That night Robin Wright (who was reporting for *The Christian Science Monitor*) and the three mercenaries who had escaped, Tilsey, Saunders and McPherson, staggered into the Intercontinental Hotel in Leo – much to the relief, tingled with professional jealousy, of the two radio correspondents on whom, five days earlier, she had stolen a march. Attractive twenty-eight-year-old blondes can wheedle their way into the front line where older and maturer males, like in this case John Simpson of the BBC and Neil Wilson of NBC, meet only with prevarication and frustrating excuses. Since their arrival in Leo, John Simpson and his colleague had seen nothing of the front and nothing of any fighting mercenaries – having to be content with such hotel contacts as the blustering Colin Taylor, always threatening to shoot journalists, the disgusting Nick Hall, who was once seen jabbing a burning cigarette into the eyeballs of a Congolese who displeased him, the sinister white youth they nicknamed 'the Cyanide Kid' and the silent, macabre Dave Bufkin with his red beret and ex-Vietnam combat gear. The three Robin Wright led in were the first fighting mercenaries they had actually seen – and these three spent the night cowering in John Simpson's bedroom, trembling at every waiter's footstep outside the door, fearing that at any moment an FNLA execution squad might burst in to shoot them down as deserters. 'What shall we do, sir?' they said. As the long long night wore on and John Simpson reassured the three that he would see them safely to the British Embassy next day, their reserve began to crack and their tongues to loosen. 'Tell everyone not to come out here,' said the shaven-headed Dougie Saunders. 'No-one should join the FNLA.' He looked around at his companions and his voice trembled: 'It's been dreadful – white men shooting white men.' Bit by bit the story started to emerge, though they hardly knew the details themselves. It had happened about a week before – fourteen British mercenaries killed in cold blood. Then their own commander, a 'Jock' called Pete, had flown off, and there had been more shootings. An RSM had been executed – Sammy his name was. But the other one, the one who'd been responsible for the killings, the Colonel, he had been ambushed and probably killed. The Colonel's name? They didn't know.

Next morning, the Sunday, John Simpson flew back to Brussels convinced that he had the biggest scoop of his life – only to find on arrival that evening that his NBC colleague had pipped him to the post. Neil Wilson had found out the Colonel's name from Robin Wright – and by Sunday evening his own radio report had been picked up by networks all over the world; from his thick Australian accent it sounded as if the man's name was 'Cullen'.

That was why, with journalists now swarming out to the Congo by every available flight and 'Cullen's' background rapidly and success-fully being investigated in England, the new batch of mercenaries were 'detained' at Leo airport on the Monday morning. When they reached the FNLA villa-compound that afternoon McAleese did not hesitate. He flew the whole group (except for one middle-aged Norwegian doctor, Arnold Dahlseng, who needed to go on to South Africa to collect medical supplies) immediately down to Sao Salvador, the one town of any importance remaining in the FNLA's hands.

The End at Sao Salvador

Militarily the situation was – in the time-honoured phrase – desperate but not hopeless. Wainhouse, 'Shotgun' Charley, 'Canada' Newby and Sergeanaro were in Sao Salvador, a scattering of old hands briefly joined by Tomkins and Lewis once again. Two Chinese-built tanks, a missile launcher and a miniature Chinese version of the 'Stalin's organ' had been contributed by Mobutu and were in place. Rennie and four other mercenaries were out at Tomboco, with two hundred black troops, twenty-three new British mercenaries (in fact including two Hungarians and a German) had now arrived – and they were followed, the next day after an overnight drive from Leo by yet more reinforcements – the American contingent.

Not that Bufkin had been able to recruit anything remotely approaching the thousand Vietnam veterans of which he had been talking. He had arrived in Leo on the Saturday with a mere six, all of whom had had to pay their own airfares; and of the six, one, Eugene Scaley, took refuge in the US Embassy that night demanding to be repatriated. The remaining five were George Bacon III, Daniel

Gearhart, who had advertised in *Soldier of Fortune*, Bufkin's 'secretary', Lobo do Sol – and two whose names have not yet been mentioned, 'Gus' Grillo, a mafioso-type of Argentinian origin, and Gary Acker, a Californian and ex-corporal aged twenty-one.

Right from the start things did not go well with the ill-fated American contingent. The newcomers decided they had been misled by Bufkin's claim to be an 'official recruiter' and were, rather contradictorily, indignant when Bufkin informed them that he was returning to the States immediately with thousands of dollars handed over to him by Holden Roberto to bring back more recruits. There were toings and froings, wavings of guns and exchanges of threats, in the corridors of the Intercontinental Hotel. The upshot was that they forced Bufkin against his will to accompany them to Sao Salvador – Oates was to go back to America as 'official recruiter' in his place. But the taste for courtmartials seemed to be growing in the doomed mercenary force; and, before leaving, Oates flew down, with Hall, to preside at Sao Salvador over Bufkin's courtmartial on a charge of misappropriating FNLA property. He was found guilty and sentenced to fight at the front without pay: in the circumstances a mild reproof.

But the ones who were not courtmartialled, though perhaps they ought to have been, were the main body of mercenaries still in the area – over forty of them, mainly of the second intake, in Leo. It is not at all clear whether McAleese, in Leo, was spending most of his time in trying to persuade them to return to the front and whether the British Embassy was countering his efforts; but I imagine that he was and they were. Their presence, a really solid reinforcement, more then doubling the number of mercenaries, might have swung the balance at Sao Salvador. As it was, they all flew back to England on the Monday night – to face at Heathrow a press barrage for many and for Freeman and Dempster close interrogation about their part in the Maquela massacre from the police. (Callan of course was the focus of the press' curiosity. He's a real nut,' said one returning and only moderately inaccurate mercenary. 'He was still alive when we left him but that was nine days ago 30 kilometres inside enemy territory and he was badly injured in both legs by a mortar bomb and then he'd been shot by a British mercenary. He must be dead.' As for Freeman and Dempster, though they admitted their 'involuntary' part in the killings, they were released on the Thursday, the Director of Public Prosecutions having announced that no charges would be instigated in the affair.) Tomkins and Lewis were out of Sao Salvador and back that same week, Wainhouse was back in Leo too with dysentery again,

Bufkin escaped on the pretext of trying to find and fit up an aeroplane to be piloted by himself and was not seen again, Rennie and his four had abandoned Tomboco to enemy armoured cars, two of the latest intake had deserted, one, Vic Gawthrop, had died of a heart attack (and was buried, macabrely, on a full-sized bed); and McAleese, the Field Commander, was hardly ever in the field. It looked as if the whole mercenary operation was collapsing.

That it did not was really due to two men, Mick Rennie, now promoted to 'Captain' and virtually in command at Sao Salvador itself, and Shotgun Charley. They planned, originally, to form three 'killer groups' – one under Shotgun Charley himself, one under 'Canada' Newby and one under Mick Wainhouse – and retake Maquela. Callan's aggressive spirit rather amazingly still lived on. Wainhouse's departure changed but did not scotch the plan. What scotched it were aerial reports of a large Cuban/MPLA convoy having moved out of Maquela heading for Sao Salvador. That was on the morning of Saturday, 14 February. The enemy were reported at Cuimba only forty miles east. Shotgun Charley took out a Landrover patrol to investigate – consisting of himself, two of the Americans, Daniel Gearhart and Gus Grillo, and two young British mercenaries of the latest intake, John Nammock and his great friend Andy Holland.

By that evening the patrol had not returned, and nothing had been heard from it. All the same 'Canada' Newby set out that night with a fighting patrol, three Landrovers strong, to attack and halt the head of the advancing enemy column. They reached Cuimba Junction before the village, camped, set demolition charges to two bridges; and then, in the confusion of the early morning and conflicting radio messages, separated, with half the patrol reporting back to Sao Salvador where McAleese had arrived. 'Canada' himself patrolled forward at high speed towards Cuimba village in one Landrover, crowded with mercenaries: two Americans, George Bacon III and Gary Acker, three Englishmen, Malcolm Dimmock, John Cashmore, and the RSM of the new intake, Dickens, and one Portuguese, Nilsson.

They did not come back either. McAleese, flown forward in the Cessna, spotted the enemy convoy of seventy-five vehicles including tanks and armoured cars, led by the mine-sweeping bulldozer, heading past Cuimba for Sao Salvador. He flew back to Sao Salvador, ordered an immediate evacuation, apologised to his men for leaving them in a tight spot and sought safety in Leo. Rennie organised the blowing-up of the FNLA 'palace'. By that evening, Sunday, 15 February, Sao Salvador had fallen to the enemy, without anything in the nature of a last stand. On the 16th the twenty-vehicle convoy under Rennie's command was at Luvo; on the 17th it crossed the border into the Congo and safety. The war in Angola was – at least from the mercenaries' point of view – over.

10

Show Trial in Luanda

'You were a foreigner. You came to a country that was not your own from a land far away, you came voluntarily, you came with guns. What are guns for? For killing. You were paid for killing. You are a hired killer, a paid assassin, guilty of aggression and invasion, guilty of crimes against peace, guilty of the crime of mercenarism.'

Manuel Rui Monteiro, *Procurador Popular*, Luanda

'Shotgun Charlie' was dead. He had been killed instantly at the wheel of his Landrover when the patrol he had taken out ran into an ambush outside Cuimba. John Nammock, the young mercenary fresh from North Kensington – he was only nineteen – heard the dying screams of his great friend Andy Holland as he hid, wounded, in the long grass. He was soon rounded up; so were the two Americans, Daniel Gearhart and Gus Grillo. Grillo, like Nammock, was wounded in the leg; but Grillo, the only ex-soldier among them who had seen action, opened fire before surrendering. The lives of the three were – at least temporarily – spared.

'Canada' Newby was dead. In a far more horrifying incident he and the seven mercenaries crowded into his Landrover had rounded a corner to find themselves face to face with two truckloads of Cuba/MPLA troops. By now the enemy had come to anticipate the white mercenaries' suicidal frontal assault tactics, and this time it was they who reacted with the greater speed. In a few brief seconds all the mercenaries were killed, all but one. George Bacon III died there, a Portuguese mercenary named Nilssens, and no less than three of the twenty-three British mercenaries who had come with the third and final intake: Malcolm Dimmock, John Cashmore and RSM Dickens. The one who almost miraculously escaped death, though he too was wounded in the leg, was the American Gary Acker. According to one version 'Canada' Newby did not die on the spot. Mortally wounded, he was loaded with the five dead bodies into an MPLA truck and driven back to Cuimba where he died several hours later in agony.

The bodies of the dead mercenaries were displayed to, and photographed by, the Cuban war correspondents on the spot. It was the biggest single disaster that had befallen what, even in his absence, it is still impossible not to think of as Callan's men.

But Callan himself was not dead. Callan, against all likelihood, was alive. He and the seven survivors of his 'killer group' had sheltered in the hut of Joao Antonio and Senda Isabel for three or four days. They did not know of course whether Sammy Copeland and, following him, Shotgun Charlie had got safely back to Maquela or not; still less could they have imagined the dramatic events that had followed there, and Copeland's death. But no rescue attempt came and despair slowly settled upon them. They sent Joao Antonio out to a nearby village, to bring six stretcher-bearers back for Callan. They came, they obeyed, they carried. The mercenaries spent their last night together in the village but when they awoke next day it was to find the village deserted. The MPLA forces were all around; and it was Joao Antonio himself who denounced them. Accounts of how they were captured differ; it seems that Lawlor, Wiseman, Marchant and Evans – all of the second intake – set off on their own and were not made prisoner till several days later. Malcolm McIntyre, the medical orderly, stayed with Callan till – at gunpoint but too late – Callan ordered him to leave; they were captured almost simultaneously. The greatest mystery of all surrounds the taking of Andy MacKenzie. Certainly he lost a leg – and also lost his companion, the eighth of the survivors, known only as 'Tobey'. The pair were probably sent off separately by Callan to seek help; for some reason neither MacKenzie nor his captors ever revealed the details of what must have been a last little battle but remains a minor mystery. Finally, 'Satch' Fortuin, who had been left behind with a sprained ankle before Callan's final attack, wandered by himself, abandoned, from village to village, generally cared for (by of course people with whom he had no means at all of communicating) till in mid-February, at about the time when McAleese ordered the final evacuation, he too was picked up by the now totally victorious MPLA. With 'Brummie' Barker, captured in his underpants at San Antonio, they held no less than thirteen white mercenaries – three Americans and ten British – in their hands. The question was: what to do with them?

The question must have been debated for several weeks as the civil war drew to its end, with in the south the invading South Africans retreating and Jonas Savimbi and his UNITA followers dispersed into the bush. It was the Cubans who insisted on a show trial for all the thirteen. The Russians were very sceptical; but the Russian advisers were few and comparatively discreet, the Cubans were many, prominent and ebulliently victorious. Almost certainly Raul Valdes Vivo, a member of Fidel Castro's Central Committee, was the moving spirit and the brains behind the trial's preparation. As for the Angolans, they would probably have preferred to shoot the captured thirteen out of hand. But they allowed themselves to be persuaded that a show trial would be not only a virtuous example of solidarity among progressive nations but, as it were, an outward and inspiring celebration of victory, almost equivalent – not that any of those concerned would have accepted the comparison – to a classical triumph in ancient Rome, complete with ritual sacrifices.

The Trial Begins

The mercenaries were not paraded through the streets of Luanda in chains to the jeers and cheers of the mobs. However on the eve of their trial a monster demonstration filled the centre of the capital, with waving banners proclaiming '*Morte Aos Mercenarios!*' and inflammatory speeches in which the name of 'Callan' constantly recurred. That was on a Thursday evening. When the trial at last began, on the morning of Friday, 13 June, the thirteen defendants were already in the courtroom, sitting quietly, handcuffed, looking understandably awed, side by side, in two rows. The foreign journalists – about fifteen from the West, mainly from Britain and twenty or so, a very separate group, from the Eastern bloc and from 'progressive' African states – craned curiously from their gallery-style box to study these monsters. They looked very harmless; and above all they looked, in the main, very young. Andy MacKenzie, who had had his left leg amputated, was in a wheelchair; two more, Nammock and Grillo, had their legs in plaster, up resting on stools in front of them. They all seemed fit and well-treated. They were dressed in tasteful sawdust-coloured uniforms and rubber-soled black boots; their heads were shaven and they wore identity cards hanging from their necks. Nammock, at twenty the youngest of them, could hardly stop grinning at the British journalists. For all of them it must have been the first, and reassuring, sight of their fellow countrymen – though the three Americans had a lawyer to defend them, Bob Cesner, an attorney from Philadelphia who had already flown out and seen his 'clients' in the jail where they had been kept, for almost four months now, in solitary confinement: the prison of Sao Paulo.

Above the dock stood the dais. The five members of the Popular Revolutionary Tribunal that were to hear the case filed in to take their seats beneath a huge picturesque gold star set against a background of revolutionary red velvet. There were two soldiers, a lawyer, a woman representing the Angolan Women's Organisation. The presiding judge, by contrast to his comrades, who were unmistakably African, was an older bald-headed bespectacled man in a black gown with a chain of office, Ernesto Teixeira Da Silva. He could very easily have been Portuguese.

A contrasting figure too was the People's Prosecutor, Manuel Rui Monteiro, a flamboyant figure with an Afro hairstyle, dramatic gestures, and ringing tones who opened the proceedings by reading out the charges against the accused. There were no less than 139 different charges on the indictment, and it took over an hour to read through the long, long list. It seemed that the mercenaries were to be charged with everything from murder to mine-laying, from looting to outrages against the dignity of the Angolan people, and above all with the crime of being mercenaries, of '*mercenarismo*', a term that was to crop up again and again in the days that followed. For this, as very soon became clear, was to be not so much a trial of the thirteen accused themselves as of the Western powers who permitted and indeed had encouraged and financed *mercenarismo* throughout the African continent; and simultaneously with the trial an International Commission of Enquiry into the phenomenon of *mercenarismo* had been organised which – the organisers obviously hoped – would attract even more attention than the trial itself.

It did not of course. All the attention, all the publicity was focused on the trial itself, and the debates pursued by the fifty-odd delegates to the International Commission were virtually disregarded – at least by the Western press – in the nearby National Science Museum.

The delegates were mainly from Third World or Eastern bloc countries, but Britain had sent two representatives, a bulky and bearded young trade unionist named Jack Dromey and a discreetly radical barrister, Stephen Sedley. They were not the only two to be viewed by the British press with a certain suspicion. Michael Wolfers had been on *The Times* and so was in a certain sense a colleague; but he was now working for the People's Government, in the Ministry of Information and kept himself apart, almost as if tainted. Wilfred Burchett was also in a sense a colleague, a famous Australian journalist who made no secret of being a communist. He was in his own way typical of the almost fashionable, almost cosmopolitan Marxist gathering that attended the trial. There must have been at an average hearing at least a hundred people seated in the audience – a hundred, that is, apart from guards, prisoners, judges, advocates, court officials and journalists – and they ranged from many jovial Cubans and a few grim-faced Russians through every shade of colour and country, enlivened by the presence of Isabel Allende, the daughter of Chile's murdered President, and of 'the glamour girls of the Revolution' as Western journalists termed the colourfully-clad *mestizas*, the half-castes who, it soon became apparent, played such an important role in the ranks of the MPLA.

The trial itself was held in the Palace of Commerce, a modern Portuguese-built building near the seafront. It was conducted in Portuguese, but there was simultaneous translation (via smart little machines with white ear-plugs, issued to all) into four other languages – English of course, for the benefit of the accused, French for many of the visiting Africans, Spanish for the Cubans – and Russian. No expense had been spared. A Press Centre was fitted up nearby for visiting journalists, with telex machines and telephone links that – in a city left almost bare of shops and food since the exodus of Portuguese settlers a year earlier – amazingly functioned. Yet despite all the careful planning things almost immediately started to go wrong for the organisers. The first was the arrival of Robin Wright, as the correspondent of *The Christian Science Monitor*. It took a day for the authorities to realise that she had not only been with 'the traitor Holden Roberto' but had been in San Antonio and indeed knew reasonably well one of the accused, 'Brummie' Barker. She was promptly expelled as a CIA agent. Yet, that incident apart, the opening day of the trial went very much according to plan. It became clear to all observers that this might be a show trial indeed but for all that it was to be seriously and fairly conducted. The People's Prosecutor would be allowed to rave (indeed as the Foucquier-Tinville of the Revolution that was his role) but the presiding judge would remain sober, fair and calm, and his four colleagues were there to listen and to assess, not to interfere.

As for the accused, they were to appear one by one on the stand, to be questioned by the People's Prosecutor and by their own defence counsel – for each had been allotted a defence lawyer by the court (apart of course from the Americans; but even in their case Gus Grillo had elected to be defended by an Angolan, so Mr Cesner was acting only for Gearhart and Acker).

That morning the first of the accused to be called to step forward, much to the disappointment of most of those present, was Kevin Marchant. Callan was of course the figure awaited; but it became apparent that the planners of the trial were reserving Callan for the next day and, as it were, practising the routine to make sure that

The mark of the mercenary throughout the ages: a devotion to war. The statue of Venice's Renaissance leader, the condottiere Colleoni.

Above, the marching songs of the French Foreign Legion are still used to implant its 'Ésprit de corps'. *Camera Press. Below left*, Legionaries of all ages parade against the traditional backdrop of the Sahara. *The Photo Source. Inset*, 'Stepson of France' in the epoch of *Beau Geste. BBC Hulton Picture Library.*

Death in the Congo. *Above*, Five Commandos' first action, a lakebourne attack on Albertville, ended with exultant Simbas gloating over two dead mercenaries (*Agence Dalmas*) whose graves were later dug and decorated by their commander, Siegfried Mueller. *The Photo Source.*

The civilian and the soldier. Conor Cruise O'Brien, with a fellow Irishman – both elements of the
UN Peacekeeping Force that so dismally failed to eliminate the Katanga mercenaries. *Popperfoto*.

Mobutu Sese-Seko, the bloodstained present
ruler of the Congo (Zaire). *Camera Press*.

'Black Jack' Schramme, a Belgian planter,
leader of the mercenaries' revolt. *Associated
Press*.

'Mad Mike' Hoare of Five Commando: Irish origins, British background, South African residence. *Camera Press*.

Siegfried Mueller, a German officer of Five Commando. *Associated Press*.

Moise Tshombe, employer of freelance mercenaries in the Congo, he revived the 'profession'. *Jean Guyaux*.

Bob Denard, best known figure for over 20 years among the French mercenaries. *Reporters Associés*.

On the banks of the River Congo, mercenary in repose. *Camera Press*.

On the banks of the River Congo, mercenary in action. But atrocities, such as the shooting of prisoners, were common on both sides. *Agence Dalmas*.

The capture of Bukavu: arrival of Schramme's mobile column comprising about 150 white mercenaries and 800 Katangese gendarmes plus 1500 women and children.

Above, after the fall of Bukavu the white mercenaries fled across the Shangugu to Rwanda where they were interred and eventually, much to their relief, flown out to Europe. The small figure in the centre foreground is 'Mini' Schmidt. *The Photo Source.*

(*Below, main picture*) Rolf Steiner, the former Legionary, inspecting his men in Biafra. *Gilles Caron-Gamma.* (*Inset, left*) General Ojukwu, the genial Biafran leader who was forced to expel Steiner. *Camera Press.* (*Inset, right*) Count Carl Gustaf Von Rosen, the Swedish idealist who very nearly reversed Biafra's fortunes. *Camera Press.*

Death in Biafra. *Above,* 'Taffy' Williams giving orders for the attack on Onitsha (10 November, 1968) to the Flemish mercenary Marc Goosens. The meditative mercenary sucking a straw is Armand Ianarelli. *Gilles Caron-Gamma. Below,* minutes later Goosens has been killed. His men bring his body. *Gilles Caron-Gamma.*

Right, Holden Roberto, the dour leader of the FNLA, who hired mercenaries in Britain to halt the Cuban/MPLA advance. *Camera Press. Below*, John Banks, the dishonourably discharged ex-paratrooper and mercenary recruiter from Camberley who was paid £200 a head levy money for every man he sent out to Angola but barely risked his own skin. *The Photo Source.*

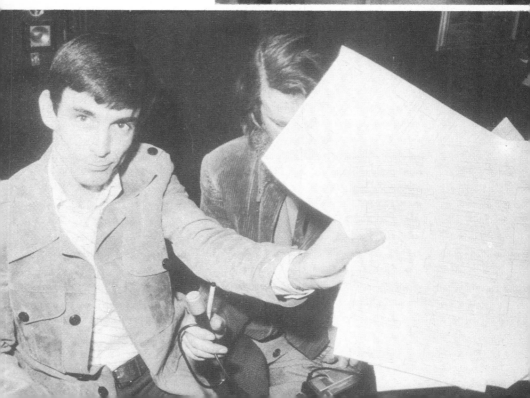

Above, a blown bridge in Angola – FNLA troops attempting to stem the tank-led Cuban advance northwards. *Popperfoto. Below*, the rival MPLA forces – Cubans and Angolans mix. *Popperfoto.*

Above, the popular Revolutionary Tribunal that judged the Angolan mercenaries. The presiding judge in the centre, Ernesto Titeixeira Da Silva, was at times almost perturbed. *Popperfoto.* *Below, main picture*, 'Callan' at the microphone pleading his cause. He was condemned to death and executed as were (*inset*) Andy MacKenzie (*top left*), shot in his wheelchair, the ill-starred 'Brummy' Barker (*below left*) and the naïve American, Daniel Gearhart(*below right*). *Popperfoto. Opposite*, one of the fortunate ones 'a mercenary escorted by a police officer on his return to Europe'. *The Photo Source.*

Above left, the puritanical President René of the Seychelles whom the mercenaries tried to overthrow. *Camera Press. Above right*, Jimmy Mancham 'The Playboy President' whom the mercenaries were hired to restore. *Camera Press. Right below*, Nicholas Fairbairn, the mercenaries' legal defender at the Seychelles trial – here pictured in typically flamboyant pose at his Scottish home, Fordell Castle. *Camera Press. Opposite*, the mercenaries on trial in the Seychelles. The 'woman mercenary' Sue Ingles was released as the trial began. *Popperfoto.* Four others, including the veteran Jeremiah Puren, but not including the bizarre Dolinchek – preceding Puren down the steps, were sentenced to death. *Argus Africa News Service.*

Above, the 'Ancient Order of Froth Blowers', on the surface rugger players with charitable leanings, flew in with AK47s concealed under Christmas toys for Seychellois children in their hand grips – had it not been for an intelligent customs officer . . . *Popperfoto. Below*, 'Mad Mike' Hoare (Alias 'Mr Tom') arriving at Natal's Supreme Court to hear the verdict of the judge and assessors at the end of his trial for hijacking a getaway plane at Mahé Airport – a very different figure from the spruce leader of 20 years earlier in the Congo. *Popperfoto.*

everything went smoothly on that first day. Marchant appeared to be a poor fish, and it was difficult to believe his story – true though it in fact was – that he had been recruited as a PT instructor by Banks. He did not mention – nor did Colin Evans when it came to his turn on the stand – that he was one of the deserters who had nearly been executed on Callan's orders. None of the observers had at the time (with the possible exception of the Cubans, who had interrogated and taken statements from all the mercenaries before the trial) the slightest notion of the relationship of the mercenaries with each other. All accepted, for instance, the truth of the statement in the indictment that Andy MacKenzie had been Callan's second-in-command when in fact of course he had merely, like Barker, been one of the original nineteen. All assumed that all the other twelve had been under Callan's command when in fact to the three Americans and Nammock Callan was as much a stranger, as much a myth, as to the assembled spectators; and to Barker he was merely a brief acquaintance. They knew nothing – and they were to hear nothing in court – of Callan's achievements as a commander; all they knew was that he was the monster who had ordered and possibly himself carried out the killing of fourteen fellow mercenaries, a horrifying story still terribly unclear in its details and motives; all of which – observers hoped – would be revealed at the trial.

It was not. For on the second morning, when a tense hush fell as Callan himself was called forward at 9.45 am to take the stand, a semi-disaster for all concerned occurred. Callan refused, as was his right, to answer questions.

'All my men who was [sic] captured, called mercenaries, were under my direct orders' [he said]. They were my soldiers and I was responsible for what they did. Mackenzie wasn't my second-in-command. I refuse to answer any question in this court. All the responsibilities for what these men did is mine alone. No-one else is responsible for anything. They only did what I told them.'

He spoke forcefully with a rough, heavy accent, but not violently or impertinently. And that was the end of that. The presiding judge confirmed his right to refuse to answer any questions. A buzz of disappointment arose – a feeling that was mingled with a certain admiration for Callan's crude courage, his presumption that he could take everything upon his own shoulders. MacKenzie, who followed him, provided more of a sensation.

'The dead mercenaries – who killed them?' he was asked.

'I, under orders' replied MacKenzie quietly, sitting in his wheel-chair.

'Did they die straightaway?' pursued Manuel Rui Monteiro.

'I think so.'

'You *think* so?' asked Monteiro, showing something of the horror that all those listening must have felt; except that in Monteiro's case the horror was of course more than half feigned. How could there be any regrets on the MPLA side that mercenaries had indulged in mutual massacre? From the Angolan and Cuban point of view if they had all killed each other off to the very last man, so much the better. It was one of the paradoxes that was to become more and more prominent as the trial proceeded, this emphasis by the prosecution on the internecine massacre of the mercenaries, a matter – to their enemies – of the most profound moral indifference.

They rushed through the accused. On the first day Marchant had been heard in the morning, Acker and Fortuin in the afternoon. On the second day Callan, MacKenzie, McIntyre, Lawlor, Evans, Wise-man and Barker were heard – over half the accused, leaving only three for the third day of the trial, clearly all due to be 'disposed of' in the morning session: two Americans and the youngest of all, the still very bright and cheerful Nammock. But then on the early evening of the second day, Saturday, 14 June, a new and startling development occurred. Four British barristers flew in to take up the defence of the British accused.

The British Barristers Appear

They appeared in court the next morning. They seemed to have stepped out of another world – as indeed they had. They obviously had no notion at all of what a revolutionary tribunal was. One even apologised – and the British press winced – for not appearing in his wig and gown. It was all they could do not to address the Comrade President as 'My Lord'. They appeared to be young, self-righteous, loud and insensitive – and it seemed obvious to observers who, after two days, felt themselves to be 'old hands' that these newcomers, so far from helping, would actually hinder their 'clients" cases. Clearly the Cuban 'managers' had reached the same decision – for, after a certain amount of argument, the tribunal decided as a 'gesture of international goodwill' that these lawyers, though late arrivals, should be allowed to represent clients who were already technically repre-sented. Clearly even the mercenaries thought so too; for after a certain amount of chopping and changing only three of them chose to be represented by British lawyers. As two of these three – Evans and Fortuin – had already been heard, the immediate result only affected Nammock: and when Nammock was heard that afternoon, the worst apprehensions of Western observers seemed to be confirmed.

For his new defence cousel, Peter Warburton Jones, a large and stout young representative of the British upper classes, behaved exactly as he would have done had the setting been the Old Bailey and the trial a criminal case before judge and jury. He demanded a recess to study documents, he complained of the brief time he had had to interview his client, he argued with the presiding judge (to the visible horror of the Angolan defence lawyers who had, for obvious reasons, a very different idea of their role) and he became 'with due respect' (as he phrased it) cantankerous. The audience had little idea of how to react; whether to laugh or jeer. It seemed a total disaster. It was not till Warburton Jones took Nammock by skilful cross-examination through his life as an unemployed young man with an Irish mother in North Kensington, his bedazzlement by John Banks and the rolls of banknotes, and his totally innocuous action in Angola, that the other side of the coin became clear: the traditional skill of the traditional British barrister in eliciting, by short questions and answers, the facts. But even so Warburton Jones went on too long, and had to be halted. Furthermore the court found it almost impossible to believe Nammock when he asserted – true though it no doubt was – that he had never heard of Angola before coming to Africa. Nevertheless Warburton Jones had broken the rhythm of the trial. The next day, the fourth day of the trial, was taken up entirely with the appearance of the two American mercenaries, Gus Grillo and Daniel Gearhart.

The pair could hardly have formed a greater contrast. Gearhart was hopelessly naive and honest, convinced that once he had explained everything clearly and fully, everyone would understand and sympathise. His attorney Cesner shuddered visibly as Gearhart insisted on answering the prosecution's questions in longwinded, almost pedantic detail rather than with the plain 'yes', 'no' or 'I don't know, sir' which had at least kept most of the British mercenaries from hopelessly incriminating themselves. Manuel Rui Monteiro tied the wretched man in knots, making great play with the $10 he had sent to a Wild Geese Club for information and even greater play with Gearhart's confused explanation of his own motives, his desire to come to Africa and Angola to study the political situation, and indeed for travel.

'So you wished to come as a tourist, so to speak?'

'Yes sir, that was it, in a manner of speaking?'

'But do tourists usually come with guns in their hands, killing the innocent people of the countries they visit?'

Yet in his odd way Gearhart was obviously sincere. He had wanted to see Africa as well as to make money; he suffered from the typically American sentiment that the obtaining of information on any subject, anywhere, and almost by any means, was a worthwhile goal in itself; and he clearly felt that he had done nothing morally wrong. He seemed confused, upset indeed, by the notion that anyone could consider him in any way undesirable or evil.

Gus Grillo on the other hand, alone of all the accused, took a highly original and intelligent line. He was anything but naive or honest. He had clearly worked out exactly what the tribunal would like to hear and he made sure that they heard it. He virtually admitted that he was an undesirable member of society but blamed for this the society that had adopted him, the United States. 'The part of American society I come from', he specified, 'was a monster.... In New York they have restaurants for dogs while people die on the streets.' This was music to the tribunal's ears – and not only to the tribunal's, for the trial was being televised and broadcast live, without censorship or cutting, throughout Angola; and here at last was one of the mercenaries practising in the best Marxist fashion self-criticism as well as condemning capitalism and its lackeys. For Grillo went on to condemn not only himself but Callan 'a wolf, an assassin' and the other mercenaries as being totally responsible (despite what Callan had said) for their acts; but even worse than the mercenaries was – a stroke of near genius by Grillo here – Holden Roberto who had betrayed a whole people. After the self-criticism came, of course, the promise of self-reform. Grillo had been lying in a hospital bed, being treated for his leg injury, and next to him was lying a Cuban soldier; then and there he had realised the difference between them: he, Grillo, was merely a despicable mercenary who had come to Angola as a hired killer whereas the Cuban comrade had come for ideological reasons to the aid of a fraternal struggle against neo-colonialist oppressors. In a flash all had become clear.

Here Grillo had gone a little too far out on a limb, by touching on a very sensitive point that all sides throughout the trial most carefully avoided mentioning. The point was this: that the Cubans too were in a sense mercenaries. They were undeniably foreigners fighting for a cause and in a country that did not directly concern them, and for pay. Certainly there were important distinctions; but there were enough resemblances, ideological verbiage apart, between the position of the Cubans fighting with the MPLA and the position of the Anglo-Americans fighting with the FNLA to make the comparison between the two distinctly embarrassing for the Cubans. Indeed one of the great questions in the quite passionate debates between the British and American lawyers and journalists present that occurred at night in the bars and restaurant of the hotel where they were lodged was whether this comparison ought to be brought out in open court. The lawyers felt that it would be counterproductive and dangerous for their clients; many of the journalists (myself included) argued that it ought to be made, that this was a political trial and that therefore all political points of view and of comparison ought to be openly aired. For, as the trial progressed, it became impossible for the Western journalists present to preserve their initial and traditional detachment; we became, inevitably, emotionally involved with the fates of the men in the dock. They were our fellow countrymen; whatever their faults, they had almost certainly behaved no worse than their opponents; furthermore, they were under threat of death and most of us came from a country where the death penalty had been abolished as barbarous and uncivilised; we had not ever been (in most cases) at a trial that might end in executions before; and we too, the journalists, like the lawyers and of course like the prisoners themselves, were feeling the strain. We could not help imagining the howls of protest that would have been heard from the Eastern bloc if the FNLA had won the civil war and if Cuban soldiers rather than white mercenaries had been put in the dock accused of roughly the same crimes.

But even the Cuban presence itself was a taboo subject. Georgie Anne Geyer, a famous columnist syndicated in several hundred newspapers in the States and a bright, effervescent friendly woman with it, was suddenly removed from the hotel dinner table one night by security police – and not seen again. Worried enquiries finally elicited from the somewhat embarrassed Angolan authorities the news that she had been held overnight and then expelled on the first available flight: her 'crime' was that of having talked informally to off-duty Cuban soldiers (who must have been delighted in this Portuguese-speaking country to find a fluent Spanish speaker) and of having telexed a report about their numbers ('spying') and, even more embarrassingly, their attitudes – they were, despite all propaganda, homesick. The following afternoon with greater formality all the remaining journalists were assembled to be informed – and it was the first he had heard of it too – that the correspondent of *The Times*, Stewart Tendler, was also being expelled – not for anything he had written but for an article appearing in the previous day's edition of his newspaper which had offended the susceptibilities of the Angolan government.

The Failure of the Witnesses

By then however the authorities hardly cared how the Western press reacted, for it had become evident that the show trial was not going to produce the hoped-for propaganda result, and that all that remained was to hurry it as quickly as possible to its end. Things had begun to go seriously wrong on Tuesday, 15 June, the fifth day of the trial, when most of the eleven witnesses summoned to appear took the stand. The object of the trial's organisers had been to get together an impressive collection of eyewitness accounts proving the mercenaries' atrocities and war-crimes; the difficulty of course was that the eyewitnesses would have had to be living in Sao Salvador, Maquela or Quibocolo at the time and would therefore have been almost automatically FNLA supporters. The enemy, the MPLA, might for the moment have won the civil war, but who was to tell when Holden Roberto might not be back again, with the Americans behind him? Clearly it had been a hard job collecting any eyewitnesses at all; and several of the witnesses when they did come onto the stand proved almost useless for the prosecution's case, having 'heard' that Callan had massacred or maltreated civilians but never having seen it, as even the mildest cross-examination elicited, with their own eyes. As for identifying the mercenaries in person, the very first witness – who made much of the blowing-up of the 'palace' at Sao Salvador (which of course had been done by Rennie on pulling out, not by any of the men in the dock) identified MacKenzie as being responsible for killing two civilians in a Sao Salvador club on Callan's orders. But he gave the date as 15 January, several days before MacKenzie had even arrived in Angola. Unfortunately MacKenzie's Angolan lawyer, Suarez do Silva, was both hopeless and obviously terrified of putting a foot wrong with the authorities; he failed even to mention this contradiction in his so-called cross-examination. It was becoming evident as the trial proceeded that only two of the four Angolan defence lawyers were taking their 'difficult revolutionary task' seriously – Spiritu Santos, an incisive and almost aggressive question-er, spurred on by the example of his Anglo-American 'colleagues' and, rather surprisingly, the tiny pale-skinned woman lawyer who had been allotted to defend Callan, Maria Teresinha Lopes. She and Callan often conferred together in whispers – more and more often as the trial went on. Callan's scowl was replaced by quite a gentle smile when he talked to her and she, stiff and reserved at first, gradually appeared to be more and more at her ease with this (in her country's eyes) embodiment of evil. It was a fascinating process to watch.

From the tribunal's point of view another major difficulty was that the judges and the People's Prosecutor could hardly hide their contempt of and dislike for most of the witnesses, their former enemies and now in a sense barely trusted quislings. This came out most clearly in the case of the seventh witness, an ex-FNLA sergeant with seven and a half years' service in Holden Roberto's army, who blamed the mercenaries for everything but insisted blatantly and boldly that the black soldiers of the FNLA had never been guilty of the least atrocity or misdemeanour. This was not at all what the court wanted to hear or (via radio and television) to be heard. The presiding judge announced next morning that, on studying the evidence, he had ordered the arrest of the witness for perjury. But even the two 'safe' witnesses, both '*Comandantes*' in the MPLA forces that had captured San Antonio, were surprisingly unsatisfactory. They gave evidence of 'Brummy' Barker's capture and proved satisfactorily enough that he was in command at San Antonio but when it came to his misdeeds as recounted to them by the inhabitants, they were very vague indeed. The best – or worst – that one of them could come up with was that the white mercenaries there had often 'raped' young girls who had gone to their house; and the People's Prosecutor, rather wisely, decided to skate lightly over this 'crime'.

But undoubtedly the most dramatic witnesses were the two peasants, Joao Antonio and his wife Senda Isabel, in whose hut Callan and the remnants of his killer group had sheltered for three or four days after the last battle. Joao Antonio was an excitable loquacious man who unlike the other witnesses spoke only in Kikongo – which of course had to be translated into Portuguese (and the court's or lawyers' questions back into Kikongo for his benefit). One of the most dramatic moments of the trial came when he identified, with outstretched finger, Callan. He parried the defence lawyers' questions well and cleverly; but even so it became fairly clear that the mercenaries had committed no atrocities in any accepted sense while staying at the hut.

'While they were in your hut, did they treat you very badly?' asked one of the 'defence' lawyers, Mercedo.

'They treated us very badly,' replied Joao Antonio. The audience waited eagerly for the translation of the details. It came. 'One urinated in the doorway.'

222 THE NEW MERCENARIES

'Who?'

'Callan. He urinated,' continued Joao Antonio with great indignation, 'many times'.

It was only when Maria Teresinha established that Callan had all
the time been lying on a stretcher, unable to rise, that the general
hubbub of indignation at this affront to human rights and human
dignity subsided.

Senda Isabel, whose evidence followed next day, was – despite, I
would imagine, a night of careful coaching by the prosecution – rather
more naive. She found it hard to identify the mercenaries (bar
Callan), she said, because 'they were fat then and they are thin now'.
They had eaten their mangoes and drunk their palm wine and she
had been forced to shell and roast groundnuts for them.

'Didn't they try to buy your love of the Angolan people for the
MPLA with money?' asked the People's Prosecutor.

It was an unfortunate question: it suggested rape, which as Senda
Isabel was very pregnant and not, to Western eyes, attractive seemed
unlikely; which she indignantly denied, and which led to her telling
the court that the mercenaries had offered money and cigarettes to
her husband, and indeed a watch. Her claim that 'another forced my
husband to take the 1,000 escudos but he didn't want to' – something
Joao Antonio had not, in his righteous indignation, mentioned the day
before – did not ring very true. All in all by the time the evidence of
the husband and wife was finished a picture had emerged not of
atrocities and cruelty but of a group of frightened mercenaries having
behaved really very well, having paid generously for the food and
drink they had taken, and having in the end been betrayed by their –
admittedly unwilling – hosts.

On the sixth afternoon of the trial, propaganda reigned – a series of
television films were shown, to the glory of the MPLA and to the
detriment of President Ford and the CIA. But what was quite
fascinating, more relevant, and from the point of view of the trial's
stage-managers a real *tour de force* was the soundtrack, played over for
the courts, of a BBC *Panorama* programme made in Britain partly in
late January at the time of the mercenaries' recruitment and partly
much later as the trial began. 'Satch' Fortuin, who in his evidence had
insisted that he had come to Angola only as John Banks' bodyguard
and had stayed on as a mercenary 'by mistake', must have quivered
inwardly to hear his own disembodied voice arrogantly telling a
Panorama interviewer, 'Christians have always been adventurous
people.' Wiseman's wife, parents and, rather touchingly, his choir-
master at school were heard. But what no doubt made the most

sinister impression was the voice of John Banks (who with the Americans Dave Bufkin and Lobo do Sol had become the absent villains of the courtroom drama) proclaiming: 'Whatever happens to the ten men in Luanda, these days if you're buying mercs you're buying British.' The 'ten men in Luanda' must have been wishing at that moment with every fibre in their beings that John Banks were there in the dock himself, side by side with his own countrymen whose fate he so casually dismissed. Certainly the British journalists present felt this feeling – as well as a growing awareness of how easily their own reports might be used, then or at some future occasion, to condemn men whom they hardly knew.

Indeed the final speech of the People's Prosecutor, heard the following day after a morning's recess, was larded with references to, and quotations from, articles and interviews in the Western press and on radio and television. *The Observer*, *The Sunday Times*, *The Times*, the *Sun*, the *Sunday People*, the *Morning Star*, the BBC, and Channel 7 in California were all cited, as if to prove from the capitalists' own mouths, the guilt of their mercenary lackeys. The speech was a masterpiece of both rhetoric and research, three hours long, uncompromising, harsh and declamatory. After the comparatively calm and at times almost relaxed and humorous atmosphere of the preceding days it brought the trial back to a pitch of tension that culminated in Manuel Rui Monteiro's emotional and draining peroration: 'Comrades,' he repeated time after time, going down the list of Angolan organisations – the Pioneers, the Women, the People's Army – 'Comrades of the Angolan Revolution, in your name I demand the death penalty for the mercenary defendants.'

The death penalty ... the death penalty ... the death penalty, again and again, with tremendous emphasis, the phrase *la pena de la morte* was repeated. Western observers, journalists and lawyers left the courtroom that evening in a state of near shock. For gradually the feeling had been building up that on the evidence presented to the court none of the proclaimed 'atrocities' had been even remotely proved (bar the extremely two-edged massacre of the mercenaries by each other) and that all thoughts of the death penalty would have to be dropped, except possibly in the cases of Callan and MacKenzie. Western observers, journalists and lawyers were jolted back into the world of 'revolutionary justice' where the actual details of who did what and when, the concepts of 'bourgeois justice' and individual responsibility, were much less important than the realities of class struggle, capitalist tools and neocolonialism.

Western observers, journalists and lawyers were abruptly reminded that this was a political trial, in which the calling of witnesses, the hearing of defendants and the attempt to 'prove' atrocities by evidence, were merely sops thrown out to appease bourgeois ideas of justice; and that the whole point of the trial was to condemn, ringingly, once and for all, the phenomenon of *mercenarismo*. Would this mean necessarily therefore, and almost in the face of all the evidence, the execution of the thirteen accused? The press was by now well aware of the tensions existing not only between the Russians and the much more hardline Cubans, but also in the ranks of the MPLA itself: between the sophisticated *mestizos* (aided indeed by left-wing Portuguese) who were its leaders, and the mass of its black followers. The intellectuals and the leadership were worried about the effect executions might have on Angola's image throughout the world: but the population as a whole, and more importantly the army, desperately wanted all the mercenaries executed. '*Toudos ou solo Callan?*' ('All or only Callan') I asked a group of men in the street in elementary Portuguese. '*Toudos*' replied their spokesman, and drew his hand grinningly across his throat.

The defence lawyers that night, Angolan, British and American, after seeing and trying to reassure their shaken clients, anxiously debated – though in separate little groups – the tone and contents of their final pleas.

Final Pleas

The first to speak next morning, exactly a week after the trial had begun, was Maria Teresinha, for Callan. She based her plea astutely on the fact that Callan, or rather Costas Georgiou, was a Cypriot, a victim of colonialism, himself a 'colonialised man' – and she spoke, unlike Suarez do Silva who followed her for MacKenzie, with obvious sincerity and feeling. For Malcolm McIntyre and Gus Grillo, Comrade Mercedo pleaded briefly for clemency on the grounds that they were members of an exploited class. Then came Spiritu Santos for most of the British mercenaries: rather boldly (for a lawyer who would have to go on living and working under the MPLA regime) pointing out that none of the charges laid had actually been proved and criticising, though without naming him, the People's Prosecutor for his 'emotionalism'. So far nothing was unexpected, not even the rather touching concern that Teresinha had obviously developed for Costas Georgiou.

But then came the speech of the day, a magnificent and most carefully prepared oration by Bob Cesner, the Philadelphia lawyer, who had obviously been holding his fire till this, the last moment of the trial. It was a lawyer's speech, through and through: it went in great detail into international law, the Geneva Conventions and the question of the rights of prisoners-of-war, the Nuremberg trials and the definition of war crimes, United Nations' Declarations and OAU Resolutions and the question of whether they had or had not the force of law, plus the Code of the Angolan Combatant and how and in what aspects it might be applied to the prisoners. By the end of Cesner's speech it seemed as if the whole case for the prosecution had, legally speaking, crumbled: the defendants had not been guilty of war-crimes, they had not been treated as they ought to have been treated; and above all, neither in international law nor in Angolan law was there any such crime, as yet, as *mercenarismo* – though there might be one day if and when the draft 'Luanda Convention', work on which had just been finished by the International Commission of Enquiry, became the basis for law. But that day was not yet. In effect, without being absolutely specific about it, Cesner was demanding for his clients – and by implication for all the mercenaries – not clemency, but acquittal.

Unfortunately the effect of his brilliant speech was slightly spoilt by his associate, another American lawyer, Bill Wilson, demanding to be heard. Wilson made a short but insensitive and fatuous intervention. As the veteran Australian journalist Wilfred Burchett said, it would have been better if he hadn't opened his mouth at all. For by this time even communists like Burchett (and to a far greater extent left-wingers like the Western members of the International Commission) were beginning to be very worried indeed about the outcome of the trial: a mixture of repugnance at the thought of the death penalty actually being carried out, worry about Angola's reputation for revolutionary purity, and a certain acceptance both of Cesner's compelling legal arguments and of the Angolan lawyers' pleas that the mercenaries were themselves members of an exploited proletariat in their countries of origin.

It was now the turn of the three British barristers. For Nammock Warburton Jones began well, apologising to the court for his own previous 'arrogance' and insisting that he had not come to Angola 'to defend a man's right to become a prostitute of war'. He criticised the British government for allowing and indeed encouraging mercenaries, spoke movingly of his own painful knowledge of a country at civil war – his own, Northern Ireland – and movingly too of his client: 'His face has been so full of hope but his heart has been full of fear.' But then he showed how little he had understood the Angolan system of

justice or its aims by declaring, as if in a British court of justice, 'I
know this court will decide this case according to the evidence and
will be most careful when it deliberates on individual evidence and
the part individuals played'; and he lost the sympathy of court and
spectators alike as he ploughed on through details and mitigating
circumstances for far too long, in sad contrast to the effective and
more generalised arguments of the American Cesner.

Clive Stanbrook, who followed for the ferrety-faced Evans, showed
himself far more sensitive to the aims and needs of 'revolutionary
justice', even though he was himself, like Warburton Jones, the
product of a highly right-wing background – Stanbrook's father was a
Conservative MP, Warburton Jones' a Lord Justice of Appeal in
Ulster. Stanbrook cited most tellingly the example of the other
Portuguese ex-colony, Mozambique, whose Marxist president,
Samora Machel, had recently condemned the death penalty even for
traitors on the grounds that even traitors could be re-educated; and if
traitors, then why not such misguided and exploited members of the
working class as Stanbrook's client, Evans? In a peroration that
carefully balanced, and could be seen to balance, that of the Public
Prosecutor, the English lawyer, in the name of Humanity, asked again
and again for clemency for these 'dregs of society'.

Finally the pedantic Herbert Kerrigan spoke for Fortuin. Kerrigan
shocked the whole court and ruined a reasoned plea by demanding at
its end the outright acquittal of his client. Thereby he showed that he
had understood nothing of the nature of a political trial. Clemency
was possible, acquittal unthinkable. Next day an editorial in one of the
two Luanda newspapers praised, grudgingly, the Western lawyers for
their calm, their techniques, and their tactics and suggested that the
final defence speeches had all been very cunningly tailored to cover
all aspects without overlapping. On the contrary to the British
journalists it seemed that the British lawyers at least were astoundingly hidebound and insular; not that there were not tensions among
them too. Stanbrook described Warburton Jones after one exasperat-
ing incident as 'the rudest man I have ever met'. But they were, after
all, secondary figures in the drama. The primary figures had still to
speak on their own behalf.

The next morning Callan at long last rose to his feet again and this
time spoke out. The presiding judge questioned him sharply and then
less sharply, almost gently. Teresinha plucked anxiously at his arm.
He took little notice of either of them. 'Ask me straight,' he kept
saying; but when he was asked straight, he paid little attention to the
question, more to a sort of interior monologue which, incoherently,

he repeated to the court. 'No man wants to die but I am prepared to die. I accept the consequences. I am responsible for everything. I must not lie. What is it you want to know? No, the truth. Costas, you will speak the truth and nothing but the truth.'

It was a painful and embarrassing scene, and gradually the whole courtroom, sections of which had been convinced that Callan was play-acting, fell silent, till at the end Teresinha went up to the presiding judge, whispered in his ear – earlier she had always been able to calm Callan when he had shown signs of excitement – and had the interrogation quietly brought to a halt. What was clearly preying on Callan's mind was the 'massacre'. 'I have killed one English soldier,' he said, 'the reason being I was told that he fired the rocket at my men which were in the Landrover where all the men which were at the beginning at the front with me. ...The reason? An ambush is an ambush. Men with many years experience do not exaggerate an ambush. ...How many mercenaries? One mercenary.'

Alone of all the relatives Callan's sister had come out to attend the trial. 'Blondie' she was immediately christened by the press; and she certainly added a touch of background glamour and melodrama to the proceedings. But (as she was under contract to a popular British paper that had paid for her journey and stay, in return for exclusive rights to her story) she kept well away from journalists. Nevertheless, and indirectly thanks to her presence, an 'explanation' emerged years later for Callan's mental state on that final day at the trial. According to this 'explanation' the Angolan authorities were determined to break down all the mercenaries' resistance before the trial. Callan alone remained defiant, and the orders were stressed all the more after his first short and impressive appearance where he accepted responsibility for the acts of 'all my men'. So, after all other methods had been tried and failed, Major Victor Correia Fernandes, the *oficial-instructor* of the trial (and the leader of one of the columns attacked by Callan's men) had flown up to Maquela, collected the remains of the executed mercenaries whose bodies had never been buried, loaded the bones and skulls and hair into four ammunition crates, and left them, labelled with insulting comments, in Callan's cell on the Friday night. This macabre move had finally broken Callan's nerve.

Personally I do not believe this story; I think the 'facts' would have become known to the other prisoners and via them to their British and American lawyers – who would have cited such barbarous methods to discredit 'revolutionary justice'. I think that under the strain of waiting and listening, the strain of an entirely passive role absolutely contrary to his nature, Callan finally cracked. But, as it would explain his obsession in court on that final morning with the massacre of the mercenaries, this story ought to be recorded just in case it is true.

Next came Andy MacKenzie, in his wheelchair. He was quiet, coherent and impressive. 'When I came to Angola,' he said, 'I came to join the FNLA army. I conducted myself as a soldier. I did not murder any civilians. Allegations of robbery and looting are not true. I admit I was part of the people who took part in the execution of other mercenaries but this was a direct order. I admit as a military man I should have had the courage to refuse.'

The rest of the British mercenaries confined themselves in the main to thanking, rather clumsily, their doctors, guards and lawyers, 'and you, Sirs and Madame on the bench' (as Marchant rather touchingly phrased it) for good treatment and a fair trial, and to apologising to the people of Angola. 'I'm very very sorry for coming to Angola. ...That's about it, sir,' said Nammock. The Americans were more articulate. Gus Grillo repeated how wicked he had been and how grateful he was: but then his intelligence seemed to take leave of him. 'Words are not enough,' he said. 'I'm prepared to fight a war, do anything else, for the People's Republic of Angola.' There was almost a collective shudder at this instinctively mercenary plea. Gary Acker embarrassingly quoted Corinthians XIII on 'Faith, Hope and Love, but the greatest of these is Love' and then sat down, eyes shining. Daniel Gearhart claimed that he had 'learnt a great deal in these last nine days,' and still clinging to his hopeless naivety, added, 'Through the generosity of this court, I might be able to help other people.'

At 10.50 in the morning the court rose. The presiding judge announced that sentence would not be pronounced till the middle of the following week.

In fact nine days passed before the court was called together again for its final brief session, nine days of rising tension and speculation, nine days of evidently increasingly bitter arguments among the various factions of the MPLA, of which only sketchy rumours reached the ears of Western observers. On the one hand only death sentences for all the mercenaries would satisfy the Angolan people. But on the other hand such an obviously unjust and blanket sentence would shock international opinion. Which was the more important? What too of black African opinion in general, which would welcome the execution of all and any white mercenaries? Was that more important than Marxist principles of re-education? It was obvious that there would be unpleasant political repercussions whatever the sentences were, and many members of the MPLA's central committee must have cursed the Cubans for bringing them this poisoned gift, this superficially attractive concept of a show trial with worldwide publicity. Could they indeed even execute Callan, a mental wreck, or MacKenzie, an invalid confined for life to a wheelchair? But if they did not execute either, on what possible grounds could they execute any of the others, against whom nothing, not even the internecine murder of fellow mercenaries, had in any sense been proved?

Sentences of Death

The court reassembled on the afternoon of Monday, 28 June. It had been a fair trial, fairly conducted; and the presiding judge was obviously ashamed of what he now had to say. He read through a text that bore no relation whatsoever to the trial or the evidence, a text that might well have been prepared months in advance: all the mercenaries had known exactly what they had been hired to do, with the complicity of their governments. They had 'spread fear, shame and outrage, mangled children, laid bare the people with bayonets'. 'Packs of dogs of war with bloodstained muzzles' could not claim prisoner-of-war status or the protection of any conventions. For they were 'foreigners with knives between their teeth who had come to spread dark wounds across the country', who had 'silenced with bullets the clear laughter of the youth'. This was frightening language; it sounded as if it might be leading up to death sentences for all, against all expectations. Then came, however, a little relief. In the cases of Nammock, McIntyre and Acker their 'low degree of intelligence and age was noted in their favour'. Gearhart, though, must have trembled when he heard himself described, ridiculously, as 'a highly dangerous character'; and Grillo must have wondered if his tactics had totally backfired when his 'accentuated malice' was stressed.

Then, after less than half an hour, came the sentences. For Nammock, McIntyre and Acker sixteen years' imprisonment. For Lawlor, Evans and Fortuin twenty-four years' imprisonment. For Wiseman, Marchant and Grillo thirty years' imprisonment. For Callan, MacKenzie, Barker and Gearhart – death by firing squad. The trial was over. Only the punishment remained.

In the comparative level of the punishments there was a certain rough justice. Nammock and Acker had been among the last batch to arrive in Angola whereas Callan, MacKenzie and Barker had been in the first. McIntyre had been a medical orderly only, and so was less severely treated than the other British mercenaries of the second intake. Lawlor was an ex-Royal Marine who had made no attempt to disguise the fact that he had taken part in the fighting and had made a good impression on the court. Evans had been ably defended by Clive Stanbrook. There was obviously a certain truth in 'Satch' Fortuin's plea that he was there by bad luck rather than by design. As for Grillo, his 'repentance' may have fooled to some extent the court and saved him from the death sentence; but it never fooled the Cubans, who knew the ins-and-outs of American society and had had (and rejected) an earlier offer by Grillo to get in touch with Lobo do Sol, if released, and together with him 'deal with' Dave Bufkin. The great shock was the death sentences on 'Brummy' Barker was and Daniel Gearhart. It now became clear why two apparently unnecessary witnesses had been called to 'prove' that Barker was in command at San Antonio. 'I've always been unlucky,' Brummy had said in his statement at the trial, 'and I've run out of luck again. I was born under an unlucky star.' He would have done better to have risked his luck and swum in his underpants for the other side of the Congo estuary rather than to have pretended to be a *Daily Mirror* reporter and, with engaging insolence, have asked his captor, Major Victor Correia Fernandes, to contact Harold Wilson, then Prime Minister, for confirmation if he was doubted.

As for the unfortunate and shattered Gearhart, his was entirely a political sentence. He had been less than a week in Angola and he had been captured before he had the chance to fire a shot. But it was unthinkable that three British mercenaries should be sentenced to death, and not a single American. Of the three Americans captured Acker was young, and, as Bob Cesner his defence lawyer had proved, psychologically ill. Grillo was the obvious candidate for the firing squad; but Grillo by his intelligent defence had in fact saved himself and by doing so condemned to death, as it turned out, the only possible alternative: Gearhart.

That night Western journalists sent off their last dramatic reports. The news that four mercenaries had been condemned to death made headlines in most countries, though it was stressed that President Agostinho Neto could still exercise the prerogative of mercy. Next day the journalists were ushered firmly onto the first available flight and out of Angola. The lawyers followed a day or two later. Only 'Blondie', Callan's sister, escorted everywhere by Major Victor Correia Fernandes, remained. Appeals for clemency reached Luanda both from Britain's Prime Minister, James Callaghan and America's Secretary of State, Henry Kissinger. A later appeal from the Queen herself was, according to Donald Belford (Callan's original recruiter who surfaced briefly in Leeds) – a Foreign Office blunder, badly advised in view of President Neto's well-known anti-monarchical views. On 9 July the President confirmed the death sentences. On the afternoon of 10 July they were carried out at Grafanil military base outside Luanda by a firing squad of military police. It is said that Callan died bravely and that MacKenzie levered himself up from his wheelchair to face the firing squad, standing, on his one leg. But Barker and Gearhart died badly, in tears, screaming for mercy.

The Angolan government gave relatives eight days to collect the bodies. In the case of 'Brummy' Barker alone, unlucky in death as in life, there were no family or relatives or friends ready to meet the expense involved. Handlers at London Airport refused to unload Callan's body when it was flown in to Heathrow. Nevertheless he was eventually buried, discreetly, in North London according to the Greek Orthodox rite. Andy MacKenzie was buried by his grieving but unashamed parents near Swindon, where his father, an RAF warrant officer, was given compassionate leave. An Angolan Relief fund was set up to compensate the families of the executed or imprisoned mercenaries but came to a dismal end when its organiser, Wilf Middleton, a former RAF corporal with an IQ of 170 who had become chairman of Mensa, worried by the problems of coping with the relief fund, committed suicide. Why he had ever agreed to become involved in these sad and tragic events that seemed almost to bring a curse upon all even remotely concerned is most obscure.

Book Three

THE INDIAN OCEAN

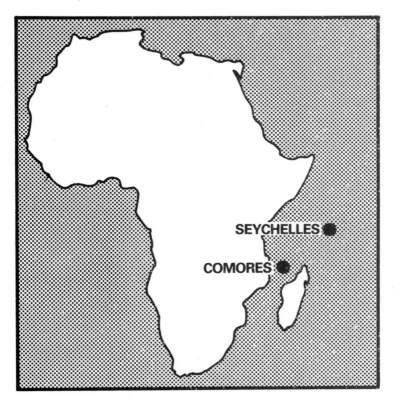

Indian Ocean showing position of the Seychelles and the Comores

11

Paradise Gained – Coup in the Comores

Bob Denard was born, probably on 20 January 1929, in Morocco or at Caen or near Bordeaux. It is typical of the man that even these elementary and unimportant facts are so contradictorily reported. Over the whole range of French mercenary activity in the past quarter of a century there hangs a cloud of obscurity of which this is just one tiny, mildly annoying, example. No French mercenary of note has ever written his memoirs. Most, unlike their British or American or South African counterparts, are reluctant to give interviews. Furthermore almost all have the confusing habit of using false names. For instance the real name of the man known in the Comores as Captain Marques, the head of the security police, is almost certainly Dominique Malacrino. Malacrino, born in 1953, is one of Denard's more recent recruits, like so many a former Legionary – too young however to have been in that breeding-ground of now-ageing mercenaries, the 1er REP. As for Denard himself, it seems almost undeniable that he is both the Colonel Jean Maurin who in late 1967 became a 'technical adviser' to President Bongo of Gabon and the Colonel Gilbert Bourgeaud who, nine years later, after the Angolan fiasco, was once again re-employed as a 'technical adviser' by the President at a salary of 500,000 CFE francs a month.

What has been astounding in Denard's career has been his ability to recover from so many fiascos that would have discredited lesser or less confident men and still come bouncing back. There had been the 'bicycle invasion' fiasco in Katanga in 1967; then a succession of failed attempts to become successfully involved with the Biafran affair. When Biafra collapsed in early 1970, Denard was over forty, unemployed without a future. Felix Houphouet-Boigny, '*Le Vieux*', the ruler of the Ivory Coast, apparently persuaded his young protégé Bongo to reward Denard with a farm, Donguila, sixty miles outside Libreville in the tropical jungle; and over the next decade Denard was certainly based in Gabon. If he was indeed, as one account has it, the son of a French peasant farmer, then his inherited instincts may have been put to good use: he became involved in the import-export meat business, with another old Biafran hand, the former Spitfire pilot Jack Malloch. Affretair, Malloch's charter company was registered in Gabon but had its main offices in Salisbury, in Rhodesia – and very soon a profitable little business was flourishing, flying out Rhodesian beef to Gabon and importing via Gabon (and against the sanctions imposed on Ian Smith's isolated regime) cosmetics and television sets into Rhodesia. Affretair's 'fleet' expanded, from a single propellor-driven DC7 to a jet-propelled DC8. But this remained for Denard just a sideline, though a sideline that he was later – both directly and indirectly – to develop.

Was Denard involved as early as 22 November 1970 in a mercenary attempt to overthrow President Sekou Touré of Guinea as many black Africans have alleged? Did such an attempt ever genuinely take place? Was it Denard who, with one companion, cold-bloodedly murdered in Libreville a year later one of Bongo's political rivals, Germain M'ba, as a recent book published in France has, unchallenged, stated? I would hesitate to say. What is certain is that there is thereafter a gap of three or four years during which nothing much at all was heard of Denard – quite possibly he was devoting himself to his farming and import–export activities; and then in 1975, 1976, 1977 and 1978 a flurry, growing to a crescendo, of mercenary activity.

All this was based on Gabon and, directly or indirectly, on the Presidential Guard there, whose formation and purpose have been described earlier (see pages 125-6). However Denard was never, under any of his aliases, the commandant of the Presidential Guard but he was at least for a period one of the Presidential Guard's small group of 'instructors' and he certainly set up with President Bongo's blessing, a '*Groupement Etrangère d'Intervention*', a kind of 'Rapid Deployment Force', in effect the nucleus of a mercenary 'Company' comprising both whites and blacks, ready to intervene in nearby countries and conflicts. This was probably in 1977 when Valéry Giscard d'Estaing came to power in France, and Jacques Foccart, for so long the *éminence grise* of France's African policy, at last fell. Foccart had clearly lost any confidence he might ever have had in Denard as a useful tool. But others had not; and with Foccart's disappearance from the scene Denard was, at least to a certain extent, given his head. In the early summer of 1975 he was active, with a very small group of mercenaries, in the Indian Ocean: of which more later. The operation was a success. In the late summer and autumn of 1975 he was active in Cabinda and Angola on a slightly larger scale. Those 'operations' were a failure; but I was perhaps wrong to describe them in a previous chapter as a fiasco. Cabinda was a bold but hurried and therefore botched attempt. On the contrary the intervention in Angola erred on the other side: it was too slow. By the time the twenty French mercenaries had been flown down from Leo to join the fray, UNITA was in as bad a way as the FNLA. Its 'capital' Huambo had fallen on 9 February 1976 and Jonas Savimbi with at most a few hundred followers had taken to the bush. It is not surprising, then, that the French with their SAM-7 missiles were unable to achieve anything effective.

What is surprising (if the story that they shot down one of UNITA's own supply planes on 13 March is true) is that they were still, five weeks later, in the field at all. Apparently two of their number were killed by a mine before all American and South African aid to UNITA ceased and they were pulled out. At least, however (as had not been the case with either Faulques or Lucien-Brun in Biafra), Denard had supplied the number of men he had contracted to supply, and they had taken part in the fighting as agreed. (In Leo incidentally they had rejected as unsuitable material the three British mercenaries who had fled from Sao Salvador and who had taken refuge in John Simpson's room in the Intercontinental Hotel. John Simpson considered the French to be of a much higher class than the British: their leader in Leo had, interestingly enough, been educated at a British public school. He refused however, typically, to give his name – and was known to Simpson only as 'Max'.)

With Angola behind him, Denard was (again according to the same French author, Pierre Pean) engaged by President Bongo for yet another assassination attempt: this time of a Haitien who had seduced *Madame La Présidente*, Bongo's wife. The Haitien had fled to Miami; Denard hired first Jean Kay and then, when Kay, something of an idealist, cried off, another of 'his' mercenaries, Thadeus Surma, a fifty-two-year-old ex-Legionary of Polish origins, for the job. It is not too clear whether the Haitien was eventually killed or not. It is not too clear what proof there is at all that Denard was in any way involved in this (or in a later, successful murder of another of the amorous Madame Bongo's lovers, carried out in France allegedly by gangsters from Bordeaux on Denard's orders). But what does seem clear is that Denard has many questions to answer; and that between a Bob Denard and a Mike Hoare, the two best known mercenary leaders of the past quarter of a century, there is more than a difference of language or culture, there is a difference of standards, a difference indeed of mercenary morality.

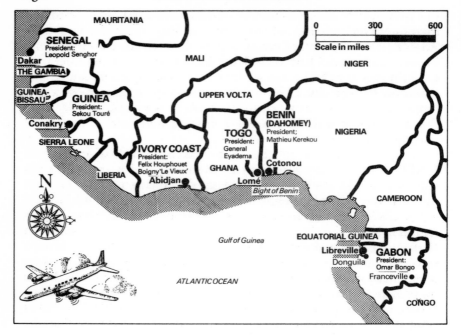

West Africa – The Gulf of Guinea

Kerekou of Benin

From this point on the mercenary ventures with which this book will deal are *grosso modo* of a very different sort: not interventions in civil wars, but attempts to organise swift coups in small states: in three small states, to be precise, in Benin, in the Comores and in the Seychelles. Two were organised by Bob Denard; one by Mike Hoare. Denard was the first – both to fail and to succeed. This chapter will now tell the story first of his failure in Benin, then of his success in the Comores.

General de Gaulle had, wisely, given the two vast French colonies of French West Africa and French Equatorial Africa their independence without fuss or delay when, in the sixties the 'wind of change' blew through black Africa; and even more wisely had split these territories into a number of comparatively small independent states. Had the British done the same with their colonial giants, Nigeria and the Sudan, or the Belgians the same with the even vaster Congo, there would in all logic have been no bloodthirsty and unforgettable separatist civil wars in this wretched trio of countries. As a result of this wise policy most of the newly-independent French-speaking African states retained – like Gabon, like the Ivory Coast, like Senegal – the closest links with France. But not all. Sekou Touré's Guinea had alone refused to join the French Community, the equivalent of the British Commonwealth; as a result De Gaulle had cut off all French aid. Others, without going so far, gradually swung to the left.

One of these was Dahomey, an impoverished strip of territory inhabited by three million or so Africans, bordered on one side by the mighty Nigeria and on the other by an equally impoverished and even smaller strip of territory, Togo. Togo was ruled, with French approval, by General Eyadema. Dahomey, the scene of fierce political rivalry between three rival leaders – one representing the 'civilised' coast, one the Saharan desert nomads of the interior, and one the ex-ruling family of the black kingdom lying in between – had been taken over, on 26 October 1972, to French dismay, by Major Mathieu Kerekou and a group of left-wing military. President Kerekou, as he soon became, rechristened Dahomey Benin, eyed neighbouring Togo (which had once been part of the medieval African empire of Benin) avidly, and, even worse, proceeded to nationalise French-owned companies. The three rival leaders were firmly under house arrest. But there was in exile, in that happy refuge of many exiles, the Ivory Coast, a former President of Dahomey, Dr Emile Zinzou, whom Kerekou had originally used as a civilian figurehead. What had been good for the goose could be equally good for the gander. Kerekou was thought to be unpopular, and indeed right-wing African presidents like Bongo were not the only ones with marital problems: in June 1975 Captain Michel Aikpe was convicted of adultery with Madame Kerekou and executed. There were rumoured to be murmurings in Benin's tiny army. A 'Dahomey National Liberation Front' was formed in the Ivory Coast under the leadership of yet another of Kerekou's fallen friends, an ex-ambassador named Gratien Pognon; its aim was to restore 'the rightful civilian government' in the person of Dr Emile Zinzou, that now-useful figurehead; and with that aim in mind the Front, on 5 November 1976, signed a contract with Colonel 'Gilbert Bourgeaud' – that is to say, with Denard – for the temporary hire of ninety 'technicians' – sixty, it was specified, white and thirty black – for the overthrow of President Kerekou's regime. Interesting financial details were included. The pre-operational budget would be $475,000, the post-operational budget $530,000; and it was noted that a project budget of $145,000 had already been paid to the colonel.

Of this project budget $5,000 had been spent on an 'observation mission' – presumably a trip by Denard in person to Cotonou, the coastal capital of Benin, to recce the lie of the land. A further $100,000 had been needed for travel and administrative expenses; and then a further $40,000 still. All this had led to the drawing-up of a plan for a two-pronged attack to be launched against Benin on 5 January 1977.

Force Omega's Alternatives

As so often in military operations, the plan lightly veiled the names of the countries concerned; but with slightly more imagination than the traditional NATO style of 'Blue Land will launch an attack on Red Land'. In this case the plan was for a preventative attack against the Republic of Banalia. Why? Because Banalia was itself about to attack the neighbouring Republic – Denard must have been reading his Frederick Forsyth avidly – of Zangaro. Zangaro's forces only numbered 1,000 men in all whereas Banalia had an army of 6,000. Fortunately, though, Zangaro had a traditional friend and ally: the Republic of Loana. Banalia was of course Benin, the wretched Zangaro was Togo, and Zangaro's friend and ally Moana was Gabon. The plan was for one group of Bongo's men (a combat company of Bongo's Presidential Guard – mainly therefore whites – already in Togo) to launch an attack, a diversionary attack, at the head of the thousand noble Togolese warriors across the frontier. Just as fortunately, Benin's 6,000 men were split into small packets, a company here, a company there, so that the attackers would not immediately be overwhelmed. On the contrary all these scattered companies would be called upon to repel the attack whereupon Denard's group of ninety 'technicians' would assault and seize the capital. The capital was garrisoned by Benin's 1st Battalion, 600 men strong, at the military camp of Guezo near the Presidential Palace; and there was also a squadron of Ferret armoured scout cars in Cotonou. The attacking force would therefore have to rely on speed and surprise: the seizure of the Presidential Palace, the elimination of Kerekou himself, then the takeover of the radio station and (this was planned with loving detail) the interruption of the morning broadcast of the 'Voice of the Revolution'. There would be a thirty-second pause; then the 'Voice of Dahomey' would take the air. 'The tyrant is dead! *Enfants des Dahomey, debóut!*' The National Anthem, 'New Dawn', would follow in three different versions (one sung by a male choir), then M. Gratien Pognon, President of the Directing Committee of the Liberation Front, would read a Proclamation in French – which would be repeated in Fon, in Dendi, in Yoruba and in four other languages.

In the event of failure the force attacking from Togo would fall back over the frontier. But how, in the event of failure, would Denard's men fall back? This of course would largely depend on how they came in; and a very interesting 'appreciation of the situation' paper analysed the various possibilities.

Cotonou, Benin's capital, had began life, like so many of the capitals of West African states, as a trading station. It was therefore on the coast and it boasted a harbour. For a West African capital it was very small, with less than 200,000 inhabitants, and therefore very compact: the airport, the Presidential Palace, the 'Voice of the Revolution' radio station, the army camp, the ministries, the embassies – all the obvious *coup* targets – were within, at most, ten minutes' drive of each other. As Cotonou was on the coast, the attacking force – Force Omega as Denard now christened it – could come in by sea, by air, by night or by day. There were therefore four alternatives, each with its advantages and disadvantages. In *The Dogs of War* in a similar situation Frederick Forsyth had had his small group of mercenaries come in by night and by sea, setting off from the mother-ship in near-silent Zodiac black rubber landing craft; and Denard considered this method. A landfall could be made very near the main target, the Presidential Palace, at 1 a.m. – and that was clearly an advantage. On the other hand night operations could very easily go wrong (Forsyth had argued in his book, and possibly in real life too, that European soldiers were excellent at night operations whereas Africans even on their own territory were useless – in its first premise at least, a dubious thesis); it would be impossible to bring in and unload heavy weapons from the Zodiacs; and, above all, if things went wrong, escape would be difficult. The other seaborne possiblity was for the mother-ship simply to sail into Cotonou's harbour by day. This, for obvious reasons – it would be too slow and the vital element of surprise would be lost – Denard rejected.

The alternative was that Force Omega should arrive, all together, by plane at the airport. The great advantage here was that they could bring their heavy weapons in with them and above all that they would have a ready means of escape. The airport was lightly defended, if at all, and it would be easy to seize control by acting swiftly once the plane had landed. Force Omega would then split into two groups: Group A, fifteen men, would guard the airport, control the road outside and set up a heavy mortar group, ready to shell the army camp

if there were any resistance. Group B, forty-five men (the thirty black mercenaries were for operational purposes ignored – they were designed for decorative propaganda, rather than for real action) would themselves split into three groups. Twenty men would assault the Presidential Palace, the seat of the government. Ten men would concentrate on attacking the President's own house, in the Palace grounds, and on eliminating Kerekou himself. Fifteen men would 'neutralise' the nearby army camp. Then the radio station would be seized, and the 'Voice of Dahomey' take the air.

That was Stage A. Stage B would follow: the occupation of the whole western quarter of the capital. Stage C would take longer: extending the new regime's control over the whole of the country; and Stage D would involve taking measures against a possible counter attack launched from abroad.

It now became apparent why Denard had been asking for, and had obtained, such large budgets. In the pre-operational budget each of the sixty white mercenaries would be paid three months' salary (most of it, clearly, a retainer) of $2,000 a month; but in the post-operational budget (Stages C and D) each of the mercenaries would be under contract at the same salary for a further four months, with – a thoughtful touch – no less than one month's paid leave. The 'bill' for salaries alone, therefore, would be $840,000. As for the thirty blacks, they would be paid out of the pre-operational budget a 'salary' of $1,200, plus a $1,000 bonus if all went well – a comparatively minor $66,000. The other major expenses would be the hire of a jet-propelled DC8 and the outright purchase of a propeller-driven DC7, which – with generous payments to the pilots and crew – would come to a total of $95,000. Though Denard did not of course mention this in the contract, the DC7 and the DC8 for which he had negotiated were the two planes of Jack Malloch's Affretair, the charter company in which he himself had an interest – and no doubt Malloch was delighted at the thought of getting rid, by outright sale, of the ageing DC7, the aeroplane which would actually be at risk during the *coup* attempt at Cotonou airport.

The question, however, remained: should the aircraft with Force Omega aboard fly by night? Or should it fly in boldly by day? Kerekou's ministers met regularly once a week at the Presidential Palace, on Wednesdays from 10.30 to midday, and there was therefore much to be said for timing the landing boldly at 11.30 am on a Wednesday, seizing cars and taxis at the airport, and – within ten minutes or at most a quarter of an hour after having landed – attacking the Presidential Palace and capturing or killing not only the

President but all alternative leaders in one fell swoop. This was the bold decision taken; and the attack was therefore planned for Wednesday, 5 January.

But three days before it was due to be launched General Eyadema of Togo and President Bongo of Gabon met secretly; and they insisted on the plan's revision. The General had developed cold feet. There was to be no second prong, no cross-border attack — until at any rate the tyrant had been eliminated and the new regime could legitimately call for aid in 'restoring order'. But Denard, though he must have been worried, would not consider abandoning his plan. A brief postponement at most. For his men had already been assembled and were training at a military base in Morocco, his pre-operational budget had been invested, and his post-operational budget was guaranteed — a most important consideration — not only by President Bongo but also by King Hassan of Morocco.

For where had the money, the million-dollars-plus that the *coup* would cost, come from? Clearly not from the impoverished Liberation Front of the exiles. Gabon had since 1973 been suddenly transformed by the oil boom from one of the poorest to one of the richest countries in Africa; and President Bongo would have been less than human if he had not wanted to speculate politically with some of Gabon's new-found wealth. The Moroccan interest was more obscure. But King Hassan had to some extent acted as France's support and indeed substitute in policing Africa — it was Moroccan troops, airlifted by French planes, that came to the aid of General Mobutu against the invading Katangese gendarmes in the 'First Shaba War' later this same year — and the King's former minister, the dreaded General Oufkir, had at the time of the 'Libyan contract' shown great interest in helping 'James Kent' to piece together again his thrice-failed scheme. Oufkir had later tried to assassinate his royal master and had himself died; but the thought of using white mercenaries to overthrow his ever-more troublesome neighbour, Gaddafy of Libya, no doubt remained germinating in the King's mind. Hassan may have seen the Benin *coup* as a means of testing the efficiency or otherwise, of French mercenaries. Denard too had of course his Moroccan contacts from his own period there in the fifties. At any rate the King put the military base of Benguerir, sixty miles outside Marrakesh, at the disposal, for training purposes, of Colonel Maurin and Commandant Mercier.

Maurin was of course Denard himself; who 'Mercier' was I have not been able to discover, but I suspect that he may have been André Cau, also known as Carrel, one of Denard's most loyal lieutenants, who certainly took part in the *coup* attempt. Among the mercenaries in training at Benguerir were at least a dozen former Legionaries, of whom the older ones – Louis Cabasso alias Carden, Franz Heinmann alias Eugene François, Alfons Holzapfel alias Lingen, Werner Kolibius alias Koli and Istvan Wagner (who chose unusually, to go under his own name) – had all been in the 1er REP. There were plumbers and bar-waiters and men with no military experience among them too; but most had seen active service of some sort or other. On the night of 10/11 January Denard was in Paris at the Sheraton Hotel, where he apparently summoned an 'O' group of senior officers and NCOs. The NCOs included such men as Hugues de Chivre alias Sergeant Rucker and Michel de Charrette de la Contrie, who chose the very Breton *nom de guerre* of Kermarec. Less imaginatively, a real old hand, a Belgian ex-Para who had fought in the Congo, Van Den Berge, simply called himself Van. The final plans were made. On Saturday 15 January training ended at Benguerir; Force Omega were flown out in the hired DC8 from Marrakesh to El Hadj Omar Bongo Airport at Franceville in Gabon. There they were transferred to the propellor-driven DC7 (like the DC8, a cargo plane without seats). It was piloted by a Swedish pilot, Bjorg Isberg, who had flown for the Red Cross (and very possibly later for Von Rosen) in Biafra. The plane had been due to take off at 11.00 that night; but the plane was old, there was a bad oil leak and take-off was delayed for what must have been an agonising two hours. Nevertheless in the first hours of Sunday, 16 January the DC7 carrying Force Omega, an ample supply of sten-guns, machine-guns, bazookas and rockets, Denard himself and, by his side, with his speech all prepared, M. Gratien Pognon (travelling as M. Jacky) was winging its way through the darkness across the Gulf of Guinea and the Bight of Benin towards Cotonou.

Assault on Cotonou

It was just after dawn when an unknown aircraft, all lights extinguished, came skimming in over the sea to land at Cotonou Airport. The handful of technicians in the control tower and the scattered airport workers and officials were bewildered, for on that sleepy Sunday morning the first flight officially due in was not expected till nearly four hours later. The unknown aircraft taxied up to Piste No. 6, the landing-bay that had been used six years earlier for the Red Cross mercy flights to Biafra. It come to a halt at 7.03 precisely, only three minutes – apparently – later than planned. The technicians were even more amazed when the doors were thrown open before any landing steps could be wheeled up and ropes slung out. Their amazement turned to alarm and their alarm to panic as armed men, black and white, slithered down the ropes, touched *terra firma*, fired their weapons noisily but terrifyingly into the air – and started running for the control tower where the said technicians were ensconsed.

Within minutes the airport was in Force Omega's hands, and the initial opposition – two Ferret scout cars that appeared on the perimeter of the airport – had been dealt with by the mercenaries' bazookas. Denard's men now split into six mixed groups of black and white mercenaries. The smallest group, the 'command group' that took over the control tower, consisted of six men: three white and three black. Colonel Maurin (Denard himself), alias – for the duration of the operation – Soleil; two white officers, Lts Verdier and Tanguy; M. Gratien Pognon, the potential liberator; Sy Sawane Umar, a Guinean exile, who had recruited a number of Guineans for the coup under the pretext of an attempt to overthrow the hated President Sekou Touré; and Adjudant 'Montagne' – in fact a former warrant officer in the Benin army, Soglo by name, who had already taken part in a failed attempt to overthrow Kerekou and who had subsequently escaped from jail in Benin.

A group of twelve – *Pourveyeurs Protection* – acted as close protection to the 'command group'; a group of nine – *Groupe Couverture Ouest* – covered the airport buildings and entrance; and a group of thirteen – *Groupe Appui Couverture* – assured the vital protection of the aircraft in which they had all landed, at the same time setting up a mortar group that could range onto the army camp, less than a mile and a half away. This meant that well over a third – indeed, allowing for last-minute drop-outs, very nearly half – of Force Omega remained at the airport itself. The remainder – and my impression is that these were nearly all whites – were split into two groups, *Groupe Bleu*, twenty-nine strong, and *Groupe Noir*, twenty-four strong. One group immediately set off along the coast road, the esplanade, for the Presidential Palace; the other group headed down Cotonou's central avenue in the same direction.

The original plans had, of course, been changed. The rash project for a landing in broad daylight on a Wednesday at a busy airport had been abandoned [wisely in my view] in favour of a dawn landing on a Sunday at an almost deserted airport. So swift sudden and unexpected had been Force Omega's arrival that it seems that they achieved without difficulty one of their major aims, which was to seize control of the airport's telephones before the alarm could be raised.

But, on the other hand, early on a Sunday morning the private cars and taxis, which the two assault groups had planned to seize as transport, were simply not there at the airport entrance; and so Blue Group and Black Group had to double down the esplanade and the central avenue, on foot. At least one of the two groups evidently decided that, with the advantages of concealment that transport would have given obviously lost and their own small numbers only too apparent, terror was now a better tactic than secrecy. They opened fire on the facades of a dozen ministries and embassies as they jogged past – a terrifying awakening indeed for the occupants.

The central avenue group, nearing its target, seized a modern block of flats, *Quarante Logements*, overlooking the Presidential Palace two hundred yards away. They set up a bazooka group at the entrance and from the fourth floor – whose scared apartment owners had been forcibly woken and hustled out – opened fire. The esplanade group meanwhile had occupied the Palace of Congress, on another side of the Presidential Palace – which was therefore caught in a crossfire. But there was no attempt at an assault. Instead – and this may have been a hasty variation on the original plan – President Kerekou's residence was mortared, and mortared most thoroughly. But momentum, vital for a small attacking force with much inferior numbers, had been lost, the Presidential Guard from inside the Presidential Palace opened up with counterfire, one white mercenary was killed outside *Quarante Logements* and, worst of all from the attackers' point of view, President Kerekou was still alive. It was known that Kerekou was *always* in his residence at 7.30 every morning; but for once – and it seems to have been merely a stroke of fate, though a very fortunate one for Benin's President – this was not true. He had spent the night elsewhere, in a house three miles away; and less than two hours after the DC7 had landed, he was on the air, speaking via 'the Voice of the Revolution' to all the people of Benin, calling on them to seize whatever weapons they might have, report to local party headquarters and set up road blocks everywhere to repel the dastardly counter-revolutionary invaders.

An hour later, by 10 am, the attempted *coup* was over. Two hours of desultory exchange of fire around the Presidential Palace had led only to a stalemate that was broken, after Kerekou's belligerent broadcast, by the appearance of citizens wielding machetes and two hundred soldiers from the military camp, Camp Guezo. Radio contact between the various mercenary groups – all officers and NCOs carried walkie-talkies – was obviously functioning perfectly; and the two assault companies, called off, withdrew to the airport apparently without difficulty. At 10 am, only three hours after having landed, the DC7 was airborne again, winging its way back to Gabon, leaving behind it on the tarmac an assortment of weapons and equipment, ammunition crates (including one labelled 'Colonel Maurin' that proved to be full of documents), six dead and over fifty wounded Beninois (soon to be proclaimed 'Martyrs of the Revolution'), two dead mercenaries, one white and one black (soon to be exposed for photographers in the local morgue) and one very scared black mercenary, forgotten, in the last minute rush to get away, on top of the control tower building where he had been left as a sentinel.

This was Ba Alpha Umaru, a Guinean, of the Peul tribe, who while working in Senegal had joined an anti-Sekou Touré exile group in 1972 after the execution by Sekou Touré of the former Secretary General of the OAU, Diallo Telli, and the subsequent oppression of the Peuls. Recruited like a dozen other Guineans by 'Monsieur Joseph' – Sy Sawane Umar – he had been flown from Dakar to Casablanca on 30 December and had had less than a fortnight's military training – his first – at the Benguerir base before the *coup* attempt. As various Commissions of Enquiry – United Nations, OAU, and Benin's own – hastily assembled in Cotonou, Ba Alpha was produced again and again to tell his story. President Bongo meanwhile scornfully and pungently denied any involvement in the whole affair – if indeed there had been any attempted coup at all and it was not all a fiction invented by Kerekou – and invited the various commissions to visit Gabon and make as many enquiries there as they might wish: an open invitation which none of them accepted. King Hassan maintained a lofty and impassive silence. Various reports were issued; and the affair was quickly forgotten – except, presumably, by the wretched Ba Alpha Umaru (whose fate is unknown), President Kerekou himself (still in power at the time of writing) – and the disappointed backers who had invested well over half a million dollars in Denard's latest failure.

Yet within two months Denard, already planning ahead, was setting up a company, based in Rue Bachaumont, Paris, entitled France Outre-Mer Services (later rechristened Horus) which was virtually a barely concealed mercenary recruiting operation. That was in March 1977. By November, only ten months after the failure at Cotonou, Denard was already planning a similar strike, on the far side of Africa. The *coup* target this time was the Comores.

The Archipelago of the 'Battling Sultans'

Few people have ever heard of the Comores, fewer yet would be able to lay a fast finger on the map and proclaim with total confidence: *voici*! or *voilà*! Among the obscure little groups of islands that dot the Indian Ocean and were engulfed, at one stage or another in the womb of the British or French Empires the Comores must be one of the most obscure. Undeservedly so, however. The four islands that make up the archipelago are, though impoverished, beautiful and varied; their history is fascinating, their inhabitants picturesque and their position definitely strategic.

It always has been strategic. In the era of the 'Battling Sultans' the Comores was basically a nest – or rather four nests – of slave-trading Arab, Persian and even Malayan pirates; and pirates have always had a beady eye for strategic positions. The Comores archipelago dominates and controls, at its northern end, that much-used sea-lane known as the Mozambique Canal, the wide stretch of ocean separating Mozambique, on Africa's eastern coast, from the great island of Madagascar. Ever since the Cape was rounded this has been and continues to be a major trading passage, the route up and down which, nowadays, the vast oil tankers pass. The inhabitants of the Comores were, though charming, a ferocious and bloodthirsty lot; and slave-trading continued up to nearly fifty years ago. This even though one hundred years earlier the French had annexed one of the four islands that formed the archipelago – Mayotte. Mayotte was not the biggest or the richest of the islands but it had what was possibly the best natural harbour in the Indian Ocean. Inevitably the 'battling Sultans' in the rest of the archipelago were drawn into alliance with, or opposition to, the French. By the turn of the century Sultan Said Ali, the most liberal and open-minded potentate on the biggest island, Le Grand Comore, had, with the backing of the French, achieved dominance over his rivals. By the time the Sultan Said Ali died, in 1916, the Comores was a French colony, he its leading figure, and Moroni, which he had founded, was on the way to becoming the archipelago's capital. Times changed, and titles varied, but power remained with the ruling family. In 1970, on the verge of Independence, Prince Said Ibrahim, son and heir of Sultan Said Ali, was President of the Government of the Comores: what in a British colony, pre-independence, would have been called chief minister.

Politics seem to be even more passionate in small countries than in large. With only a quarter of a million inhabitants the Comores was undeniably a small country; but it was riven, as many archipelagoes are, by inter-island rivalry. The families of Anjouan, one of the two large islands, hated with an ancestral loathing the leading family of Le Grand Comore. Anjouan was rich, a spice island invested in and

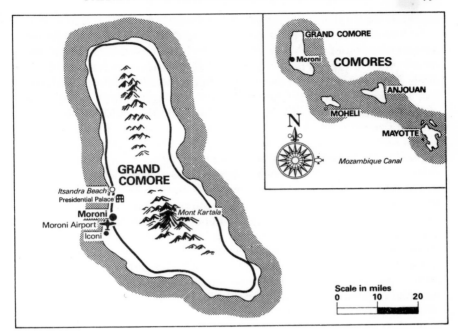

Le Grand Comore and inset of the four islands

exploited by French plantation owners: they backed one of the
leading Anjouan notables, Ahmed Abdallah. Le Grand Comore was
twice as large, contained half the population but was poor. The
people of Mayotte, the third island (the fourth, Maheli, is small and
unimportant), used to French rule, employed by French government
services, distrusted both of the other larger islands but in particular
the French plantation owners of Anjouan who coveted their own land.
There were more formal names for the political parties that eventually sprang up, but they were known generally (and simply) as the Parti
Vert and the Parti Blanc. The Parti Blanc were Prince Said Ibraham's
supporters; the Parti Vert Ahmed Abdallah's. Both those gentlemen,
it should be stressed, were robed and dignified Islamic ancients,
outwardly on the most friendly terms; but Ahmed Abdallah was, in
addition to being an island notable, a French Senator with (rather
surprisingly in view of his local plantation-owner backers) strong
support from the French Socialists. In one of those unforeseen upsets
that can happen in any elected assembly, the Prince was in 1972 voted
out as President of the government and Ahmed Abdallah was voted
in. Even more unforeseeable was Ahmed Abdallah's next move; he

suddenly and unilaterally declared the Comores independent.

It looked like – it probably was – a Mitterand-backed move, designed to embarrass Mitterand's recently triumphant opponent, the newly elected President of France, Valéry Giscard d'Estaing. Certainly Ahmed Abdallah, a gnome-like figure, would hardly have dared risk such a step without being assured of support in France; and indeed this mini-UDI did embarrass Giscard. He could hardly order French troops in when the Comores were in any case due to become independent very shortly; and he could hardly reimpose as the islands' ruler Prince Said Ibrahim, who retired to live in self-imposed exile in France. So the French government accepted, with a shrug of the shoulders, this political pinprick; but cannot have been displeased when the inhabitants of Mayotte immediately declared that they wished to remain under France's benevolent rule and protection. What was France to do? Impose an illegal independence on the inhabitants of Mayotte against their will? Hardly. The manoeuvre had rebounded; the premature Declaration of Independence had led to a mini-state mutilated of its most important asset, unity; Ahmed Abdallah's prestige, instead of rising high, sank very low.

Ali Soilih's Takeover

Less than four weeks later, on 3 August 1975, Ahmed Abdallah's regime was overthrown in a bloodless coup. The moving spirit behind the *coup* was a young man of a totally different generation, Ali Soilih, and of a totally different kind: genial, prematurely balding, large, with Black African (that is to say slave) blood in his veins, but for all that a member of the Parti Blanc. The old nobleman, Prince Said Ibrahim, in whose name the *coup* was carried out, refused however to accept power originating from a *coup d'état*; he died shortly afterwards on a pilgrimage to Mecca. His son and successor, the third of the line, Prince Kemal Said, a man with an extraordinary facial resemblance to the late Emperor Haile Selassie of Ethiopia in his younger days, was living in another of France's overseas ex-colonies, Djibuti on the Red Sea. He did not return to the islands immediately; he waited to see how the situation would turn out. He was sure that Ali Soilih, his contemporary, would rule well: Ali Soilih was an easy-going semi-intellectual, much influenced by the May 1968 Paris students' revolt, non-violent, joint-smoking, open-shirted, open-minded, and very popular. Meanwhile there remained an immediate problem; the deposed President, the wily Ahmed Abdallah, had fled to his own island of Anjouan and Anjouan was in revolt. Fortunately Ali Soilih had a French friend of his own age, Le Bret, installed on the Grand Comore, a *'gars de bonne famille'*, indeed a cousin by marriage of France's President, Valéry Giscard d'Estaing. Le Bret had founded the local airline, Air Comores. His chief pilot was a man named Morançay, who had flown relief supplies into Biafra. Morançay had his contacts in Gabon. Le Bret used them.

So in that August of 1975, that is to say three months before his Cabinda contract, six months before his Angolan contract, a year and a half before the Benin failure, Bob Denard first set foot on the Comores. He was 'lent' by President Bongo, no doubt with the French government's approval. He arrived with three other white mercenaries (almost certainly including René Dulac, Le Grand, also known as Vincent, and quite possibly Thomann and Lafaille who in November were to go into Cabinda under 'Vincent's' command). He met Ali Soilih at Moroni, he crossed to Anjouan with a hundred Comoriens in tow; and, virtually speaking, he came, he saw, he conquered. The era of the 'battling sultans' was long past, the islands' warlike traditions had long disappeared, and the notables were used to conducting their disputes, however bitter, by intrigue rather than by force of arms. Nevertheless three or four of Ahmed Abdallah's followers were killed before the ex-President surrendered. Anjouan returned to the fold. Ahmed Abdallah after four months' house arrest was packed off first as ambassador to Idi Amin in Uganda then – which must have been much more congenial to the old gentleman – to exile in Paris, with a large cheque signed by Ali Soilih in his pocket as a gesture of goodwill and consolation. As for Bob Denard, within weeks he was back in Gabon with successful and very discreet little action to his credit, presumably a large cheque from the new government in his pocket too – and the memories of a spice-tanged tropical paradise where manners were perfect and morals most attractively lax lodged firmly (if memories can be lodged in that part of the anatomy) in his heart.

At the beginning of 1976 Ali Soilih, who had been using another aged nobleman, Prince Mohammed Jaffar, as figurehead, arranged to be elected Head of State himself; and from then on the nature of the regime began to change. Curiously the Comores must have been the only state in the world where the extravagant ideas and ideals of May 1968 were actually tried out and where, in the words of the famous students' slogan, *'L'imagination prend le pouvoir'*. In complete contrast to a man like Ayatollah Khomeiny (whose time had of course not yet come) Ali Soilih swept away the veil, and all puritanical Islamic traditions. More dramatically still, he handed over power in the island to the _____nd's youth. It was not to the Head of State but to a collective of schoolchildren that the flabbergasted American Ambassador in Moroni found himself presenting his credentials. Pot was legalised. Jeans replacing flowing white robes. A *'Marche Rose'* was organised, a non-violent mass infiltration, to bring Mayotte back to the fold. It failed. However much the people of Mayotte may have disliked Ahmed Abdallah and his backers, they disliked even more this extraordinary version of Maoism in action that had even the Chinese Ambassador to the Comores jittery with apprehension. By 99.4 per cent the people of Mayotte voted to stay under French rule. In the other islands a certain anti-French tinge for the first time developed. Numerous French *co-opérants* left. At the end of the year Prince Kemal Said, in a sense the natural head of state, flew down to Moroni. 'You can't go on like this, Ali,' was his message to a man for whom he still had great sympathy. *'Tu es un bourgeois,'* retorted Ali Soilih somewhat inaccurately, *'tu n'as rien compris.'*

What most shocked Prince Kemal Said was the sight of a handful of imported Tanzanian troops; he left the islands after three days, convinced he could do nothing to moderate his contemporary's actions and afraid of being arrested. Yet, as Kemal Said always stressed, Ali Soilih's was more of an idealist than an oppressive regime; only one man was ever executed, and that a sorcerer who (according to the Prince) deserved death. Agriculturally speaking the economy boomed. Politically speaking Ali Soilih was convinced that, provided he kept the Russians at bay – as he did despite all their blandishments, a true child of May '68 in that – the French would make no attempt to overthrow him. He foiled an attempted *coup* on Anjouan; he quarrelled with his mighty island neighbour Madagascar (most justifiably – hundreds of Comorans who had settled there were massacred at Majunga); he rechristened the Republic *'democratique, laique et sociale'* and he continued to attack religion. He even organised on 28 October 1977 a referendum which showed – it must have been one of the few true results ever to emerge in a one-party African state – that only 55 per cent of the voters supported him. Yet in a sense it was the honesty of this openly proclaimed result that led to his downfall. The end of the year was marked by rumours of plots and arrests – as was only to be expected in a country where nearly half the population, and that probably the older, more economically powerful half, was openly against 'the revolution'. The early spring was marked by riots and deaths on the Grand Comore. And in the late spring, assured of important support for the 'counter-revolution' they proposed to instal, the mercenaries struck.

Assault on Moroni

This is the only instance I know of in modern mercenary history where a mercenary leader – Denard – acted in the worst traditions of his 'profession', selling his services first to one side and then without scruple to the other. That said, it must be admitted that Ali Soilih had himself changed and that all his French friends – feeling that he was going too far, too fast, too wildly – were deserting him. What is somewhat repugnant is that they did not all do so openly. His friend Le Bret, who had contacted Denard in the first place, was Ali Soilih's semi-official ambassador-at-large; but it seems that even Le Bret was involved in the betrayal – as were his chief pilot Morançay and another acquaintance of Denard already installed on the Grand Comore, Christian Olhagaray, a Basque adventurer who had much earlier worked in Gabon for President Bongo's predecessor, Leon M'ba. On the other hand, in any coldly calculated analysis it must be admitted that inside aid, which had been lacking in Benin, is probably vital to the success of any sudden *coup* that involves an invading force. That does not make those who treacherously provide that aid any more attractive as human beings.

Far less is known of the planning, the payments, the details and the execution of the Comores *coup*, that succeeded, than of the Benin *coup*, that failed. All that is certain is that almost exactly the same number of white mercenaries were used (this time black mercenaries were not included) and what is probable, though not certain, is that most of them were the same individuals who had taken part in the Benin attempt. For though the leadership of the Benin attempt was bitterly criticised by the white mercenaries themselves at the time, it had not been a total fiasco. It had failed, admittedly; but all *coups* risk failure. When they fail there is usually a heavy price to pay in casualties – but in this aspect the Benin *coup* had been exceptional. Though there were rumours of forty mercenaries wounded, they had all been evacuated speedily and successfully. The withdrawal – always the most difficult and dangerous part of any military operation – had been remarkably planned and brilliantly executed. The failure of the *coup* had been largely due to bad luck, combined with bad intelligence: the fact that President Kerekou had not been sleeping in his mortared residence that night. Admittedly there had been a lack of punch in the assault and a failure to capture the all-important radio station from which Kerekou had broadcast and rallied his people. But even if the Presidential Palace in Cotonou had been taken by assault, even if the '*Voix de la Revolution*' had been interrupted, as planned, by the '*Voix de Dahomey*', the *coup* would still almost certainly have failed with Kerekou alive, at liberty, and able to rally his supporters.

In the Comores, even more than in Benin, the whole force of the regime was bound up in one man. Ignoring all other objectives, Denard decided, rightly, to concentrate entirely upon seizing the person of this one man, the President, the Head of State, Ali Soilih. The great advantage this time was that, with inside information from traitors in Ali Soilih's immediate trusted circle, he could be absolutely sure where the President was to be located – as it happened, in the Presidential Palace.

Moroni, like Cotonou, is a small capital, lying on the sea, with a natural harbour. Just to the south of the capital is the airport. The Presidential Palace is rather further away than at Cotonou, well to the north of the city centre, but again, as at Cotonou, reasonably close to the shore. The four alternative means of 'invasion' were therefore again studied. This time however – and no doubt as a result of the lessons learnt at Cotonou – Denard plumped for total (rather than merely relative) surprise; and this meant a discreet landing by sea, at night, rather than the intimidating but inevitably public landing by air, at dawn. In addition of course, a most important factor, he and three others already knew the terrain and knew the 'target'. They had been to the Presidential Palace, they had met Ali Soilih, they would not be landing at night, always a muddling affair, on unknown soil in search of a president known only by photographs. They planned therefore to land at 1 am from Zodiacs at Itsandra beach, to the north of the capital but close to the Presidential Palace.

According to a version later leaked by Denard's adjudants, the 'mother-ship' was a trawler, purchased for the operation in France, that had set out thirty-five days earlier from a small port in Brittany and rounded the Cape. This seems, to say the least, unlikely. Far more probably the 'Clandestine Liberation Force', as Denard named his commando, had assembled in neighbouring Mayotte; and the 'mother-ship' was given the departure signal by wireless by Christian Olhagaray, who ran a small shipping company at Moroni. The contract had been signed by an exile group, the 'Rassemblement des Comoriens en France', and Ahmed Abdallah had flown out to the nearby French-owned island of Reunion to await the turn of events. This was a comparatively shoe-string, small-budget operation. There was no need for training, no need for heavy weapons, no need for a vast budget. Each mercenary was paid 10,000 francs (almost £1,000) in advance and carried only a sawn-off shotgun. The army commander, a Moroccan by origin, was in the know, and seems to have kept the Tanzanian troops, the only real threat, away from the scene of action in Anjouan. The Foreign Minister, Mouzaoir Abdallah, who had also been sounded out, was carefully abroad. Ali Soilih was practically a man alone, a man around whom a void had been created. Guided in by Olhagaray's transmissions, the 'mother-ship' approached the coast of the Grand Comore on the night of 14/15 May. Silently the Zodiacs were launched and conveyed the mercenaries, as planned, onto Itsandra beach. This time nothing went wrong. Nothing had been expected to go wrong. Before dawn Denard was able to open the twenty-four bottles of Dom Perignon which he had been carrying with him in justified anticipation of a successful *coup* to celebrate.

Ali Soilih had been in the Presidential Palace, as reported, guarded only by four bodyguards. The 'Clandestine Liberation Force' disembarked and made its way by foot, without difficulty, across the three miles separating the beach from what had previously been the French High Commissioner's Residence. Surprise was total. In the brief scuffle that followed one mercenary was wounded, the only casualty on the attackers' side. One bodyguard was killed. There is a story that Ali Soilih was found in bed with two young women and executed there and then on the spot, and they with him. That was not the official version. At the time it was announced that he had been arrested and was being held at the Palace; fifty more arrests followed swiftly before dawn. Prince Kemal Said, who had been in contact both with Ahmed Abdallah, his father's old enemy, and with Bob Denard in Paris, was telephoned at 4 am in Djibouti to be told that the *coup* had been successful and that Ali Soilih was a prisoner. The Prince favoured a public trial for his friend. Several days of confused political manoeuvring followed, for no-one was sure how Ahmed Abdallah would be welcomed. Then it was announced, in the time-honoured formula, that Ali Soilih had been shot 'while trying to escape' – in fact executed, it was later said, by an ex-legionary named (or, more probably not named) Vanne, a Belgian or else a Dutchman, probably therefore a Flamand. On 21 May Ahmed Abdallah, the former President, flew in to be welcomed by a cheering crowd of no less than 30,000. On 24 May Ahmed Abdallah and another of the coup's backers, Mohammed Ahmed, were proclaimed co-Presidents of a Politico-Military Directory for what now became by way of contrast to the late Democratic, Lay and Social State the Federal and Islamic Republic of the Comores. Here in full are the names of the Permanent Members of the new Politico-Military Directorate: Abbase Djoaddouf, Said Hassane, Said Hachim, Saidi Madi Kaff, Hadji Hassan Ali – and Colonel Said Mustapha M'hadju.

A Mercenary Paradise

The Comores are remote, difficult to reach, and free from journalists. It took some time for it to be realised that Colonel Said Mustapha M'hadju, Minister of Defence of the Federal and Islamic Republic, was none other than Bob Denard himself in his most elaborate and imaginative disguise yet. It was, literally, that. He was to be seen in white robes and a turban – jeans were of course out, and veils back in again, the schoolchildren at their desks, and everything in its place, as it had been before – and he claimed to have been converted to Islam. He even made the pilgrimage to Mecca and added a Hadji to his already elaborately impressive alias. It is possibly not true that he took possession of both Ali Soilih's car, a new Citroen, and of Ali Soilih's wife, Mazna – that he drove the one as ostentatiously as he married the other. But it is certainly true that he acted as if the Comores were his own personal fief. And so, in a way, they were. His fifty mercenaries in the main stayed on. They formed, on Gabon's lines, the new Presidential Guard commanded by a Belgian, Commandant Charles – the only armed force, once the Tanzanians had been peacefully expelled, in the islands. But for Denard himself it was a little too good to be true. The OAU, outraged, refused to accept the Comores back into its ranks while a notorious mercenary figured in its government, and on 28 September Colonel Hadji Said Mustapha M'hadju was seen off at Moroni airport by the President (now the sole President) Ahmed Abdallah and all his former cabinet colleagues. At a moving farewell ceremony the President called the Colonel a 'hero' who had saved the Comores, its people, the Muslim religion and 'all that is humane in this country' – an inhabitual accolade for mercenary leaders.

And that, it might have been thought, was that. But such was very far from being the case. It was significant that Denard flew out on an Air Gabon cargo flight which was collecting Rhodesian beef and had been diverted to pick him up. The mercenary leader was now approaching fifty; as he had said on French television, in one of his very rare interviews (on 5 June, three weeks after the *coup*, when French journalists had uncovered his identity), 'I hate the traffic jams of Paris but I adore the scent of the ylang-ylang.' He was soon, much more discreetly, back again in the Comores where he set up a meat-importing company, Socavia, that had the monopoly on meat imports from South Africa. And many of the other mercenaries did likewise. They had already set to, in the aftermath of the counter-revolution, reorganising the islands' administration from street-cleaning upwards; and they stayed on to become 'men of affairs', in many cases marrying two or three wives, owning two or three houses, effectively filling the void left by the ejected French plantation owners of Anjouan and the temporary French *co-opérants* on the Grand Comore, neo-colonialists on a new but yet (in that pirate archipelago) surprisingly traditional pattern.

And there they are still, seven years later, discreetly controlling the Presidential Guard and, under Captain 'Marques', the islands' security police. It is a mercenaries' dream, a mercenaries' paradise: a lush and comfortable tropical existence. They protect Ahmed Abdallah, now well on into his seventies. They hold the monopolies of various trades with South Africa. Denard himself, though technically under a *mandat d'arrêt* in France since 1981 when Giscard was defeated and Mitterand elected President, can often be found – if his alias can be penetrated – in the Hilton Hotel in Paris on his frequent visits to his motherland. The only potential threat to the mercenaries' continued idyllic existence comes from Prince Kemal Said, who was fobbed off with the post of Ambassador to France but resigned, to plan – of all things – an Australian-based mercenary counter attack that would replace Denard's mercenaries with his own. This first attempt ended in an ignominious failure: on 13 November 1983 John Pilgrim, of Southend-on-Sea, and two others, were charged in Perth in Australia with offences under the War Crimes (Foreign Incursions and Recruitment) Act.

Strong French forces are still based at Reunion, and a detachment of the Foreign Legion garrisons Mayotte. It seems certain that Denard's last and most successful attempt in his long and varied career as a mercenary leader could not have succeeded without the semi-official support of the nearby French authorities; it seems equally certain that any attempt to overthrow the discreet mercenary regime now in power in the Comores would hardly succeed unless and until French policy changes. But for all that Colonel Said Mustapha M'hadju would be wise to remember the words of one of his predecessors, one of the leaders of the mercenary *Grandes Compagnies* that pullulated in medieval France, the Bascot de Mauleon. 'I know of very few Companions bar myself,' the Bascot told Froissart, the fascinated medieval historian, 'who have not, somewhere or other, died a violent death.'

12

The Planning of Operation Anvil

'Like most of my plans it had tinsel around the edges.'
Mike Hoare, *Three Years with 'Sylvia'*

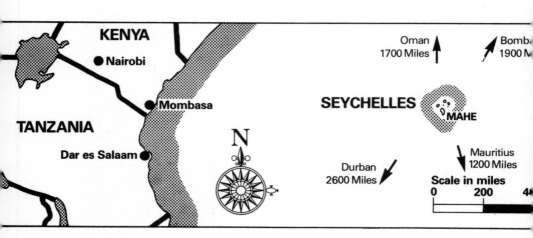

KENYA

● Nairobi

●Mombasa

TANZANIA

Dar es Salaam ●

Oman
1700 Miles

Bomb
1900 M

SEYCHELLES

MAHE

Mauritius
1200 Miles

Durban
2600 Miles

N

Scale in miles
0   200   4

The Seychelles and the East Coast of Africa

When he was a comparatively young man, before he had ever dreamt of becoming a mercenary, Mike Hoare had fallen in love with the Seychelles.

> Let me begin [he later wrote] by telling you something about the Seychelles and why I went there in the first place. There are ninety-three islands in the archipelago and they are formed by the tips of under-water mountains protruding through the sea. Coconut and bread fruit trees grow everywhere and the islands are lush with foliage which grows profusely in a climate drenched twice yearly by the monsoons.
>
> Hot and humid it can certainly be, after all Mahé, the principal island, is practically on the equator – four degrees south if my memory serves me right. Dense mangrove and takamaku trees on the edge of lovely white beaches, with cloves and vanilla high up in the hills and surrounding it all crystal clear water. Sounds enchanting, doesn't it? Well it is – a regular paradise.

In those days, in the 1950s, the Seychelles slumbered in the Indian Ocean, almost untouched by modern civilisation or development. The British India Steamship Line ran two ships between South Africa and Bombay, the *Kampala* and the *Karanje*, and they touched at Mahé on alternative months. Their arrival and their departure, with both passengers and mail, marked the great monthly excitement at Victoria, the tiny capital which boasted in its main square, Gordon Square, the tiniest statue of Queen Victoria on public display in the British Empire, one foot tall. British governors ruled lethargically over this backward dependency with the support, barely needed in view of the general good humour and peacefulness of the population, of a smart and excellent little police force. The official language was, of course, English; but the inhabitants spoke between themselves a form of French dialect, Creole. For the islands, previously uninhabited, had been colonised two hundred years earlier from the larger French island-colony of Mauritius far to the south; and the French planters, the *grands blancs*, had brought with them their own slaves. Then, before Napoleon became Emperor, a Royal Navy squadron seized the Seychelles and at Mahé the finest natural harbour for hundreds of miles. Thereafter British governors in Government House lived in general harmony with the *grands blancs*, the Savys, the Michaux, and the rest, with whose language, customs and way of life they interfered as little as possible.

By the middle of the twentieth century when Mike Hoare arrived for a nine-weeks' holiday with a 16 mm Bolex camera – a luxury in those days – and an ambition to make a documentary on island life, the coconut plantations, the main source of revenue for the landowners and of employment for the islands' men, had fallen on bad times.

The girls were very often beautiful [he wrote] and ranged in colour across a wide spectrum, which was not surprising seeing that their forbears had been drawn from all parts of Africa, Arabia, India and Europe. Many were extremely attractive, and there in very large numbers to boot. Fish were ten a penny, and girls were ten for one fish, went the local and unnecessarily harsh saying, a state of affairs brought about by the economics of the island. To find work it was essential to emigrate to the mainland: on the island it was almost unobtainable. So there were very few men about.

Mike Hoare appears to have much more of a rounded and engaging personality, with a noticeably wry sense of humour, than the somewhat cliché'd and two-dimensional figure of Bob Denard. He must still have been married to his first, English, wife at the time; he was obviously however bored with his post-war life as an accountant and a respectable family man in Durban. His passion was for adventure in general and in particular for sailing. His film project came to nothing: but he did hire and sail a wooden dinghy the *Miranda* around the crystal-clear lagoons of the Seychelles. He sunk it too, in twenty foot of water, three miles from shore, capsized by a sudden gust of wind as the sun was setting. His two crewmen, Jean and Pierre, brothers who had served in the British Army in Cyprus in a Seychellois Pioneer Battalion, thrashed around the *Miranda*'s mast, one foot of which protruded above the waves, screaming with their terror of *les demoiselles*, the tiger sharks that often swim quite close inshore. Hoare trod water for one hour, two hours, trying not to think of the barracudas and the sixteen other varieties of shark that infest this part of the Indian Ocean. He and his crew, hoping against hope, were rescued, of course, in the end by a lucky chance and three pirogues of young boys; and in gratitude Hoare spent fifty pounds – 'a veritable fortune', the local French priest assured him – on a three-day-long beach party for his rescuers. He went home, to Durban, to take a share in a secondhand car business and to set up, more actively, a Safari company. He went to Katanga, separated from his first wife, and married a South African girl, Phyllis Sims, by whom he had two more children to add to his original three. He became famous as a mercenary leader. In his mind the Seychelles faded to a happy if spectacular memory of nine weeks in paradise.

The Presidency of James Mancham

During his time there Hoare had stayed in a bungalow in the grounds of the Hotel Seychelles, on the most beautiful stretch of beach in the main island, Beauvallon Bay. The owner of the hotel, Gerry Le Grand, had come from South Africa, convinced that there was a vast tourist potential in the Seychelles if only they would open an airport. In the end 'they' – the British authorities – did. But it took a long, long time. Mahé International Airport, as it was grandiosely called, actually opened on 4 July 1971, though it was not officially opened till March the following year when the Queen paid her first and last visit to what was still, just, a part of her Empire.

The opening of the airport changed the whole way of life in the islands. The Seychelles did, almost immediately, undergo a tourist boom. Smart new hotels sprang up in the decade that followed: a cluster of three on Beauvallon Bay: the Coral Strand Hotel, the Beauvallon Bay Hotel, and the Fisherman's Cove Hotel, and out a mile or so past the little lagoon-style airport, the Reef Hotel, on its own. Roads were built, work increased, tourists, developers and speculators poured in; and politics inevitably reared their head.

The *grands blancs* had seen with regret their old style of life fading away: though a plantation owner like Henri Michaux, a *grand blanc*, could still boast – or rather state without boasting – that he had had over sixty children of his own on his plantation and that his grandchildren could be counted in their hundreds. But though the *grands blancs* retained their social prestige, their economic power base had disappeared. A few by property speculation made new fortunes. The future however obviously lay with the commercial classes rather than the landowners; and from the ranks of the commercial classes sprang the epitome of the islands' *nouveaux riches*, Jimmy Mancham.

Mancham's father had been, in the words of one of the oldest British inhabitants, 'just a grocery store owner'. But the grocery store had prospered, a chain of stores had developed, and Mancham's father set his son on the traditional upward path for intelligent young men in any British colony by sending him to study law in London. In due course Mancham qualified as a barrister-of-law at the Middle Temple. He was a flamboyant, bearded young man of great charm and dynamism, proud of his racial mixture and his streak of Chinese blood, intent on cutting a dash in the great world outside and on bringing prosperity and glamour to the islands. In November 1970 the Seychelles' second ever elections were held. Shortly afterwards Jimmy, as everyone called him on the islands, became at the age of thirty-one the Seychelles' first Chief Minister. His party won ten out of the fifteen seats in the little local parliament. Next year came the opening of the airport; the year following the visit of the Queen. Mancham loved the pomp and the ceremony, the luxury, the power, the connections with the rich and famous and above all the girls. Heather Jane, his English-found wife, did not last long. Soon it was the turn of a Yugoslav starlet Olga Bisera, of Helga Von Mayerhofer, a New York jewellery designer, of Michele First, the model, even of Fiona Richmond, 'Britain's nudest dancer'. 'So I'm happy with another woman,' Mancham told journalists. 'Is that a crime? You must remember these are the Seychelles, not stuffy Westminster. I'm only human, a common trait in politicians, despite what people think.' Yet in a way it was the girls that ruined Jimmy; even the easy-going locals said that he ought to have been more discreet. Moreover he always chose what he described, with almost touching snobbery, as 'young ladies of international stature' whereas his political opponents were in his view 'only going out with some village girls'.

The Seychelles is a small place, and this sort of remark wounds. When they came back almost simultaneously from London together, Mancham and another newly qualified Middle Temple barrister, France-Albert René, used to do the rounds of the Seychellois bars together. But that was in the early Sixties, before Mancham could afford to sneer at René's choice of girls. René was four years older, also an extremely handsome and very attractive man, but of a very different cast of features and mind. His father had been a rich Frenchman from France, M. Lanier; René was illegitimate, no disgrace in the Seychelles, and half-French, half-Seychellois, no disgrace either. He too had married an English wife in England, Karen, whom he discarded in favour of, eventually, one of the Savys – hardly a 'village girl' therefore, though certainly no café society girl like Jimmy's preferred set. There were far greater divergences, though, than their attitude towards women between the two fellow barristers and former friends. René had originally trained for the priesthood and always had a more serious turn of mind. The political party which he founded and led, the Seychelles People's United Party, wanted independence from the British, preached social justice and was highly suspicious of capitalist development and of tourism. Mancham and (as the 1974 election proved) just over half the Seychellois population with him, were perfectly happy to remain under British protection as long as they could run their own internal affairs. 'Do we want Independence?' Mancham thrice asked a vast rally (by Seychellois standards) in Victoria's stadium and thrice the answer came roaring back from thousands of throats: 'No, No, No!'

Nevertheless the British government forced Independence on the Seychelles; and on 29 June 1976 Independence came. 'You must know when I move into the Governor's Residence on Tuesday it is

going to be the swinging-est State House in the whole world,'
Mancham told the delighted guests who arrived to celebrate. They
included, apart from the Duke and Duchess of Gloucester, a bevy of
the international jet set, Adnan Khashoggi's brother, Essam, and a
'friend', a British businessman discreetly anonymous, who presented
the new Head of State, President Mancham, with a blue Rolls Royce
Corniche in which he left Independence Stadium (he had arrived in a
more modest Jaguar) to the cheers of his supporters.

Earlier on Independence Day he had joined hands with his new
Prime Minister, Albert René – for the British had insisted on a
coalition government – in a more serious gesture.

'In this spirit,' he proclaimed, 'I call upon my Prime Minister to
hold my hands as a once and for all demonstration of our mutual
respect, as a resolve of our determination and that of the parties we
represent to work together for the common good and as a symbol of
lasting national unity.'

One year later, while he was in London attending the Commonwealth Leaders' Conference – to be even more precise, while he was,
in his own words, in bed with a 'tousled blonde' in the Savoy Hotel –
he was telephoned by his Arab friend Khashoggi to be told that there
had been a coup in Victoria. The President – or rather the
ex-President as he had just become – had been overthrown in his
absence and that, despite all the hand-holding and proclaimed
mutual respect, by none other than his own Prime Minister, Albert
René. Swinging time was over.

René's Regime

In retrospect it is difficult to blame René too much for this Judas-type
conspiracy. The Seychelles are a relaxed place and the Seychellois a
relaxed people who were at ease with Mancham's genial style; but
many of them felt he had gone too far when he had allowed whole
clusters of out-islands to be sold to Arab business men or to members
of the Shah's family. They approved when the new President, René,
re-appropriated these islands without compensation. They approved
when René introduced social security, health clinics and free education. But they approved much less when he instituted a one-party
state, censored the rival newspaper, and set about abolishing the
religious fee-paying private schools. And they approved not at all
when he formed an army and called in the Tanzanians to 'train' it.

The Seychelles of course had never had an army. They had never
needed an army. As Mancham had pithily put it, 'the only weapon of

the Seychellois people is their laughter'. There was a British-trained police force and a police armoury containing the only firearms on the islands, about two hundred rifles, at Montfleury in Victoria. That was why René's coup had been so surprisingly easy. Sixty of his supporters had flown in from the out-islands on the Sunday night, 4 June 1977 and in the early hours of the Monday morning, at 2 am on 5 June, they had simply seized the armoury at Montfleury, and all was over. They were armed with twenty Kalashnikovs that had been smuggled onto Mahé from Dar-es-Salaam; in the brief struggle one policeman was killed and two men were wounded, one on each side. But once the armoury was in the 'Revolution's' hands that was that: there was simply no possiblity of resistance. The Commissioner of Police, Mr Patrick Somerville, and four other British police officers were arrested and expelled. The Chief Justice of the Seychelles, Mr Aidan O'Brien Quinn, who was unwise enough to describe the Prime Minister's 'task-force' to the press as 'people with long criminal records', followed within a few days. The only other casualty appears to have been the brother of the Anglican Minister who was dragged into a courtyard and for obscure reasons shot. But of course the real casualty was the whole way of life in the Seychelles. For the first time murder and violent death had, like the serpent, intruded into the politics of paradise; and it ought never, to be forgotten that it was René and his party, not Mancham and his supporters, who were responsible for this ruinous development.

The problem the new government now therefore faced was this: that it would be as easy to overthrow them as it had been for them to overthrow their opponents – unless of course an army was created. So, with the help of President Nyerere of Tanzania, an army was created. Not a large army – it was at most six hundred strong – but still a new and oppressive element that would never have been needed if Britain had not unwisely imposed an unwanted independence. The police force, some 450 strong, kept to their British traditions though their British officers had departed: they despised the ill-disciplined, idle and ragged army and they, like the populace at large, loathed the loutish, aggressive Swahili-speaking Tanzanians who were imported technically to train the new army but in fact as a sort of presidential bodyguard. Ogilvy Berlouis, who had once worked as an office boy for the British-owned company Mahé Shipping, a small man with a big head, generally feared, became Minister of Youth and of Defence in President René's new government.

'Mad Mike' Takes a Hand

Mike Hoare had, by the early 1970s, apparently abandoned forever his mercenary ambitions. He had, presumably with what remained of his Congolese money, bought and refurbished a Baltic schooner and for three years fulfilled one of the dreams of his life by sailing her around the Mediterranean, with his second wife Phyllis and various of his children as crew. But by early 1974 he was back in South Africa. The Baltic schooner was sold. He wrote a book about her, a very attractive book called *Three Years with 'Sylvia'*; but books rarely keep a family alive; and by 1975 Hoare was wistfully dreaming of a comeback, with his eye on Angola. He made contact with a young and ambitious operative of BOSS, South Africa's much-feared Bureau of State Security, named Martin Dolincheck. But though Dolinchek was keen to play a part in any intrigue that might increase his own importance, in the end the head of BOSS, General Hendrik Van Der Bergh, warned Hoare off. The former mercenary was not, the general cabled, 'to meddle in State affairs'.

But, as Dolinchek later put it, 'Guys like Mike Hoare – they live for this kind of operation. They go to bed praying that something will turn up.' It is impossible to say whether Hoare immediately thought of the Seychelles as a possible target when the news of Mancham's overthrow and René's coup came through on 5 June 1977; or whether the idea gradually developed. Indeed it may originally, and most ironically, have been put there by René himself. For only five days after the coup the new President was accusing Mancham of recruiting mercenaries for a counter-coup, an allegation which Mancham immediately and almost certainly truthfully, from his London exile, denied. René, he said, was 'a victim of his own over-reactive mind'; and he added, with less prophetic truth, 'I have been fighting a diplomatic battle and will continue to do so.'

Less than a year later Denard launched his successful coup in the Comores; and I personally always felt that it was this success by his despised rival of the Congo days that induced Mike Hoare to make the Seychelles his target. After all, the similarities were only too evident; both the Seychelles and the Comores were newly independent small archipelagoes in the Indian Ocean; in both the legitimate, elected right-wing government has been overthrown by violence and in both a left-wing regime had been installed. If anything, the Seychelles with only a fifth of the population of the Comores was the easier target; and if Bob Denard could overthrow Ali Soilih's regime with fifty mercenaries in one night, why could not he, Mike Hoare, as easily do the same in the Seychelles?

I still believe that this age-old rivalry with Denard spurred Hoare on. But, more recently, conclusive evidence has come to light that Hoare was already plotting a mercenary coup in the Seychelles *before* the success of Denard's coup in the Comores. For on 12 May 1978, that is to say *two days before* the Comores coup, Hoare was writing as follows to a prominent Seychellois exile:

Dear Gonzague,
    I am enclosing Plan No. 2 which I would like you to consider. It seems a very workable plan to me. ...Tender my respects to Mancham and tell him my services are entirely at his disposal if he needs me.
                                            Mike.
PS Beware of a man named Banks in Britain. He is very dangerous and bad news in our line of country.

Gonzague – Gonzague D'Offay – had been Minister of Internal Affairs under Mancham's short-lived Presidency; and this letter is conclusive proof that less than a year after Mancham's overthrow Hoare was already hard at work preparing plans for a mercenary coup in the Seychelles and in close touch directly with leading right-wing exiles and indirectly with Mancham himself. Indeed it seems that Hoare had revisited the Seychelles as a tourist the previous September, that is to say three months only after René's coup, and presumably on the strength of that reconnaissance had drawn up not only Plan No. 2 but Plan No. 1 – whatever they may have been. It is not at all clear whether at the time the letter was written Gonzague D'Offay was in Durban, where many Seychellois exiles were gathering, or in Australia or in Paris, other centres of activity (indeed in Paris about this time a Seychelles Liberation Committee was formed) or in London; but the reference to John Banks 'in Britain' and the advice to steer clear of him would seem to imply Paris. As for John Banks, he ought to have been flattered that Hoare deigned to consider him as a rival mercenary leader who was worth warning the Seychellois off.

Hoare's concern was partly justified in that Banks had been very active in 1976 and 1977, in and out of intrigues with his old cronies Dempster and Tomkins, one more fantastic than the next: a parachute raid and rescue on Luanda prison; blowing up Cabinda oilwells (Gary Van Dyk, a South African living in England, set up a training centre for this abortive venture at Pine Valley Farm near Okehampton in Devon); forming a new anti-communist mercenary recruiting organisation, ACRO. Later he was to become very bad news indeed: involving himself in the terrorist scene; in attempts to trap Carlos for the Israelis (which Tomkins and Dempster, to trap him in his turn, denounced to the PLO); allegedly in activities connected with the IRA; and definitely in unsavoury plots involving assassination in Somoza's Nicaragua. By 1981 he had been on the run for several months from an open prison where his blackmailing activities had landed him. Hoare's diagnosis of three years earlier had proved only too accurate a forecast as far as John Banks was concerned.

Hoare himself was having a busy year in 1978. Apart from preparing plans for a coup in the Seychelles, he was hired as technical adviser on far and away the best mercenary film ever yet to be made, *The Wild Geese*. In the film, based on the Irish-born Rhodesian-based Daniel Carney's novel, Richard Burton played the leading role, of a Mike-Hoare-style figure, an ageing mercenary leader called out of retirement for one last venture, a swift mercenary raid (rather on the lines of the abortive Libyan Contract) to rescue an ex-president from a prison in Albertville in the Congo. Among the actors – the cast included Roger Moore and Richard Harris – was one with whom Hoare struck up a close friendship, a man some twenty years younger than himself named Tullio Moneta. Though born in Yugoslavia – curiously enough like Martin Dolinchek the BOSS operative – Tullio was basically an Italian, an impressive athlete six foot five inches tall, who had been a champion discus thrower in Italy before emigrating to South Africa and becoming, in South Africa, a well-known television actor; he still retained, however, a strong Italian accent. He was also a karate expert and it was via karate that Tullio Moneta knew a man of his own age, in his late thirties, a 5th Dan named William Dunlop Paul who owned a string of health studio clubs and had, more importantly, close connections with South Africa's commando force of which he had once been a member. From playing a mercenary in a film to becoming a mercenary in reality there seems to be only the slightest imaginative jump, particularly in a country like South Africa which was, at that time, awash with rumours of mercenary plots and generally indignant at the state of affairs in what had previously been one of South Africa's favourite tourist destinations, the Seychelles. While Hoare continued in his role as technical adviser, Tullio Moneta and William Dunlop Paul travelled down to Capetown to meet the last commander of Five Commando, George Schroeder.

Schroeder was now a businessman in the Cape; but, like almost all ex-mercenary leaders, he seems to have had a nostalgia for the good old days. He too had a plan for a Seychelles coup that involved two Hercules cargo planes with two amphibious troop carriers on standby and he offered Moneta and Dunlop Paul 20,000 rand down and 20,000 rand on successful completion of the 'mission' to join his team. (There were – and are – approximately two rand to the pound; at the time a rand was about equal to a dollar. As most of the figures will from this point on be in rands, it is worth bearing these rates in mind. 1,000 rand therefore would be about £500.) These were large sums but the two were not impressed with Schroeder or with his plans; they did not like the man, they considered him politically ill-informed and they preferred in the end to work with Hoare – who would almost certainly have talked of *his* plans to Moneta during the shooting of *The Wild Geese*.

The November Plot

Nevertheless all these plans apparently came to nothing until, well on into the following year, in November 1979, President René announced in the Seychelles that he and his government had foiled a plot 'sponsored from abroad with the cooperation of mercenaries standing ready in Durban'. At the time, to the world in general, this seemed a mere invention, a pretext dreamt up by René to crush internal agitation against his regime – even the schoolchildren were demonstrating against the hated National Youth Service that would take them from their families – and to imprison his opponents. Sure enough, over eighty Seychellois were arrested and held, in the main, for nine months without being charged or tried before being exiled. But, with hindsight, it seems more than likely that there was a real plot against René. Whether it was Hoare's Plan No. 1 or Plan No. 2 or even No. 3 or No. 4, I doubt; it seems far more likely that it was French-inspired. France after all had been the original colonial power in the Seychelles, French and Creole were still more widely used as languages than English, France had, with its Indian Ocean fleet and troops at Mayotte and on Reunion, a far stronger position in the area than Britain; and it was almost certainly with France's approval and complicity that another left-wing regime on another Indian Ocean archipelago had the year before been successfully overthrown. Furthermore it was a Frenchman, Schroeder had told his visitors, who had first approached him with the suggestion of a mercenary coup; and in the Seychelles, on the discovery of the November Plot, twelve Frenchmen out of the thirty-man crew of the *Topaz*, the Seychelles' only naval vessel, were arrested. So was the

man in charge of training the Harbour Police, M. Jacques Che-
valereau. The thirteen Frenchmen were deported two months later
after allegedly admitting preparing a *coup* – which they denied on
arrival in Paris. But the whole thing does rather whiff of the Denard
touch. Could he have been hoping to extend his power from the
Comores to the Seychelles? Could he even have been planning –
which would have been possible with the cooperation of the Harbour
Police and the neutralisation of the naval vessel – the descent of a
boatful of mercenaries, complete with heavy weapons, who would sail
north from Moroni, on Victoria itself? That was one of the four
alternatives he had originally considered for the Cotonou *coup*; and in
the Seychelles it could have succeeded. Had it done so – if there is
any foundation at all in this speculation – then Denard would have
become a figure of unrivalled power and menace in the Indian Ocean.

The End in Rhodesia

A month after the failed November Plot in the Seychelles events
occurred elsewhere in Africa that were to have a bearing on future
mercenary plans. In December 1979 the bitter war in Rhodesia at last
came to an end. UDI was terminated, the ceasefire held, Lord
Soames flew out from Britain as Governor to preside over the
elections that would lead to the independence of what now became
Zimbabwe – and hundreds of whites who had fought the black
guerillas of Nkomo and Mugabe in the Rhodesian army were faced
with an uncertain future. They began to consider their position.
Their position, they knew, would be insecure in a black-ruled
Zimbabwe, particularly if they had served in any of the units most
reputed for their ferocity and ruthlessness in hunting down the
guerillas who would now almost inevitably become the masters of the
new country.

Consider, for example, the case of Mike Webb, an Englishman just
turned thirty at the time. Webb was in effect a high-class professional
soldier, a man whose life was soldiering. He had joined the British
Army and had been commissioned into the 15th/19th The King's
Royal Hussars, a regiment that, like all Britain's cavalry regiments,
only accepted gentlemen of the traditional breeding and background
as officers. Five years later he had resigned his commission and
joined, with the rank of captain, the Trucial Oman Scouts. By doing
so he had technically become a mercenary but a mercenary of a very
official sort, for Sultan Qaboos' army was with British government approval almost entirely British-officered. After only a year,

however, in March 1975, Mike Webb again resigned his commission; and this time he took a further step towards becoming a fully fledged mercenary by joining the Rhodesian Light Infantry.

White-ruled Rhodesia lacked white manpower; and as in the mid-Seventies the war against the guerilla forces of Joshua Nkomo based in Zambia and those of his rival Robert Mugabe based in Mozambique grew more ferocious and more murderous, conscription of the local white settlers proved insufficient to fill the ranks. Therefore, at first discreetly, then much more openly, Ian Smith's regime began to recruit professional white soldiers from all over the Western world. Most, like Mike Webb, were British. They were of course fighting for a country that was technically a British colony in rebellion against the British Crown; but they can hardly be described as traitors. For Rhodesia was quintessentially British in style and way of life, and proud of it. Perhaps that is why so very few South Africans joined the Rhodesian army – there has always been a strong mutual antipathy between the Boers of South Africa and the British of Rhodesia despite their common boundary, shared interests and similar colour of skin. But a certain number of Americans came to Rhodesia, recruited indirectly via articles and advertisements in *Soldier of Fortune* and more directly via Major Robert Brown, the magazine's publisher, who came himself to Salisbury in June 1977 to discuss recruiting with Colonel Lamprecht, head of Rhodesia's recruiting office.

The pay was at the time not high – a mere £40 a week – and the contract long: three years. But as the war against the guerillas intensified, the pay rose to $800 a month minimum, up to $3,000 maximum, and the number of foreigners serving with the Rhodesians, either as 'volunteers' or as 'immigrants', to no less than fifteen hundred. British and Americans apart, a number of other whites from different parts of the world were recruited. One of Denard's right-hand-men, Major L'Assomption, formerly of Gabon's Presidential Guard, appeared at the end of 1977, leading a group of French mercenaries recruited by Roger Bruni (now dead), ex-REP and ex-Yemen, from the offices in Rue Bachaumont. Precise figures are difficult to come by but it seems that the RLI – the Rhodesian Light Infantry – was largely composed of West Germans and Danes and that both the Selous Scouts, a ferociously ruthless guerilla-killing unit and Grey's Scouts, who patrolled steathily on horses, were in effect mercenary units.

The foreigners were mercenaries, of course, but they were joining a structured, regularly paid regular army as individuals; and so they can hardly be said to constitute mercenary war-bands in the sense that Hoare's men and Denard's men had done in the Congo. Mike Webb joined the RLI and then, after three years, switched in 1978 to Rhodesian Special Forces. A certain air of mystery surrounds Special Forces. It was not a guerilla-hunting unit nor a commando group specialising in cross-border strikes into Mozambique like the Rhodesian SAS, the apple of the commander-in-chief General Peter Wall's eye (he had commanded C Squadron of the Malayan Scouts in the 'emergency' there and had modelled this unit on that). Special Forces continued to function after the ceasefire of November 1979 up to and through the elections of February 1980. On 4 March the victor in the elections, the Marxist-orientated Mugabe, was asked by Lord Soames – his last act of importance as Governor – to form a government. There had been rumours in the interim of a last desperate fling by the still white-commanded army, a *coup* in Salisbury to preempt Mugabe's installation as Prime Minister. It came to nothing. The white units – the Rhodesian Light Infantry, the Selous Scouts and of course the Special Forces – were dissolved. Mike Webb – one of many – headed south, away from possible reprisals, across the Limpopo into the Republic of South Africa. Rhodesia's C Squadron SAS headed south too, and were immediately enrolled, most of them, in a rather special unit of the South African Defence Force (as the Republic's armed forces were called), the Reconnaissance Regiment, stationed at The Bluff just outside Durban, overlooking the Indian Ocean.

Others of the SAS – though whether from Rhodesia or Britain is not quite clear, twenty in all it is said – joined as officers the notorious 'Buffalo Battalion', No. 32, South Africa's most mercenary unit, commanded by Colonel Carpenter, an American, Vietnam (and possibly Congo) veteran, officered – apart from the SAS – by Americans and Australians and formed by no less than 1,200 black Angolans. This unit was later to be 'exposed' by two deserters; a Briton, Trevor John Edwards, and an Angolan, José Ricardo Belmundo. Though deserters' atrocity tales must always be taken with a pinch of salt, it seems that the black Angolans were FNLA veterans, transported from the north of Angola to fight side by side with UNITA forces in the south. If this is so, then inevitably the setting-up of the Buffalo Battalion must have been a joint CIA–South African operation, which would of course account for the nationality of its commanding officer.

A word of explanation is necessary here about the Citizen Force, South Africa's army. As its name implies, it is not a regular standing army in the traditional European sense but rather an extension of the time-honoured Boer concept by which all male citizens, in time of war or crisis, take up arms to defend the State. In practical terms this meant – and means – that there is a skeleton staff of full-time professional officers and NCOs, the Permanent Force, but that the mass of the army, trained by compulsory military service and by compulsory annual camps, is on stand-by, ready to be called up at a moment's notice for a campaign or for an operation.

Units such as the 'Buffalo Battalion' in the Caprivi strip or the bounty-hunting Koevoet (Crowbar – mainly ex-Selous Scout offi-cered, with, as troops, 'turned' ex-SWAPO guerillas) in South West Africa, raised for a special purpose and a special theatre, obviously lay outside this system; as did the theoretically independent budding 'armies' of the Bantustan homelands. Ron Reid-Daly, the former commander of the Selous Scouts, found a new mercenary niche as commander of the Transkei Defence Force, with Tim Bax, also ex-Selous Scouts, becoming the CO of the Transkei Regiment – his second-in-command being a thirty-two-year-old American.

Also theoretically outside the Citizen Force/Permanent Force system were the traditionally most prestigious units of Afrikanerdom, the Commandos. Training for the Recce Commandos, as the various units of the Reconnaissance Regiment were called, continued on and off for no less than sixteen years. Most of their members were civilians – citizens – with ordinary jobs in or around Durban, but they were not permitted to leave the country or even their homes without the permission of their commanding officer and they were used to being suddenly summoned to report to barracks at The Bluff for short, sharp operations – usually, it seems, cross-border raids into Mozambique or Angola or perhaps even further afield on 'special missions'. As South Africa's otherwise surprisingly free press is muzzled by laws of exceptional severity when it comes to military matters, it is almost impossible to discover what exactly the Recce Commandos did and how and where they were used. But they certainly considered themselves an élite, and an operational élite at that.

The Rhodesian SAS veterans did not, however, apparently fit in too well with what was very much an Afrikaner-dominated Afrikaner-speaking force; and when their one year's contract came up for renewal in March 1981, it was not renewed. This meant that Natal in general and Durban in particular, the former centre of British power in South Africa to which the ex-Rhodesians naturally gravitated, was by early 1981 full of disgruntled ex-soldiers who had led an adventurous life in Rhodesia, who had had to become reconciled to the idea that the South Africa army did not want them, and who were trying half-heartedly to reconcile themselves to civilian life and civilian employment. Mike Webb had become, without enthusiasm, an insurance salesman. Others, Rhodesian born and bred like Aubrey Brooks (who had served in the Selous Scouts), had left Zimbabwe a little later with his family and his wife, Di. Brooks had tried to set up a printing business in Durban; but like many of the exiles was under-capitalised, for it was impossible to take money out of independent Zimbabwe. They used to meet, many of these ex-Rhodesians who still retained Zimbabwe citizenship, in the Riviera Hotel on Durban's waterfront. The Riviera was owned by a Briton, Ken Dalgliesh, who had been a policeman in Rhodesia, a Special Branch inspector. Dalgliesh had seen the end coming earlier than most and had emigrated to South Africa in 1975. Rhodesian reunion evenings were, from March 1980 onwards, celebrated nostalgically, at the bar of his hotel every week.

Hoare's Plans Mature

It is now time to draw together the various strands that form the complex but fascinating background to the planned Seychelles mercenary coup of November 1981. Mike Hoare, from his home in a small village outside Pietermaritzburg, the capital of Natal, was undoubtedly the moving spirit in the whole venture. Undiscouraged by the failure of the November Plot in 1979, he got in touch with the new group of exiles – those Seychellois who were later expelled by René's government after months in prison without trial. They had, in June 1980, formed a far more dynamic exiles' group than the original Paris-based Seychelles Liberation Committee. It was called the *Mouvement pour La Résistance,* and its leading activists were, in London, Paul Chow Singh, a young man in his thirties of – obviously – very mixed blood who had run a bookshop in the Seychelles and acted as stringer for foreign wire services and, in Durban, Gerard Hoareau. Chow acted more as a spokesman and propagandist; Hoareau was the more ambitious. He had been Assistant Secretary for Foreign Affairs under Mancham and Chief Immigration Officer under René till his arrest in November 1979. Exile politics, however small the country involved, are always tricky and riven by personal rivalries; and Jimmy Mancham in his Putney home by the River Thames always kept his distance from the *Mouvement pour La Résistance.* Hoareau for his part appears to have despised Mancham but to have seen that it was vital to use him as a figurehead if René

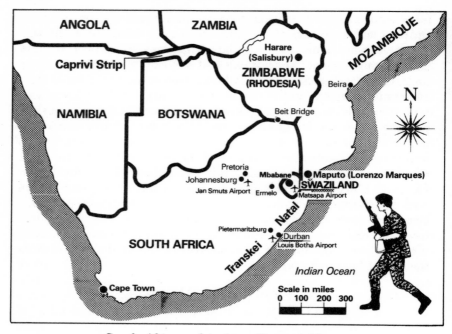

South Africa and its immediate neighbours

and his left-wing regime were to be overthrown. The situation was further complicated by the existence of a large community of Seychellois exiles in Australia including Robert Frichot, a wealthy young barrister from a 'big family' who represented the *grand blanc* interest. Precisely who Mike Hoare had most dealings with it is impossible to be sure. But certainly in the months before November 1981 he went out to Perth to meet Frichot, visited London to meet Mancham and kept in constant contact with Gonzague D'Offay, the 'money man', and with Gerard Hoareau and the other Seychellois exiles in Durban. As early as July 1980 Hoare was able to show Tullio Moneta in Johannesburg a letter from 'the exiles' authorising himself, Hoare, to draw up a plan for the overthrow by a mercenary force of President René's regime in the Seychelles. One month later Charles Njonjo, Kenya's Minister for Constitutional Affairs, secretly visited South Africa.

No mercenary coup can hope to succeed without at least the tacit complicity of the country in which the mercenary force is recruited and the active complicity of a country bordering the target country, the objective. That at least, I hope, is clear from all that has gone before. The South African government as such – the prime minister and the cabinet – may not have known that a mercenary coup was being plotted on their territory against the Seychelles but that may simply have been because they had no desire to know. Certainly their intelligence services, both military and specialised, both knew and were directly involved, as the sequel will show. But the Republic of South Africa could only have a minor interest in what happened in the Seychelles. Kenya on the other hand had a major interest. The Seychelles were almost equidistant – about six hundred miles – from Mombasa, Kenya's major port on the Indian Ocean and from Dar-es-Salaam, Tanzania's capital. Tanzania had been since independence Kenya's great and annoyingly influential rival in what was formerly British East Africa. Oversimplifying wildly, one might say that Tanzania was socialist verging on Maoist (certainly much-influenced by the Chinese) whereas Kenya was capitalist and pro-Western. Among the most pro-Western of the Mzee's* successors was the elegant, suave Kikuyu, Charles Njonjo known – only half-affectionately – among Kenya's élite as 'Sir Charles'. Kenyatta had been succeeded as President by a man who was generallly, if wrongly, considered to be a mere stopgap, the inconspicuous Daniel Arap Moi. The colourful Njonjo, invariably to be seen with a carnation in his buttonhole, was thought to be the power behind the throne, the strong man of the regime and a potential president himself. For any black politician to make a trip to the bastion of apartheid, South Africa, particularly at that period, was personally unpleasant and politically full of danger if the 'secret' should leak out. There must have been extraordinarily strong reasons for a man as ambitious as Njonjo to take the risk; as he was later to take the risk of issuing visas for South Africans to enter Kenya. It is almost certain that what induced him to come was the need to meet the leaders in Durban of the *Mouvement pour La Résistance* and very probably Mike Hoare himself to discuss Kenya's part – Kenya's vital part – in the proposed overthrow of President René and his left-wing regime in the Seychelles.

Politically the plan finally decided on was this: that Jimmy Mancham, whom Charles Njonjo knew and liked – they were in political outlook much of a muchness, 'men of the world' both – should be restored to his rightful position as President of the Seychelles with Gerard Hoareau as Vice-President and Robert Frichot, from Perth,

---

* Mzee was the title given to President Jomo Kenyatta, the Old One, the father figure of Kenya's Independence, himself a Kikuyu tribesman, who had died in 1978.

as Prime Minister – the Vice-President holding, at least in Hoareau's view, the real power in the new regime. The coup would be carried out by mercenaries led by Mike Hoare who would act rapidly and decisively and then withdraw. Kenya would have troops and police standing by ready to fly in and 'restore order' should there be any serious resistance to the new regime or any danger of the Russians or the Tanzanians intervening directly. South Africa would be rewarded with the restoration of landing rights (withdrawn by René) for South African Airways, and with increased trade. Kenya would profit by an extension of the nation's sphere of influence – a matter which, incidentally, could not fail to rebound to the personal prestige and advantage of 'Sir Charles' in his (as it was then thought) looming struggle for power against his fellow Kikuyu and rival, the Vice President Mwai Kibaki. As for Mike Hoare, he would be rewarded with the knowledge that he, like Denard, had made a successful comeback as a mercenary leader; with the prospect of retiring in his old age to the island paradise which he had always loved; and, of course, with money.

It was the question of money, however, that delayed for over a year the implementation of the plan. Basically the trouble was simple: there was not nearly enough of it. Hoare's original plan had envisaged a budget of no less than five million dollars; a sum large enough to equip, arm and transport an impressive mercenary force and to prepare at the same time a popular uprising in the Seychelles. But the difficulty with exile groups is that by the very fact of being exiles they are, at least comparatively, impoverished. The Americans, though mildly alarmed by the size of the new Russian Embassy in Victoria and mildly annoyed at President René's drastic rent increases for their satellite tracking station installed on a mountain in Mahé, were not prepared to back a coup or a civil war as they had been in Angola. The British and the French, had they been approached, might well have informed René of the threat – in the case of the British out of distaste for Mancham, in the case of the French out of distaste for English-speaking mercenaries rather than their own variety. Neither the Kenyan nor the South African government nor any of their departments, though prepared to help in other ways, put up a single penny. It was later rumoured that Adnan Khashoggi had financed Hoare's plan; if so, he seriously under-financed it; and I doubt it. Hoare even wrote to his acquaintance Robin Moore, the American author of *The Green Berets* and *The French Connection* in an attempt to raise money; but Moore was not prepared to follow Frederick Forsyth's possible example and risk the profits from his own bestsellers on a mercenary adventure. In the end instead of five million dollars there was less than half a million available: 400,000 rand apparently, and not all of that at once. With such a comparatively pitiful sum (in my view probably all contributed by Seychellois exiles and by the *Mouvement pour La Résistance*), Hoare's options were severely restricted. It would necessarily be an inexpensive operation, indeed so inexpensive as to be, many would argue, almost doomed from the start. But Hoare was growing older and he had been planning his coup in the Seychelles for three years. In June 1981 he and the colleague he now thought of as his second-in-command, the actor Tullio Moneta, flew out to the Seychelles, as tourists, on the trip that was to decide whether or not to go ahead with the planned operation; and, if so, how to put it into effect.

They had chosen June in order to watch the Independence Day parade of 29 June and to gain a first-hand impression of the Seychelles army, its numbers, weapons, equipment and general appearance. After the parade Hoare, satisfied, flew back to South Africa. Tullio Moneta stayed on for nine days, holding clandestine meetings with opponents of René on the island, visiting the American satellite station and the Russian Embassy (no less than 105 strong), returning with maps of State House – the President's 'Offices' in the centre of Victoria – and of the airport, details of the garrisons and anti-aircraft defences, and an impression of a 'jittery' President René rarely appearing in public and living in what had once been the British Governor's Residence but was now the Presidential Palace way up in the hills above the capital, guarded by Tanzanians.

Tullio Moneta returned to meet Mike Hoare at the mercenary leader's family home outside Pietermaritzburg, the Old Vicarage, and to find Hoare in close contact via Martin Dolinchek with the South African intelligence services. Intelligence services all the world over are a source of confusion if only because of their multiplicity and their rapidly changing names and personnel. The ill-famed BOSS had disappeared in the internal Afrikaner struggle for power that led to the replacement of Vorster as South Africa's Prime Minister by his long-serving Minister of Defence, P.W. Botha. Or rather BOSS had not disappeared; it had simply been twice renamed less gratingly, first as DONS, then as NIS – National Intelligence Service – and its overlord General Hendrik Van Den Bergh replaced by a younger civilian, Dr Neil Barnard. But the organisation's changes of name were as nothing compared to those of its employee Martin Dolinchek – alias Malcolm Donaldson, alias Eddie Smith, alias Martin Van Rensburg, alias Martin Van der Merwe, alias (during Bobby Kennedy's 1966 tour) Frans Zajc – ostensibly representing the Yugoslav news agency Tanyug which in fact had no correspondent covering the visit. Dolinchek had been born at Krajn in Yugoslavia in 1948 and of course his ability to speak Serbo-Croat and Russian was, theoretically at any rate, an asset to any 'intelligence operative'. He loved to describe himself as an 'intelligence operative' and to adopt, along with his aliases, mysterious airs. He had long been a bit of a joke among the South African press corps who kept a weather eye well-open for *agents provocateurs* in the government's service; and there was certainly no mystery in Durban or among fellow members of his jogging club about which 'government organisation' Dolinchek was working for. It was he originally who had sought out Mike Hoare in 1974, to pose questions about the Congo (and secretly tape-recorded the interview) – presumably off his own initiative as answers about the Congo could have been of little or no interest to BOSS at that stage. But Hoare and he kept in contact; indeed as early as July 1978 Dolinchek was consulting General Hendrik Van der Berge about a proposed coup in the Seychelles. He was told at the time that BOSS had no interest in any such affair; and it seems that for all Dolinchek's attempts to interest the NIS three years later the result was almost exactly the same.

Not quite however. Hoare was invited to meet the Deputy Director of the NIS, N. J. Claasen. They lunched together in a Durban hotel; and Claasen informed Hoare that the NIS could not support the operation, Operation Anvil as Hoare, romantically, had christened it. This was disappointing. What however was far less disappointing, positively encouraging, was Claasen's next remark: that the whole affair had been handed over to South Africa's military intelligence.

Hoare, elated, made his final plans. It was now the month of September. He visited London and met Jimmy Mancham in a London hotel. He was not impressed at the opening remark with which Mancham greeted him: 'Hello Mike, how do you like my jacket?' Mancham, Hoare told Dolinchek on his return, was in his opinion a political disaster, self-indulgent, with an insatiable sexual appetite. He would however be only a figurehead and it would give the coup legitimacy if he were restored. He visited the Seychelles again, briefly, from 12–15 September, and tied up a few last details with Jean Dingwall, a local businessman and organiser on the spot of the *Mouvement pour La Résistance*. And then finally on 26 September he was summoned to Pretoria by Claasen to meet in the Zanza building two representatives of military intelligence, Brigadier Daan Hammam, the Director of Military Intelligence for Special Forces, and Brigadier Martin Knoetze. Hoare's plan was now very simple: with the military co-operating fully all his worries about men and weapons and training programmes would disappear – and with them most of his worries about money. He would use, on 'loan' from the SADF as he had once proposed doing in the Congo (see p. 75) 150 South African troops, members, he would suggest, of the Reconnaissance Regiment, who were used to and trained for this sort of rapid in-and-out operation. And they would of course be equipped with weapons supplied on the instructions of military intelligence. Furthermore as a refinement those weapons would all be Eastern bloc weapons from the stockpile of those captured by the South African forces which had been operating in Angola. And Hoare had, ready to hand, together with his own personally observed assessment of the Seychelles army, a list of the weapons required.

The two brigadiers demanded from Claasen a written Minute from the Prime Minister's office which the Deputy Director of the NIS promised to obtain. It should be pointed out that P.W. Botha had not only been Minister of Defence for fourteen years but was at the time in addition to being Prime Minister also Minister of the National Intelligence Service. As such, he presided over the regular meetings of the National Security Council, generally regarded as the Republic's major policy-making body. There is no evidence that the two brigadiers ever obtained the written Minute that would have formally covered their activities, but there is evidence that Hoare had previously been introduced to a gentleman named Alec Van der Wyck who had submitted a Minute describing Hoare's proposals to the cabinet. These are arcane matters, of interest mainly in the sequel when the Prime Minister formally denied before South Africa's House of Assembly any knowledge whatsoever of the proposed Seychelles coup. That P.W. Botha distanced himself from it is clear: that he knew nothing of it is, despite his formal denial but in the face of what evidence we have and in the face of his own vast experience in both intelligence and defence matters, barely believable.

The formalities complete, the two brigadiers plied Mike Hoare with questions. How, above all, did the mercenary leader plan to get his attacking force onto the islands? Mike Hoare had clearly been considering very carefully the various alternatives, as Bob Denard had done. Victoria, the capital, was on the sea like both Cotonou in Benin and Moroni in the Comores; and, as there, the airport was a little way outside the capital. The invasion could therefore be launched by sea or by air, by night or by day, with the usual advantages and disadvantages. The difficulty was that Kenya, though prepared to support a successful coup, was not prepared to offer itself as a launching-pad for the invading force itself – which would consequentially have to set out from distant South Africa. A seaborne invasion would mean therefore a long and difficult voyage, with increasing risk of discovery once the out-isles of the vast archipelago were reached and considerable risk of a breakdown in discipline or morale or both among the cooped-up mercenary force. Hoare must have thought back to his period as technical adviser on the film of *The Wild Geese* and considered the advantages and disadvantages of parachuting in, the method Richard Burton and his fictional mercenaries had used. But even if the South African Air Force had been prepared to lend a plane, which it was not, and even if his proposed troops had all been trained paratroopers, which they were not, Mahé was a mountainous wooded island, not at all suitable terrain for parachuting onto. The other alternative seemed to be, as at Cotonou, a landing at Mahé International Airport. But, unlike Denard, Hoare had no access to a spare DC7 or DC8. Furthermore the distances were so great that refuelling would be necessary. If so, where? Furthermore could one be sure that, in a highly sensitive area like the Indian Ocean, the approach of an unauthorised and unknown aircraft skimming across hundreds of miles of ocean would .not be picked up by radar and reported to the Seychelles government long before the aircraft could land? The air approach seemed, though faster, almost as risky and dangerous a proposition as the sea approach.

Hoare had thought it all out, however; and had come up with a highly original scheme that would reduce both the risks and the difficulties to almost zero. The basis of the scheme was this: that the men and the weapons would go in *separately* and would only combine once both were on the islands. The men would go in by air; and the weapons would go in by sea. The men would go in, in batches, as tourists; and the weapons would go in concealed in the hold or fuel tanks of a motorised ocean-going yacht. In other words there would be no invasion as such but rather an uprising; and all the problems associated with an invasion and a landing would be sidestepped. It was a most ingenious idea and it appealed to the brigadiers, particularly when Hoare explained how little South Africa would be formally involved. First of all the weapons used would be of the sort with which the Seychelles army was already equipped. Secondly, as soon as the coup was successful, the 'tourists' would revert to being tourists – and by the time the emergency was over, the new government installed and the airport open to curious journalists, the 'tourists', their job done, would already be back in South Africa. As far as the outside world was concerned, all the evidence would point to an internal uprising that had overthrown an unpopular government.

Better still, there was to be as little bloodshed as possible. There would be no attempt to kill President René as Ali Soilih had been killed on the Comores. It was known that René would be visiting France in the last week of November and, as Hoare later put it, 'in the best tradition of African coups the attempt was to be made when the head of state was away'. There would, as Hoare must have been well aware, be a poetic justice in this: just as Mancham had been overthrown by René in his absence, so René in his turn would be overthrown in his absence by Mancham. It was a very neat plan.

The only thing the brigadiers objected to was the number of men involved. They thought it could be done with half the men, with 75 instead of 150; and Hoare agreed. It would in any case be a far less conspicuous group on an island no longer used to the arrival of South Africans *en masse*. But Hoare stressed the urgency of obtaining the arms. The yacht would need a month to sail to the Seychelles; so, if the coup was to be launched in November, he must have the arms by early October.

At 9 am on 6 October one of the most curious scenes in this whole affair occurred, a scene in which cosy domesticity blended with potential menace. A five-ton lorry, driven by Sergeant Van der Merwe in plain clothes, drove into the little drive of the one-storey suburban bungalow-style house called The Old Vicarage. The sergeant presented SADF Form DD 12 to 'Mad Mike', headed Lynwood near Pretoria, the DMI's office, and listing the contents of the lorry; the mercenary leader signed the 'delivery note' and he, his sons, and the sergeant proceeded to unload and store in The Old Vicarage's modest cellar sixty unused Rumanian AK 47 assault rifles with folding butts, fifteen used Hungarian AMDs, very similar, seventeen green ammunition boxes stencilled with yellow paint containing 23,800 rounds, ten RPG rocket launchers with 102 rockets, forty Chinese hand-grenades and fifteen two-way radios. The weapons had, as promised, arrived.

Hoare phoned Martin Dolinchek and invited him to come and test-fire them, which they did on a disused airport outside Durban, together with Hoare's elder sons and his wife's brother. All but one were perfect. Hoare had clearly been warned by military intelligence to steer clear of their rivals, the NIS; he spun Dolinchek a yarn destined as much to impress as to mislead about having obtained the weapons from Adnan Khashoggi. But at the same time he wanted to use Dolinchek, whose abilities and ambition he obviously admired. Would Dolinchek, he asked, act as his intelligence officer on the spot? Would he go to the Seychelles in advance of the main body? Not officially, Dolinchek replied, that would be quite impossible. But he would do so privately. He would concoct a story about going elephant-hunting on the Botswana border and would take leave from 5 November to 17 December. He set about obtaining, to deceive his own superiors, a false passport; and via a personal contact, a secretary in the Department of the Interior, he obtained one in the name of Anton Lubic. He offered to obtain a false passport for Hoare. But Hoare had already twice been in and out of the Seychelles without difficulty on his own passport, lightly doctored. It was an Irish passport – Hoare, like many British post-war expatriates, had never formally become a South African citizen – and Hoare, whose name of course might have awakened suspicious echoes of bygone days, even in the sleepy Seychelles, had himself altered the H to a B and added a final l. Dolinchek a totally humourless man, was horrified at the amateurism, the lack of professionalism of 'Thomas Bernard Michael Boarel'; and certainly it makes a striking contrast to Denard's array of aliases and false identity papers. But it worked.

No mercenary operation, indeed no military operation of any sort, ever proceeds exactly according to plan. The first blow to fall on Operation Anvil was almost a fatal one. Brigadier Hammam telephoned Hoare and warned him not to send the weapons in by boat. Hoare had set aside, and indeed possibly already spent, no less than half his total budget on the ocean-going yacht – 150,000 rand for the yacht itself, 50,000 rand for the captain and crew. But, money considerations apart, the warning – which must have been backed by facts picked up by military intelligence, possibly about Seychellois harbour security – struck at the whole essence of Hoare's scheme. For if the weapons could not go in by sea, separately, how on earth were they to be smuggled in? Hoare mulled over the problem. He came up with a daring half-solution which very wisely he kept for the time being strictly to himself.

Meanwhile equally important was the question of the men. The key figure here was Major Willie Ward, of the Permanent Force, formerly Sergeant Major of No. 2 Recce Commando, then a major in the 1st Recce Regiment. A meeting was set up at the Kyalami Ranch Hotel near Johannesburg. The two brigadiers seem to have left this part of the operation entirely to the mercenary leader, though they may well have dropped a preliminary word in the right ear. Dunlop

Paul, the health studio club owner, Tullio Moneta's friend, approached his contact in No. 2 Commando, Sergeant Brian Walls, a Johannesburg jeweller. Walls contacted Ward. Tullio Moneta arranged the actual meeting. Hoare expounded his plan and his needs. Ward enthusiastically offered to raise seventy of his men for the operation. Pieter Dooreward, a Citizen Force staff sergeant in No. 2 Recce Commando and, though aged only twenty-eight, a veteran of over twenty 'special operations', was also present, and also enthusiastic. No. 2, incidentally, specialised in the use of communist weapons. The system Hoare proposed was that the men should under his own overall control be divided into two groups, one under the command of Tullio Moneta, the other under the command of Willie Ward with Pieter Dooreward to back him up. Ward would, like Moneta, receive 40,000 rand; Dooreward less, 20 or 30,000 – payable of course on successful completion, with one tenth down in advance. Other 'officers' would be paid on the Dooreward scale, whereas the men would be offered, on the same terms, 10,000 rand each. Furthermore, Hoare announced, Brigadier Knoetze of Military Intelligence, had offered them a training ground in north Transvaal. Training for Operation Anvil could begin therefore within the next two weeks, on 7 November.

At first everything appeared to be going swimmingly. Willie Ward, accompanied by an ambitious local Nationalist politician named Norman Reeves, visited in Durban Gerard Hoareau, the future Vice-President of the new regime. But then – *post hoc? propter hoc?* – the second blow fell. On the pretext, which was true, that no arrangements had been made for evacuating the mercenary force if the operation went wrong Ward backed out. And so, with only four weeks to go till D Day, Mike Hoare was faced with a major crisis: the need to put together, rapidly, a purely mercenary team. A lesser man might at this stage have been inclined to throw up his hands in despair and abandon the whole project. Not so 'Mad Mike' Hoare. He was determined, come what might, whatever the obstacles, whatever the difficulties, that Operation Anvil should go ahead.

13

Paradise Lost – Coup in the Seychelles

'I should have taken Richard Burton and Roger Moore along with me and we'd have had a happy ending.'

Mike Hoare

On the last day of October three apparently innocuous tourists flew into the Seychelles – Mike Hoare's advance guard. Two were men, one was a woman. The woman was frail, grey-haired, British-born, a mother of four – and at the time the girlfriend or, as the authorities later more pompously put it, the common-law wife of the older man. She called herself Sue Sims but in fact the name on her passport was Susan Ingle. Her 'husband', Bob Sims, was the brother of Phyllis Hoare, Mike Hoare's wife. He was aged 49, by profession a jockey and trainer as his father had been before him. Hoare clearly believed in keeping his affairs as much as possible within the family. The Sims had rented, for a month's holiday in the Seychelles, via Colin Whiting, a Durban associate of Gerard Hoareau, a small villa in a remote mountain village named La Misère high up in the centre of the island of Mahé. 'Remote' is of course a very comparative term in an island of the size of Mahé which is at its widest point less than three miles wide and only twenty miles long. 'Fairview', the villa, was at most half an hour's drive from the airport. But it was certainly not easy to find, inconspicuous, though with splendid views down towards the airport and the capital, Victoria – just the place for a quiet holiday and a quiet couple.

The third tourist, Barney Carey, was a much more conspicuous figure, a publican from London – for years he had been the landlord of The Gloucester Arms – a big man, aged thirty-eight, twice married, who had come out in 1980 to Pietermaritzburg to join his father in a small repairs business. But there was much more to

Carey's background than this, much more to Carey's contacts with Hoare than the mere coincidence of address. Certainly he had spent years of his early life in Africa, certainly he spoke Swahili. He was rumoured to have been in the Congo at the age of nineteen and then in the Yemen. His own accounts of his past, and his friends' too, have, to say the least, varied. But the dates fit: Barney Carey may very well have been in Five Commando and, like Hoare himself, come back to the mercenary business after a gap of almost twenty years.

The two men, in addition to their ordinary luggage, each carried a tan-coloured cricket bag, full of clothes and personal effects. The cricket bags had false bottoms five or six inches deep. In each bag was concealed an AK 47 with folding butt and two ammunition chargers each holding 30 rounds. Mahé International Airport welcomed 2,500 South African tourists every year. It is – or rather was at the time – a small, relaxed airport despite its grandiose name. Tourists visas are stamped on passports with a smile and a word of greeting; tourists' baggage is waved through, the only prohibition being on spear-guns which are illegal for fishing in the Seychelles. Within minutes Mike Hoare's ingenious plan for smuggling arms and ammunition into the Seychelles had been tested and been found to be workable. The 'dummy run' had been successful.

Barney Carey stayed only a week, at the Reef Hotel on the coast to the south of the airport, before flying back to South Africa and reporting to Mike Hoare. The Sims stayed on, quietly, barely seen by their neighbours at La Misère, the owners of 'Fairview', the Savys. The two cricket bags, with their contents, were stored carefully away. Sue Sims – Susan Ingle – went down to Victoria, to the Standard Bank and there played her part in the affair by opening a bank account in her own name. The Swiss Bank Corporation in Geneva had telexed $10,000 to be held at her disposal on the instructions of their client M. Thomas Hoare. Dolinchek, the self-styled profession-al, later condemned this as he had condemned Hoare's technique of altering passports as 'childish'. 'You should use cash,' said Dolin-chek, 'not bank accounts. It's contrary to ground rules. It's like leaving fingerprints on the scene of the crime. It's just not done.' But, as in the case of the passport, Hoare had one retort – the best: it worked.

Next to appear in the Seychelles, on Saturday, 14 November was Dolinchek himself, travelling, as 'Anton Lubic' on a South African passport, No. D631473 issued on 12 October by Mrs Van Heerden, his contact in the Department of the Interior in Durban. His task was, in his own typically overblown phrase, 'to evaluate the political social-economic and military situation for Mike Hoare'. He had been booked via Budget Tours in South Africa on a two-week package holiday, the first week to be spent at the Reef Hotel, the next on the other side of the island at the Beauvallon Bay Hotel. The coup was less than a fortnight away. Hoare had seen him off at Louis Botha Airport, Durban's airport; and had handed him a letter for Bob Sims plus a bag, a heavy bag containing, Hoare said, 'communications equipment'. 'I realised Hoare had crossed me once more,' said Dolinchek later, 'and I was carrying my personal weapon. But it was Hobson's choice.' Mike Hoare had indeed decided on his technique; were he to warn his men that they would have to smuggle in their own weapons, they would undoubtedly – and understandably – have cold feet. In this, the second trial run, he was experimenting as much with psychology as with the system. If even the uppity Dolinchek rather than pull out at the last minute would accept an added risk, then there was little danger that the rest of his men would baulk.

On arrival at Mahé airport Dolinchek took an extraordinary risk. He went through the red 'something to declare' channel, to declare the cigarettes and liquor he had bought duty-free; and the customs-officer not only mentioned spear-guns and the need to deposit them but searched his bags. They failed to find the concealed weapon. Hoare must have been jubilant when he telephoned Seychelles 23591, his brother-in-law's number at 'Fairview', and heard of this double success. Not only had a third weapon passed in successfully but, even when searched for, it had not been found. Outside the airport Sims was waiting. He had met Dolinchek before, both at the racecourse and at the deserted aerodrome near Durban where together they had test-fired the AK 47s in the company of Hoare and his sons. Dolinchek handed over the bag and the letter – which instructed Sims to pay Dolinchek's car hire and personal expenses. Understandably, with the tension, Sims was a bit drunk – much, however, to Dolinchek's disapproval. He called Dolinchek 'my little boy'. 'I firmly believe,' noted Dolinchek, 'there is a time to work and a time to drink.' But however much he might disapprove of Sims' behaviour and Hoare's methods, Dolinchek accepted two cheques from Sue Ingle – one for a thousand rupees for personal expenses, one for 1,600 rupees for car hire. He began his investigation of social-economic conditions by swimming and refusing American tourists' offer of an all-night party. On his second day he made contact with the native population. 'Local boy grabbed me by my balls,' he noted in his diary. 'Asked me if I was queer. Name Gee. All is normal; beautiful place, beautiful people.'

Back in Natal Mike Hoare, meanwhile, was drawing the strands of his operation rapidly together. He had established a safe house and an inconspicuous paymaster on the Seychelles. He had an operative in position. He had, above all, twice tested a method of passing in arms and ammunition that was, compared to his original more grandiose ideas, both simple and inexpensive. It could of course never be applied to RPG rocket launchers and their shells; the strike force would simply have to make do with AK 47s, a minimum of ammunition – sixty rounds only per man – and a few hand-grenades. But if the coup could be organised swiftly and bloodlessly, that would be more than enough. It would be a 'pushover', Hoare had assured Dolinchek; and so he continued to assure the other members of the 'team' that despite his earlier difficulties, he was now successfully assembling.

Hoare's Team

That team divided, roughly, into three very different groups of men. First and most naturally of all Mike Hoare turned to the 'old hands', men who had served under him in the Congo and of whom Barney Carey was probably one. There were surprisingly few of them* so many years later, who were still in the mercenary market. One, the oldest of all, at fifty-seven not much Hoare's junior, was Jeremiah Puren. Puren was still in the secondhand car business, running a 'repossession centre' in Durban's Smith Street. My guess, though Puren always denied it, was that he had been in continual contact with Hoare ever since Hoare's return to South Africa; indeed there is evidence that Puren too had visited the Seychelles, with radio equipment, in 1979, though whether before or after the November Plot is not clear. But in his late middle age Puren had become both respectable and a maverick. He was the father of three sons, still married to his Belgian wife Julia, and chairman of The Bluff Ratepayers Association – The Bluff where the Reconnaissance Regiment had its headquarters. But he had also been a local candidate for the marginal, extreme right-wing, British-style, New Republic Party. 'You can't take an old crazy like Jerry Puren on this,' Dolinchek had told Hoare and Hoare *per* Dolinchek had replied: 'Only over my dead body will he go in.' Whatever Hoare may or may not have told Dolinchek, Puren was definitely in, once again to play –

---

* Tullio Moneta, Hoare's second-in-command, may have been in Five Commando himself. If so, he kept rather quiet about it. According to one account he was the mercenaries' cook there.

as always throughout his mercenary career – a somewhat mysterious role.

Another ex-Congo mercenary was Peter Duffy, a news photographer described as 'the best sneak pics man in the business', who worked mainly for Durban's *Sunday Tribune*. He had in fact served a contract in Five Commando not under Hoare but under Peters; so had Peter Rohwein, whom Duffy contacted on his coffee farm in Zimbabwe – a German, born in Minsk, who had left Five Commando at the same time as Duffy and apparently, curiously, in Hoare's company when 'Colonel Peters shot a man just for no reason, just to impress people' – a reference most probably to the never-forgotten affair of Captain Hugh Van Oppens (See pages 81-88). Kurt Priefert – another German, a crossbow champion in South Africa – was almost certainly in the Congo too, though it is not clear who recruited him. Des Botes, at fifty-two the oldest bar Hoare himself and Puren, had another traditionally useful combat speciality: Botes ran his own karate school in Johannesburg and had once been South Africa's karate champion. Peter Duffy, Gordonstoun-educated, was not only a bouncy photographer but a physical fitness fanatic too, who had studied karate under Shigero Kimuru and was a leading expert of the Shokokai style. Not that he was an ascetic, far from it. He loved people and girls and parties. He 'seemed to be the man', Hoare wryly decided, 'most able to carry conviction as the leader of a beer-drinking group.'

For that was the cover under which Hoare planned that his main group should go in. Forty-five men plus himself and Puren – that was to be the strength of the main group; and forty to fifty men arriving all together, mainly young and fit, would be bound to arouse suspicion even in the easy-going Seychelles. It may have been, as he later claimed, Dolinchek's idea or it may have been Duffy's – they were planning to work together on the island – but who's ever it was it was a brilliant refinement, the scheme that the forty-five men – rugger players, hence young and fit, three teams, hence forty-five strong, plus their two older 'managers' – should be spending a fortnight in the Seychelles on a package tour as a beer-drinking group. It was probably Duffy in any case who came up with the further twist that the beer-drinking group should have a jokily formal and impressive title, one that must have appealed to himself as an associate of journalists and that would appeal in due course to journalists throughout the world: Ye Ancient Order of Frothblowers.

So the 'Frothblowers' were born. It remained to fill their ranks. Major Willie Ward might have backed out but that did not mean that all was lost on the side of the Recce Commandoes. Tullio Moneta and William Dunlop Paul approached Ward's potential number two, Pieter Dooreward, directly; and Dooreward agreed to sound out a dozen men, mainly – like himself – Afrikaans-speaking. His friend Vic de Beer, a lieutenant in One Recce Commando, issued the call-up papers which its Citizen Force members were accustomed to getting before going on a special operation that, so they thought, would cover them; Two Recce Commando's commanding officer, Commandant Davie Van Der Spuy, was bypassed on, as De Beer later put it (thereby presumably doing his future military career no good at all) 'the need to know' principle. Half a dozen men from two Recce Commando were enlisted plus two ex-Parabats, bored with civilian life, Patrick Henrick and Johan Fritz, plus no less than three young doctors, all connected with the Recce Commandos, Steyn de Wet, Chris de Jager and Theodorus Van Huysteen. These, with one or two others, formed what I would roughly describe as the Afrikaner group: all trained soldiers, most of them used to working together.

The third and numerically the most important group were the ex-Rhodesians. It was Puren who first approached Ken Dalgliesh, the owner of the Riviera Hotel where many of them met every Thursday for 'Rhodesia Night'; and it was Dalgliesh and Mike Webb, the former British cavalry officer, bored out of his mind with selling insurance, who recruited almost all the others: Rhodesians like Aubrey Brooks, formerly of the Selous Scouts, Englishmen like Roger England, formerly of the Rhodesian SAS and before that – a throwback, the only throwback, to the Angola mercenary era – a long-serving member of the 3rd Paras, and even Americans like Charley Dukes, ex-Rhodesian SAS too, ex-One Recce Commando for a year but at the time a bouncer (he was well over six foot tall and had hoped to be a professional boxer but had failed, knocked out in the second round of his first major fight by a black in Bulawayo) at 'Father's Moustache', the night-club bar in Durban's Malibu Hotel.

For the ex-Rhodesians Mike Webb's participation and enthusiasm was almost a guarantee of success. Among many others he recruited Peter Hean and Richard Stannard. Hean, aged thirty, 'a fearless resolute soldier', had as a major commanded a battalion of the RLI; he was at the time manager of a Pretoria textile firm. Stannard, though two years younger, had an interesting career already behind him, first with the British special press and propaganda operation in Ulster, then as a captain in the Selous Scouts and a much-decorated hero of the Rhodesian war, finally as an officer with South African forces in Angola, service for which he was later to be awarded the

Honoris Crux, the Republic's Victoria Cross. He immediately resigned his job as the manager of a retail store in Durban. Simon Willar, Scots born, had like Stannard been a captain in the Selous Scouts; his father, Colonel Mac Willar, was a senior intelligence officer in Rhodesia. These were all experienced fighting men, indeed more expereinced than the Afrikaner group, and what will immediately be noticed is the number of obviously excellent officers enrolled. With such men as these in his team Hoare could be satisfied that there would be no risk at all of a repeat of the disorders and ill-discipline that had turned the Angola affair into bloody chaos. On Wednesday, 18 November he gathered the 'old hands' and the new officers together at the Riviera Hotel for a meeting. His most important announcement was that they would be flying to the Seychelles precisely one week later, on Wednesday, 25 November, on the weekly Air Swazi flight from Matsapa airport, across the border in Swaziland.

The Advance Party

But first Hoare had decided – though he did not of course announce it to the assembled mercenaries – that he needed not one but two more trial runs yet to test his weapon-infiltrating system; and, incidentally, to get more men onto Mahé and acquainted, in advance of the main group's arrival, with the layout of the island.

So on Saturday, 21 November Barney Carey flew back in for the second time, taking with him a list of instructions from Mike Hoare and no less than three fellow mercenaries: Des Botes (who at fifty-two would have been, however fit, decidedly old to pretend to be a rugby player), Ken Dalgliesh, and Aubrey Brooks. Dalgliesh and Botes had this in common, that they had both been in the Rhodesian Police (Special Branch); Brooks was in a sense the odd-man out, though he was Dalgliesh's friend. But he had a very important technical skill; he had worked, after demobilisation, as master controller at Salisbury's broadcasting station, and he knew exactly how broadcasting stations functioned.

Mike Hoare had told them to be sure to take cricket bags with them. He himself arrived at the airport with four brand-new cricket bags which he substituted for theirs. Once again everything at the other end went smoothly; even though with four of them the odds of something going wrong, of discovery, were four times as high. Nothing went wrong. The only thing the newcomers did not appreciate was Dolinchek's disapproval when he joined them at the

Reef Hotel later. 'Not my type of people,' he described them as, 'very undisciplined, on the loose side: not that I'm a moralist'. Even less did they appreciate Dolinchek's attempt to stop their drinking. Barney Carey, whose livelihood drink had, after all, for many years been, apparently warned Dolinchek that if he pushed it he would get a bullet in the back once action started; and Dolinchek beat a strategic retreat.

Not that Dolinchek should be underestimated. He had made contact with the local soldiers over a drink or two, he had while at the Reef located the Tanzanian mini-barracks at Pointe La Rue, the main army camp lying between the airport and the Reef Hotel, and most important he had studied the Russian Embassy in Victoria and its occupants. This was where his ability to understand Russian was helpful; and he listened in to Russian officials at a football match as well as getting the general Seychellois opinion – highly unfavourable – of the Russians; 'they even accuse them of stealing their fish,' he noted. What he and Duffy apparently planned to do was, during the confusion of the coup, to bluff their way behind the high walls of the Soviet compound and photograph whatever documents they could find – a highly risky venture but with Duffy an expert photographer and Dolinchek speaking Russian, a possible one. Hoare presumably approved and saw this as a way of improving his position with the South African authorities. Indeed the general suggestion may have been made by military intelligence. For it is impossible to believe that the various branches of South Africa's intelligence services were ignorant of or totally uninvolved in Hoare's coup. Dolinchek apart, there were at least three mercenaries who finally came in with Hoare who were thought by the others to have some intelligence connections: 'Blue' Kelly, a burly Australian, generally suspected of being an NIS agent, Kevin Beck who had certainly been in intelligence, and, almost inexplicably, Jan Olaf Sydow of military intelligence – inexplicably because he spoke only Swedish – though many Swedes, it must be added, speak fluent Russian as well.

Another somewhat inexplicable event was the next and final trial run. On the Sunday, the day after his own return onto Mahé, Barney Carey went out to the airport to meet two more incoming mercenaries, the tall American Charley Dukes and the stocky English ex-paratrooper Roger England – the pair had served in the Rhodesian SAS together. The minor mystery is this: why did they fly in, as they did, via the French-owned island of Réunion, France's major military base in the Indian Ocean? There seems no reson why they should not have come in the day before with Carey and his three. In any case

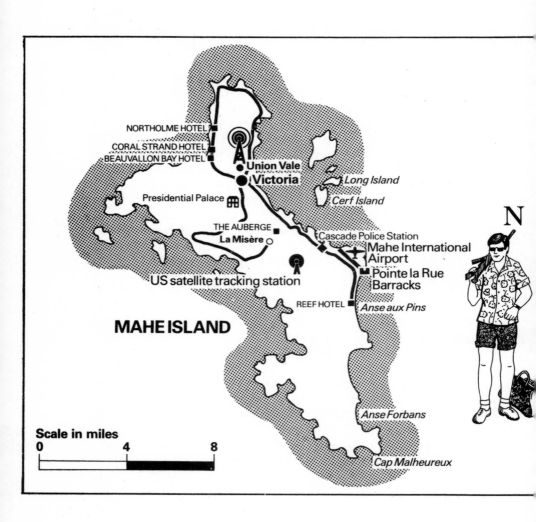

NORTHOLME HOTEL
CORAL STRAND HOTEL
BEAUVALLON BAY HOTEL
Union Vale
Victoria
Long Island
Presidential Palace
Cerf Island
THE AUBERGE
La Misère
Cascade Police Station
Mahe International
Airport
US satellite tracking station
Pointe la Rue
Barracks
REEF HOTEL
Anse aux Pins
MAHE ISLAND
N
Anse Forbans
Scale in miles
0   4   8
Cap Malheureux

Mahé

there were, once again, no difficulties with customs. On four separate occasions now, arms and ammunition had been successfully smuggled in in false-bottomed bags; and there were now nine AK 47s, each with sixty rounds, on the island – four up at 'Fairview' with the Sims (for Barney Carey had passed his second trip's bag to Bob Sims) and five at the Reef Hotel. There were nine members of Hoare's advance guard on Mahé too – the middle-aged couple in the safe house at La Misère, Barney Carey and the five mercenaries under his command at the strategically located Reef Hotel, and Dolinchek all on his own at the Beauvallon Bay.

Carey however at some stage seems to have moved to the Coral Strand Hotel, next door to the Beauvallon Bay, on the other side of the island. He had more to do than drink and reconnoitre. The list of instructions Hoare had written out for him at the airport before departure mainly concerned his own and Sims' role in welcoming Hoare the following Wednesday: 'Barney take me Auberge – Bob to draw funds 18,000 rupees – Bob to arrange car for me – Bob to bring all arms to meet plane.' But at least three of the items were both more cryptic and, almost certainly, more significant. 'Movement Blue not White'; 'Bob to introduce Anton'; and thirdly a list of names; 'Rollye Marie, Raymond Bonté, Claude Vidot, Philip Lucas, Macdonald Marengo.' This list was far and away the most significant entry; it was a list of the five majors who commanded the Seychellois army under the Minister of Defence, Colonel Ogilvy Berlouis.

'Movement Blue not White' had certainly to do with the local support to be expected from clandestine members of the *Mouvement pour La Résistance*, and the significance of the colour change will become apparent. 'Bob to introduce Anton' – Sims to introduce 'Anton Lubic', Dolinchek – but to whom? Not, obviously, to his fellow mercenaries in any case. As for the names of the five majors, this proves at least that Hoare's local intelligence service was functioning well. But it indicates much more than that. Either it indicates that these were the five men who would have to be arrested or eliminated if the coup was to be successful; but in that case it would have been enough to specify 'the five majors' without spelling out (and most accurately) their names. Or, much more probably, it indicates that these were the men who either were to be discreetly approached or had already been discreetly approached for their support, active or passive, in the coup attempt itself. The five majors were the men who would physically be issuing orders to the Seychellois troops – if they could be bribed, flattered or threatened into reacting slowly or not at all, then the chances of the coup's success would be enormously enhanced. What this list does not show is how exactly a local uprising was to be organised or local resistance to the coup sabotaged. But what it does prove beyond any shadow of doubt is that Mad Mike's coup was a carefully planned affair in which all factors had been taken into consideration. It was not (as so many of his critics have implied) an ill-prepared improvisation.

The Detailed Plan

On Monday, 23 November a second meeting was held in South Africa to which all the mercenaries not already in the Seychelles were summoned. Here, with the aid of a papier-mâché model of the island of Mahé, Hoare expounded the final plan. The main group, the Frothblowers, were booked into the Reef Hotel for a pre-paid fortnight's package tour. They would be not only a drinking-cum-rugger club but also a charitable group, doing their bit for South Africa's public relations by taking in toys, advance Christmas presents, for the black kids in the Seychelles – an ingenious new touch, extra 'cover', an extra excuse for their presence. Peter Duffy would be the tour leader; Hoare himself was booked into the Auberge, a remote inn in the hills, not far from La Misère. For a few days they would simply enjoy themselves in the sun as tourists. Then at zero hour on D day they would strike. The coup would probably be all over in an hour or two. The airport would immediately be closed – except to the new government which would fly in from Kenya and be followed, if necessary, by a planeload of Kenyan troops and a planeload of Kenyan police. The mercenaries meanwhile would have reverted immediately to their role as tourists. They would enjoy another week's relaxation in the sun. Then, when the airport was reopened, they would fly out as they had flown in, as simple tourists, back to South Africa where they would, within fourteen days, be paid the 10,000 rand still owing to them. They would return therefore bronzed and relaxed after a fortnight's paid holiday on an island paradise, interrupted only by a short sharp spell of 'work', to a considerably richer life. There was a hint that a few, like Hoare's personal bodyguard, a forty-five-year-old Englishman named Donald Kenny, who had seen service in Rhodesia in both the Rhodesian SAS and Grey's Scouts (and before that very possibly in Five Commando), might be used to stay on and train a 'reformed' Seychellois Army à la Denard. It was an alluring prospect.

Hoare emphasised that there was to be, if possible, no bloodshed. They were there to liberate the Seychellois from an unpopular government and to restore the rightful President; and they could count on the support of most of the local people. They would therefore be using light weapons, assault rifles and hand-grenades, only; and these mainly as 'frighteners'. An advance party was already on the island. That advance party, under Carey's command, would seize the Seychelles Radio station that lay just a mile to the north of the capital, Victoria, at Union Vale. It was guarded by sixteen soldiers at Union Vale barracks; but Carey and his men had already carefully reconnoitred the surroundings and were confident they could easily seize both the radio station and the barracks just above it. Once the station was secured, Aubrey Brooks would play over the air a tape-recording that he, Hoare, now had with him: it would announce that René's regime had been overthrown by a popular rising; and then Jimmy Mancham himself, the former President, would be heard proclaiming that he was back on the island – a white lie, insofar as he would in fact still be in Kenya at this point – and appealing for calm.

Meanwhile Group II, commanded by Mike Webb, eighteen men strong, would have seized the airport and the main army barracks at Pointe La Rue, just to the south of the airport and to the north of the Reef Hotel. Richard Stannard would be Webb's second-in-command; and his team would be divided into three sub-groups. The main sub-group, twelve men under Peter Hean, would neutralise the Seychellois army barracks and secure the airport perimeter. A stick of four men, commanded by Simon Willar, would assault the two houses inside the Pointe La Rue camp where the Tanzanian soldiers were lodged: they would be the most dangerous opponents but it was hoped that, at zero hour, noon, in the heat of the day, they would be caught off their guard, dozing. Finally two men, both in the Rhodesian airforce, Vernon Prinsloo who had been a captain and Charles Goatley who had been a helicopter pilot, would seize the control tower and allow only those planes which they authorised to land. Numbers were small but with speed, surprise and, no doubt Hoare hinted, with local complicity, as well as with the expertise of soldiers trained in the Rhodesia war, success should not be difficult.

Tullio Moneta would be commanding Group III which would attack targets in Victoria itself; essentially army headquarters, the barracks in the capital, State House and a mile and a half outside, the Presidential Palace, guarded by, *per* Dolinchek, 'ten guards, not too awake'. The Presidential Palace however would be a secondary target; for the attack would probably be launched while President René was abroad. The most important objective by far was State House, which would be the target for the sub-group of Recce

Commando men led by Pieter Dooreward. The aim would be to seize, at one fell swoop, the entire Cabinet which would be there in session at midday on the Friday. They were to be taken prisoner unharmed – unless of course they resisted. At this stage Hoare passed around photos of President René and the Cabinet members. Apparently he pointed out two who were particularly dangerous, probably Ogilvy Berlouis, the Minister of Youth and Defence, and James Michel who combined the post of Minister of Education and Information with that of the army's Chief of Staff. It is interesting that Hoare passed round René's photograph too; there was of course always the danger that René might cancel his trip abroad or that the coup would have to be launched before his departure. But there must be a suspicion that talk of a bloodless *coup* was merely window-dressing, and that René and the two 'dangerous' ministers were to be killed, no doubt 'while attempting to escape'. According to Kevin Beck, they were told that all three would have to be 'taken out, eliminated or spirited away' – for if not, Mancham would refuse to return to the islands. Beck admittedly is hardly the most reliable of witnesses; but later, chillingly, Bob Jones-Davies confirmed that he would have killed Seychelles Cabinet ministers if ordered to do so.

Once the three groups had successfully seized their targets, Mike Hoare would establish his own headquarters in Victoria, in the Cable and Wireless offices that controlled all overseas phone-calls and telex messages. His own HQ Group was to consist of three men: Kenny for close protection, Sydow the Swede for undisclosed reasons, and an Austrian named Sven Forsell, who can only in the most remote sense be called a mercenary at all. Forsell, an ex-opera singer, was a would-be film director who for years had been planning a documentary on mercenaries; an old friend of Tullio Moneta's, and like Moneta living in South Africa and working on South African television series. Hoare, who always had a not-totally-disinterested sympathy for journalists and film producers, invited him along for the ride. He was to carry no weapon; and Hoare himself was to carry no weapon either. Once headquarters were established in the Cable and Wireless Office (manned – if that is the word – almost exclusively by young and attractive Seychellois girls as I can personally testify), then Hoare would take personal control, of the entire operation and in particular would flash the success signal across the Indian Ocean to Kenya. There had been last-minute difficulties with the Kenyan side of the operation; the two turbo-jet-propelled aircraft originally scheduled had been stood down and at least one of the Kenyan 'backers' had pulled out. But Njonjo had paid another rapid visit to

South Africa, Hoare allegedly one to Nairobi (he stayed, if the story is true, at the Hotel Fransea in Moktar Daddah St.), and apparently two weeks before the coup all had been sorted out.

The new government would be standing by at Nairobi ready to board a Beechcraft Super King 200, callsign Caroline Alpha, leased from Captain Peter Lucas of Sunbird Charters. Hoare would send through the codeword for success, 'Cloudburst' which would be acknowledged by 'Fairy Bell'. The Beechcraft would then take off and disgorge at Mahé airport, now securely held by Webb's men with Prinsloo in the control tower, the returning President Mancham, his ambitious Vice-President Hoareau and most if not all of the proposed new cabinet. Meanwhile Kenyan troops and police would be at Mombasa ready to fly in if and when formally requested to do so by the new government – the 'ace in the pack' Dolinchek rightly called Kenya. No-one bar the mercenaries and the cabinet would know that Mancham had not actually been on the island when his voice was heard over the air; but as the gap between the broadcast and his actual arrival would only be a few hours, no-one would in any case much care. It was a carefully prepared operation, with targets and the sequence of events, the chain of command and expected enemy reaction all meticulously defined. Hoare added one further encouraging touch: local support could be expected as soon as the coup succeeded, with members of the *Mouvement pour La Résistance* taking over such duties as the guarding of prisoners from the mercenaries. In order to avoid confusion the Resistance members would have been instructed to wear blue shirts; and just in case they had forgotten to do so, Peter Duffy and Jeremiah Puren would be bringing suitcases full of blue shirts with the 'team'. (Hence the message to Barney Carey to inform him that Blue would be substituted for White for the 'Movement'.) The briefing was over.

The Frothblowers Fly In

Hoare had organised the whole Frothblowers' package tour through Budget Tours of Johannesburg and had paid them 14,000 rand in advance to cover the round trip and the hotel bookings. The men met, on Tuesday, the day after the briefing, at 2 pm at Louis Botha airport on the outskirts of Durban. From there they were taken by coach to the Ermelo Holiday Inn about sixty miles outside Swaziland where they were to stay for the night. At 8 pm Peter Duffy as 'tour leader' called them together to explain the procedure next day, with Jeremiah Puren in the chair. At 10 pm the men were dismissed while group leaders and sub-group leaders were held behind for an 'O' group. At 4 am the next morning, in the early hours of Wednesday, 25 November they were woken up, bleary-eyed; and then and only then, at a time when psychological resistance is notoriously low, they were issued with new cricket bags – on the side of each one of which was inscribed the initials A.O.F.B. (Ancient Order of Frothblowers) – and told that they would be carrying their own weapons through the customs. At this stage, one – but only one – of the mercenaries backed out, 'Sergeant' Chris de Jager of No. 2 Recce Commando. 'A nasty surprise,' he called it. But as he was one of the three doctors, and doctors are not expected to be physically brave, and as the other two in any case stayed on, the defection was not too serious. The remainder – now forty-four men in all – were driven across the border into Swaziland, crossing, unsearched, at Oshoek; and at 9 am local time Royal Swazi Airlines' one and only plane, a Fokker Friendship, took off from Matsapa Airport, Manzini on its regular scheduled flight to the Seychelles, stopping off at the Comores. The Frothblowers were on their way.

Swaziland lies roughly two hundred miles north of Durban and is separated by only a narrow strip of Mozambique from the Indian Ocean. But it is still a long haul north of almost a thousand miles to the Comores and at least half that distance again from the Comores north-east to the Seychelles. The Royal Air Swazi flight was not due in at Mahé International Airport till shortly before sunset that evening. Earlier Dolinchek had telephoned the airport, to be told that only two flights were expected, Air Swazi and Air India, and that Air Swazi was due to arrive as scheduled at 5.30 pm. Long before that he was out at the airport, sitting in his hired car, reading *Punch* and the local Seychellois daily paper, *The Nation*. The other members of the advance party were there too, tense, apart. So was Bob Sims, down from La Misère with four AK 47s and their chargers in his boot. There was always the risk that the whole plot might have been betrayed to the government – in which case a 'welcoming party' of troops would certainly arrive to surround the incoming plane as it landed. If this were to happen, the task of the mercenaries already on the island was to create, by gunfire, a diversion at the moment of landing. Dolinchek's particular role would be to act as the Colonel's bodyguard and escort. Three times he asked Sims for his 'personal weapon' without result. 'I think he was numbed with fright,' said Dolinchek later. 'He didn't say nothing.'

No lorryloads of troops however swung suddenly across the tarmac as, exactly on time, the orange and white Fokker Friendship came in to land and taxied to a halt. Less than a quarter of an hour later 'a fairly short gentleman, a bit aged, with light hair and a small goatee beard' came striding cheerfully out to meet his brother-in-law and friends. This was 'the Colonel', 'Mad Mike' Hoare himself, or (to the Seychellois official who stamped his visa) Mr Thomas Boarel. The first stage of the plan had succeeded, without a hitch.

While Hoare chatted to a much-relieved Bob Sims and to Barney Carey and while Dolinchek, who had mentally allotted himself the role of the Colonel's chauffeur, tried officiously to present his 'intelligence report' only to be waved aside till the following morning, the mercenaries, laughing and joking, marshalled by Jeremiah Puren, came out into the open airport concourse carrying their over-heavy grips. Three minibuses were waiting to take the whole group (bar the Colonel whom Sims was going to drive to the Auberge) to the Reef Hotel, less than two miles down the road. They started loading their grips, with the drivers' help, onto the minibuses. The manager of the Reef Hotel had (he later informed me) laid on a cocktail party especially to welcome so large a group; indeed, ironically, the Seychelles' Minister of Tourism was due himself to show them round the following day. Everything appeared to have gone exceptionally smoothly.

But the gods must have been jealous. Neither the Colonel nor any staff officer preparing any contingency plan could possibly have foreseen what happened next. One of the mercenaries, one of the last off the plane, Kevin Beck, came safely through Passport Control. But he then turned through the red channel of Customs, the 'Something to declare' channel rather than, as all the rest had done, the green channel, with 'Nothing to declare'. Why did he do it? It has never been made clear. There are two possible explanations. The first is that the mercenaries had had too much to drink on board the flight; in other words that Beck, and others, were, to say the least, merry and liable to make mistakes. Certainly there had been an incident the night before in the Ermelo Holiday Inn where a drunken mercenary had challenged another guest to a fight despite all their officers' previous injunctions to keep a low profile. According to Dolinchek the Colonel himself had said on arrival: 'Martin, I don't think the guys will last till Friday. We'll have to do it tomorrow. I've got a load of drunkards on board' – to which Dolinchek had retorted, 'You've got more drunkards here in the Seychelles.' But this hardly sounds like Hoare's authentic tone. It may very well have been just Dolinchek airing his pet prejudice after the event. For the mercenary officers on board have always denied that their men had been allowed to drink.

The other possible explanation was in a way more unforeseeable still. It is that Beck, like many South Africans, had never left South Africa and had therefore never in his life gone through a Passport or Customs control; so he simply drifted, unaware of what he was doing, of the ghastliness of his mistake, into the wrong channel. Furthermore, like many South Africans, he may not have been able to read English very well and so simply may not have been able to interpret what the signs said. In any event there he was with (he apparently insisted) nothing to declare – a suspicious insistence in the circumstance – on the wrong side of the customs desks. Despite his protestations the young Indian customs officer, Vincent Pillay, who had reported for duty one hour earlier that afternoon, insisted politely on searching his grip.

Two or three other passengers, Peter Hean and Sven Forsell among them, had been following Kevin Beck and waited, aghast, to see what would happen. Peter Duffy, as tour leader, did more. He pulled toys from his own bag and attempted to divert Pillay's attention by pressing a squeaky rubber duck. The diversion did not succeed. Beneath the socks in the grip which he was examining, six inches from its bottom, Vincent Pillay's fingers felt the hard outline of a weapon. He hesitated, apparently, and looked nervously round. Then, plucking up courage, he asked Beck to accompany him to the guardroom.

Even then, even in the guardroom, all was not lost and Beck might still have bluffed his way out. The polystyrene was pulled out revealing the dismantled AK 47. But – and this is nearly the most incredible incident of this whole incredible tale of the discovery – the woman police constable in charge, WPC Flavia Potin, took the weapon simply for a spear gun and was in the process of writing out a receipt whereby Beck could reclaim it on leaving the islands when her more observant superior, Sergeant Esparon, took a closer look and presumably did not at all like the look of what he saw.

'What is this?' he asked Beck.

'I told him quite honestly,' said Beck with utter accuracy later, 'I had not seen it before.' Then Beck added – was he trying to joke? was he drunk? was he simply scared? – 'I don't know what it is but there are forty-four more with bags like mine outside.'

That was how, through a combination of bad luck and one man's stupidity, the whole carefully laid plan, that seemed to have had such a promising a start and might so easily have succeeded, was, by an utterly unforeseeable event that even a Frederick Forsyth would hardly have dared to imagine, prematurely and, from the mercenaries' point of view, disastrously exposed.

Mahé: Dusk to Midnight

Sergeant Esparon, holding the AK 47 muzzle downwards in his hand, came running through the front of the airport shouting that the buses must not leave, that 'they' had guns. It was Jeremiah Puren, a 'tall white-haired man with sideburns and a moustache, wearing a hat, jacket and tie', who reacted most quickly. 'Come on, boys. Move it, boys,' he shouted. He must already have been alarmed at the delay and had his own AK 47 almost assembled. As the mercenaries dived for their grips and their guns, Puren, leaning against the second minibus, at a range of sixteen feet shot Sergeant Esparon in the shoulder, four inches above the heart. That, the first shot – or rather the first two shots – 'Yah, Yah' it sounded like to the sergeant – was fired at about ten past six, forty minutes only after the Air Swazi flight had landed. Night falls quickly in the tropics and by this time the sun was sinking below the horizon and the light was fading. The confusion and chaos that followed was made many times worse by the growing dark.

'Don't shoot civilians!' Puren shouted. But in the panic that followed as airport staff and passers-by ran here and there screaming; as more and more mercenaries in their shorts and tennis shoes appeared with guns in their hands; and as shooting broke out, not against any target as such but simply in order to frighten, to assert control, one of the mercenaries, Johan Fritz, was shot by accident by his own side – possibly because he stumbled. He was twenty-four years old, the eldest son of the head of General Mining's Gold and Uranium Division, from 'Millionaire's Row' in Westcliff, Johannesburg's richest suburb. His friend Patrick Henrick, who had done his military service in the Parabats with Fritz, saw him lying there bleeding. He yelled for Steyn de Wet, the doctor. But when the doctor came, there was nothing he could do. 'Is he okay?' asked Dunlop Paul. 'No,' replied Steyn de Wet. Johan Fritz, a 'model child', who had been bored with farming the family farm near Rustenberg in the Orange Free State and who had longed for a little excitement, was dead.

That was the only casualty, bar the wounded Sergeant Esparon, there at the airport. The mercenaries quickly herded staff and passers-by, about sixty Seychellois in all, into one of the passenger lounges and disconnected all telephones bar one. Vincent Pillay slipped away onto the road, stopped a passing car, dropped off at nearby Cascade Police Station to tell the police what was happening; and then, after his historic day, unlikely ever to be equalled again in his career as a customs officer, wisely went home. Dolinchek sat in his car for five or ten minutes and then drove off. 'I realised people in Hoare's party didn't know me,' he explained, unconvincingly, later, 'and they might shoot me, so I drove away. ...If I had had my personal weapon,' he added in an attempt to put a better face on it, 'I would have stayed with Hoare.' But Sims had apparently already driven off, back to La Misère in the hills. And, like Sims, but with less excuse – he had no woman to look after – Dolinchek retired from the fray, driving south to the Reef Hotel where he 'had a few beers', awaiting, in safety, as a spectator, the turn of events.

For now, of course, all Hoare's carefully laid plans had been ruined and the element of surprise had been totally lost. The cocktails at the Reef Hotel remained unserved, the rooms reserved for the Froth-blowers were never occupied. There was now no chance, from Hoare's point of view, of familiarising the men with the island and of launching the coup a day or two later. Indeed the question of launching the coup – impossible in any case in the dark – now became secondary to ensuring his men's immediate survival. Hoare had no way of knowing that Sergeant Esparon's colleagues had attempted (before the guardroom phone was disconnected) to phone Army HQ and Police HQ only to find all lines engaged so that Pillay's alarm at Cascade Police Station was therefore the first to be raised. He had to assume that the army, at Pointe La Rue, at the southern end of the airport, had been alerted and would shortly be moving in to attack his men. So he immediately ordered four of the advance party (who of course in their days on the island had studied the camp's layout) to drive to the gates of Pointe La Rue camp and there 'seize the barracks'. Ken Dalgliesh, Charley Dukes, Roger England and Aubrey Brooks, all four now with their AK 47s assembled and ready, drove out fast in their hired car. The Colonel paused to organise Mike Webb and Richard Stannard, with the dozen or so Rhodesians in their group, to follow in the commandeered minibuses and then himself set out, chauffeured by Barney Carey (who, like Hoare, was unarmed) and accompanied by the Austrian film-maker, Sven Forsell. But he was delayed, apparently, by the appearance of Jean Dingwall and possibly one or two others of the local *Mouvement pour La Résistance* supporters with whom consultations, in the new situation, were immediately necessary. Meanwhile Webb and Stannard heard an exchange of gunfire ahead as they drove the mile and a half that separated the airport entrance from the Pointe La Rue gates. They debussed their men 150 yards away and advanced in extended line, hesitantly, spreading out across the unknown lush tropical countryside.

The bearded Brooks, Dukes, England and Dalgliesh had leapt out of their car inside the Pointe La Rue entrance gates, firing in approved mercenary style from the hip. In Dukes' expressive phrase there were about 50–100 Seychellois soldiers running around inside 'like chickens with their heads cut off'. A few were wounded; none seriously. They did not run around disorganised for long, however. Within minutes the mercenaries were in their turn under heavy fire. They fled, scattering into the deep grass and trees on the hillside opposite, leaving their yellow Colt the main target of the concentrated barrage. By the time the Colonel and Barney Carey drove up, it was to find Dukes wounded in the arm and bleeding badly, supported by a shaken Ken Dalgliesh. Of the other two, of Roger England and Aubrey Brooks, there was in the gathering dark no sign. These were Barney Carey's men, and Carey decided to stay behind and look for them while Hoare drove Dalgliesh and the wounded Dukes back to the airport. The attack on the army barracks had obviously failed: indeed the revving-up of engines inside could be heard. Further back Webb had identified a heavy 12.7 mm firing from inside the camp. Rather than risk an assault on far superior numbers now clearly ready to riposte, he wisely decided to retreat: to pull back to the airport and 'consolidate'. It was now the turn of the Seychelles Army to counterattack.

Their counterattack took the form of a sortie by an armoured car, a Soviet BRDM, that eventually roared out of Pointe La Rue with soldiers sitting on top. Timings become very confused, and reports of movements too, now that night had fallen. Some mercenaries later claimed that two armoured cars attacked them. In fact it seems that there was only one, roaring around the airport entrance, then reversing, then back again onto the tarmac of the runway, in and out, the soldiers on top dropping off and taking apparently to their heels as they were fired upon, but the armoured car itself firing its cannon utterly impervious to AK 47 bullets. Without RPG rocket launchers – which Hoare had had to leave behind – there was no way it could be destroyed.

While Webb and Stannard deployed their men on the southern airport perimeter and exchanged desultory fire with what they later claimed to be infiltrating Tanzanians, Bob Jones-Davies with five or six other mercenaries had set up a roadblock, of cars and granite blocks, on the main road outside the airport. It was when the armoured car tried to breech this that it finally came to grief. It reversed away, and one wheel stuck in the roadside gutter. Armoured cars are not tanks. They are almost as vulnerable to ditches as ordinary cars – certainly as Landrovers. Despite revving up the BRDM would not budge. It was there – still dangerous but immobile – and potentially most useful if only the mercenaries could now capture it.

Patrick Henrick, with Tullio Moneta, had been trying, unsuccessfully, to make Molotov cocktails from the bottles in the airport bar to deal with the BRDM. Now that it was immobilised, hatch down, he and other mercenaries surrounded it, banging on the outside with their guns, shouting at the crew to come out and surrender, promising them they would not be harmed. Not surprisingly the crew preferred to stay safe inside rather than trust their lives to the promises of a murderous gang (as no doubt they believed) of white mercenaries. Then Henrick and Alex Deacon climbed on top, poured petrol over the vision ports and set it alight. From inside the vision must have been frightful. What happened next is obscure. But what I deduce happened, from hints dropped on various sides (though both parties officially prefer to gloss over the incident), is that the mercenaries threatened to pour petrol down the gun barrel and set it alight, thus incinerating all inside. Still the commander, Lt. David Antat, refused to surrender. Then one of his own crew, terrified at the thought of being burnt alive, shot him; and the rest surrendered. Certainly Antat (and Antat alone) was killed: and certainly neither the Seychellois authorities nor the mercenaries have ever explained precisely how he met his death. It is tragically ironic, if this account is correct, that of the two men who died in the Seychelles coup attempt – one on each side – both were killed not by the enemy but by their own men. The mercenaries set the dazed crew members free.

Despite all the efforts, however, to push, haul or tow the armoured car out of the gutter and give Hoare's men some much-needed mobility, it remained obstinately stuck and immobile. Furthermore, though six rockets were found in the armoured car, there was no rocket launcher; no protection therefore against further attacks by other armoured cars. Not that that came. After this first furious flurry of action, that may have been over by eight or half-past-eight (nobody on either side appears to have been keeping a time-check) there was a total lull. In a sense the military situation was a temporary stalemate. The mercenaries controlled the airport. The army controlled the barracks to its south. Neither was prepared, in the night, to move against the other. To the north of the airport, the government, by now fully alerted, controlled the capital and the radio station and had already imposed a total ban on all movement. Further to the south Dolinchek was still drinking at the Reef Hotel, and Roger England, isolated, had decided to save himself by swimming back to his hotel, also the Reef, from the beach near the barracks. In the jungle above Pointe La Rue, Barney Carey was to spend the night searching without success for both England and Brooks; meanwhile Aubrey Brooks was lying in the bush, semi-conscious, badly wounded with a bullet through his right thigh. Back in the aiport Hoare had set up his command post at the Aviation Seychelles Traffic Office near the Transit Lounge where the hostages and prisoners were being held.

Outside the airport, from a phone cabin at the Shell Station across the road, Jeremiah Puren – without informing Hoare – was trying to get in touch with the British pilots of the Air Swazi Fokker Friendship, Captain James Farquharson and Flying Officer Bob Kerr. They and the three Swazi airhostesses, Nanette Dhlamini, Pinkie Mpungose, and Liz Dludlo had left the airport before firing broke out. They too were at the Reef Hotel. Understandably bemused, the pilots were not willing – even if they had been able – to return to the airport and at the risk of their own lives rescue the stranded mercenaries by flying them out. Nor did the government, whom Farquharson contacted, want them flown out. For President René and his hardline supporters were by now rightly convinced that the attempted coup had aborted, that the mercenaries who had landed were neither numerous nor well-armed, that no local uprising had taken place or was now likely to take place in their support, and that in effect the invading rats were caught in a trap.

A certain lassitude, indeed almost a certain apathy, was by now beginning to overtake the mercenaries. They had been up since 4 am. Their initial exhilaration had faded. They could see that their position was poor, though by no means desperate. It was at this stage that differences began to surface between the professional soldiers and the old hands. Professional soldiers, like Mike Webb, were worried by the low stocks of ammunition left and the lack of a plan. Old hands, like Peter Duffy, knew from Congo days how opportunities might always turn up and how improvisation had so often succeeded in mercenary operations when plans had failed. In any case there was, it seemed, nothing more to be done that night: the morning might bring new counsel.

Vernon Prinsloo had, as planned, 'captured' the control tower as soon as firing had broken out by the simple expedient of announcing his presence via the microphone outside to the three terrified women inside. They had told him there was nothing to control in any case till four hours later when the incoming Air India flight would land; but all the same he had the decency to dig out the very nervy young Director of Civil Aviation, Maurice Lousteau-Lalanne, from the crowd of hostages and dispatch him to the control tower to replace the girls. Shortly before ten o'clock Prinsloo suddenly remembered that the Air India flight would soon be approaching. He, his 'second-in-command' Charles Goatley and David Greenhalgh (who had been a lieutenant in the RLI) found the door to the control tower firmly locked and barred. Greenhalgh and Goatley climbed onto the roof; and as they skinned down through the windows (thoughtfully shot out earlier by Patrick Henrick) a very curious sight met their eyes. The Director of Civil Aviation was cowering under a table, holding – as well – a dustbin lid over his head; apparently he had been in that posture ever since the armoured car in its perambulations had loosed off a round at the control tower. They persuaded him to emerge and to tell them the Air India callsign.

Captain Umesh Saxena, the pilot of Air India Flight 224 from Salisbury to Bombay, had been calling up the Mahé control tower frantically but (in view of Lousteau-Lalanne's posture) without success; a hundred miles out and at 9.57pm he had decided to divert his Boeing 727 to Mauritius when the Seychelles at last came on the air. Goatley was experienced enough in air traffic control to reassure the worried captain that all was well. Breaking contact, he told Prinsloo that the Boeing – it was a big plane, a Boeing 727, with a crew of fourteen but, with only sixty-five passengers, half-empty – would be coming in to land shortly. Lousteau-Lalanne protested strongly: it must not, he argued, be allowed to land – the lives of the crew and passengers would be endangered. Prinsloo contacted 'headquarters' on his walkie-talkie and was told to bring the plane in. This is where the story becomes confused. Prinsloo thought he spoke to Hoare and that these were Hoare's orders. Over the radio of course Prinsloo could only guess that he was talking to Hoare. In fact the 'Sunray' – the commanding officer – with the British accent who was on the receiving end of Prinsloo's message and who gave the order to talk the Air India Flight down was almost certainly Mike Webb. The significance of the order was, of course, this: that the Boeing with its enormous range could, once refuelled, be used as a means of escape. Therefore whoever gave the order for the Boeing to be talked down must already − which was certainly not the case with Hoare − have given up the coup for lost and been planning to quit. The Boeing would be the golden, the only, indeed almost the heaven-sent opportunity. In reply to Lousteau-Lalanne's renewed almost hysterical protests Goatley simply retorted, 'The flight must land.'

The landing lights were switched on in the control tower − to reveal a new obstacle, two landrovers and a small truck driven out there earlier by the Tanzanians and still blocking the runway. Goatley radioed the pilot to 'land deep'. The port wing of the Boeing just scraped the second landrover as, at 10.45 pm, Captain Saxena touched down. Peter Duffy was sent out by Hoare with a couple of companions to board the aircraft and explain the situation.

The aircraft's lights were switched off, the blinds drawn, and the passengers, only mildly aware that something was a little wrong, were told to remain quietly in their seats. Saxena and his co-pilot, Captain Misra, were shortly afterwards escorted by Dunlop Paul to the Aviation Seychelles Traffic Office in the airport building while Alan Mann and Kurt Priefert cleared the runway. Hoare had set up his headquarters at the Traffic Office for the single reason that it had the only working telephone connection with the outside world − the 'hot line' as it was soon to become. He introduced himself as 'Mr Tom' − a mild attempt at disguise. 'You have arrived at a very unfortunate time,' he told the two pilots. 'The flight should never have landed. We are in the middle of a revolution.'

Saxena had been an airforce pilot himself and was not a man to panic, as his cool control in the unusual circumstances of the landing had shown. This was just as well because now, unexpectedly, the Seychellois Army re-entered the fray, even though at (from their point of view) a distance. A .75 mm recoilless rifle, apparently situated north of the airport, on the outskirts of the capital, sent shells crashing around the terminal buildings. As the mercenaries dived for cover from the flying glass, it was Hoare who panicked. Not that he panicked for his own safety; he panicked − and he was right to panic − over the risk of a shell hitting the stationary Boeing. He sent for Lousteau-Lalanne and he sent for Patrick Elizabeth, the Airport Duty Officer, and, having seen them both, he ordered Patrick Elizabeth to telephone the Commissioner of Police in Victoria and demand a truce. For, as Hoare shakily confided in an aside to Tullio Moneta, if the Boeing 727 exploded, he would be blamed for every man, woman and child burnt alive. 'There will not be a place on earth I could go,' he said. He was absolutely right. Had that disaster

happened – and it did not – Hoare, who had allowed the plane to
land, not the Seychellois Army, the actual direct agents of its potential
destruction, would have been held up to universal obloquoy. It is yet
another reason for believing that Hoare himself never gave the order
for the plane to land, the order that placed him in so fearful a
dilemma. It is also a reason for thinking that by this stage the
Seychelles authorities – possibly President René himself, possibly the
more ruthless Ogilvy Berlouis – were very well aware of the precise
situation at the airport and were content, once the Boeing had landed,
to play a game of cat-and-mice with the mercenaries by carefully
continuing the shelling.

The precise details of what happened next are unclear. Even
Hoare claims to be uncertain whether he spoke over the 'hot line' to
the Commissioner of Police, James Pillay, or to President René
himself. At any rate by 11.30 pm, three-quarters of an hour after the
Boeing's touchdown, a ceasefire had been agreed. The Boeing would
be allowed to take off – provided there were no mercenaries on board.
But as a *quid pro quo* Hoare himself would have to stay by the
telephone and phone the President in person at the moment of
take-off, thus proving that he and his men were still on the ground. If
not, the shelling, even at the risk of the innocent lives of all the
passengers, would be resumed. That was the deal. It showed a
surprising confidence in their military abilities on the part of the
Seychellois. It might have been thought that they would have been
delighted simply to be rid of the mercenaries in this comparatively
harmless way of a flight out – honour satisfied on both sides. On the
contrary the Seychellois now seemed intent on keeping the mercenaries on the island for their imminent destruction.

Hoare himself was perfectly prepared, once rid of the incubus of
the Boeing, to stay on and fight it out. 'The Old Man wants the plane
out and at first light we will attack,' the word spread among the 'old
hands'. The plan was for an all-out assault at dawn on the Pointe La
Rue camp. The 'old hands', such as Peter Duffy, were all in favour of
giving this a try; after all, the mercenaries had not seriously joined
battle yet, and all the experience of the Congo days led them to
believe that dash and noise would always carry them through –
particularly against an army such as that of the Seychelles, no
members of which had ever seen any military action at all. Many of
the rank-and-file mercenaries too were against any sort of a deal with
René. As Nick Wilson later said, 'the position was far from hopeless'.
But the 'old hands' were outnumbered by the ex-Rhodesian and
Afrikaner Recce officers, men who had always been used, even in

in-and-out cross-border raids, to the back-up of a regular army, to helicopters to lift them out when in a tight spot, above all to the knowledge, so reassuring psychologically, that they were backed by the superior weapons of superior forces. Here, by contrast, at Mahé Airport they were underarmed, outnumbered, backed by no-one and – if the Boeing were allowed to depart – literally without a means of escape, with their backs to the wall. They would be forced in the morning to fight and against all odds to win; or to die; or to surrender. Their conventional military mentality, all their training, held them back from so stark a choice.

'We should have issued the Recce boys with a pair of flippers each to keep them happy,' said one of the 'old hands' later, derisively. But no mercenary leader can impose his will against the general wishes of his sub-commanders – particularly when he is ageing and has not himself been in action, unlike them, for many years. His sub-commanders talked of the Tanzanians, of the possible arrival of a Russian gunboat. Wearily, bitterly disappointed, Hoare agreed to an evacuation. Nick Wilson had positively to be forced to withdraw. But others were convinced that the Air India flight had been laid on specially to rescue them. Patrick Eurelle had been told that Kenya would provide an escape aircraft if things went wrong; and assumed that this was it. John Mackay thought it was a South African Airways flight in disguise, laid on by Botha himself. Kevin Beck claimed afterwards, more reasonably, that he had been assured that Air India would be paid 175,000 rand by the South African government to fly Hoare's men off in an emergency. Ideas, to say the least, were at this stage very confused.

The Flight Out

Afterwards the mercenary leaders always maintained that the two Indian pilots agreed almost cordially to fly them out to whatever destination they might choose. 'If you save us, we will save you,' Peter Hean heard Saxena say. It seems very likely he did say it – and meant it. It seems probable enough that in their relief at the thought of getting away alive and safe from a very sticky situation that was no concern at all of theirs, with their crew, plane and passengers intact, the price to pay – giving fifty white men a lift – must have seemed very low indeed. Indeed Misra even told Hoare: 'Mr Tom, you are a lovely man.' On the other hand Saxena was later to testify that he had been warned: 'Follow our orders and you will not be harmed. Disobey and you will lose your life.' Here again it seems probable enough that one of the mercenary leaders should have used this sort of language; and the threat was of course, even if not stated so brutally, in any case implied.

Two questions remained to be settled: weapons and destination. Hoare ordered that weapons were not to be taken aboard; but Hoare was beginning by now to lose his authority. Mike Webb and Tullio Moneta countermanded his orders: weapons *were* to be taken aboard; else as Tullio Moneta graphically put it 'we would have been sitting ducks' if attacked at the moment of take-off. There were contradictory reports of how Captain Saxena reacted to this; but it seems most likely that he agreed to the mercenaries bringing their AK 47s on board provided all explosives were left behind.

The question of destination was debatable. Saxena for obvious reasons suggesting continuing the flight to Bombay. Kenya? Very dubious. Sir Seewosagur Ramgoolam's Mauritius? A possibility. Oman? Mike Webb vetoed that: the Sultan would not welcome the arrival of a group of mercenaries and in any case the RAF base there would send up fighters to intercept the flight before landing. In the end the obvious decision was made: to head for home, to return to South Africa.

Peter Duffy had been supervising the refuelling. Lousteau-Lalanne found a car to take Misra out to inspect the runway and check that it had been cleared. There remained only the problem of the take-off itself, of the ceasefire condition that no mercenaries would be aboard the departing plane, and of Hoare's guarantee that he would be standing by the phone and would speak to René at the moment of take-off. It was Saxena who suggested that 'Mr Tom' make the phone-call and sprint across the tarmac, and he would have a rope-ladder hanging down ready for him to clamber up into the cockpit. But Hoare would have none of it. 'Mad Mike' insisted that he would stay behind as pledged. All his plans had crumbled. The past years were wasted. The future for Hoare himself, the failed leader, must at that midnight have seemed bleak indeed. What thoughts ran through his head at that moment it is impossible even to surmise. Rohwein, the former Congo mercenary, offered him a hand-grenade.

'What's this?' said Hoare.

'Well, maybe you need it.'

'What the hell would I need it for?'

Neither a lone last stand nor suicide appear to have been in the Colonel's mind. Nevertheless Tullio Moneta told Kurt Priefert to watch him 'in case he runs off into the bush'. But at the moment of departure, with all the mercenaries aboard, 'Two of my men', as

Hoare later and with dignity put it, 'would not hear of my staying and obliged me to return with the group'. In fact Moneta ('Colonel, you are coming with us,' he declared) and Priefert simply frogmarched Hoare to the plane. He ordered Kenny to burn the tapes he was carrying. He seems at the last moment to have remembered his 'documents'; and Puren ordered Botes to go and fetch them. Too late. When the Boeing finally safely took off, without landing lights, some time after midnight much to the relief of the passengers, who found the seats beside them occupied by jovial young men, and to the relief of the crew – 'My goodness gracious me,' said Stannard, backslapping the captain when Saxena came to check that all was well while Dalgliesh boisterously ordered champagne – a roll-call was held. Forty-five live mercenaries were on board, including the badly wounded Dukes, and one dead body, that of Johan Fritz. But the 'documents' were missing – and so, more mysteriously, was Jeremiah Puren.

Hoare relapsed into understandable depression on the long flight south. Webb, sitting beside him, summoned Charles Goatley and sent him forward to the cockpit, with instructions to make sure that Saxena and Misra were in fact flying towards South Africa. For if by any chance it had treacherously entered their heads to divert back to their airport of origin, Salisbury in Rhodesia, that would have been 'disastrous'. No-one needed reminding twice of how Mugabe and his men would deal with a 'gift' of forty-five white mercenaries, descending from the skies: the very thought was enough to send shudders down the strongest ex-Rhodesian spine.

The thought may fleetingly have crossed Captain Saxena's mind; a successful hijack of fleeing mercenaries would after all, apart from turning the immediate tables, have made him one of the Third World's heroic figures. But, if so, wisely he did nothing about it. In the early hours of the morning he contacted Jan Smuts airport, at Johannesburg, to announce minor engine trouble and request permission to land. He was ordered to head for Durban's Louis Botha airport. It was only when approaching Durban that, apparently with Goatley's agreement, he pressed the transponder that is fitted to all international flights and is used as an alarm signal to signify that the aircraft emitting has been hijacked. From the mercenaries' point of view this may have seemed a wise move to make: it would mean that the airport would be closed and that they would have to deal not with the civilian authorities but directly with the military. From Saxena's point of view only the fact that he was being hijacked, that he was acting under constraint, would, he explained to Goatley, protect his reputation as an Indian accepting assistance from the outcast regime of South Africa. The pilots were 'nice fellows', said Hoare – 'with', it was noticed, 'tears in his eyes'. According to Dalgliesh he 'looked like a broken man'.

At 4.57 am local time the Boeing touched down in thick mist, at Durban. The plane was isolated by armed railway police (traditionally responsible in the Republic for all public transport security operations) under Colonel Mouton; and Dalgliesh and Duffy, on Mike Webb's orders, took charge of negotiations that, to their amazed chagrin, were both long-drawn-out and difficult. Long before the 'siege' was over, local pressmen, alerted to a potential hijack, were pressing around the airport buildings. The police refused them permission to go near the isolated aircraft. 'What's Duffy doing down there?' cried one of the photographers in anguish, having spotted a rival. 'Who authorised him to get in?'

The passengers and crew were after two hours allowed out. 'Mr Tom,' Captain Saxena said, 'I do hope we meet again.' Outside, he talked briefly but in a very friendly way to newsmen, playing down all questions of a hijack – later he claimed that he was uncertain how long he, his crew, his passengers and his plane might be detained in what was for him hostile territory unless he was very careful as to what he said. In the plane Pieter Rohwein emptied a whole bottle of whisky as the mercenaries waited. At 11.30 am they emerged, handcuffed, and were immediately flown to Waterfloof Air Base near Pretoria. From there they were driven in two trucks to Zonderwater Prison outside Cullinan.

Meanwhile, at about the same time, back in the Seychelles, from the mountainside covered by deep jungle overlooking the airport, Barney Carey was watching the Seychellois Army brush aside a posse of police waving large white flags to put in 'a very good commando raid' on the empty airport terminal – empty, that is, of all but the sixty terrified 'hostages', still cowering in the transit lounge, uncertain what was happening and not yet daring to come out. 'They must have put about thirty to forty shells into the building,' said Carey with awe later. 'They shot the hell out of it. They really tore the place to pieces.' The hostages, including poor Lousteau-Lalanne (whose nerves months later had still not recovered from the whole episode; he could not bear – shades perhaps of 'Mr Tom's' frantic appeals for a ceasefire – even to look at a telephone) were released, miraculously unharmed by this last assault. But at least one fisherman out at sea was killed by the uncontrolled gunfire – his boat according to terrified eyewitnesses cut in two.

The soldiery, having successfully launched a classic two-pronged attack preceded by the textbook artillery softening-up against a building whose only unfortunate defect was that it had been evacuated many hours earlier by all enemy forces, proceeded to relieve their understandable frustrations by breaking into and looting the duty-free liquor shop. 'A bit of a shambles,' commented another spectator watching from more comfort, Dolinchek. 'You had a good manoeuvre there,' he later, patronisingly, told a Seychelles officer, 'but that was the real McCoy.'

By now – though the magic name of 'Mad Mike' Hoare had not yet surfaced – news of a failed mercenary raid on the Seychelles was flashing around the world. The wire services reported 'heavy fighting' around the airport that morning as – apparently – the cornered mercenaries desperately resisted the determined Seychellois attacks. There was as yet no link-up with the reports of a hijacked Air India plane that had landed in Durban. Then in the afternoon news came that the Mahé terminal was 'stormed'. A group of Seychellois journalists were escorted out to the airport after its 'fall' to inspect for themselves the heavy damage caused; and the destruction and looting, for which, they were told, the mercenaries were directly responsible. As their jobs depended on the Seychelles government – the Ministry of Information controlled all means of communication on the islands – they had little incentive to question this information. However one journalist stumbled across – in the ladies' toilet which he was all the same 'investigating' – an interesting find: two reels of tape, one completely burnt, one half-burnt, with various strips and shreds lying on the floor tiles. Within hours these tapes were in the hands of M. Baudouin, the Seychelles' Director of Information, and being carefully pieced together by his technicians. Kenny, Hoare's bodyguard, had in the rush of the departure botched his job; and Jimmy Mancham's complicity in the attempted coup was about to be proved.

Meanwhile, in London, Mancham was that Thursday denying all involvement to the journalists who phoned him for his comments. He admitted only that he had been contacted two days earlier by an anonymous caller who had told him, in Creole, that: 'The Movement is on the march.' But how did it come that Mancham was in London that Thursday when by rights he ought to have been already in Nairobi, waiting for the success signal to be flashed that would bring him and his new government flying back in triumph to the Seychelles?

There is here another minor mystery to add to the list of unanswered questions still surrounding the attempted coup in the Seychelles. It is complicated by the fact that a *Daily Express* reporter claimed to have talked that same Thursday to Mancham not in London but in a remote hideaway in, of all places, Majorca.

So was Mancham in London at all? Modern communications being what they are and journalists being, despite their reputation for cynicism, generally trusting creatures, one can imagine Mancham returning calls perhaps taken minutes before by his secretary in Putney as if from London – but in fact from very considerably farther away, indeed from another continent. One can imagine the *Daily Express* reporter, probably with a photographer in tow, being turned away from his door with a hastily devised holiday story and the promise of a call back. Or one can even imagine that Mancham was telling the truth, the whole truth and nothing but the truth. If so, he was the only governmental figure – of all the many governmental figures involved in the affair – to be doing so, as the next and final chapter will tend to demonstrate.

14

Trials and Tribulations

'You tell me what laws the mercenaries broke in South Africa. They only shot out some windows and ran around in the bush.'
Louis Le Grange, Minister of Law and Order in South Africa

Those who plan a mercenary coup and fail pay a stiff penalty. Hoare and his men were held without charge at Zonderwater Prison for almost a week. Conditions are not pleasant in South African jails, even for white detainees. They were stripped on arrival, kept in tiny cells, in solitary confinement, 'like common criminals', commented Hoare afterwards, 'and given the most disgusting food I have ever seen in my life', washed down with Roiboos tea. At the end of the regulation forty-eight hours Major General Zietsman, head of the detective branch of the South African police, summoned Hoare. 'Mike,' he said, 'get your men together and tell them to cooperate on statements. In return we will allow you thirty minutes a day in the open air and later perhaps we will give you your boots back.'

What must have hurt the mercenaries far more, though, than the bad food and the lack of exercise or boots was the fact that they, who, had they succeeded, would undoubtedly have been treated as heroes, were being held as terrorists, under Section 6 of the Terrorism Act – and that not in the country that they had attacked (which would have been understandable) but in the country that had half-instigated the coup. They were totally disowned. On the Friday the Prime Minister, P.W. Botha, denounced the 'adventure'. On the Saturday the US State Department demanded 'prompt and severe punishment' for the instigators of the hijack. For the hijack rather than the failed coup itself was by now the point at issue; South Africa had severe laws against hijacking and behind the scenes the seven nations who had signed the Bonn Agreement of 1978 were threatening, as that Agreement laid down, to cease all flights to any country that did not punish hijackers. These seven nations were the United States,

France, Britain, West Germany, Italy, Japan and Canada. Had all flights from these countries ceased, the effect would have been almost catastrophic.

But had there been in any real sense a hijack at all? By Sunday, though Hoare's name had still not come out (and Mrs Puren was telling inquisitive reporters that her missing husband was on a business trip in Europe) the general sequence of events had become known. Admittedly *Le Monde* in Paris was still referring to ten hours of battle on the island and *The Observer* in London, more specifically and even more inaccurately, was describing how after the defence forces had 'ringed the airport', it was 'not till 4 a.m. that fierce fighting broke out which lasted till 1 p.m.' But back in Bombay Captain James Martin, the spokesman for Air India (whose famous Flight 224 had finally reached its destination on the Friday evening, only a day and a half late) poured scorn on the idea that there had been any 'collusion' between the crew and the mercenaries. 'As far as we are concerned this is a straightforward hijacking', he said.

The South African government was faced with a dilemma. Under their own severe laws hijacking carried a minimum five years' mandatory sentence. Clearly something had to be done to satisfy international opinion. On the other hand South African opinion (exemplified by the immediate reaction, as quoted at the head of this chapter, of the Minister of Law and Order when first questioned by journalists about the events in the Seychelles) was swinging more and more in favour of the mercenaries, as it became clear how very little damage the attempted coup had actually done, particularly when compared to so many of South Africa's covert but official cross-border raids. It was generally considered a sporting attempt that had failed. There was great sympathy for Mr and Mrs Fritz, who buried their son Johan with dignity, and considerable sympathy for the mercenary leader who had taken pains to ensure that his body was brought safely back – particularly when it came out that the mercenary leader was Hoare himself, the ageing folk-hero of what had almost become part of South African mythology, the Congo adventure.

By Wednesday, 2 December the South African government had resolved its dilemma. The doors of Zonderwater Prison were opened. The mass of the mercenaries were sneaked out without being charged – but with orders to keep their mouths shut – or else. Hoare and four others were released on bail (in Hoare's case 10,000 rand, guaranteed by his nephew, Leo Baxter of Denton Hall, to where he was immediately whisked by private helicopter, thus avoiding the press). They were charged with the offence of 'manstealing' – which carried no mandatory jail sentence. Honour appeared to be satisfied; and diplomatic niceties too. Next day the Prime Minister formally denied that he had in any way authorised, or that the Cabinet had been informed of, the coup attempt. He added – for rumours were abounding – that laws would be passed to stop South Africa's part-time soldiers from taking part in any future mercenary operations. Hoare and the other four were ordered to answer to their bail on 7 January. It looked as if their six nights in Zonderwater, unpleasant though these had been, would be the first and last period they would spend in a South African prison; as if, therefore, they could breathe a sigh of comparative relief.

In the Seychelles

The same could not be said for the mercenaries who had remained behind in the Seychelles. A week after the attempted coup they would have considered a spell in Zonderwater Prison as comparative paradise.

Barney Carey, unarmed – he had never been armed – was picked up as the police and army swept through the dense tropical bush overlooking the airport on the afternoon of their 'commando assault' on the terminal buildings. An hour and a half later they arrested Aubrey Brooks at Anse Aux Pins. He had laid up for the night and most of the day; then, weak with loss of blood from a badly bandaged wound, had staggered into the hut of a Seychellois named Lionel who had – as soon as he had recovered from his fright and managed to get Brooks' weapon away – informed the authorities. A twenty-four-hour curfew was still in force, the Seychelles government had announced that Tanzanian reinforcements had flown in to help them with 'mopping-up' operations; and the four remaining members of the 'advance party', who had (successfully as they thought) resumed their identity as harmless tourists, lay low in their hotels or at La Misère.

Both Brooks and Carey were badly beaten up by the soldiers who arrested them. Brooks was kicked, punched and stripped, beaten with rifle butts, threatened with having his eyes plucked out and his genitals cut off. Two soldiers bound and tied his legs behind him and kept kicking him on his wounds. Later, he was told he was to be executed. 'It was very quiet,' he said, 'and I wondered if this was death.' On Friday night after a day and a half of beatings he was transferred to Victoria Hospital, where his arms and legs were manacled to the bedframe. There on the Saturday Carey joined him. Understandably the weaponless Carey had been less badly beaten; but he was still suffering from multiple bruises and abrasions and broken ribs, as the doctor who examined him indignantly diagnosed. The Seychelles were not used to official violence or to hospital patients manacled and held under armed guard. Dr Desmond Fosbery, in addition to being a Fellow of the Royal College of Surgeons and the former government surgeon on St Kitts, was a Buddhist, an earring-wearing individualist and a famous character on the islands. That night Barney Carey, who understood Swahili, heard the Tanzanians guarding them talking of killing them. He asked their nurse Betsy to call the doctor – and Fosbery came in and stayed, to protect them, till the early hours of the morning. Next evening the same thing occurred. 'The soldiers prepared six bullets for each of us,' recounted Carey. Once again their lives were saved by the doctor, 'who after having many words with the soldiers told them they would have to shoot him first, if they wanted to shoot us'.

On the Monday, at noon, though Dr Fosbery insisted that his patients were in no fit state to be discharged, he was tricked into phoning Army HQ and, while he phoned, their guards abducted the two mercenaries. They were driven to Pointe La Rue and there they found Roger England. It was England's car, left at the airport, hired in his name, that had led to his interrogation. He was arrested by the police in his room at the Reef Hotel on Friday afternoon and handed over to the army, on their insistence, on the Saturday. He was not beaten badly, as the other two had been. But he was handcuffed, kept in a tiny cell, without toilets, two foot square; and then when the other two arrived, all three were hooded, handcuffed, occasionally beaten, kept for long periods without water and told at least twice that they would be shot at dawn. It was not till the following Thursday, that is to say Thursday, 3 December, the day after their ex-comrades had been released from Zonderwater Prison in South Africa, that they were finally handed over to the police; and their sufferings ended. There was no love lost at all between the long-established British-trained police in the Seychelles and the newly created Tanzanian-influenced army. There was to be no suggestion at any time that the police ever maltreated any of their prisoners.

The police had already rounded up, the previous Saturday, the day after England's arrest, the remaining three mercenaries on the island – Dolinchek back at the Beauvallon Bay Hotel and the Sims up at La Misère. Probably it was England who revealed, under questioning, their names and whereabouts; though any single male South African still on the island, like Dolinchek, would have been automatically suspect. The curfew was still in force day and night. The airport was closed, the Seychelles virtually cut off from the outside world, and the two thousand-odd tourists in the islands prisoners in their hotels, not even allowed to go down to the beach. For the Seychelles authorities were convinced that there were at least three mercenaries still at large on the island, no doubt trying to lose themselves among the tourists. The authorities by this time even knew their names – Dalgliesh, Dukes and Botes, the three still-uncaptured members of the advance party. What they did not know was that these three had escaped on the Air Indian flight. What they never suspected, however, what only the mercenaries back in South Africa knew, was that one mercenary, not a member of the advance party, had deliberately missed the return flight and was in fact still on the island: Jeremiah Puren.

So the curfew remained in force. The tourists however had to be allowed out. Many of them were unable to pay their hotel bills for this unwillingly-prolonged stay and the situation was becoming for the authorities, besieged by frantic hotel managers, highly embarrassing. So the airport was opened and on Wednesday, 4 December a thousand tourists flew out in a vast 'rescue operation' organised by the international airlines. They may hardly have noticed, in their relief at escaping from the 'island paradise', the wretched orange and white Fokker Friendship standing, its cockpit and fuselage wrecked by shells, on the tarmac at the airport. For the real material casualty of the whole affair had been Royal Swazi Airlines, now out of business, their sole plane shot up – though neither the Swazis nor the Seychellois were to emphasise this point – by a heavy weapon that could not have been fired (for they did not possess any) by the mercenaries, but only by the Seychellois themselves.

By the weekend the authorities were convinced that the threat to their security was over and that no more 'mopping-up' operations were needed. It was the moment to rejoice, to celebrate the Revolution's triumph over the infamous forces of evil. That Sunday a vast demonstration was organised in the stadium where a little over five years earlier Independence had been celebrated with a handshake between President Mancham and Prime Minister René. This time the crowd, 10,000 strong, one in three of every man, woman and child on Mahé island, roared, 'Get us Mancham! Give the mercenaries to us!' 'Capitalist Imperialist Racist Traitor Killer', ran the placards, 'You Must Die!' It looked like Angola all over again. It looked like Angola even more when President René announced to deafening applause that 'The mercenaries we have captured will be tried before a People's Court. We will do with them what the people tell us to do!' Next morning *The Nation* of Monday, 7 December carried the headline 'Death For Paid Foreign Killers, Cry The People'; and over the headline, with more wit than was usual, ran its daily slogan revised for the occasion: 'The only good mercenary is a dead mercenary. Let us make them all good ones.'

But the Seychelles is not – could never be – an Angola. It seems that not only did the British High Commission, the Seychelles Bar and the Judiciary protest at the idea of a People's Court but also – which may have carried more weight – both the islands' Bishops. René himself, as a barrister-at-law and Member of the Honourable Society of the Middle Temple, may have felt a qualm at the impulse that had driven him towards 'revolutionary justice', and towards a wild claim that in view of the killing of Lieutenant Antat the charges would be murder. Antat had been named, posthumously, a Hero of the Revolution – but even in a People's Court there was a danger that the whole story of his killing might emerge and the whole charge therefore backfire. The idea was quietly discarded. The mercenaries were not seen again for almost a month. Then on Tuesday, 5 January 1982, barefoot and handcuffed, thin and in certain cases still bruised, they appeared in court, to be charged, banally, with importing arms contrary to the laws established, and to be remanded in custody for a fortnight. The one point of interest in their first appearance in early January was the presence among them of a seventh mercenary, Jeremiah Puren, finally captured.

Puren had not in fact been arrested. He had presented himself at Cascade Police Station near the airport on the Thursday following the mass demonstration. According to his own story he had taken to the hills when firing had begun.

'I am not a fighting man and am afraid of shooting,' he had told the police – and had wandered around lost and in hiding till near-starvation had forced him to give himself up. 'I am not at my best,' he said pathetically when M. Baudouin presented him, clad in blue shorts, desert boots and no socks, to local journalists, 'I have just spent fourteen days in the bush.'

'I understand he was very hungry,' added the Seychelles' Director of Information, keeping an apparently serious face.

Amazingly neither then nor at any time later did the Seychelles authorities question, officially at least, this very tall tale. Tullio Moneta was later to say that Puren told him that he, Puren, had a good cover in the Seychelles; and Des Botes that he had deliberately decided to leave his weapon behind. My personal belief is that he was sheltered by supporters of the *Mouvement pour La Résistance*. There is some evidence that one of the reasons Hoare was reluctant to leave was because he was still hoping for a local uprising the morning after if only the mercenaries had stayed on. Was Puren dispatched by Hoare to attempt to organise that local uprising? Or did he simply think that he would have a better chance of escaping by himself, later, when the hue and cry had died down? If so, why did he give himself up at all?

The only thing that is certain in this still-mysterious business is that the Seychelles authorities were at the time playing down any idea that the coup might have had any support on the islands. Jean Dingwall, the local 'resistance leader', was arrested; but contrary to all expectations he was never brought to trial. He appears to have been long detained, then quietly released. Two hundred other suspected supporters of the *Mouvement pour La Résistance* had also been rounded up, but only for a matter of hours. It seems therefore that it simply did not suit the book of the Seychelles authorities to enquire too closely into where Puren had been, whom he had contacted, and how he had survived – nor indeed to enquire too closely into Puren's background at all. They had after all in Puren a prisoner with a notorious mercenary past: an historic catch. But his past, and his background, were never brought up publicly either then or later. He was simply treated like the other mercenaries and indeed, being a white-haired old man, as rather less dangerous – this despite the evidence that it was a white-haired old man who had fired the first shot at the airport and nearly killed Sergeant Esparon. It is all very perplexing.

Puren was mildly maltreated after being handed over to the military, and told he would be executed on Christmas Eve. By Christmas the military had won back control from the police of all the mercenaries bar the 'woman mercenary'. Sue Ingle was held at the Central Police Station in Victoria, and well treated. The rest, the six men, were held in solitary confinement, in bad conditions but at least free from beatings, at Union Vale Camp up in the hills above the radio station which they had planned to seize, while the case against them, and its conduct, was being prepared. One of the 'five Majors', Macdonald Marengo, commanded the camp.

On 4 February, however, all seven, on their third appearance in court, were charged with treason only to be once again remanded in custody. Dolinchek when asked by the presiding magistrate if it would be 'convenient' for him to reappear in court on 19 February burst into loud laughter. But, despite his attempts at joking, his – and their –

situation had changed drastically for the worse. Treason is the only crime for which the death penalty, under Seychelles law, can be imposed. The hardliners had won a delayed victory. The mercenaries were to be tried, not indeed by a People's Court but by the Chief Justice of the Seychelles, for their lives.

Forty-five in Pietermaritzburg

In South Africa meanwhile the tables had once again drastically been turned, and this time to the escaped mercenaries' disadvantage. On 1 January the Attorney General of Natal, Mr Cecil Rees, issued warrants for the arrest of all the forty-five mercenaries who had landed at Durban's airport within his jurisdiction on the morning of Thursday, 26 November. It took several days to track them down and serve the warrants, in all parts of the Republic; for the thirty-nine who had been released from Zonderwater without charge a month earlier had naturally asumed that the whole misadventure was, for them, over. They had scattered. But none had left the country. All were now charged with serious offences against the Civil Aviation Act of 1972; and all were released on bail ranging from 500 rand to, for Hoare, an increase to 20,000 rand. All were ordered to appear before Durban's magistrates' court on 18 January, to be served with the detailed charges and to be informed of the date and venue of their trial. The previous minor charges of 'manstealing' against Hoare and the four others were dropped.

Why this sudden switch of legal policy? What was behind this decision to prosecute, and prosecute severely, not only the ringleaders but all the mercenaries involved? South Africa's is a complex society, constantly – like Heracleitus' river – in a state of flux, and there is no simple, single answer to these questions. Partly no doubt it was the result of continuing international pressure to have the mercenaries 'properly' punished. The United Nations had dispatched a Commission of Enquiry to the Seychelles the previous month, December; its members had interrogated the imprisoned seven mercenaries and witnesses on the island (and had incidentally endorsed the Seychellois government's 'bill' for damage to the airport totalling 7,693,000 rupees which with extraordinary effrontery – in view of the fact that the damage had been almost entirely caused by his own forces – President René was attempting to present to 'the West' in general and Britain in particular). Normally the South African government paid little attention to the United Nations and its enquiries ('I have great respect for the United Nations as an impartial body,' said their imprisoned agent, the shameless Dolinchek); but the implication that they themselves (as well as the Kenya government) had been directly behind the attempted coup could only be scotched by severity against its actual executants. Furthermore undoubtedly the South African government wanted to crack the whip not only at unauthorised adventurers but also at its own forces' reservists.

Then there had been the internal pressures. The English-speaking press, led by the *Rand Daily Mail*, had professed itself shocked at the decision to let the mercenaries off so lightly, in the face of world opinion. Even *The Citizen*, which generally supported all official decisions, headed its editorial 'What a Poor Show' and implored Botha to 'throw the book' at Hoare and his men. Mr Kobie Coetsee, the Minister of Justice, had in early December fired, in response, a warning shot. The charges of 'manstealing', he said, were merely provisional and might be replaced; and other charges might still be brought against the thirty-nine released; as in fact happened.

Finally there was the position of the Natal authorities themselves. Whatever the central government of the Republic might advise or warn, Natal's attorney-general was absolutely free, at least in theory, to reject its advice and warnings and to proceed as he and his colleagues in Natal's provincial government might consider best. If they thought it wise, or right, to bring charges against all the mercenaries, there was nothing that the Prime Minister could do, whatever his own reservations, to prevent them. Natal was ruled by a very British-style élite, respectable, rich and long-established, and there was among them a distinct vindictiveness against the various social classes from which the mercenaries were drawn – lower-class Afrikaners, newly arrived and impoverished Rhodesians, and mavericks such as Hoare himself who had never been fully accepted into Natal society. My impression is that there was a remarkable desire among these people to teach Hoare and his associates a lesson which they would never forget, and that they little cared what embarrassment they might in the process cause to the Republic's Afrikaner-dominated government and Afrikaner-officered military forces, for which they felt neither affection nor responsibility.

On 18 January the forty-five accused, dressed mainly (bar the self-styled poet Kurt Priefert) in dark suits, and far more subdued than they had been on previous occasions in court, heard the four charges – which carried sentences ranging from five to thirty years' imprisonment – read out to them, after which the State prosecution summarised the background. Some of them, according to observers, 'visibly blanched'. They were not asked at this stage to plead. They were once again remanded on bail for summary trial before Natal's Supreme Court seven weeks later.

Pietermaritzburg, not Durban, is the judicial and administrative capital of the Province of Natal. It lies up in the hills in the hinterland, about fifty miles from the coast. By contrast to the sprawling, dynamic, humid conglomeration of Durban, Pietermaritzburg is small, cool, 'historic' and discreet. It has the reputation of being the most English town in the Republic, with its red-brick Gothic town hall, its cobbled lanes, its Woolworths and its old-fashioned War Memorials to 'Our Glorious Dead'. In Longmarket Street a Union Jack flies outside the Victoria Club: 'Good God, no,' I was informed 'we would never have had that fellow Hoare as a member here.' Hoare and his family lived only a few miles outside Pietermaritzburg, in a small village, Hilton, set in Home-Counties-style countryside.

The Supreme Court, where the trial began on 10 March, is a small building on College Road on the outskirts of the town, looking rather like a Victorian school outside and like a church, with its high ceiling and oak benches, inside. South Africa does not have the jury system. The accused were tried by the Judge President of Natal, Neville James, and two assessors. Before they were asked to plead guilty or not guilty, the Attorney General announced that charges against two of the accused had been dropped; they would, instead, be added to the list of the State's witnesses. These two were the two doctors, Steyn De Wet and Theodorus Van Huysteen. There was a certain justice in this; they had done nothing violent, nothing morally wrong bar the initial decision to become involved at all, and they were the only two with professional careers at stake that could have been ruined by a jail sentence. They were not in the end called upon to give evidence against their former comrades. Yet the preferential treatment given to them must have rankled with the remaining forty-three. Those forty-three all pleaded not guilty on all four counts.

I do not propose to recount step by step the trial that followed. It lasted for over four months, it was both confused and monotonous, it contained little high drama, and it was fundamentally vitiated by the refusal of the Indian government to allow the Air India crew, and in particular Captains Saxena and Misra, to appear in South Africa as witnesses for the prosecution. Yet their evidence, their confrontation with Hoare and the others, was absolutely vital. For of the four charges laid against all the mercenaries three concerned matters for which, in the absence of Saxena and Misra, the prosecution could produce no real evidence at all bar hearsay. The fourth charge was that of 'jeopardising good order and discipline at Louis Botha airport'; and here the prosecution made much – a string of State witnesses to the fore – of the long-drawn-out 'surrender' negotiations and the fact that Durban's airport had had to be closed to all other traffic for five whole hours. But it was a very legalistic charge; and in the end only Hoare and Duffy were to be found guilty of it. Peter Duffy must have regretted the moment when he volunteered (because he, as a journalist, knew most of them) to negotiate with the airport authorities. Hoare of course was by this stage virtually out of the game. I doubt whether any fair-minded jury would have found either of them guilty on this particular count. The appalling weakness of South Africa's proudly independent judicial system is that it gives legalistically-trained minds the ultimate power.

The other three charges were both more interesting and more debatable. Hijacking strictly as such was not included among them. The general view among South Africa's legal experts was that hijacking could only take place 'in flight'; and that 'in flight' was to be defined as from the moment when an aircraft's outer doors were closed prior to take-off. If therefore an agreement were made, even under the threat of force, while on the ground, this would not technically constitute a hijack.

But legal texts can be twisted to cover most eventualities. The first count alleged that the accused had 'unlawfully by threat of force or intimidation' seized or exercised control of Air India Flight 224 during a stopover in the Seychelles. The second count alleged that they had endangered the safety of the aircraft and of its crew and passengers, its good order and discipline, by boarding it at Mahé Airport; and the third that they had possessed weapons on the plane without permission – to wit, thirty-eight AK 47s, 2,345 rounds of ammunition and three Chinese hand-grenades.

To consider the last of these charges first: it seems clear that the AK 47s were taken on board with, in the end, Saxena's permission – and in any case neither they nor the three hand-grenades (which may easily have been taken on board by mistake) were used to threaten or endanger either passengers or crew. It was a totally different case from that of the normal armed hijack, where smuggled arms are suddenly produced and crew and passengers menaced with death unless the plane is diverted. In this case the diversion had already been agreed; the arms were arguably for the aircraft's protection only.

On the second count the prosecution's general argument was that by the very act of boarding the plane, the mercenaries endangered its safety; for a fight with 'the Tanzanians' could have followed. This, while theoretically true, was a very hypothetical argument – based on what *might* have happened, always disputable, never disprovable, rather than on what actually *did* happen: nothing.

The first count however, was the real crux of the whole affair; and here, in a sense, it was simply Hoare's word against Saxena's. For Saxena did give evidence, though in a very unsatisfactory way. The whole trial in Pietermaritzburg was suspended for most of April while the three-man prosecuting team, led by Cecil Rees, and the three defence lawyers flew out to the Seychelles to hear evidence given 'on commission'. By this bizarre legal device the Judge President of Natal empowered one of the Seychelles' three judges, Judge Frank Wood, to conduct, as it were, a hearing on his behalf – almost a trial within a trial. The Indian government allowed Saxena and Misra to come to the Seychelles for this, not so much accompanied as guarded by their Indian lawyer, Mr Madon Gujadhur; and after confusions and diplomatic 'illnesses', after Judge Wood had heard certain Seychellois witnesses like Lousteau-Lalanne again tell their tale, at last at the end of April Saxena gave his evidence. To no-one's surprise he denied any collusion or agreement at all with the mercenaries. It would have been, evidently, the end of his professional career with Air India if he had done otherwise. But a trial where the main, essential prosecution witness is heard at a distance, never seen by the Judge presiding, never confronted directly with the defendants, is a botched trial. Back in South Africa, Sven Forsell, himself the son of an Austrian high court judge, was to give evidence of his conversation with Saxena and Misra in the airport terminal. 'So you could take us?' he asked. 'No problem if you get us out of here,' they replied. He had reported this to Hoare. 'Thank you, Sven,' Hoare had said.

Forsell's evidence has the ring of truth to it. The mercenaries can hardly be said to have 'seized control' of the aircraft 'by threat of force or intimidation' if the pilots themselves had vountarily agreed to fly them out. The only 'threat of force' around at the time was that emanating from the 75 mm recoilless rifle shells being fired from the outskirts of Victoria, and very 'intimidating' they must have been too. But this was a threat not by the mercenaries against the passengers and crew but to mercenaries, passengers and crew alike. The whole situation may have been – obviously was – provoked by the mercenaries' arrival; but that is a very different matter; and they were not being tried, as the South African authorities always insisted, for having attempted to organise a coup in a foreign country. There was no law under which they could have been tried. Coup plotters are normally only legally at risk if caught by the country against which the coup was being plotted – and then, of course, only if it has failed.

By early May, Michael Hannon, a smart Johannesburg lawyer who had been hired by most of the mercenaries to lead their defence, had retired from the case. He had not distinguished himself and had often appeared confused, particularly in the Seychelles; it was something of a waste of the 40,000 rand that Hoare, according to certain accounts, had paid him on behalf of them all. But what formally occasioned his withdrawal was not so much a lack of further money to pay his very high fees as a 'conflict of interest' among his clients. To begin with, the forty-three remaining accused had presented a united front, filing into court in almost military fashion, respectfully behind their leader. But by the time Hoare himself came to give evidence in early May, cleavages had occurred among the defendants. Many, most vociferous among them Kevin Beck, were claiming that Hoare had totally misled them, that he had told them that the *coup* was officially backed, and that therefore they had nothing to fear. 'I am sure I would have said,' nuanced Hoare in mid-May, 'that if the operation went wrong, we were not friendless and our friends in high places would help us.' He was by now, like Kurt Priefert, defending himself – and that rather unskilfully, for Hoare was legally naive and still, apparently, believed that he and his men were bound to be acquitted. With his own total legal expenses rumoured to be nearing 80,000 rand he could no longer afford a lawyer. He had had to sell the family Rover. But his wife Phyllis still continued to bring the accused mercenaries flasks of tea and necessary sympathy. Local counsel, Piet Oosthuizen and Steve Janson, replacing Hannon and his junior Eddie Stafford, continued to defend the rest.

'With great reluctance' Hoare told the story of his meetings with N.J. Claasen of NIS and with Brigadiers Hammam and Knoetze. He even announced that he would sub-poena them as his witnesses but later dropped this move. It would certainly have embarrassed the South African government. Was he threatened with a heavier sentence if he did so or promised a lighter one if he did not? He can by this stage of the trial have had few illusions about its eventual outcome. He was according to some accounts growing both frightened and angry. He had already had several snappy exchanges with the Attorney General.

'Mr Hoare, you have several catchphrases you continually use,' said Rees at one stage.

'You, sir,' retorted the normally courteous Hoare, 'have pitifully

few'. In his final summing-up the Attorney General, by many
accounts an unpleasant man, described Hoare as a 'cunning schem-
er', and, without giving any instances, as 'an unmitigated selective liar
with a smooth and persuasive tongue'. It was too much for the
Colonel. He protested passionately, when his turn came to speak, at
having to sit there listening to a string of personal insults which, he
added, Rees would never have had the courage to voice except under
the protection of a courtroom. He virtually challenged Rees to step
outside and settle their differences as gentlemen should. Then on 16
July he launched into his own carefully prepared but embarrassingly
overblown final plea.

> I see South Africa as the bastion of civilisation in an Africa subjected to a
> total communist onslaught. In the last twenty-two years I have watched –
> in many cases physically battled against – its inexorable encroachment
> into free Africa and its conquests by default.
>   The enemy is at the gates. I prophesy that this country of ours will fall a
> prey to Marxist doctrine before the end of the century unless South
> Africans of all races become actively engaged in the fight against
> communism.
>   I see myself in the forefront of this fight for our very existence. I see my
> men as a noble band of patriots motivated by the same desires.

One hopes that some of the 'noble band' had the grace to look a little
ashamed of themselves. The trial was adjourned on 18 July. On 29
July the Judge President summed up. He accepted that Colonel
Hoare was a dedicated anti-Marxist. But he was no knight in shining
armour. He had expected to be well paid for what he did. He would
have received 100,000 rand if the *coup* had been successful and 'his
reputation as a mercenary would have reached new heights'.

But the *coup* had been miserably botched. Colonel Hoare had
gambled with the lives and safety of his men by asking them to
smuggle rifles through customs at Mahé airport and by having no
contingency escape plans if they should be discovered, as in fact
happened.

'You are an experienced soldier and commander,' concluded the
Judge President, 'and you obviously realised that although the prizes
for victory may be high, the penalties for defeat are even higher.' He
proceeded to find Hoare guilty on three of the four charges and to ask
him what if anything he had to say in mitigation – before those
ominous and 'higher' 'penalties for defeat' were imposed.

The Judge President's summing-up calls for various comments.
First it was hardly his role to say that the *coup* had been 'miserably
botched' – a point totally irrelevant to the charges. But a comment not

easily forgotten, designed, it seems, only to wound the pride of a man already downcast and defeated. It was in any case the only point that Hoare took up in his brief and dignified plea in mitigation. 'My Lord,' he said, 'I did my duty as I saw it. I brought my men home safely and I am proud of that. I have nothing further to say.'

Yet Hoare might well have taken up, more directly, other points. He had in fact been paid as his personal fee only 15,000 rand, though he expected, he had told the court, the new government once installed to 'show its appreciation' with 100,000 rand for himself and 50,000 for his second-in-command, Tullio Moneta – the rewards of three years' planning and very possibly less, he might have added, than the Judge President received for only one year's work. Fifteen thousand rand, the actual fee, was by no-one's standard, certainly not by the standards of mercenaries such as Denard, a fortune; Hoare was not, and would not have been, even if he had earned the whole 100,000, a rich man. Did he offer to pay Air India, Rees had asked him? No.

'Do you think Air India is a charitable organisation?' pursued the Attorney General.

'No,' Hoare had retorted, 'they are not a charitable organisation and I am not a millionaire.'

It was only too true. As for the smuggling of the AK 47s through Customs, that had been a carefully prepared gamble, the success of which all the odds favoured. The lack of any contingency escape plan was arguably a major weakness; yet on the other hand many famous military commanders have deliberately sabotaged their means of escape in order to force their men to stay on and fight without thought of fleeing. This *may* not, however, have been Hoare's case at all. In one curious, overlooked, statement in the witness box he had mentioned that he had $55,000 set aside to fly his men off the Seychelles if something went wrong. This was not as much as the 175,000 rand that Kevin Beck suspected the South African government had paid Air India to do the same; but it is a curious half-confirmation of Beck's suspicion. What is even more curious is the information contained on Hoare's passport, an Irish passport issued on 6 March 1973 in Berne and extended in 1978 for a further five years in London: it gives his occupation as: 'Chartered Accountant with Air India in Calcutta'. This was a point never brought up either by Air India or by himself. There may have been much more to the contingency escape plan, much more collusion, than has ever yet come to light.

When Steve Janson, speaking in mitigation for thirty of the other accused, pointed out quite rightly that the crime was unique in the annals of aviation history and unlikely to be repeated, the Judge President interrupted. 'This was a case of being in the frying pan and finding it too hot and jumping into the fire. They were in a mess and they had to get out,' he commented dismissively. But earlier, he had half-praised most of the mercenaries as impressive, decent young men, led astray by a desire for adventure as well as easy money. He reserved his rancour for Hoare and for Peter Duffy, whom he described as 'a most unreliable witness' who 'in essential matters was untruthful'. Hoare and Duffy were each sentenced to five years' imprisonment on the first charge, of endangering good order and discipline at Durban airport. The rest were, on this charge, acquitted.

They were also acquitted, all of them including Hoare and Duffy, on the charge of bringing weapons without permission aboard the plane. But they were all found guilty, all of them, of endangering the safety of the plane, its passengers and crew at Mahé Airport. For this offence they were all sentenced to six months' imprisonment.

On the main count, that most equivalent to hijacking strictly speaking, unlawfully seizing and controlling the plane, seven including Hoare were found guilty, and the rest were acquitted. Hoare was sentenced to no less than twenty years' imprisonment, to run concurrently with his other sentences and with half suspended on account of his age – ten years in all, then, a fearsome sentence for a man aged sixty-three whose only real 'crime' from the South African point of view was failure. Mike Webb and Tullio Moneta were sentenced to five years. Arguably, they had actually 'controlled' the plane more than Hoare. And in accordance with this scale of diminishing control, Ken Dalgliesh was sentenced to two and a half years and Vernon Prinsloo, who had given the order for the Boeing to be talked down, to one year. Charles Goatley was sentenced to two and a half years, mainly on the grounds that he had sat in the pilots' cockpit, with his gun and wearing headphones (which he denied) and thus 'controlled' the flight. Most surprisingly of all, Pieter Dooreward was sentenced to five years too, though it is hard to see for what. The Afrikaners had in the event played a very small part indeed in the whole affair. The real reason no doubt was government pressure, this time yielded to, to crack down on the ten Recce Commando reservists by severe punishment of the senior among them; no more unautho-rised ventures were ever to be lightheartedly undertaken was the implied message.

The condemned men began their prison sentences the following day, on 30 July – the majority mightily relieved that they would have to serve (with remission for good behaviour, available in sentences of under two years' only) a mere four months, the minority depressed and bitter, but all – one supposes – with a certain sympathy for their leader, faced with twice the price inflicted on any others to pay, and with little or no future left not only as a mercenary leader but indeed as a human being. The Judge President, Neville James, went into retirement shortly afterwards, able to boast – had he wished to do so – of a spectacular and possibly fitting climax to an otherwise undistinguished career that would merit him at least a minor place in South Africa's history. He had preferred to accept as true the evidence of an absent witness, objectively most unlikely to be truthful, to that of defendants whose stories in general agreed. He had ignored the presumption of innocence and the reasonable doubts that in an English court of law would almost certainly have saved the accused. He had tempered a questionable verdict with gratuitous insults and a pitilessly harsh sentence. He had, in fact, presided not over a fair trial but over a dubious and disorganised one that did no credit at all to South Africa's often vaunted legal system. On 6 August he himself heard and dismissed Hoare's application for leave to appeal, on the grounds of a biased trial, against his own judgement.

One man, however, stepped lightheartedly from Pietermaritzburg's Supreme Court, acquitted – quite rightly – on all charges. Charley Dukes must that day have blessed the bullet that incapacitated him from disturbing 'good order and discipline' at any airport or aboard any plane, and that had indeed led indirectly to his safe return to South Africa. For if, like most of the 'advance party' he had stayed on in the Seychelles, he would have been in a far, far worse position.

Seven in Victoria

To temper the confusion caused by two separate trials that most newspaper-readers understandably felt at the time, particularly over numbers and places, it may help briefly to recap here the whole affair. Fifty-four mercenaries in all were involved in the attempted coup in the Seychelles. Of these nine were already on the island on the evening of Wednesday, 25 November 1981; and one, De Jager, had backed out at the last moment in Swaziland. Forty-four therefore landed at Mahé Airport; of these, one, Johan Fritz, was almost immediately killed. Fifty-two mercenaries in all were, as dusk fell, still involved. Forty-five flew back to South Africa on the Air India flight and were tried, by the South African authorities, basically for hijacking. Seven remained on the Seychelles and were tried, by the

Seychelles authorities, basically for treason. The two trials occurred simultaneously, and it was this that caused most confusion; but the trial in South Africa overlapped the trial in the Seychelles at both ends. The Seychelles trial was far, far shorter. It began in mid-June when the Pietermaritzburg trial had already been under way for several months and it ended three weeks later in early July, before the final pleas in the Pietermaritzburg trial had even begun. What with weekends, Independence Day on 29 June, and adjournments, the Seychelles court sat for only thirteen days and many of those were very short sessions indeed. But, though shorter, it was also far more dramatic than the trial in South Africa – a legal battle, the result uncertain till the very end, with men's lives at stake.

Bar this one major similarity nothing could have been, on the surface, more unlike the trial of the mercenaries in Angola than the trial of the mercenaries in the Seychelles. The Angola trial before the Popular Tribunal had been revolutionary in tone and intent. The Seychelles trial, before judge and jury, was traditionalist to an almost caricatural extent. Where in Luanda the People's Prosecutor had ranted and roared, in the Seychelles the Attorney General, Bernard Rassool, was invariably calm, unrhetorical and utterly without aggression. The trial was presided over by the Chief Justice of the Seychelles, Mr Justice Earle Seaton, a courteous elderly Jamaican with a mild American accent* resplendent as a cardinal in his scarlet robes. The defence was conducted by a Queen's Counsel from the United Kingdom specially imported for the occasion, begowned and bewigged, a gentleman named Nicholas Fairbairn with, as his junior, a local advocate, Mr Kieran Shah. The trial was held not in the tiny Supreme Court but in the larger Assembly Chamber in National House, on Victoria's outskirts, which had galleries for both press and public. The prisoners were dressed in dark suits. The only obvious similarity with the Luanda trial was that they too arrived and departed under heavy military escort; and during the hearings were handcuffed by their left hands to the dock rail in front.

This trial opened on Wednesday, 16 June 1982; and quickly resolved itself into a duel of wits between the Counsel for the Defence and the Chief Justice. Nicholas Fairbairn was of a very different calibre from the British barristers who had flown out to Luanda. For a start he was older and far, far more experienced. 'I have defended all sorts of people accused of all sorts of major crimes,'

* Seaton had practised in Bermuda – hence the accent. He had been imported as Chief Justice by René from Tanzania after a 2½ year vacancy following the expulsion of the previous Chief Justice, O'Brien Quinn. He was therefore very much the President's man.

he confided unworriedly, 'including hundreds of cases of murder and one of piracy, but this is the first time I will be defending people accused of high treason.' He opened his attack on the first day of the trial, arguing strongly, forcefully – and to observers it seemed most logically – that there was no case for the accused to answer: whatever else they might be guilty of, they were not and could not be guilty of high treason in the Seychelles because they were aliens and hence owed no duty of allegiance to the Seychelles state. He quoted Archibald, he quoted Halsey, he quoted Russell. The Chief Justice meticulously noted the references. 'Well, what have you to say to that, Mr Attorney General?' he asked courteously.

Mr Rassool had come prepared. Section 39A of the Seychelles Penal Code defined as guilty of treason any person – without stipulating their nationality – who 'levied war against the Seychelles or did certain acts preparatory to levying war against the Seychelles'. For two and a half hours the legal arguments continued, lawbooks and penal codes to hand, far over the heads of most of the spectators (some sixty or seventy of the hundreds queueing had been squeezed into the public gallery), of the press, and indeed of the seven accused. Down among the lawyers the official observer from the OAU, an opulent lady with a variegated wardrobe and shapely arms, Madame Esther Tchoota Moussa of the Cameroons, began leafing through illustrated French magazines. There would clearly be no vitriolic denunciations of *mercenarismo* to be expected in this courtroom. Mr Fairbairn orated on the 'jurisprudential understanding of the crime of treason'. The Chief Justice nodded sagely, announced that he would consult the authorities and give a ruling next day, and adjourned the court.

That first session set the slow, almost stately tone that the trial was, despite sudden leaps and bounds, generally to follow. The first three days, the Wednesday, Thursday and Friday, were all devoted to legal arguments. Every lunchtime Nicholas Fairbairn, clad despite the sweltering heat in dark jacket, striped trousers, waistcoat and watch-chain, held court on the terrace of the Pirates' Arms, the social club of Victoria, astounding even the brash South African press corps with his scabrous stories, his condemnations of 'this ghastly Socialist paradise' and his pitiless mimicry of both his political friends and enemies at Westminster. For Fairbairn was not merely a lawyer; in his own entry in *Who's Who* he described himself as 'Author, farmer, painter, poet, T.V. and Radio broadcaster, dress designer, landscape gardener, bon viveur and wit'. In that impressive list he omitted only 'politician'. He was in fact the Tory MP for what had previously been the ultra-respectable Alex Douglas-Home's constituency in Scotland – Kinross and West Perthshire, a constituency which, Fairbairn was fond of pointing out, had more inhabitants than the Seychelles but no international airport, embassies abroad, or other costly extravaganza. He had bought a ruined castle with a title attached – Baron Fairbairn of Fordell he was entitled to call himself, and thereupon embossed his luggage with the initials F.OFF – had married the daughter of the 13th Chieftain of Clan Mackay, and subsequently divorced her; had become Her Majesty's Solicitor General for Scotland – Mrs Thatcher liked him; and then early that year had lost the post, partly because of his controversial decision not to prosecute in a notorious Scottish rape case, partly because his private life had become too embarrassing even for the Tories: his secretary Pamela had for love of him draped a rope around her neck (without any permanent ill effects) outide his London home. Almost exuberantly indiscreet on most personalities and topics, Fairbairn was not so about one: how and why he had come to be briefed for the Seychelles defence at all. He had, he said somewhat mysteriously, 'important contacts' in South Africa. He had certainly seen Mike Hoare earlier that month, for Hoare had dedicated a copy of *Three Years with 'Sylvia'*:

> For Nicholas Fairbairn, Q.C.
> with everlasting gratitude and admiration for a man of courage: from Mike Hoare, Col.
>
> Hilton, RSA.
> June, 1982.

An interesting and unexplained inscription. He was certainly in close contact with a firm of Durban attorneys; but the mercenaries' families had little or no money and he appears to have been paid, no doubt via these attorneys, by a South African popular magazine in return for 'exclusive rights' to his clients' inside story. He was also, and probably much more profitably in the long run, acting for the Lloyds insurance syndicate in London, that wanted to reclaim the still-stranded Fokker Friendship belonging to Royal Swazi Airlines – a knotty legal negotiation. Money apart, however, I believe he saw the Seychelles trial as both a challenge and an opportunity: a challenge to fight and win a sensational case, an opportunity both to save the lives of men with whose views he sympathised, and by doing so to redeem his own slightly shaky legal and political reputation.

He lost the first round. Courteously but predictably, quoting two Lord Chancellors of England, Loreburn and Jowitt, the Chief Justice ruled that the charge of treason could stand. Fairbairn immediately put forward a second, probably less expected objection: that a fair trial would be impossible because no impartial jury could be empanelled. What with all the publicity on the radio and in *The Nation* condemning the mercenaries, and what with – a telling point – the mass 'kill them, kill them' demonstration of 7 December which one in three of the island's inhabitants had attended, the jury – any jury – would already be automatically conditioned to believe that the mercenaries were guilty – particularly, added Fairbairn, in a country with only one party where members of the government had already publicly announced what they expected the verdict to be. But on the Friday the Chief Justice overruled that argument too; and, the preliminary legal fencing over, the court adjourned for the weekend.

Fairbairn, however, had won, behind the scenes, a partial victory. Journalists from overseas had been eagerly awaiting the appearance of the 'woman mercenary' in the dock; imagining a sort of glamorous gun-slinging Pasionaria – in any case a dramatic story on which to fasten. The Seychelles authorities had hamhandedly never let it be known that the 'woman mercenary' was frail, middle-aged, grey-haired and obviously frightened. They would have exposed themselves to worldwide mockery and derision if they had allowed her trial as a dangerous enemy of the state to proceed. On the second day therefore the Attorney General announced that all charges against Sue Ingle had been dropped. She remained one night more in the Central Police Station, with her pet cat, 'protected' from journalists; and was then discreetly flown back to South Africa. It had to be done. But the hardliners in the Seychelles government were not pleased; and they became even less pleased with Mr Rassool when it became apparent, on the Monday, that a certain amount of behind-the-scenes wheeling and dealing, a certain amount of plea-bargaining, must have taken place over the weekend.

For on the Monday Fairbairn played his trump card. The court assembled to hear the six remaining accused plead; and it was naturally expected that they would plead not guilty to the charge of high treason and that then the trial proper could begin. Instead, to general amazement, one after the other they pleaded guilty – all except Bob Sims, who pleaded not guilty to high treason but guilty to importing arms illegally into the Seychelles. It seemed suicidal; and it must have seemed suicidal to many of the accused too when Fairbairn, in his visits to them at the army camp, had persuaded them to follow this course. For by pleading guilty they were, on the face of it, condemning themselves to death. But then, on reflection, the subtlety of Fairbairn's manoeuvre became apparent. With the pleas of guilty the whole process was virtually over and done with: all that would remain was a speech by Fairbairn in mitigation, and then sentencing. There would be no show trial at all, no witnesses describing the landing at the airport, no evidence of Kenya's or Mancham's involvement, no gradual working up of passions against the accused as day succeeded day. Nothing. The whole purpose of the trial, from the point of view of the Seychelles government, would be defeated. It would be a non-event politically and internationally. Furthermore how would it look abroad if the Chief Justice were to impose the death sentence on shadowy figures whose particular misdeeds were unknown because never recounted? It would look brutal. Indeed it would look barbarous. It was a gamble that Nicholas Fairbairn took, and that he persuaded his clients to take: to play it low key. But it was a brilliantly calculated gamble; and it very nearly came off.

That it failed was due to one man: Dolinchek. Dolinchek had refused to be represented by any lawyer, maintaining at first that the South African government, his employers, ought to provide a lawyer to defend him; and later refusing even a local one. 'I don't need a lawyer to lie on my behalf,' he said, 'I don't lie.' So he, the odd man out to the very last, was defending the – by implication – only honest man of the seven accused: himself. Confusingly he pleaded guilty – but not really guilty. This confusion gave the Chief Justice the pretext he needed to adjourn the hearing and to consider, overnight, Dolinchek's position. There were rumours, later, that as soon as a day's proceedings were concluded the Chief Justice immediately sidled off to report to President René at State House and receive his instructions for the next day. These rumours were certainly never confirmed, and probably purely malicious. But it is hard to imagine, equally, that that night passed without any consultation between the highest legal and political authorities. Certainly next morning, Tuesday morning, the Chief Justice announced that after due considera- tion he had decided to rule that Mr Dolinchek had entered a plea of Not Guilty. The trial therefore would proceed – the trial admittedly of Dolinchek alone. But in Dolinchek the court and the country had, it seemed, the ideal sacrificial victim: a self-confessed spy from a country theoretically at least loathed and feared. At this stage few would have put much money on Dolinchek's prospects of survival.

But, before the other mercenaries were dismissed, temporarily, from the dock and the courtroom and Fairbairn (except as an observer) with them, the Attorney General announced that the charge of treason against Sims had been withdrawn. It would have been difficult to do otherwise after allowing his companion, Sue Ingle, to go scot free. On the other hand his plea of guilty to importing arms – four AK 47s had been found hidden in the grounds of La Misère – was registered. For Sims, therefore, there was no longer any risk at all of the death penalty – another client saved by Fairbairn. On the other hand this very fact served only to infuriate the hardliners even more against the suspiciously unforceful attorney-general whose father had been a personal friend of the Mancham family. And the hardliners were not only to be found in the party or the military. 'Kill them, kill them, kill them,' a fierce young Seychellois, matching his gestures to his words, told me. 'If they do not kill them, I tell you this: I will personally demonstrate against the government.' That, though uncommon, was certainly reminiscent of Angola.

The Chief Justice having outmanoeuvred his most dangerous opponent, the much-desired show trial could now proceed. But with Nicholas Fairbairn reduced to a frustrated and impuissant silence and with Martin Dolinchek more or less clay in the court's hands, the Chief Justice could afford to show himself most meticulously concerned for the defendant's rights. The days that followed were punctuated by continual courteous murmurs of 'if this is agreeable to you, Mr Dolinchek,' or 'I wonder if you have quite taken this point, Mr Dolinchek,' or 'pray interrupt me if there is anything here you do not follow, Mr Dolinchek'. And in indirect reponse to Fairbairn's views on the obvious bias of any jury, the Chief Justice spent no less than a whole day quibbling over their selection. First he disqualified two jurors because they were related to witnesses or policemen; then, on his 'advice', no less than three more disqualified themselves as being already convinced in advance that the accused was guilty; and finally, at the very last moment, the foreman of the jury was ignominiously dismissed for having failed to tell the Chief Justice that he was a member of the local militia. As if to make impartiality doubly sure, the Chief Justice ordered that for the duration of the trial the jury finally selected – six men and three women – should live together, without any contact with the public or indeed members of their families (this reduced one jury woman to tears). In fact they were put up in the government-owned Northolme Hotel, near Beauvallon Bay. It was all something of a charade. Free from casual outside pressure they may have been. But they lived under the watchful eye of an army officer and escort; and there could be little doubt of what the army's view was: they wanted Dolinchek found guilty and the mercenaries executed.

Not that the army can by any means have been happy with the six days of Dolinchek's trial – an opportunity for the police, far more experienced, naturally, in legal procedure than the army, to produce not only a succession of far more coherent witnesses than the few rather incoherent soldiers who were called, but also to bring into the open the 'list of the five Majors' in Hoare's notes to Carey. Significantly, the list was given in full, without comments, in the following day's issue of *The Nation*, though *The Nation* often censored in its daily reports on the trial the more embarrassing aspects of, for instance, Dolinchek's own evidence. It was almost as if President René was issuing an open warning to the five majors that they were under suspicion and that he preferred to rely on Commissioner James Pillay's officers and men. One of these five, Major Rollye Marie, appeared in court to give evidence of the finding of the arms at La Misère – a large, capable man. He made no reference to the list, nor did the Chief Justice nor did the Attorney General. It just lay there, as it were, on the table, a silent indictment, a legal weapon that might, in the infighting of Seychelles political life, one later day be used.

The trial organisers had their moments of triumph: the evidence of Vincent Pillay and Sergeant Esparon, for example, with their graphic descriptions of how the Frothblowers had been uncovered; and the production of seventeen AK 47s, complete with ammunition and the grips in which they had been abandoned or hidden, more out of place and sinister perhaps in the courtroom, almost within reach of the handcuffed mercenaries in the dock, than they would have been in action. Mike Hoare's passport was produced too, plus written indications of Kenya's involvement – the 'documents' which had, in the rush of departure, not been recovered. But undoubtedly the most spectacular moment, the moment around which in a sense the whole show trial had been planned, was the playing-over of the tape-recordings reconstructed from the burnt and torn spools that, if the coup had been successful, would have been played over the seized radio station. The words and phrases, in French, English and Creole, were very jumbled and bitty; but there were three distinct male voices there. The first a radio technician gave evidence as recognising: 'That voice is very familiar,' he said. 'I've recorded him on several occasions before.' It was the voice of Gerard Hoareau. The second was 'a friend of mine. We have talked on many occasions before.' Paul Chow. The third – its most audible phrase was 'today a free nation' – the technician also immediately recognised.

'How can you recognise it?' asked the Attorney General.

'I think anyone who hears that voice can recognise it,' replied the technician, 'I've recorded things for him, heard his voice, a lot of times.'

'Whose voice is it?'

'Mr James Mancham.'

For all those listening, for everyone in the Seychelles, there could be no further reasonable doubt possible: the former President, despite his denials at the time, must have been directly implicated in the preparation of the coup attempt. The government had proved its major political point; Mancham was a dangerous 'enemy of the people'; and in that sense the whole setting-up of the trial had been worthwhile.

All this of course was basically irrelevant to Dolinchek's own trial. Witnesses and evidence were introduced on the pretext that it had to be proved that war was levied, on the night of Wednesday, 25 November, against the Seychelles. Fairbairn, had he been defending Dolinchek, would no doubt forcefully have objected. But the Chief Justice, with his deadpan explanations to the jury of how Item A should now after identification be listed as Exhibit B, and with his silky courtesy towards the defendant, preempted all possible criticism. The only moment in the whole trial which occasioned a display of judicial peevishness came (if I remember rightly) during the poor Lousteau-Lalanne's once-again-repeated story. 'The Colonel?' said the Chief Justice. 'Who is this Colonel to whom these continual references are being made? What Colonel is this?' Had Hoare remained behind in the Seychelles and been captured, his trial there would have been in every sense a historic trial. He was what the French call *le grand absent* in the whole proceedings, and the rest were poor substitutes. But in the Colonel's absence Dolinchek undoubtedly became the star turn. He answered in his own way the Chief Justice's rhetorical question. Hoare, he said, was 'an overglorified soldier who got his Colonel title from Mobutu Sese Seko'. 'For a conspiracy-type operation,' he added dismissively, 'he was not up to standard.'

Dolinchek's whole attitude to Hoare resembled that of a rejected and embittered suitor towards a once-admired, now lost, object of love. It had been very different before when he had cast himself in the role of the Colonel's right-hand-man. As he said of his first meetings with Hoare, and his own part in the conspiracy, 'of course it takes two to tango'. He had added in his diary: 'If my government knew I was discussing this with him, they would chew my balls.' The diary, hidden by Dolinchek on the island before his arrest, then produced by him as a sop to the authorities, was a source of considerable light relief when extracts were read out in court. Dolinchek asked that a part of it should not be read out, because it would be 'embarrassing for my family' and the Attorney General gravely, to the vocal disappointment of all the South African journalists in the press gallery, agreed.

Had his fellow-prisoners been in the dock, but they were not, they would hardly have appreciated Dolinchek dismissing them in his evidence as 'rubble' or referring to Sims as 'a stupid man called Bob'. When he came to describe how he had, in the Reef Hotel, criticised Carey and his men – 'Drunkards only interested in birds. I told them there were lots on the trees' – and how they had responded, both the court and the translators (for, the sake of certain members of the jury everything had to be translated into Creole) were left far, far behind. 'Those guys,' explained Dolinchek, 'who were threatening me with a zap-off, they were skimmering – a good Afrikaans word.' That occasion the Chief Justice let pass; but on others he had to intervene, to ask Dolinchek for an explanation of his language. For instance: Chicoms? 'An intelligence abbreviation, my Lord,' the accused gravely explained, 'for Chinese Communists.' Dolinchek was extremely insistent on his status. 'I am not a mercenary,' he told a somewhat flabbergasted courtroom, 'and I will never be one because it is below my dignity. I am a professional intelligence officer.'

The drama was not only in the dock. Among the spectators attending the trial every day was a grey-haired Englishwoman who had come out specially from South Africa to see Dolinchek condemned. She was convinced, rightly or wrongly, that he had been involved in the assassination of her son, Dr Richard Turner, a banned liberal lecturer at Natal University, shot down mysteriously at his home in January 1978. She was not the only woman specially there. Di Brooks, a dark-haired woman of twenty-eight always fashionably dressed, usually smiling, had flown out, alone of the wives or relations, to be present at her husband Aubrey's trial. On leaving Rhodesia they had together tried to set up a printing business in South Africa. But 'the debts piled up', she told me, 'and that's probably why he got involved in all this'. Her opinion of Hoare is worth giving, if only as a contrast to Dolinchek's: 'a gentleman, an absolute gentleman'. She was allowed most days to pay a brief visit to her husband at Union Vale Camp, usually escorted by Nicholas Fairbairn. She found him resigned to his fate, whatever that might be, and reading the bible – a sort of religious conversion, bordering occasionally on exaltation, that Fairbairn worriedly confirmed. Alone in their solitary cells, in what Fairbairn described as 'abominable conditions' – handcuffed day and night, without light and with little air, having to scrabble on the floor for their food, jeered at and promised death by their captors – the other mercenaries, knowing that one way or another their fate was sealed, had to wait out with growing mental tension the long days of Dolinchek's trial.

This came to an end with the final pleas on Thursday, 1 July. The Attorney General for the prosecution was brief, civil, but firm in calling for the death penalty. Dolinchek, addressing the jury, grovelled. He had been misled.

> I know I committed a ghastly wrong to all of you [he said]. I can only hang my head and say I'm truly sorry. . . . I now believe Mancham's government harboured a lazy and crooked bunch of parasites who wallowed in super luxury and opulence and gallivanted the world of high jinks where corruption was rampant. What a catastrophe, what a calamity for your gentle nation if Mancham and his accomplices were to return! I'm glad we were foiled in our plan to impose this bunch on your liberated people.

A recantation of the sort that by Gus Grillo before the People's Tribunal in Luanda had seemed astutely machiavellian appeared in the much calmer atmosphere of the Seychelles merely faintly ridiculous. The press gallery could barely stifle their indignant guffaws at the hypocrisy of Dolinchek's peroration.

> In conclusion, [he said] I humbly ask your Lordship to allow me to offer my hand of brotherly friendship. There is a time in every man's life to stand up and be counted, to take sides. From now on my place will be in the ranks of anti-aparthied forces to save Africa from a certain holocaust.

This must have been the most surprising recantation since St Paul's conversion on the road to Damascus. The Chief Justice, unblinkingly, announced that he would, if Mr Dolinchek were agreeable, adjourn the case till the Monday following to consider and prepare his judicial summing-up. 'Indeed, my Lord,' said Dolinchek with unctuous deference, 'your wish is my command.'

The court reconvened, after a long and sunny weekend, on the afternoon of Monday, 5 July. The Chief Justice ran briefly through all the evidence, pointing out that Dolinchek had not taken part, like most of the rest of the accused, in the fighting around the airport or the barracks but that he was, by his own admission, a party to the conspiracy to overthrow the Seychelles government. He concluded his summing-up shortly after three o'clock. The jury retired. Exactly half an hour later, they returned.

'Mr Foreman, have you reached a verdict?'

'Yes, Your Lordship.'

'What is it?'

'We find the accused guilty as charged.'

'Is that an unanimous verdict?'

'Yes, Your Lordship.'

Dolinchek, previously standing, was asked to sit. 'Now then, Mr Dolinchek,' said the Chief Justice, 'I do not propose to sentence you this afternoon – though I know that in your situation I would like this to be over with one way or the other.' Pleas in mitigation for the other accused were still to be heard; then all the five now found guilty of treason would be sentenced together. The court would reconvene the following day for the final act.

This was Nicholas Fairbairn's chance to redeem the situation. He rose to address the court on Tuesday afternoon, conscious that he was the cynosure, both in the courtroom and outside, of all eyes and ears. He skated lightly over the careers, characters and family situations of Brooks, England, Carey and Puren, and even more lightly over their motives and their past military careers, emphasising their humanity. Then he drew breath. 'The matter to which I must now turn,' he said, 'is equally relevant but perhaps more distasteful'; and for the first time the court, and the press, heard the details of how the mercenaries had been beaten up and maltreated after capture. As the long recital continued, the Seychellois in the public gallery began to show signs of protest. But none of the account of the army's brutality – Fairbairn carefully made the point that the police had always behaved impeccably – was to be reported over the radio or repeated in *The Nation* next morning; this time discretion ruled. As for outsiders, the non-Seychellois press, they found it difficult to be too shocked by what in a sense is a risk that must be accepted by any mercenary if captured, or to be too impressed by Fairbairn's legalistic point that 'if the State claims allegiance, then the State must also offer protection'.

Finally, Fairbairn, step by step, and with caution, turned to the offence of treason itself. 'Those who gain power by tainted hands,' he concluded amidst a profound and attentive silence, 'must show mercy to those who attempt to regain it.' But he went no further than that. He named no names and he made no precise comparisons. He did not point out, as he could have done, that René himself was guilty of treason against Mancham and that only by 'levying war' and by bloodshed – the exact crime of which the mercenaries were accused – had René and his supporters come to power. A Cicero or a Demosthenes would have made immense play with the open secret on the islands that René, under Mancham's presidency, had used his own position as Prime Minister to smuggle weapons into the islands – the ten Kalashnikovs with which his supporters were armed – via the airport, in almost exactly the same way, *mutatis· mutandis*, as Hoare had attempted to do, but with greater success. British lawyers of modern times are not used however, unlike their Roman and Greek predecessors, to attacking men of state head on. Fairbairn did not dare to be specific. He was already worried, as he confided afterwards, that he had gone too far in the detail of his descriptions of the army's brutality when his clients would, that very evening, be back under Major Macdonald Marengo's untender control. But that, he felt, was a risk that had had to be taken. It would of course have made a far greater impact on both the courtroom itself, on the Seychelles, and on world opinion if he had come out with an open and detailed denunciation of the hypocrisy of René's regime, itself installed by a coup, instigating a trial of any sort against those who had attempted – in the name moreover of the legitimately elected President – to do the same thing. But he did not. He left it unfortunately merely as a hint and an allusion, hanging in the air. He ended with an unremarkable plea for leniency.

Dolinchek on the other hand, who now again had his turn to speak, ended with one of the most remarkable pleas that a man of his type may ever have addressed to court of law. 'Lastly, my lord,' he said, 'if the death sentence is passed on me I appeal to your Lordship direct that I should be executed by a military firing squad as befits an officer or gentleman.' At this last request even the Chief Justice appeared to wince. He adjourned the court briefly before pronouncing sentence. At 4.30 in the afternoon he returned to the courtroom. All rose, then sat. The five found guilty of treason, unhandcuffed, remained standing.

'The accused,' said the Chief Justice, 'allowed themselves to become involved in levying war against a small country that was not their own. All of them must have known that what they planned would have risked the lives of hundreds of people.' This seemed to me at the time, and still seems on reflection, a remarkable exaggeration. 'I take into account,' added the Chief Justice, 'the eloquence of their learned counsel.' He did not however, answer, refute or indeed take into account at all the arguments, whether express and implied, that Fairbairn had put forward in mitigation. It was an empty phrase.

'I believe however,' he continued without any change of pace or tone, 'this type of crime calls for deterrent sentences. If people engage in these kind of activities because they are lucrative the penalties must be as heavy as they possibly can be.'

He paused; and eyes turned surreptitiously towards Di Brooks, apparently calm, flanked by a Seychellois policewoman and the impassive British Consul.

'Aubrey Vincent Brooks,' said the Chief Justice, 'I hereby sentence you on Count 5 to suffer death in the manner authorised by law.' Sentences of death on Carey, England and Puren followed. There was no awful solemnity, no black cap, no reference to 'being taken from this place and hanged by the neck until you are dead', no appeal to God to have mercy on their souls. It was all spoken in a conversational tone of voice; almost like a word of advice from an older man to a young friend. The only surprise, to many unpleasant, was that Dolinchek, 'because he has shown a spirit of contrition', was sentenced not to death but merely to twenty years' imprisonment – rather as if a hypocritical sinner had half succeeded in hoodwinking a somewhat naive father confessor. The convicted men, pale but showing no emotion, were escorted out of the courtroom into the bright sunlight and, constantly photographed, into the waiting military vehicle. Di Brooks, was taken out that evening by a shocked Nicholas Fairbairn and her South African lawyer, newly arrived; Fairbairn fulminating against the duplicity of the Chief Justice and openly worried that he had himself chosen the wrong tactics. My opinion (never confirmed by him) is that he had always imagined that he had fixed up a behind-the-scenes deal with the authorities and had been given some sort of guarantee, probably by Bernard Rassool, the Attorney General, that if his clients pleaded guilty, they would not be sentenced to death. But if the Attorney General did give a guarantee of this sort (and clearly for reasons of legal etiquette even Fairbairn would never have had the gall to approach the Chief Justice directly), he was in no position to enforce it. Indeed Mr Rassool did not survive as Attorney General very much longer. In view of his unconvincing performance in the trial he was dismissed in the autumn, and later, I believe, went voluntarily into exile and has now joined the ranks of the opposition.

For the passing of the death sentence was not of course the end of the affair in the Seychelles. The question remained, posing much more of a long-term dilemma than in Angola; would the sentences ever be carried out? 'Now it's all over,' said one Seychellois, 'we wish they would just send them back to South Africa and forget all about it.' Such was the general attitude of the ordinary people. On the other hand President René had to consider that a pardon of any sort would inevitably encourage his exiled opponents to try again whereas executions actually carried out would certainly act as a deterrent to would-be mercenaries in the future. He had to balance the interests of tourism and aid and trade, and the islands' reputation as a tropical paradise, which would be almost irretrievably scarred by executions of white men, against the pressures of his own party hardliners, of the army, of the Tanzanians on the islands (now reinforced to a strength of perhaps five hundred), of President Nyerere, his ally, and of the OAU in general: all favouring death. A further complication was that the Seychellois authorities were faced with rather a macabre practical problem if the executions were to go ahead. For the accused had been sentenced to die in 'the manner authorised by law': hanging. But no executions had been carried out on the islands within living memory and not only had the gallows rotted but there was no-one remotely capable of acting as a hangman on the islands. A foreign 'professional' would therefore have to be imported, a distasteful procedure and one likely to lead to a bad press.

Perhaps fortunately for the President the legal system itself imposed a delay and solved his immediate dilemma. Fairbairn had before leaving the Seychelles lodged an appeal against both conviction and sentence. The appeal would have to be heard by the three peripatetic judges of the Appeal Court, one Irishman and two Mauritians, but it could not be heard until the autumn. No immediate political decision on whether to go ahead with the executions or not was therefore either necessary or possible. Fairbairn set great store by the appeal, believing that on strictly legal grounds he would win his argument that there had been a mistrial. Others however were much more sceptical and did not see how the Appeal judges could do anything but support, with whatever qualms, the Chief Justice of the Seychelles, his conduct of the trial, his summing-up, the verdict and his sentence. The date for the appeal hearing was set: 20 September.

The appeal however was never heard. Two events intervened – one minor and one major. The minor event, but one that at first must have been most nervewracking for the condemned mercenaries, was this: shortly after the trial had ended they were without explanation taken from their prison camp to the office of the President himself. This was the first time the mercenaries and the man they had planned to overthrow but who now held virtually the power of life or death over them had come face to face. It seems that René waved at them – it must have been the last thing they were expecting – an article in London's most renowned political weekly, *The Spectator*, which of course none of them had ever set eyes on before.

The article was entitled 'Fairbairn in the Tropics' and gave a detailed account of Fairbairn's views on the Socialist regime in the Seychelles in general and on the army's brutality in particular. It was an accurate article, if anything understating Fairbairn's views on the 'depraved conditions' imposed on his clients by a 'depraved government'. I should know; I wrote it, little imagining it would have repercussions. But it made René see red. He would never, he apparently said, allow Fairbairn to set foot again on the islands – a man who after all in order to appear for the defence had had to be admitted to the Seychelles Bar and so had had, most ironically, to take a formal oath of allegiance to the President of the Seychelles Republic, to himself, President René. The mercenaries must, he insisted, drop their appeal and sack Fairbairn. They must also hold a press conference and deny that they had been beaten up by the army. In return he would spare their lives.

The four condemned men were of course in a horribly unenviable position. The implication was that if they went ahead with the appeal, with Fairbairn as their lawyer, as was their undoubted legal right, and if they lost, then the President would not exercise the prerogative of mercy. No-one would have wished to be in their shoes, unadvised and friendless, at this particular moment. They had no real choice: they fell in with the President's wishes. Fairbairn, to his fury and frustration, was dismissed, the appeal was dropped, and the prisoners held a press conference (attended mainly by local Seychellois journalists and so not widely reported) denying that they had ever been maltreated. No official Presidential announcement followed, however, to the effect that their lives would be spared and their sentences commuted to terms of imprisonment. They simply had to hope that René would keep his word.

The second and major event helped the mercenaries much more directly than my article had done indirectly. There had been unrest in the army for some time; and on 17 August 1982 the soldiers guarding the mercenaries at Union Vale mutinied. They seized, at 6 am, the radio station and broadcast over it an appeal to the President, 'as Commander in Chief of the Army and as the Father of the Seychelles' to help them. They were sick, they said, of being treated 'like pigs' by their officers; and in particular they demanded the dismissal and punishment of two of the 'five majors'. René was in the out-islands at the time, on Almirante, and the mutinous soldiers, as a means of pressure, seized over two hundred hostages at the radio station and threatened to kill them and blow up the petrol storage tanks outside Victoria unless their demands were met. For they had also demanded the dismissal and punishment of two of the ministers, including their own official commander 'Colonel' Ogilvy Berlouis, the Minister of Youth and of Defence. He of course being on the main island summoned his Tanzanian 'allies' to suppress the mutiny.

The mutineers had not only released the mercenaries they had been guarding but had actually asked them to take the lead in the mutiny as their officers. Strangely enough very much the same sort of thing had happened in Angola a year after the trial there, when in the so-called Nito Alves *coup* attempt Sao Paolo prison in Luanda had been 'liberated' and the surviving mercenaries there offered their freedom, and arms. Wisely they had refused both, stayed in their cells, and sat the failed coup (later bloodily punished) out. But in the Seychelles the opportunites were far greater. By taking the lead in the mutiny the mercenaries might at last have sparked off a popular uprising and been in a position to overthrow – as had been their aim only nine months earlier – the whole regime. It would have been a gamble but a reasonable one: except of course for the fact that the penalty for losing would without a shadow of doubt have been immediate death, and that most of the mutineers appear to have been drunk most of the time. So they too declined. Not only did they decline but it seems that Dolinchek and Carey slipped out from Union Vale and gave information on conditions inside to the advancing 'loyalists'. Shells were falling on the barracks and the prison and by midday the fighting was over, at the cost of nine killed: no hostages, but five mutineers and four loyalists. Not a major rebellion then nor a vast loss of life but still a further dramatic increase in the scale of deadly violence originally inaugurated by René himself. How the surviving mutineers – and there may have been as few as thirty of them in all – were treated I do not know and hate to imagine. But the mercenaries of course had proved their 'loyalty' to President René and his regime. 'You'll never hang as long as I'm here,' René told the prisoners on his return. And Aubrey Brooks apparently replied: 'May I make a suggestion, Sir? We dig in outside your grounds.'

There were even rumours that Dolinchek might be asked to take over the island's security services. René, however, did not go as far as to employ the mercenaries hired to overthrow him on his own behalf. Indeed he did not even formally commute the death sentences. For there were still, even despite the failure the previous November, exiles and mercenaries actively involved in threatening his regime. In London that September Hoareau and Chow and other exiles were meeting to try again with a plan involving three hundred mercenaries to be sent in by ship. As an advance guard they did send in one, Mike Asher, with five kilos of high explosive concealed apparently in an imported van. The plan was for members of the *Mouvement pour la Résistance* to destabilise the regime, already shaken by the August mutiny, still further by a terrorist bombing campaign for which Asher would train local underground supporters. Asher, instead, blew himself up at the remote beach of Anse Forbans with one of the underground, Simon Denousse, on 20 October. Asher had not only come from South Africa but had been one of those originally considered for enrolment in Hoare's team. Despite everything, therefore, would-be mercenaries in South Africa were still actively involved in plots against René's government, and René, though kept abreast of these plots (Hoareau and Chow's telephone calls in the Carlton House Towers in London were all taped and recorded, very possibly by the Italian Secret Service, the SID) could not afford to be too trusting towards 'his' mercenaries. He seems, though, to have become and to have remained on good personal terms with them. 'Barney', he said, having summoned Carey personally, 'I'm afraid I've got bad news for you. Your wife is divorcing you.' This cannot have been entirely unexpected; Sandra Carey had been close to a break-down during her husband's trial and imprisonment and was bitter against him for ever having involved himself in the venture. It was, however, a very humane touch on René's part to take the trouble to break the news in person.

So though the threat of execution no longer seriously loomed over the mercenaries, they were neither pardoned nor released. Instead they were sent that October, all six of them – Sims, incidentally, had been sentenced to ten years for importing arms – to an imprisonment that more resembled exile on the remote Platte Island where there was already an army training camp. They were locked in their hut every night – but at dawn every day the doors were unbarred and they were free to wander. They lived on fish six days a week. They swam in the tropical seas – not far, though, for fear of their most effective guards, the sharks. It was a very different sort of life from that of their 'colleagues' who had been suffering for years in Angolan prisons or for months in South African jails. For the mercenaries in the Seychelles, trials, and tribulations were – except for the greatest tribulation of all, the loss of liberty – over.

Epilogue

THE FUTURE OF MERCENARY SOLDIERS

15

Endings – and Beginnings

Shortly afterwards the releases began. On 17 November 1982 thirty-four of the mercenaries imprisoned in South Africa were freed – those sentenced to six months at Pietermaritzburg, released after four. Then in December a far more dramatic event occurred: Gus Grillo and Gary Acker were released by the Angolan government in an extraordinarily complicated exchange operation that involved two Russians captured by UNITA, ninety-five FNLA soldiers and one Cuban captured by the South African forces in Angola, the bodies of three dead South Africans, and the release of a Catholic Archbishop. It was a triumph both for the State Department and for the International Committee of the Red Cross and a bad reflection on the Foreign Office: for the seven British prisoners remained in Sao Paolo prison, with the bitter resentment that can be imagined. They had been there in what a visitor described as 'appalling conditions', living on a diet of rice and noodles, 'very low' psychologically, physically ill – though not maltreated – for over six years.

In April 1983 Vernon Prinsloo, having served eight months of his one-year-sentence, was released. Then in the summer, as an act of clemency by René, all the six mercenaries on Platte Island were told that they were to be freed. 'Aubrey,' said the President to Brooks – it seems almost incredible but I am assured that he did say it – 'you can always come back here, you'll always be welcome. But next time I hope you'll come as a genuine tourist.' The only one who expressed, understandably, a certain alarm was Dolinchek. 'I will have to face the music – or a concert – down there after my trial here,' was how he put it. He must have been remembering how in his peroration he had claimed that the enemy was Apartheid, and that 'back home the people are crying out to be liberated'. But once he was back home himself, he seems to have totally forgotten about his proud boast – which I hope this book, if he reads it, will remind him of – that henceforward he would be in the forefront of the struggle side by side with the anti-Apartheid forces. Dolinchek had been dismissed, Prime Minister Botha himself had confirmed in July 1982, from his post as –

in his own favourite phrase – an 'active duty officer' with NIS for absence without leave, as well as for 'action contrary to' state security. But white South Africans seem on his return to have treated him with amazing tolerance. Even members of his jogging club did not boycott him; indeed they generally believed that he was back once again in favour with his old employers.

In November Ken Dalgliesh, Mike Webb and Charles Goatley were released on parole after having served only just over half of their two and a half year sentences.

In December came a curious little incident in South Africa obviously designed to show that the South African government was as a matter of long-term policy rather than short-term expediency clamping down on all mercenary activities. Five 'foreigners', British and Rhodesian, were detained and interrogated by security police after reports that they were trying to organise another Seychelles mercenary venture. This was on the orders of the Minister, Louis Le Grange, who had certainly changed his tune from the days when he could indignantly ask the press what South African laws the Seychelles mercenaries had broken. He did not allege that these five had broken any laws as such but his government, he said, took a serious view of the alleged plans and 'were not prepared to allow any such developments to take place within this country'. The five were subsequently expelled. I have been told that three of them were ex-RLI, but I very much doubt whether Dalgliesh, Webb or Goatley were even marginally involved. Being released on parole, as they had been, is a double-edged state of affairs; any transgression, or suspicion of transgression, and the parolee is smartly back inside to serve the rest of his sentence. It was far more relaxing for the six from the Seychelles who ran no such risk of any further imprisonment. That Christmas Aubrey and Di Brooks, earlier reunited, exchanged Christmas cards with President René and considered returning to the Seychelles for a 'second honeymoon'.

Three months later, in March 1984, the British mercenaries in Angola were finally released. They returned without fanfare to Britain, leaving only 'Brummy' Barker's grave behind them in Luanda as a physical memento of those eight years. It was a delayed triumph, but a triumph for all that, for the Foreign Office's quiet diplomacy. For there was nothing complicated about the deal; indeed the only advantage obtained by the Angolan government was the rather nebulous one of improved relations with Great Britain. There does not even appear to have been a bribe offered in the form of increased aid. John Nammock, whose leg wound had never healed, was photographed on crutches, being welcomed with joy by his Irish mother in North Kensington.

Finally in May in South Africa Peter Duffy, Tullio Moneta and Pieter Dooreward were released also on parole. They had served just under two years of their five-year sentences. All the many mercenaries who had been in prison in so many different parts of the world had now been released – some escaping the death penalty, others freed after only a fraction of the thirty years which they had been condemned to serve, all with their sentences so notably reduced as to indicate that society had in private and in practice pardoned them the 'crimes' which society had raged against in theory and in public.

All, that is to say, except one man, one mercenary, the oldest, the most famous and the least likely to be in a position ever again to repeat his 'offence'. When I visited South Africa in the middle of 1984, Mike Hoare and Mike Hoare alone was still in jail. I walked around the white-washed walls of Pietermaritzburg Central Prison, set at the end of Pine Road, on the outskirts of the town, looking for all the world like a large misplaced Foreign Legion fort. The notice outside the heavy gate mentioned visiting hours. I wondered whether it would be wise to apply direct to the prison governor for permission to visit and talk to his best-known prisoner or whether first, to approach his wife. In the end I drove out to the Old Vicarage and introduced myself to Phyllis Hoare. She was a friendly, likeable woman, obviously younger than her ageing husband imprisoned only a few miles away, the mother of two good-looking boys; neither of them showed the slightest sign of being ashamed of or reluctant to talk about their father. But there was no chance, Phyllis Hoare assured me, of my visiting her husband. She herself had only two authorised visits of half an hour each month.

I had imagined naively that prison conditions might be relaxed for an elderly white prisoner of distinctly right-wing views in a South African jail. I was quickly disabused. The prison regime, I was told, was certainly less harsh than that of Zonderwater Gaol and the governor, a colonel, was helpful where he could be. Hoare, who had developed a bad heart and might need open surgery, had been moved down to Pietermaritzburg from Pretoria a few months earlier for compassionate reasons. But all the same whereas political prisoners, black or white, belonged to a distinct category and had certain privileges, Hoare was technically a common criminal and was treated as such.

'Mike wanted to do a degree,' said his wife, 'anything to keep his mind occupied. But it's not permitted.' Indeed he was not permitted books or papers or reading or writing matter of any sort, only the Bible.

'But what does he do all day long?' I asked, horrified at what seemed to me, as a writer and reader a greater depravation even than that of liberty itself.

Phyllis Hoare found it hard to say. 'Fortunately he managed to smuggle Shakespeare into the prison at Pretoria,' she mentioned. 'He learnt lots of it by heart. He recites. He says it's the only thing that keeps him going. The warders think there's a madman around when they hear Mike reciting *Hamlet* to himself in his cell.'

What about other conditions, food for instance?

'We're not allowed to discuss prison conditions. We usually spend our half hours talking about legal things and the hopes of getting Mike out of there.' This seemed almost as saddening an answer as the response to my first question, and a veritable clutching at straws. But why had Mike Hoare not been released too like the forty-two found guilty at the Pietermaritzburg trial? Why were the South Arican government insisting on keeping her husband behind bars when all the other mercenaries had been released, long before expiry of their sentence, and when his was, in view of his age and health, an obvious case for compassion?

She hesitated. 'I think,' she said, 'it's because they are afraid that Mike may write a book about the whole affair.'

By the time this book appears on the South African book-stands, it may very well be that Mike Hoare will have been released. If not, I hope that the South African government will not be so foolish as to keep him in jail for the reason his wife fears. There can be very little that Mike Hoare can add in any book he may write that will implicate the South African authorities in the Seychelles affair any more than they have already been implicated by what has already come out, at the trials, in the press and indeed in this account. If they continue to use Hoare as a fall-guy – and that in effect is what they have done – it will only rebound to their own public discredit and private dishonour.

I have made no secret of my feeling that a Seychelles coup was morally justified, given the means by which René had risen to power himself; that it might – though this is more debatable – have positively benefited the Seychellois people, that Hoare wanted no bloodshed if it could possibly be avoided, that his plan was indeed designed to avoid bloodshed; that he had acted as a responsible commander throughout; that his trial in South Africa was as much a show trial for political purposes as the trial in the Seychelles had been; that the accusation of hijacking was an unjustified misuse of a term normally applied to a very different context involving demands for money, the release of terrorists, or the diffusion of propaganda statements – of a different order in any case from a mere demand for a ride; and that on the evidence of the actual accusations with which he was faced he should never have been found guilty. I hold no special brief for Hoare or any other mercenary – except the feeling that they too are human beings and should be treated with justice. In this particular case of the Seychelles *coup* and after having studied it as carefully and from as many sides as possible, I feel most strongly – and imagine that my readers will feel – that the punishment is disproportionate to the 'crime', pitiless in view of Hoare's age if imposed to anything like the full extent, and above all hypocritical in view of the nature and known activities of the government that is imposing it. For what could be more ironic than that President René has pardoned the mercenaries whom he caught though they were trying to overthrow and possibly to kill him while South Africa continues to imprison the mercenary leader who posed no threat to them at all, whom indeed their military minions encourage?

If Hoare is released, however, and if he does, as seems likely, write a book, I hope he will attempt to clear up the various minor mysteries raised but not answered in this account. Had I been able to talk to him, I would have asked one thing more – and this is a major point that I think he has almost a historical duty to answer. My additional query would have been this: had Hoare made any plans to have the coup supported by Denard? Or if not by Denard in person, then at any rate by French mercenaries from the Comores? There was certainly talk on Mahé of a planeload of French mercenaries standing by and, alternatively, a 'second wave' of mercenaries due to come in by sea, by French launch. Later Hoare himself made one, though only one, significant remark, or perhaps slip, at his own trial. He was explaining that there was in any case no need for him to have taken the Air India Boeing because he could, instead, have used the Air Swazi Fokker Friendship, piloted by his own men. 'I could always have refuelled in the Comores,' he said, most significantly. Certainly there were several hints of a Comores connection in the evidence given at the Pietermaritzburg trial; including a never-explained tale of two women who stayed overnight at the Ermelo Holiday Inn and caught the same flight as the Frothblowers next day, debarking at the Comores.

On the other hand, according to Captain Fergusson's statement in the Seychelles there was 'some confusion' at the Comores, where, he thought, one man and one woman got off. Confusingly too there was also talk of a Frenchman who *got on* at the Comores and who was indirectly responsible for Beck's luggage being searched – an odd story that was never mentioned in any evidence, formal or informal, in the Seychelles. In one sense it would have been amazing if there had been *no* connection with the Comores and if Hoare had made *no* plans at all for a 'second wave'. It ought to be remembered too that fifteen years earlier it was Puren who, landing at Bukavu to join Schramme, had clearly been liaising with Denard in Angola. Puren was always Denard's link-man. I have a feeling in my bones, backed by these hints and premises, that the reason Puren stayed on and Hoare wished to stay on had to do with their expectation, concealed from all others, of a reinforcement by French mercenaries which, in the circumstances, was called off. Had such an elaboration to the scheme existed, it would have given the proposed coup an even greater chance of success. As it was, if all had gone reasonably well from the mercenaries' point of view and above all if they had kept reasonably sober in the tense days of waiting at the Reef Hotel before the attempted coup, I still believe it, far from being doomed to failure, could for better or for worse have been successful.

After every mercenary débâcle there is a dying-down of mercenary activity. But recent history indicates that this lull is only temporary. After the Angolan tragedy it seemed inconceivable that any Englishman or American with a minimum of commonsense or any instinct for self-preservation would ever again get involved in any sort of mercenary activity. But nothing seems to put off would-be mercenaries – neither the danger of death in action, of execution if captured, or massacre by their own commanders, of treachery by their own employers or of severe punishment in the event of failure by the very instigators of their activity.

Furthermore, any attempt to ban mercenaries or mercenary recruitment appears doomed to be ineffective. In the United States the Neutrality Act and in the United Kingdom the Foreign Enlistment Act are virtually dead letters. After the Angola affair a commission was set up to consider the whole question of mercenary recruitment in Britain. It consisted of three lawyers headed by Lord Diplock. Its report, the Diplock Report, which recommended stern measures, was much derided. No action whatsoever followed. In France the recruitment of mercenaries for a foreign government is, technically, an offence, but in the one case in which arrests were made, of Thierry du Bonnay, the organiser of a 'camp' of mercenaries in the Ardeches in 1966, the French courts decided that Tshombe, in whose name the men were being recruited, though a foreign *leader* was not a foreign *government* – therefore no offence had been committed. But the truth is that all governments including those loudest in their condemnation of mercenaries are by nature inconsistent in their views. They have seen how effective mercenaries can be and how useful as instruments of policy, for, though unreliable, they can be disowned absolutely. In any case when the mercenary fever seizes a nation, as happened in Switzerland in the late fifteenth century, no government regulation can stop it. Diets and Cantons issued formal prohibitions, cities locked their city gates to stop the outflow, but in one year alone, 1492, over 20,000 Swiss poured down the Alpine passes to take service on all sides in the Italian wars – an unheard-of number utterly undeterred. One can imagine the vast impact such numbers would make in our own day should they ever appear. Whatever the laws, whatever the international conventions, whatever the deterrents, mercenary activities will continue as long as governments or counter-governments see a use for mercenaries and as long as would-be mercenaries are themselves ready to be used.

This book has told the story of only the most publicised mercenary events of the past quarter of a century. There have been literally hundreds of other mercenary ventures or plots during the same period, ranging from an attempted Dutch mercenary attack on Surinam to raids on Laos prison camps, from interventions by freelance adventurers in the Lebanese civil wars to officially-backed employment in Central America, from 'training officers' and 'technicians' hired in their hundreds by the Shah of Iran when in power to bounty-hunters of the Shah's head when the wretched man was out of power. But none of these events has produced great mercenary leaders of the style of Hoare, Denard or even Callan – I use the word 'great' in a purely technical sense – and few, if any, have been of more than marginal importance.

The mercenary world is permanently awash with activity. At this very moment even as you are reading this book, you can be very sure that a score of mercenary coups are being planned or discussed or meditated in London or Paris alone, the two world centres of exile politics. Occasionally these plans are revealed: as in 1981 when a group of ten American mercenaries were detained by the FBI en route to topple Eugenia Charles' left-wing regime in the tiny Caribbean island of Dominica (their leader Michael Perdue was to receive $150,000 and a concession for the backers, Nortic Enterprises Ltd, from the exiled ex-prime minister, Patrick John); or as in

1982 when ex-President Binaisa of Uganda was plotting to overthrow President Milton Obote with a two-pronged landing on Kampala and Entebbe airfield, launched from the Congo. This was backed by US businessmen from the Southern States; and the five hundred mercenaries involved were to be recruited by Raymond Ingram's International Security Agency in Britain. It came to nothing at the time; but new faces, new names are continually cropping up in the mercenary business and this is just one single example that has come to the surface of a whole web of subterranean activity. No-one knows where and when the next dramatic mercenary intervention will be. All we can be reasonably sure is that in a world where the great colonial empires have collapsed, where the two superpowers are reluctant to become directly involved in any conflict that may lead to a direct clash between their own forces, where scores of small and militarily backward rival states exist in which struggles for power are more likely to be settled by force of arms than by the ballot box, then the conditions for the use of mercenary soldiers do objectively apply, and the opportunities for their use will in all likelihood increase rather than diminish.

Prophecy is always dangerous – but it would not be surprising if in Africa continual turmoil should lead to what has not yet occurred: major wars between rival states. In these conditions it is likely that native mercenary leaders will emerge, as happened in medieval Italy when the foreign mercenary leaders of 'the Companies' – French, German, Breton, Hungarian and English – were gradually replaced by native Italian *condottieri*. These *condottieri*, as is well known, dominated Italian history for almost a century; and indeed even founded their own states. The initial signs of a similar process are already apparent in post-colonial Africa, with the Katangese in Angola and with Gaddafy's Islamic Legion in Libya and Chad. I would not be surprised to see the emergence of black mercenary leaders rising as it were from the ashes of the Denards and the Hoares in the next military generation: the Age of the Black Condottieri. But whether history will repeat itself, whether this phenomenon will eventually lead, as it did in Renaissance Italy, to a flowering of individual talent and the creation of a new civilisation, whether 'mercenaries' will actually be in the long run of benefit to Africa is of course another, though fascinating, question that cannot possibly be answered yet – or here.

Appendix

CONTRACT OF AGENTS IN THE SERVICE OF THE DEMOCRATIC REPUBLIC OF THE CONGO

BETWEEN THE DEMOCRATIC REPUBLIC GOVERNMENT OF THE CONGO, represented by the Prime Minister in agreement with the National Securtity Council on the one side, and Mr: *Name, Christian name, place of birth, date of birth, nationality, left or right-handed, father's full name, mother's maiden name, profession, marital status, wife's name, wife's address, children's names and ages, last address, address of next of kin, bank account number, bank address, previous military experience, rank held in foreign army* on the other side, hereinafter referred to as the Foreign Volunteer, the following has been agreed to:

Article 1. Conditions to be fulfilled in order to be eligible for enlistment.
To be eligible for enlistment into the Congolese national army, the Foreign Volunteer must have been in a Regular Foreign Army and be accepted by the Commander-in-Chief.

Article 2. Military pledge required by this contract.
a) A Foreign Volunteer must pledge himself to serve in the Congolese National Army in a military capacity.
b) The military pledge involves learning the rules and regulations of the Congolese army.

Article 3. Submission to the Laws of the Republic.
A Foreign Volunteer must submit to the Laws of the Republic and the judgement of their military tribunals, the same applying to infractions of common law as for infractions of military law. The Order in Council of December 18, 1964, decrees severe punishment for the waste of arms and ammunition, pillage, theft and violence towards civilians. In certain particularly odious cases of pillage and violence the death penalty or imprisonment for life could be imposed. Every infraction of common or military laws will automatically involve the application of the clause, Article 9, paragraphs a) and c) of this contract. The Foreign Volunteer must acknowledge and declare that he understands Chapter 2 of the Order in Council of December 18, 1964, in relation to the rules and regulations of Congolese military discipline, and that he understands their terms in this capacity in the end, and see that he must submit to all of their provisions.

Article 4. Rank awarded to Foreign Volunteers.
Promotion a) At the time of the signing of the contract, the signee is awarded the same rank which he held in the Foreign Army, provided that he has

effectively carried out the function for this rank. The contractor cannot take into account honorary ranks awarded by a Foreign Army.

b) Proof of a person's rank in a Foreign Army must be provided by original official documents or certified copies accepted by the Congolese military attaché or the Chief of Service G.I of the A.N.C. Non-certified photostat copies are not valid.

c) The awarding of rank at the time of signing this contract is made according to the following scale:

Foreign ranks	A.N.C. ranks
Private and Corporal	– Volunteer
Sergeant	– Sergeant
1st Sergeant to Adjutant	– Adjutant
Sergeant Major	– Adjutant Chief
Warrant Officer	– Corresponding Rank
Officer	– Corresponding Rank

d) The Foreign Volunteer enlists at the rank of Volunteer. If it is considered that he merits it, a Foreign Volunteer may be promoted to a higher rank. Only the Commander-in-Chief has the authority to promote, on the recommendation of the Corps Commander of a Foreign Volunteer, taking into account the necessity of leadership.

Article 5. Functions of the Foreign Volunteer.

The nomination of rank does not entitle a person to carry out the functions of that rank. These functions are independent of rank. The functions to be carried out are determined by the C. in C. for the better interests of the A.N.C.

Article 6. Various things are forbidden.

It is forbidden for a Foreign Volunteer to:

a) Bring their families to the Congo without previous permission of the C. in C.

b) Engage in any lucrative business activity while they are within the territory of the Republic.

c) Edit a newspaper or any other periodical of any nature whatsoever, or contribute to its administration or composition.

d) Participate in any political strife.

e) Publish any anonymous articles in newspapers or any other periodical, to write books or to give interviews.

DURATION OF CONTRACT, RE-ENLISTMENT, CESSATION OF CONTRACT, ETC.

Article 7. Duration of contract.

The present contract is for a term of six months following the date of signature.

Article 8. Re-enlistment.

A Foreign Volunteer may ask for a renewal of his contract for a further six months. He should make his application in writing within two months of the expiration of his contract. The request should be addressed to the C. in C. and sent through the normal channels. The C. in C. has the final decision.

Article 9. Causes for the annulment of the contract.

a) The contract will be annulled in all cases in which sentences have been pronounced for infractions of military regulations, as shown in Chapter 2 of the Order in Council, December 18, 1964, and infractions of common law by a sentence of less than six months imprisonment have been pronounced.

b) Full causes for a possible annulment of the contract. Bad conduct; grave insubordination; repeated bad discipline. All infractions are conditions of Article 6 of this contract.

c) The annulment of contracts shown in paragraphs a) and b) may be pronounced by the C. in C. or his deputy without prior notice. When a contract is withdrawn, the Foreign Volunteer concerned will be expelled *ipso facto* from the territory of the Republic. The costs of repatriation will be charged to the Foreign Volunteer who is expelled.

Article 10. Cancellation of contract.

The government of the Democratic Republic of the Congo reserves the right to cancel this contract before its expiration for any obligatory cause, or any cause beyond the control of the present contractor.

Article 11. Indemnity for the cancellation of contract.

In the case of the preceding article the Foreign Volunteer is entitled to a cancellation-of-contract indemnity equal to fifteen days' salary (Article 15) and fifteen days' daily indemnities (Article 17) for each month of service up to a maximum of three months. This indemnity is transferable, in its entirety, into Belgian francs.

Article 12. Notice of termination of contract.

a) Should either party fail to comply with the terms of this contract, the wronged party may terminate the contract. Failure to comply with the terms of this contract render the state of execution, and a continuation of mutual good relations impossible. The party breaking the contract is not bound to pay any indemnity to the other.

b) Should the Foreign Volunteer be guilty of any fraudulent act, making false statements, concealing any physical disabilities or any infirmities whatsoever at the time of his enlistment, or of inflicting any injury to himself after enlistment, the contract will be terminated.

c) Notice of termination of contract by the wronged party must be given in writing in the manner prescribed hereafter. If the Foreign Volunteer takes the initiative in terminating the contract, the termination will not become effective until the sixteenth day after the notification in writing has been submitted to the first authority in the hierarchy unless this first authority is in a position to remedy the reason for the Foreign Volunteer's decision to terminate his contract. If the field C.O. or his deputy takes the initiative in terminating the contract, the termination only becomes effective the day after this termination of contract has been given in writing to the Foreign Volunteer and passed through the normal channels.

Article 13. Cessation of contract.

The Foreign Volunteer may ask to break his contract for personal reasons only when this is caused through an Act of God. The request must be sent through the normal channels to the C. in C. or his deputy, who has the final decision. If the request is accepted, the cessation of contract will not take effect until the day after the favourable decision has been communicated to the Foreign Volunteer in person through the normal channels.

PECUNIARY ACTS

Article 14. Remuneration. (See Article 26)
  a) The Foreign Volunteer is entitled to a monthly salary, various indemnities and certain advantages in kind.
  b) These remunerations are susceptible to variations of the index.

Article 15. Monthly salary while in action.

The Foreign Volunteer will receive a monthly salary in advance at the beginning of each month. The salary while in action will consist of: a basic salary, and a six-monthly augmentation for voluntarily re-enlisting.
  c) The monthly basic salary is fixed according to the following scale:
        Volunteer – 10,053 francs × index
        Up to
        Lieutenant Colonel – 37,916 francs × index[1]
  d) From the seventh month of service, and for each six-monthly period following, the basic salary is augmented by two thousand francs multiplied by the index. A new augmentation of the same amount is awarded for each following term in favour of a Volunteer who has re-enlisted.
  e) Each month is taken as thirty days. When the contractor has to work out the daily salary and indemnity shown in this chapter the daily salary is equal to one thirtieth of the monthly total. The exact amount is calculated as shown in paragraph b) of Annex 2.

Article 16. Wife and family allowances.
  a) The Foreign Volunteer is entitled to the following allowances payable in advance at the same time as he receives his salary:

Wife – monthly allowance of	2,127 francs × index
First child	1,277 francs × index
Second child	1,360 francs × index
Third child	1,530 francs × index
Fourth child and others	1,787 francs × index

Example: A Volunteer, married father of five children for whom he is responsible, will receive a total of 9,868 francs multiplied by the index. This

---

[1] Only the two extremes of the salary scales are quoted. A second lieutenant received 21,250 francs × index.

family allowance is payable only for legitimate children of the Foreign Volunteer for whom he is responsible.

Article 17. Daily indemnity for board and lodging.

The Foreign Volunteer is entitled to a daily indemnity of two hundred francs multiplied by the index. This indemnity is in place of an allocation for lodging; it is payable in advance at the same time as the salary is received.

Article 18. Daily danger pay.

The Foreign Volunteer is entitled to danger pay as follows, payable in arrears:

a) While in a danger zone 500 francs × index.

b) While in an insecure zone 200 francs × index.

These zones are determined at the beginning of each month for the previous month by Q.G.(A.N.C.) G.₃, who also determines the dates of the beginning and end of danger and insecure zones.

Article 19. Indemnity for billets.

a) The Foreign Volunteer on operation cannot claim an indemnity for billets.

b) While he is not on operation and is not accommodated in a hotel or state building, but is in a place where he has to pay personally for lodging, he is entitled to a daily indemnity of two hundred and fifty francs multiplied by the index.

Article 20. Advantages in kind.

a) The Foreign Volunteer is entitled, in principle, to free food.

b) When food cannot be given to a Foreign Volunteer and he is obliged to purchase his own, he is entitled to a daily indemnity for food fixed on the following scale:

120 francs × index when he is in a sedentary post.

175 francs × index when he is on patrol.

Article 21. The Index.

The Index mentioned in the preceding articles is actually fixed at 4.69. It is, however, liable to variation. A new index is fixed by the Prime Minister. Annex No.2 of this contract gives the full salary with the various indemnities at the index at 4.69 included.

Article 22. Monetary deductions for punishment.

The following monetary deductions may be made by the Chief of the Corps after receiving a written report from the Platoon Commander.

a) For infraction of those disciplinary rules which demand monetary deductions on the basis of: one thirtieth of the salary (Article 15) and daily indemnities (Article 17) for each day under house arrest. One fifteenth of the salary (Article 15) and daily indemnities (Article 17) for each day under close arrest.

b) The total monthly monetary deductions cannot exceed two thirds of the total monthly salary plus daily indemnities.

Article 23. Travelling Expenses.

The Democratic Republic of the Congo will pay all travelling expenses of

Foreign Volunteers from the place of enlistment to the place of execution of the contract.

Unless they make a contrary decision the contractors will pay travelling expenses for the repatriation of Foreign Volunteers from the place of execution of the contract to place of enlistment.

The mode of transport will be, in both cases, the least onerous to the treasury.

SOCIAL ADVANTAGES

Article 24. Lump sum compensation in the case of the death of a volunteer.

In the case of the death of a Foreign Volunteer as a direct and exclusive result of action while on service, the following is granted to his beneficiary:

a) One million Belgian francs, approximately twenty thousand Swiss dollars, for the wife of a married Foreign Volunteer who at the time of enlistment was not legally separated or estranged – proof of this must be provided by an attestation from the Burgermaster, Mayor or other Authority; for the next of kin in the case of an unmarried, widowed, divorced or separated Foreign Volunteer who has not named any other beneficiary; for the person named in this contract by the Foreign Volunteer who is unmarried, a widower or a divorcee.

b) One hundred thousand Belgian francs for each legitimate child. The Government of the Democratic Republic reserves the right to make all arrangements for the compensation of the children to be made to an official institution in their country who will be charged to manage the estate until the children reach their majority.

Article 25. Insurance.

The Government of the Republic will give to an injured Volunteer free insurance up to a maximum of one million Belgian francs plus one hundred thousand Belgian francs for each child he is responsible for. This insurance will be paid out according to the degree of injury laid out in the following article.

Article 26. Compensation given to those totally and permanently injured.

In cases of wounds involving a total and absolute loss of sight, the entire removal or complete loss of the function of both hands or feet, or one hand or foot, complete paralysis, incurable mental illness excluding the possibility of carrying out any form of work or occupation, the Government of the Republic will pay 100% of the total insurable amount.

Article 27. Compensation awarded to those partially and permanently injured.

In cases of partial and permanent injury compensation is fixed as follows, as a percentage of the total:

a) The total and absolute loss – that is the complete loss or complete loss of the function of – the right arm 75%, left 60%, the right forearm

65%, left 55%, the right hand 60%, left 50%, a thigh 60%, one leg 50%, one foot 40%, one eye 30%, the right thumb 20%, left 13%, the right index finger 16%, left 14%, the right middle finger 10%, left 8%, the right small finger 8%, left 6%, the big toe 5%, all other toes 3%, the hearing of one ear 15%, the hearing of both ears 40%. For a left-handed person, on condition that this has been declared before receiving the wound, the scale fixed for the right members will apply to the left members.

b) The partial loss of one of the members or organs mentioned in a). Compensation will be paid in proportion to the loss of usage as a percentage, but not exceeding 60% of the whole amount. All wounds causing permanent or partial injury to the organs not mentioned above will be compensated for after the degree of incapability has been assessed by examination before a medical board, taking into account the preceding scale.

c) The total amount of compensation for permanent partial injury cannot be more than three quarters of the total insurable amount, whatever the case of the number of organs or members lost, whether total or partial.

Article 28. Compensation in cases of temporary injury.

a) In case of temporary injury the Foreign Volunteer is entitled to his salary, compensation and other allocations as laid out in Articles 15, 16 and 17.

b) A temporary injury. As shown in this Article, it must be recognized that it is impossible for the volunteer to carry out any activity whatsoever. This should be duly ascertained by a medical certificate.

Article 29. Accumulation of compensation.

Compensation for the deceased, totally and permanently injured, and partially injured, can in no case be accumulated. Payment of compansation as shown in Article 28 ceases on payments of compensation detailed in Articles 23, 26 and 27.

Article 30. Treatment of illnesses.

Medical treatment, surgery and hospitalisation of a person under contract is paid for by the Government for the duration of the contract and during the leave period. Any treatment paid for in a foreign country will be reimbursed upon presentation of the medical bill.

Article 31. Leave.

a) At the normal expiration of his contract of 6 months, the Foreign Volunteer is entitled to 20 days paid leave. He may spend his leave in the country where he was enlisted.

b) While on leave he is entitled to his salary and to indemnities as shown in Articles 15, 16 and 17.

c) Travelling expenses are paid for by the State, this journey being considered as the termination of the contract.

TRANSFERS, TAX IMMUNITY, SETTLEMENT OF COMPENSATION FOR THOSE KILLED AND WOUNDED

Article 32. Guarantee of Transfers.
a) Each month the foreign volunteer may have the following remuneration transferred into a foreign currency: 50% of the monthly salary, 100% of the wife and family allowances, 50% of the daily indemnity due for one month, 50% of danger pay due for one month.
b) In case of temporary incapacity the Foreign Volunteer will be hospitalised, treated or convalesce in the Congo. He may have the following remuneration transferred into a foreign currency: 50% of the monthly salary, 100% of the wife and family allowance, 50% of the daily indemnity due for one month. However, the monthly salary and indemnities due in virtue of Article 28 for the Foreign Volunteer who is hospitalised, under treatment or is convalescing in a foreign country, will be transferred in total into a foreign currency for the duration of his term of convalescence.
c) After six months of service, in the same way as for the expiration of his contract, the foreign volunteer may transfer into a foreign currency the money saved during the six months period. However, the amounts transferable may not exceed: 25% of the amount received as laid out in Articles 16, 17 and 18: 100% of the leave pay and indemnity as laid out in Article 31.
d) In cases where a contract is broken or terminated, the Foreign Volunteer may transfer the money saved during his term of contract. However, the amount transferable may not exceed 25% of the money received, as laid out in Articles 16, 17 and 18.
e) In cases where the contract is cancelled, the Foreign Volunteer may further to the amount laid out in paragraph c) transfer 75% of the indemnity mentioned in Article 11.
f) Transfers laid out in paragraphs a),b),c),d) and e) above are subject to the approval of $G._1$.

Article 33. Settlement of compensation for those killed and wounded.
The settlement of compensation as laid out in Articles 24, 26 and 27 is effective, subject to the approval of $G._1$: within a maximum of three months from the date on which compensation as laid out in Articles 24, 26 and 27, is granted: within a maximum of three months from the date on which the amount of compensation has been set out by the Medical Board (compensation as laid out in Articles 26 and 27).

Article 34. Transfer Expenses.
Transfer expenses resulting from the application of Articles 32 and 33 are paid for by the state.

Article 35. Tax Immunity.
Salaries, allowances and compensation of any nature as laid down in this contract are free of all tax.

FINAL REMARKS

Article 36. Litigation.

In cases where the subject, interpretation or execution of any clauses in this contract are contested, the dispute will be heard before a tribunal.

> Signed at   Date
> For the Democratic Republic of the Congo in .... original copies
> > The Prime Minister –
> > The Foreign Volunteer –

Note 1. The Foreign Volunteer must append in his own hand the words 'read and approved', *lu et approuvé.*

MINOR POINTS FROM ANNEXES TO THE CONTRACT

Article: Extension of Contract.

Volunteers may for personal reasons prolong the duration of their contract indefinitely. The Battalion commander has the right with the agreement of the C. in C. to prolong for administrative or security reasons a Volunteer's contract. However, these Volunteers are entitled to all advantages laid out in this contact.

> Signed: Bobozo L. Major General, Commander in Chief.

Article: Promotion.

The scale of promotion for Volunteers joining the A.N.C.s is as follows: Volunteer, Sergeant, Adjutant, Adjutant-Chief, Second Lieutenant, Lieutenant, Captain, Commandant, Major, Lieutenant-Colonel. It is obligatory to abide by this scale, no person may jump two ranks in a single nomination.

Article: Requirements for indemnities.

Official Congolese death certificate, doctor's certificate of death, witnesses' report, report of commanding officer [and many more for South Africa and Rhodesia: affidavits, etc.etc. This article is headed: *from Albertville*].

Books – A Short Selection
with Acknowledgements

MURRAY, Simon, *Légionnaire* (Sidgwick and Jackson, 1978; pbk ed.: New English Library, 1980).
    This is a quite outstanding account of life in the Foreign Legion, vivid, readable and convincing. It has also been published by Editions Pygmalion in France. I would particularly like to thank Mr Murray for permission to quote long extracts from his book.

WREN, P.C., *Beau Geste* (John Murray, 1924).
    I would like to thank John Murray for permission to quote equally long extracts from this, which with the two other novels of Wren's Foreign Legion trilogy, *Beau Ideal* and *Beau Sabreur*, needs no words of praise from me.

O'BRIEN, Conor Cruise, *To Katanga and Back* (Hutchinson, 1962).
    By far the wittiest and best-written book to have emerged from the whole Congo imbroglio. Conor Cruise of course was no friend to either mercenaries or to Katanga but his account is almost equally critical of his own employers, the United Nations.

HOARE, Mike, *Congo Mercenary* (Robert Hale, 1967).
    A factual account of Five Commando that rather skates over the crises and the seamy side of mercenary activities. Invaluable all the same as the only account by a modern mercenary leader of his own activities. The book was issued in a paperback edition by Corgi Books under the simple title of *Mercenary* in 1968 and has gone through, to date, seven reprintings.

HOARE, Mike, *Three Years with Sylvia* (Robert Hale, 1971).
    Hoare's sailing book is written in a much more relaxed and open style. I have quoted from both his books and would hereby like to acknowledge my debt to both author and publishers.

GERMANI, Hans, *White Soldiers in Black Africa* (Details unknown).
    This is a slim, vivid, often shocking account of Five Commando's activities by the eccentric who later became their medical officer. Unfortunately it was published in – if I remember correctly – South Africa only and is therefore rather difficult to get hold of.

SMILEY, David and Peter KEMP, *Arabian Assignment* (Leo Cooper, 1975).
    A rattling account of the semi-official semi-official semi-mercenary British involvement in the Yemen civil war.

FORSYTH, Frederick, *The Biafra Story* (Penguin, 1969).
    The famous thriller-writer's first book was published as a Penguin Special in 1969 before the fall of Biafra and reissued in 1976. It is a personalised, polemical, non-fiction account of the civil war in Nigeria from, as the title implies, the Biafran point of view. Frederick Forsyth went on to write the

best-selling mercenary novel *The Dogs of War* which was first published by Hutchinson in 1974 (Corgi paperback edition 1975, many times reprinted).

ST JORRE, John de, *The Nigerian Civil War* (Hodder and Stoughton, 1972).

Though this deals only incidentally with mercenaries, it places them solidly within the context of the fighting. An authoritative book by a well-known correspondent of *The Observer*.

SEALE, Patrick and Maureen McCONVILLE, *The Hilton Assignment* (Temple-Smith, 1973; pbk ed. Fontana/Collins, 1974).

A reconstruction of the abortive mercenary attempt to 'spring' a group of Gaddafy's prisoners from their Libyan jail. Also written by two highly reputable *Observer* journalists, which lends it credibility.

BANKS, John, *The Wages of War* (Leo Cooper, 1978).

Not a good book; and misleadingly sub-titled 'The Life of a Modern Mercenary'. In fact it stops at the beginning of the Angolan contract, Banks' chief claim to fame – or ill-fame.

STOCKWELL, John, *In Search of Enemies* (W.W. Norton, New York, 1978).

The unauthorised but all the more convincing account of the CIA's involvement in Angola, by the officer in charge of the links with UNITA. Often muddled about the role of the British mercenaries but good on the Portuguese and the French.

RAY, E. (Ed.) *Dirty Work: The CIA in Africa* (London, Zed Press, 1980; New Jersey, Lyle Stuart, 1978).

A most informative, if slanted, short book on the same area as Stockwell's *In Search of Enemies*.

DEMPSTER, Chris and Dave TOMKINS, *Firepower* (Corgi, 1978; 5 reprints).

This book, by two of the British mercenaries who played a major part in the whole business, is absolutely vital for any understanding of the mercenary involvement in Angola. Though I often disagree with the two authors, I owe an enormous debt to them for my own account which I hereby gratefully acknowledge.

The Diplock Report, Command 6569 (XX1) (HMSO, August 1976). The report of the Committee of Privy Councillors set up to enquire into the recruitment of mercenaries in Britain. The committee was chaired by Lord Diplock, an Appeal Judge, and included two senior backbench MPs, Sir Derek Walker Smith, Conservative, and Sir Geoffrey de Freitas, Labour. Should be studied by all mercenary lawyers.

BURCHETT, Wilfred and David ROEBUCK, *The Whores of War* (Penguin, 1977).

Wilfred Burchett, the well-known Australian Communist journalist, has of course given an utterly different picture – mainly of the Angolan mercenaries – to that presented by Dempster and Tomkins. This is well worth reading if it can be found; and is less rhetorical than the also-interesting *Angola: Fin del Mito de Los Mercenarios* by Raul Valdes Vivo, the member of Cuba's Central Committee who reputedly organised the Luanda trial that Burchett attended (Imprenta Federico Engels, May 1976).

GERAGHTY, Tony, *Who Dares Wins* (revised, expanded ed., Arms and Armour Press, 1983).

The fourth chapter of this book is entitled 'The Mercenaries 1962–1978' and has interesting snippets of information, particularly about ex-SAS mercenaries – including a brief account of a really farcical coup attempt in yet another Indian Ocean archipelago, the Maldives, by nine ex-SAS in 1980. But Mr Geraghty makes no reference to his own rather frightening encounters with the Angolan mercenaries.

PÉAN, Pierre, *Affaires Africaines* (Editions Fayard, 1983).

This book caused an immense controversy when it came out in 1983 in France, consisting as it does largely of a documented attack on France's ally, President Bongo of Gabon. It describes Bongo's Presidential Guard in great detail; and Bob Denard is one of the major villains of the piece. Its author's account of the attempted mercenary coup at Cotonou is largely taken from documents first published in full by the excellent and always well-informed progressive journal, *Afrique-Asie*.

No book dealing even indirectly with the Comores coup or the Seychelles affair has, as far as I know, appeared. James Mancham's autobiographical account *Paradise Raped* (Methuen, London, 1983) includes only an account of how the coup affected him. I would like to end this brief list of mercenary-connected books first by acknowledging gratefully my debt, large, small or minimal, to all those listed above, their authors and publishers; and secondly by recommending the mercenary novel that I have myself found by far the most tense and true to life of the many that have been written: Daniel Carney's *The Wild Geese*, published by Heinemann in 1977 and in a paperback Corgi edition next year. Corgi seems to have acquired almost a monopoly in the paperback mercenary field!

STOP PRESS

As this book was going to the printers, it was reported that Hoare, having served over a quarter of his sentence and being over sixty-five years of age, was to be released under a General Presidential Pardon.

He was freed on Tuesday 7 May, 1985. Prison, he declared, had revitalised his soul and refreshed his liver; he was totally unrepentant about his Seychelles venture and his decision to bring his men back 'at whatever cost'.

More relevantly to this section, he announced that he *does* plan to write a book 'to set the record straight'. It will be awaited with great interest – particulary if 'Mad Mike' neither avoids or glosses over the questions posed in the last chapter of this present work.

Index